COGNITIVE-BEHAVIOURAL THERAPY FOR ADHD IN ADOLESCENTS AND ADULTS

COGNITIVE-BEHAVIOURAL THERAPY FOR ADHD IN ADOLESCENTS AND ADULTS

A PSYCHOLOGICAL GUIDE TO PRACTICE

SECOND EDITION

Susan Young and Jessica Bramham

WILEY-BLACKWELL

A John Wiley & Sons, Ltd., Publication

This edition first published 2012

Wiley-Blackwell is an imprint of John Wiley & Sons, formed by the merger of Wiley's global Scientific, Technical and Medical business with Blackwell Publishing.

Registered Office
John Wiley & Sons Ltd, The Atrium, Southern Gate, Chichester, West Sussex, PO19 8SQ, UK

Editorial Offices
350 Main Street, Malden, MA 02148-5020, USA
9600 Garsington Road, Oxford, OX4 2DQ, UK
The Atrium, Southern Gate, Chichester, West Sussex, PO19 8SQ, UK

For details of our global editorial offices, for customer services, and for information about how to apply for permission to reuse the copyright material in this book please see our website at www.wiley.com/wiley-blackwell.

Library of Congress Cataloging-in-Publication Data

Young, Susan, 1957–
Cognitive-behavioural therapy for ADHD in adolescents and adults : a psychological guide to practice / Susan Young and Jessica Bramham. – 2nd ed.
p. cm.
Rev. ed. of: ADHD in adults / Susan Young, Jessica Bramham. 2007.
Includes bibliographical references and index.
ISBN 978-1-119-96074-4 (hardback) – ISBN 978-1-119-96073-7 (paper)
1. Attention-deficit disorder in adults–Treatment. 2. Attention-deficit disorder in adolescence–Treatment. 3. Cognitive therapy. I. Bramham, Jessica. II. Young, Susan, 1957– ADHD in adults. III. Title.
RC394.A85Y68 2012
616.85′89–dc23

2011053429

A catalogue record for this book is available from the British Library.

Set in 10/12pt Times by SPi Publisher Services, Pondicherry, India
Printed and bound by CPI Group (UK) Ltd, Croydon, CR0 4YY

C9781119960737_131123

CONTENTS

LIST OF FIGURES, TABLES AND BOXES

Figures

Tables

Boxes

ABOUT THE AUTHORS

Susan Young is a Senior Lecturer in Forensic Clinical Psychology at the Institute of Psychiatry, King's College London and an Honorary Consultant Clinical and Forensic Psychologist at the high security Broadmoor Hospital. In 1994 Susan set up the clinical psychology service at the Maudsley Hospital's National Adult ADHD Service and has extensive clinical experience in the assessment and psychological treatment of youths and adults with ADHD. Susan participated in the British Association of Psychopharmacology Consensus Meeting (2007) to develop guidelines for management of transition for ADHD adolescents to adult services. She was a member of the National Institute for Health and Clinical Excellence (NICE) ADHD Clinical Guideline Development Group (2009); her main contribution being to provide expert guidance on psychological treatment of children and adults with ADHD. Susan is Vice President of the UK Adult ADHD Network (UKAAN), which aims to support practitioners establish adult ADHD clinical services. Susan has published articles in scientific journals, three psychological intervention programmes and has authored two books. She is currently leading a research group, supported by the Department of Health, which aims to develop projects that will establish the evidence base on ADHD and offenders and approaches to their management in the criminal justice system.

Jessica Bramham is a Lecturer in Clinical Neuropsychology in the School of Psychology, University College Dublin. She leads the Adult ADHD Service at St Patrick's University Hospital Dublin. She previously coordinated the National Adult ADHD Service at the Maudsley Hospital in London and was a Clinical Lecturer at the Institute of Psychiatry, King's College London. Jessica has a doctorate in Clinical Psychology and PhD from the Institute of Psychiatry and a MA from Cambridge University. Neuropsychological assessment is a particular interest. She is involved in researching cognitive functioning and the presentation of comorbid disorders in adults with ADHD.

FOREWORD BY MARGARET WEISS

'The journey started with the words "You have ADHD". To the client these words were not just a diagnosis, but a framework for self-understanding.' These words taken from the authors' module on terminating therapy are a statement of the central thesis of this book. This is a clinically driven manual for understanding and helping adults with ADHD. The strength of this manual is that it is clinically driven. The authors are not constrained by a particular view of how change occurs, the structures of the DSM or ICD, the ideology of a particular method of therapy, or a narrow arena of functional impairment.

Young and Bramham define three ways in which change may occur. Biological change may occur either through maturation or as a result of taking medication, in which case one observes a direct improvement in symptoms. Environmental change can occur when the patient's milieu is modified in such a way as to minimize the impact of symptoms or optimize the visibility of strengths. Psychological change occurs through the use of cognitive, behavioral, psychoeducational and interpersonal techniques that provide a scaffolding for building skills that were not previously present. The authors further simplify this schema for understanding change by noting that it can occur from the outside in, as well as from the inside out.

Psychiatrists who prescribe medication and CBT therapists are most interested in change from the inside out. The focus of these authors is not on any one direction of change. Instead they have focused on the dialectic between symptoms and functioning that is unique to this particular group of patients. This is a book by clinicians who have learned about ADHD from their patients. The result is a practical manual that can be as easily referenced in individual, group or workshop formats. The instrumental tools that accompany each module are made available to the reader on a website for ease of presentation.

What emerges from this perspective is clinical wisdom. One can see and feel both the patient and the therapy. Sometimes the authors sound almost simplistic in stating the obvious 'Achievement is a strong reinforcer', 'Self monitoring can increase a skill', 'Recognizing and preparing for problematic tasks makes a difference'. Yet each one of these statements represents tasty therapeutic spice.

The treatment described in this book would help some of the people, some of the time, with some of their problems. The change that would come out of this therapy would be meaningful and enduring.

Our understanding of how patients with ADHD get better has at times been characterized by cognitive errors. Getting better is not black (no change) or white (remission). For the vast majority of patients change is qualified. Getting better is not a race to the finish line, in which how fast you get better is more important than how long you maintain that improvement. This is a struggle, or a journey as the authors frame it, in which time, persistence, creativity, resilience, and insight empower the greatest change in longer -term developmental gains. These authors have a developmental perspective on ADHD, but they also have a developmental perspective on how to optimize enduring functional change and quality of life.

DSM and ICD define the paradigm that allowed ADHD to obtain visibility. As a result of the research underlying the diagnostic systems for ADHD we were able to move from a moral view of laziness into a neuropsychologically informed understanding of executive function and inhibition. However, DSM and ICD have been both a friend and a foe. The history of ADHD is defined by a chronic and essential tension between a narrow definition of the core symptoms and broader schemas of the associated symptoms carried by this population. Contemporary research in ADHD has benefited profoundly from use of a narrow definition of ADHD. On the other hand, clinicians such as Rosemary Tannock, Tom Brown and Paul Wender are often pulled out of this cosy research nest by the clinical demands of patients who have other complaints and complex neuropsychological deficits. This book exists in that tension. It targets a population diagnosed by the symptoms and addresses clinical deficits in a wide range of associated symptom areas.

Adults with ADHD may be anxious, even when their anxiety is either not specific enough or not severe enough to meet criteria for an anxiety disorder. Young and Bramham observe that ADHD symptoms lead to difficulty with anxiety and depression, while anxiety and depression divert power away from the working memory engine that mobilizes attention and inhibition. You cannot divorce internalizing and externalizing symptoms and still engage and carry a patient with ADHD through therapeutic change. When someone with ADHD has to do something they are not equipped to handle (homework, taxes, housework, taking a test, driving, being on time) they will sense their own danger and remember their own failures.

One of the more energetic controversies of recent academic and clinical forums is the differential between bipolar disorder and ADHD. One has to wonder why this particular problem continues to generate such interest. It was therefore with some delight that I observed these two psychologists wrestle with this demon. They describe patients with ADHD as ‘passionate’ (a very un-DSM word), such that when they are low, they are ‘passionately low’. They note that ADHD is often associated with dramatic mood swings within the hour rather than within the week. One might even say that they have impulsive mood swings. The clinical reality for people who work with ADHD is that these patients often suffer impairment from mood and anxiety symptoms. These symptoms overlap with but are not identical to the disorders described in DSM or ICD. Since Young and Bramham first described this phenomenon, more recent research by Barkley and Surman has validated that emotional dysregulation and emotional impulsivity are in fact central to the disability associated with ADHD.

The focus of treatment for ADHD has been on symptoms rather than functioning. This truly puts the cart before the horse. Symptom-based assessment is only a conceptual gateway to knowing how to help someone get better at day-to-day living. The trick to helping patients is to target the areas where they have problems. This is the underlying structure which defines the modules of the Young-Bramham program. Most patients do not need (or could not handle) the whole of this program, however, any patient would benefit from some of it.

The modules provided include many of the most common problems these patients complain of: time management, procrastination, anger management and interpersonal problems. The authors always start with symptoms and end with functioning. For example, the module on attention starts with a discussion of the varieties of attention deficits and how these manifest clinically. What follows is a description of how to support the development of executive function skills. The module on sleep starts by describing sleep itself, the sleep problems we see in patients with ADHD and ends with a description of time tested, common sense sleep hygiene. This is all the more original given that while adults with ADHD commonly complain of sleep problems, there is almost no research on the sleep problems specific to ADHD in adulthood.

The modules deal with many different problems. The authors note that although circumstances will dictate the usefulness of one or another module, the skills that develop are cumulative. When patients address one problem, they obtain a framework for establishing change that permits them to rework the same skills in another arena of impairment. The core modules on treatment, attention, impulsivity and termination of therapy are likely to be relevant to any patient.

The section on impulsivity starts with a description of impulsive behaviour, affect and cognitions, and ends with practical strategies. If the patient has consequence blindness, reinforce the immediacy and salience of rewards. If the patient makes impulsive decisions, have them write down the pros and cons of decisions before acting. If the patient jumps to conclusions, teach them to review the evidence. Patients with ADHD could not learn these skills when they were symptomatic, but nor do they necessarily reverse a lifetime of habit when the neuropsychiatric potential for change becomes available. For someone with ADHD to grow, the symptoms have to be manageable, expectations need to match potential, and the patient has to make up many lost years of potential skill development. The disabilities that accompany ADHD are varied enough to leave room for multiple treatment options.

The module I enjoyed the most was the discussion of social relationships. This is a description of ADHD symptoms seen through the distorting lens of the non-ADHD companion. If the patient zones out, they are not interested. If the patient is staring, they are aggressive. If the patient is fidgeting, they are trying to bother you. If the patient forgets to call, they do not love you. It is also a description of the profound social handicaps that ADHD symptoms engender such as hanging out with the wrong crowd, promiscuity, difficulty with pragmatic language, trouble listening. This is one of the first attempts to describe ways in which we might assist adults with ADHD with their interpersonal difficulties.

I appreciated the authors sensitivity to what is one of the greatest sources of psychological injury in ADHD: isolation. Patients with Asperger syndrome often come in as adults and discuss their wish to have a friend, but they are not actually lonely. They have grown into an awareness that there is an aspect of human gregariousness that they are not a part of, but they do necessarily feel what it is they are missing. By contrast, patients with ADHD are intensely social and what they see is denied to them. The authors have made an important beginning in making the patient's experience of social rejection a focus of treatment.

There are many aspects of ADHD we do not understand. A good clinical book will by its nature defy categories. It will also be enriched by insights that make no theoretical sense. For example, the authors note that patients with ADHD may apologize for misdemeanours they have neither processed nor understood. I am reminded of the husband who does not remember what he said to his wife, or the child who tells the principal he 'didn't do it' and is not lying in as much as he does not know at that moment that he actually did do it.

Of all the clinical wisdom in this book, by far the best is that the authors practice what they preach. Motivational interviewing and cognitive behavioural therapy are contingent upon helping the patient see the cup as half full. Yet as clinicians how often do we focus our interview on what is wrong rather than what is right? Young and Bramham capitalize on the greatest strength of ADHD patients: courage and resiliency. The authors note that these are patients who try and try again. Some patients with ADHD have great successes to attach to their name. Some have very few. All of them have tried and tried again and this is a powerful therapeutic niche. Young and Bramham use a metaphor to describe this. They say that patients with ADHD are 'life's true entrepreneurs'. This is true, and like all entrepreneurs they risk bankruptcy as well as wealth.

The authors note that adults with ADHD 'often feel that they are "survivors" of a syndrome that has left them with significant personal, social and occupational consequences. This is anecdotally known as the "hangover" of ADHD'. There is long-term damage to self-esteem that ensues from a childhood corrupted by inattention, hyperactivity and motoric, cognitive and behavioural impulsivity. The focus on strengths capitalizes on the opportunity to rewrite a life history of injury and disability as a history of bouncing back. ADHD patients can be proud of their resiliency.

The constant refrain in lectures on ADHD has been to highlight the impairment, so as to make an invisible disability transparent and open the way to provision of credibility, accommodation and service. This has been important and successful. However, highlighting the functional impairment associated with ADHD has also had dangerous consequences. First, it has led to confusion between the consequences of ADHD and conduct disorder. Second, it has left clinicians with a feeling of therapeutic nihilism and thus indirectly increased the stigma associated with the disorder. Third, it has led to a reactive initiative where ADHD is perceived as a gift and 'being' ADHD has become a culture in its own right.

People with ADHD have a disability, but they are human and human beings react to disability with plasticity. This is not a strength of ADHD, it is a strength of being human. The blind may be musical, but being musical does not make being blind a gift. Struggling with ADHD is long and lonely. The last module of the book helps the therapist recapitulate with the patient where they are in the space and time of development, and the meaning of the relationship that has developed. Termination is a difficult and significant moment in every short-term therapy, but it is all the more salient for patients caged by symptoms in a cell of social isolation. The authors know how to deal with the bittersweet aspects of a therapeutic success that foreshadows the difficulty of letting someone go it alone when life is never going to be easy.

There are many types of therapy in the food court of psychology manuals. This one borrows from psychoeducation, cognitive behavior therapy, interpersonal therapy, behavior therapy, social skills training, anger management, motivational interviewing, problem-solving, cognitive remediation, relaxation therapy, sleep hygiene and coaching. It is perhaps a sign of our times that the only major psychological intervention that I did not see was dynamically-oriented psychotherapy. ADHD does not grant immunity from conflict. While psychodynamic psychotherapy may not be an effective treatment for ADHD symptoms, ADHD does not preclude patients benefiting from psychotherapy for life problems.

Patients with ADHD will enter therapy thinking about medication, on medication, or having failed medication. Any psychological treatment has to help them integrate the experience of taking a pill to assist with focus and restraint. An effective treatment needs to capitalize on the strength and limitations of the context of attributions around medication. Patients may use medication and psychoeducation as a way of excusing them from the forced effort required for change. Good psychological treatment is an antidote. This book is grounded in the questions patients ask. 'What is ADHD and what is me?' 'Should I tell people or should I keep it a secret?'

Medication treatment is a rapidly evolving area and no book can do justice to the latest innovations. If the patient does not take the pill, has misguided expectations, or sees himself as in a contest with the pill, medication will not be as effective. The authors have tried to formulate a way of providing a pharmacotherapy alliance.

Research on psychological treatment of ADHD is very much in its infancy. Yet the very early and methodologically limited studies of psychological treatment consistently showed improvement in symptoms, improvement in skills and deterioration in self-esteem. Insight brought its rewards, but also carried side effects. The side effect of realistic assessment of oneself is diminished grandiosity. Shrinking narcissism is good for the soul if one endures, but if the patient's only strength is the capacity to try, try again then it is not without its dangers. Young and Bramham learned this well. You cannot get better if you fail to bounce back. Throughout every module one hears the therapist negotiate between the twin dangers of unrealistic grandiosity that leads to repeated failure and despair that precludes continued effort.

Every day we are confronted with the impossibility of making up the difference between the hopes and dreams of our patients and what we can realistically provide. It is therefore with fear and trembling that we are now starting a psychotherapy program. From this strategic point of view some therapy is better than no therapy. We have to find a way to provide education, skills and coping strategies to many people, with many different problems and levels of functioning. This is a manual that lends itself to being delivered in a group or workshop modality. With limited manpower and explosive demand, this allows us to find a way to begin to deliver the essentials to our patients in a cost effective manner.

The group forum has potential to deal with the here and now of social interaction. Group treatment capitalizes on peer support. It is easier to illustrate how symptoms put a stamp on life history when more than one example is under discussion. Most of all, if one of the trademarks of disability is isolation, then the brand equity of good treatment is companionship. The hardest part of ending a group for patients with ADHD is that for many of the patients there, this will have been their first experience of being understood. They fear it will be their last. This is the first published manual I am aware of dedicated to providing a guide to psychological treatment that can be accommodated in group and workshop formats.

The single most difficult task for a patient with ADHD is to prioritize. Patients complain that they procrastinate, lack motivation, become easily distracted, and cannot stay on task. There are many coping strategies that are useful to deal with these problems. However, when the rubber hits the road, the hardest thing to explain to a patient is how to know what matters most. The early formulations of cognitive behaviour therapy described cognitive errors. They did not provide instruction in cognitive talents. Seeing the wood for the trees is a talent that underlies both the strength and the weakness of cognition in the face of an attention deficit. The problem-solving, CBT and motivational sections of this manual attempt to draw out therapeutic manoeuvres not just for getting it right, but getting what is most important.

In the past year publications by Solanto, Safren and Emilsson have all demonstrated that CBT for adults with ADHD is highly effective. The publication of the manuals by Solanto and Safren differ from this book in that they describe a fixed program in which one treatment fits all. By contrast, the approach taken by Young and Bramham is unique in that they have provided therapists with a clear description of the problem, the tools for therapy and an approach to therapy. However, they recognize that adults with ADHD may have core symptoms in common, but differ significantly in terms of the areas in which they need assistance. This is the only manual that provides 'modules' that can be adapted to the needs of patients who have distinct difficulties in a particular area. They go beyond teaching executive function skills to also addressing interpersonal relationships, sleep, addiction, and other issues that may be the most significant problem for a particular patient. This is a book then that can be adapted by clinicians to meet the needs of patients of both genders, adolescents as well as adults, and patients who are both high functioning and low functioning. This book is open to interpretation by each therapist and flexible enough to help most clients. The therapeutic approach is multi-faceted, appropriately reflecting the complexity of individuals who have ADHD. What the Young Bramham programme contributes is perspective. They have worked out what is most important and why it matters. In so doing they also helped us to begin to work out how to help patients develop this skill.

Margaret Weiss
Clinical Professor, University of British Columbia

FOREWORD BY SAM GOLDSTEIN

For many years it was reassuring for professionals and parents to believe that the problems caused by ADHD simply represented a poor fit between some children and their environments. It was comforting to reassure parents that the problem would be outgrown and with patience and treatment, ADHD was not likely to cause children significant lifetime adversity. Over the past twenty years the belief that ADHD is just a childhood condition quickly outgrown by late adolescence has been increasingly tested. A significant number of individuals, male and female alike, suffering with ADHD in their childhood, continue to suffer and lead lives less than their capabilities often into their geriatric years. Though a number of early pioneers advised professionals to consider the plight of many adults with histories of ADHD, it was not until the concept of ADHD was popularized in the lay press and media that serious attention began to be paid to the condition. Though some would argue the condition and its treatments are controversial, within the scientific and mental health community little controversy remains (Asherson *et al.*, 2010). The body of literature attesting to the emotional, cognitive, vocational, academic, substance use and criminal risks of the condition is quickly growing. As editor-in-chief of the *Journal of Attention Disorders* I have observed that in each of the past 8 years we have received an increasing number of articles researching adult ADHD issues and are devoting an increasing number of our journal pages and special issues to the condition in adulthood.

Though one-third of adults with ADHD may progress satisfactorily into their adult years, another one-third continues to experience some level of problems while the final third continues to experience and often develops significant problems related to ADHD and other comorbid conditions. Despite popular myth, ADHD is neither an asset driving greatness nor even a minor inconvenience for those affected individuals. By combining a number of outcome studies, it is reasonable to conclude that only 10 per cent to 20 per cent of adults with histories of ADHD experience few problems. Sixty per cent continue to demonstrate symptoms of ADHD and experience social, academic and emotional problems to at least a moderate degree and 10 per cent to 30 per cent develop more serious comorbid disorders as well as antisocial problems in addition to their continued difficulty with ADHD and other comorbidities. Many of these negative outcomes are linked to the continuity, severity and persistence of ADHD symptoms. Though males may experience more problems with disruptive and aggressive behaviour, females with ADHD appear to suffer equally or to a greater degree in all other arenas of life.

In 2002, Dr. Ann Teeter-Ellison and I had the pleasure to edit the first comprehensive, clinical volume addressing adult ADHD, *Clinician's Guide to Adult ADHD: Assessment and Intervention* (Goldstein and Teeter-Ellison, 2002). At the time, there were a limited number of peer reviewed, research studies focusing on adults, even fewer research tested methods for evaluating and most importantly treating adults with ADHD through combined medical and psychological interventions. It was our intent in this volume to begin aggressively addressing these issues by offering authors with promising though not completely tested ideas, particularly in regards to psychological and psychosocial treatment, the opportunity to contribute to our volume. A number of years earlier I had the opportunity to meet and spend time with Susan Young in London. Susan was focusing her treatment efforts on developing a model of psychotherapy for adults with ADHD. Susan agreed to author a contribution to our text. Her chapter (Young, 2002) provided one of the first, published comprehensive approaches to treating adult ADHD through a cognitive behavioural therapy model. In her chapter, Dr. Young reviewed the typical impairments confronting adults with ADHD, provided four extensive case examples and then set out to outline a cognitive behavioural therapy approach for treating adults with ADHD based on her work and her published article applying cognitive behavioural therapy in the treatment of adults with ADHD (Young, 1999). One of the aspects of Dr. Young's approach that appealed to me was that she emphasized that psychotherapists and mental health professionals should seek out and help adults with ADHD take advantage of their strengths as a means of creating balance in their lives and learning to cope with their symptoms and impairments. She noted at the conclusion of her chapter that, with the help of caring professionals, adults with ADHD 'have choice and opportunity to develop these talents and adapt the environment to suit their personal needs. What they often lack is the vision and courage to do so' (p. 158).

In the following years, Dr. Young joined forces with Jessica Bramham and other colleagues in expanding her work. They have worked diligently to continue studying adult ADHD and to create a psychosocial model to treat adult ADHD utilizing a cognitive behavioral framework (Bramham *et al.*, 2009; Gudjonsson *et al.*, 2009; Young, 2005; Young and Gudjonsson, 2008).

The first edition of this volume was well received. Reviewers noted that the program outlined in the initial volume offered a useful and practical set of tools for clinical practice. This second edition represents an important second step in standardizing the psychosocial treatment of adults with ADHD. The Young-Bramham program has been empirically validated (Bramham *et al.*, 2009). Similar to the work of American researchers Safren *et al.* (2005a) and Safren *et al.* (2005b), Dr. Young and colleagues have continued the important process of validating a cognitive behavioural approach to treating adults with ADHD (see also Emilsson *et al*., 2011; Young *et al*. (forthcoming). This approach has been found to not only offer personal insight and psychological relief but also the reduction of symptom severity and daily impairment.

This expanded second edition extends the Young-Bramham treatment model into the adolescent years, a critical time setting the stage for an important transition for this population (Young, Murphy and Coghill, forthcoming). New to this volume are outlines suggesting delivery of strategies and interventions in a group format as well as separate modules designed to develop and facilitate attention and memory. Each chapter has been extensively revised and updated. New references have been added. Examples relevant to adolescents as well as adulthood have been expanded. The structure of each module has been reorganized and streamlined following a consistent format. Finally, the chapter on assessment of ADHD in the initial volume has been eliminated to make space for the additions and extensions noted above.

The hypothesis that ADHD represents a lifetime condition has been tested and verified. Current theory for the aetiology of ADHD is consistent with a lifetime presentation reflecting developmental rather than pathological differences between affected individuals and the general population. The consequences of living with the burden of a significantly disabling condition, and one that leads to impaired self-discipline, has resulted in demonstrated problems across all arenas of life for adults with ADHD. The condition serves as a global risk factor limiting the potential for academic and vocational achievement as well as acting as a catalyst for comorbid psychiatric and life problems. Though much work remains to be done to understand the developmental course, risk and protective factors involved in the adult outcome of ADHD, the expanded second edition of this volume will continue to serve as a bright beacon guiding professionals in their care of adolescents and adults with ADHD in what has been an often dark and murky journey.

Sam Goldstein
Salt Lake City, Utah

PREFACE

We have frequently been asked for advice from clinicians working with adult ADHD clients in many different settings, including general adult mental health services, learning disability services, children's transition to adulthood services, forensic services, neuropsychiatry and neuropsychology services. These days we are being increasingly asked for advice from educational and occupational settings, prison and probation services. We wrote the Young-Bramham Programme to develop a conceptual framework and a unique approach for assessing and treating people with ADHD and associated problems. The book was first published in 2007 and focused on adults with ADHD. However, feedback from colleagues across the world was that they were successfully applying the programme for use with young people in their adolescent years. This led us to systematically revise the programme modules to make the book more 'user friendly' for therapists who are also working with adolescents. We have also responded to feedback suggesting that we provide template sessions for modules to be provided in group format and these can be found at the end of each chapter.

A lot has happened since the publication of the first edition in 2007. The scientific knowledge about ADHD has mushroomed and it is now widely accepted to be a condition that affects many people across the lifespan. The UK NICE Guidelines, published in 2009, provided clear guidelines for ADHD across the lifespan and the requirement for adult mental health services to recognize the disorder and provide diagnostic and treatment services. The Guidelines also drew attention to the importance of psychological interventions as a firstline treatment for children, for those with mild symptoms, and as an important complementary treatment for adults with ADHD. A key priority of the Guidelines was that drug treatment for children and young people with ADHD should always form part of a comprehensive treatment plan that includes psychological, behavioural and educational advice and interventions. NICE recommended that for older adolescents direct individual psychological interventions, using cognitive behavioural and social skills paradigms, may be more effective and acceptable to the young person. They recommended that active learning strategies should be used for a range of treatment targets, including social skills with peers, problem-solving, self-control, listening skills and dealing with and expressing feelings. These recommendations endorse the cognitive behavioural paradigm that is employed by the Young-Bramham Programme and introduced in this revised book for ADHD adolescents and adults.

Both of us are clinical psychologists and clinical neuropsychologists and we have spent several years working in a national referral service for adults with ADHD at the Maudsley Hospital in London. Between us, we have assessed and treated many hundreds of people with hundreds of people with ADHD have gained considerable insight into their problems and developed skills in working with this client group. In the book we have drawn on our knowledge and experience and provided case examples for illustration. All case examples provided throughout the book have been adapted so that clients remain anonymous. The book is accompanied by the Young-Bramham Programme Companion Website, which provides all the materials outlined in the chapters. These materials can be downloaded for use in sessions and by clients outside the sessions.

The Young-Bramham Programme is intended to help clinicians who have some knowledge of psychological approaches or cognitive behavioural therapy with clients with mental health difficulties, but who may not have worked with many adolescents or adults with ADHD. It will also be useful for therapists who have some knowledge of childhood ADHD, who are interested in how the disorder progresses and potential treatment strategies for ADHD 'graduates' or young adults. It is always gratifying to get feedback directly from clients, and it has been pleasing to hear that the book is pitched at a level that makes it accessible to clients as a 'self-help' book and has been used in this way for people to develop techniques for managing their own difficulties.

We have learnt a great deal from our clients and, in the Young-Bramham Programme, we hope to convey many of our positive experiences working with clients with ADHD. For us, their determination to access services, their motivation to change and receive psychological therapy has provided a consistent incentive to share our knowledge and experience.

Susan Young
Jessica Bramham

ACKNOWLEDGEMENTS

First and foremost, we wish to thank our clients who have shared with us their experiences, hopes and problems. We are grateful to those who supported us during the preparation of the first edition of the book and now with this revised edition. In particular we are grateful to Jane Adams, Seamus O'Ceallaigh, Philippa Bramham, Professor Gisli Gudjonsson, Josip Lizatovic, Helen Fleck, Amie Doidge and Catherine Lorek.

We dedicate this book to our children, Charlotte, Aengus and Élis, with the knowledge that you reach your dreams one step at a time.

PART I

BACKGROUND AND TREATMENT

1

INTRODUCTION

This book aims to provide clinicians with a comprehensive psychological guide to practice when working with adolescents and adults with ADHD by providing cognitive behavioural therapy (CBT) to treat core symptoms of the condition and its associated problems. As ADHD is a heterogeneous disorder, each individual is likely to present with a different constellation of symptoms with a range of psychological strengths and weaknesses. For this reason, this book consists of stand-alone modules that can be delivered in individual or group format and which together form the Young-Bramham Programme. The Young-Bramham Programme provides an innovative and intensive practical approach to the presentation of ADHD using cognitive behavioural and motivational interviewing techniques, which are described in detail using case examples. Each module is presented in a separate chapter of this book and can be used independently or in conjunction with other modules.

Practitioners often report feeling underequipped to treat this client group and there remains a limited literature on psychological treatment for adolescents and adults. Up to two-thirds of ADHD children continue to suffer with symptoms into adult life, many of whom experience residual problems which warrant treatment (Young and Gudjonsson, 2008). In addition, there are many young people who do not receive a diagnosis until they are adults in spite of having presented on numerous occasions to health services (Huntley and Young, submitted; Young, Toone and Tyson, 2003). ADHD has often been missed in the past, and misdiagnosis abounds. Aside from these clinical groups, there are additionally many individuals who have symptoms that fall below the threshold for formal diagnosis, but who nevertheless may benefit from psychological treatment to address their problems and functional impairments. Thus, the Young-Bramham Programme was developed as an intervention suitable for individuals with a formal ADHD diagnosis, individuals who are in partial remission of their symptoms, and individuals who present with an undiagnosed constellation of ADHD symptoms and related problems.

Cognitive-Behavioural Therapy for ADHD in Adolescents and Adults: A Psychological Guide to Practice, Second Edition. Susan Young and Jessica Bramham.

A second reason for writing the book was that we have talked to our clients and listened to their life histories. They have such stories to tell and it is clear that for many the pathway is far from easy, yet over and over again we have recognized characteristics of determination, resilience, ingenuity and creativity. We interviewed some of our patients and their partners with the aim of analyzing their experience of receiving a diagnosis and treatment for ADHD in adulthood and, for their partners, their experience of supporting them through this process. After feelings of relief and a sense of hope and expectation for the future, they were disappointed with treatment as this was not a panacea. They were not 'cured' and core functional problems persisted associated with organization and time-management skills, procrastination and low self-esteem (Young, Bramham and Gray, 2009; Young *et al.*, 2008). Thus our long experience in delivering psychological interventions to adolescents and adults with ADHD, together with our extensive research on the topic, led us to develop the Young-Bramham Programme to address the persisting problems that people experience regardless of whether they receive medication or not. We are not saying that this programme will fully bridge the gap and provide a 'cure' for adults and young people with ADHD, we are however confident that the strategies and techniques provided in the Young-Bramham Programme will provide additional and valued support.

THE COMPANION WEBSITE

The Young-Bramham Programme book is supplemented by a Companion Website, which provides practical and pragmatic exercises that allow the client to identify personal specific problems and methods to address them. Strategies which involve writing ideas down or making lists of potential consequences target difficulties in organizational skills and memory problems which are inherent in ADHD. The therapist therefore needs to maximize the opportunity to create lists and structure plans during sessions. Examples, charts, diaries, figures, diagrams and illustrations are presented in both the book and on the Companion Website (the latter in a format suitable for use in sessions) to clarify information, and/or to improve accessibility and understanding of the concepts and issues presented. The Companion Website provides psychoeducational handouts and blank copies of relevant materials introduced in the programme. It can be accessed with the password provided. The materials can be downloaded, copied and used in treatment sessions to determine, evaluate and treat specific symptoms, problems and strategies. The materials will help the therapist and the client to collaboratively tailor the Young-Bramham Programme interventions according to the clients' specific needs.

ADHD IN ADOLESCENCE AND ADULTHOOD

ADHD is an established neurodevelopmental condition characterized by inattention, hyperactivity and impulsivity or a combination of these problems that commences in childhood and often persists into adolescence and occupational lives. There is a clear treatment pathway. It is recognized that life span conditions such as ADHD should have a planned transfer of care from child, through adolescent, to adult services as young people move from one service to another at specified age milestones (Nutt *et al.*, 2007).

International Guidelines on ADHD

There are published international guidelines providing advice on the assessment, treatment and management of people with ADHD (NICE, 2009; Seixas, Weiss and Muller, 2011). In the United Kingdom, the National Institute of Health and Clinical Excellence (NICE) published guidelines on ADHD in 2009 and for the first time provided guidelines for ADHD across the lifespan with the requirement for adult mental health services to recognize the disorder and provide diagnostic and treatment services. The Guidelines also drew attention to the importance of psychological interventions as a first-line treatment for children, for those with mild symptoms, and as an important complementary treatment for adults with ADHD. A key priority of the Guidelines was that drug treatment for children and young people with ADHD should always form part of a comprehensive treatment plan that includes psychological, behavioural and educational advice and interventions. NICE recommended that for older adolescents direct individual psychological interventions, using cognitive behavioural and social skills paradigms, may be more effective and acceptable to the young person. They recommended that active learning strategies should be used for a range of treatment targets, including social skills with peers, problem-solving, self-control, listening skills and dealing with and expressing feelings. These recommendations endorse the cognitive behavioural paradigm employed within the Young-Bramham programme that is applied to adolescents and adults.

ADHD Symptoms

The symptoms of ADHD are inattention, hyperactivity and impulsivity however ADHD is a heterogeneous disorder and there are broad individual differences as to how these symptoms present. Additionally, with maturity there is often a shift with hyperactivity and impulsivity modifying more than attentional symptoms (Marsh and Williams, 2004). Adolescents are more likely to fidget than run around aimlessly and problems with organization and time-management become more apparent. The progression of ADHD is also heterogeneous with some individuals experiencing full remission by adulthood, some partial remission and others none at all (Faraone, Biederman and Mick, 2006; Young and Gudjonsson, 2008). While some symptoms may appear to spontaneously remit with age, relative differences that are associated with significant functional impairments may remain; indeed around two-thirds of ADHD children will experience some persisting symptoms as young adults that will be associated with significant impairment (Faraone, Biederman and Mick, 2006).

Comorbidity

For young people with ADHD comorbidity is the rule rather than the exception, as up to two-thirds of ADHD children have one or more comorbid conditions, including oppositional defiant and/or conduct disorder, anxiety, depression, substance misuse, tic disorders and autistic spectrum disorders (Biederman, Newcorn and Sprich, 1991; Elia, Ambrosini and Berrettini, 2008; Goldman *et al.*, 1998; Pliszka, 1998). Multiple presentations to health and social services have been reported by individuals who were not diagnosed until adulthood (Huntley and Young, submitted; Young, Toone and Tyson, 2003) suggesting ADHD symptoms are being missed or misdiagnosed in children. Yet for those who are identified in childhood, treatment with stimulant medication may not be fully protective as follow-up data from 208 ADHD children treated with stimulants found that 23 per cent had a psychiatric admission in adulthood (mean age of 31). Conduct problems in childhood were predictive (hazard ratio HR = 2.3) and girls had a higher risk compared with boys (HR = 2.4) (Dalsgaard *et al.*, 2002).

While many comorbid conditions can be effectively treated by psychological interventions, we have found that therapists often feel apprehensive about intervening in the same way with clients with ADHD. This may be because they lack confidence in providing treatment for individuals who may present with high rates of comorbid psychiatric problems and additional overlapping, complicating psychosocial factors. We therefore decided to write this book to share our knowledge and provide guidance for practitioners who are working with adolescents and adults with ADHD.

Aetiology

The reason people develop ADHD is not clear and most likely involves a range of genetic, environmental and psychosocial factors (NICE, 2009). ADHD often runs in families and studies have shown that it is highly heritable (Steinhausen, 2009). Genes play an important role in brain development and a number of different genes are thought to be involved and that are linked to the dopamine and serotonin systems in the brain (Stergiakouli and Thapar, 2010). Environmental factors may also affect brain development such as smoking, drinking, and substance use during pregnancy, preterm birth, low birth weight, birth trauma and maternal depression. These factors can interact with genetic/neurological factors to increase the risk of developing ADHD. The causal link between psychosocial factors and ADHD is unclear but it seems that disruption to early attachment, social adversity and deprivation may be associated with the development of ADHD (Rutter, 2005).

Sex Differences and ADHD

In childhood more boys than girls are diagnosed with ADHD with a ratio of around four to one reported in research; by adulthood however this difference becomes much less skewed (Kessler *et al.*, 2006). This may be due to a referral bias in childhood with more boys being referred for clinical assessment due to their greater externalizing problems. Boys are more likely to present with disruptive behaviour and conduct problems leading them to attract the notice of health and educational professionals (Biederman *et al.*, 1999; Gaub and Carlson, 1997). In contrast, girls are more likely to present with attentional problems, internalizing problems and disruption to peer relationships (Rucklidge and Tannock, 2001; Taylor *et al.*, 19961; Young *et al.*, 2005a, 2005b).

By young adulthood females are more likely to engage with health services for mood and anxiety disorders and/or due to pregnancy. This more frequent engagement may also be a contributory factor to the observed sex ratio adjustment in males and females being diagnosed with ADHD. Nevertheless the early sex differences in presentation of externalizing and internalizing symptoms appear to persist as higher rates of ADHD males are reported to be engaging in antisocial or criminal behaviour (Young *et al.*, 2011) compared with ADHD females who have higher rates of psychiatric admissions (Dalsgaard *et al.*, 2002).

These findings endorse the provision of sex specific treatments as opposed to structured 'one size fits all' treatment paradigm. The Young-Bramham modules are highly suited to this approach as therapists may select interventions appropriate to the individual presentation of their female and male patients. It is particularly striking that for people with ADHD, strengths and weaknesses in coping skills may be contrary to those typically reported (i.e. females usually being more prone to using emotional coping strategies and males tending to be more adept with problem-focused strategies). Indeed female adolescents adopt a variety of ineffectual coping strategies (Young *et al.*, 2005a). Thus it is important that the therapy addresses individual coping styles and facilitates clients to select, develop and apply functional strategies to overcome their problems.

ADHD and Intellectual Functioning

ADHD is experienced by people throughout the intellectual spectrum. This means that people with high intellectual functioning also develop ADHD. However it is often mistakenly believed that high functioning individuals cannot possibly have ADHD leading them to experience a similar struggle as their lower IQ peers in attempting to get recognition and treatment for their symptoms. Their personal histories, academic and occupational attainment may be very different and without impairment in childhood but, without a doubt, what they both share in common is that they are underperforming in their personal potential and this causes confusion and distress.

In our experience the high functioning person with ADHD is more likely to present to services for diagnosis and treatment later on in life, often in adulthood. This is because they have usually learned and applied constructive compensatory strategies, such as those outlined in the Young-Bramham Programme, to support them in their endeavours. Children with high IQs are also more likely to attend selective educational establishments that are attended by other bright children. Here, they are likely to have benefited from smaller class sizes with greater structure and less opportunity for distraction; they may have had greater opportunity for individual tuition through higher teacher to pupil ratios and/or additional input by teaching assistants. This means that they may fare comparatively well academically (but usually with some inconsistency) and problems do not become evident until much later in their occupation when they are expected to take responsibility for organizing their own work and/or leading others. For individuals who remain symptomatic, this can be the point when things breakdown. Others continue to adapt and find ways to overcome challenges by applying functional strategies. For them, a breakdown in these strategies may be precipitated by external factors in their occupation (high pressure of work and long hours), and/or because their personal resources have become diminished due to the development of physical or mental health problems and/or triggered by serious life events (such as bereavement, redundancy and divorce). Then, like a row of cards, everything collapses; the person becomes unable to apply compensatory strategies and may start to engage in dysfunctional strategies (such as drinking excessive alcohol or taking drugs). It is not long before the companion of 'impairment' becomes unavoidable.

Turning to the other end of the intellectual spectrum, confusion often arises from international differences in terminology regarding the comorbidity of learning disabilities and ADHD. In Europe, the term learning *disability* is used synonymously with the North American term 'mental retardation', whereas in North America, the term learning *disability* is more consistent with the European understanding of specific learning *difficulty*. Specific learning difficulties are characterized by a skill, such as reading, spelling, writing, arithmetic being differentially affected in the context of otherwise adequate mental functioning, that is, the individual's overall functioning is not globally low.

Some clinicians suggest that ADHD and learning disabilities are indistinguishable (e.g. Prior and Sanson, 1986) and that the core features of ADHD are expressed as a learning disabilities characteristic. However, it is now established that people with learning disability can present with ADHD if their attentional ability, hyperactivity levels and impulsivity, are below those expected given their developmental level. Furthermore, it is now recognized among many clinicians that individuals with pervasive developmental disorders are also more likely to present with ADHD symptoms warranting a comorbid diagnosis but the two diagnoses are currently mutually exclusive in DSM-IV. It has therefore been proposed that these criteria are changed in future revisions in order to accommodate the possibility of comorbid pervasive developmental disorder and ADHD (Goldstein and Schwebach, 2004).

Psychostimulant treatment of adults with learning disabilities and ADHD seems to be effective and well-tolerated (Jou, Handen and Hardan, 2004) but larger studies are required in order to fully determine their efficacy. Guidance regarding psychological intervention with clients with comorbid ADHD and learning disabilities is very limited in the current literature. While the Young-Bramham Programme is primarily devised for use with nonlearning disabled individuals, this does not preclude use with learning disabilities clients with ADHD but several adaptations would be required.

First, attentional and response inhibition difficulties may be more pronounced for people with learning disabilities (Fox and Wade, 1998; Rose *et al.*, 2009) which will further limit their ability to sustain attention in sessions. Thus if possible, the sessions need to be on a 'little and often' basis, that is, frequent, brief time periods, such as half an hour twice per week. Second, the primary therapeutic approach should be behavioural, as many individuals with learning disabilities have difficulty in accessing and applying cognitive strategies. Behavioural experiments in sessions, practical examples and simple explanations are particularly important for successful intervention with this client group. The therapist may also wish to recruit the assistance of a family member or carer who can reinforce outside the session what has been learned, as well as support homework tasks.

Specific learning problems such as dyslexia and dyscalculia have also been reported as more prevalent in individuals with ADHD (e.g. Rabiner and Cole, 2000). As a result, some individuals may be assessed for their specific learning difficulties while their underlying ADHD symptoms remain unrecognized for some time. While there is comorbidity between ADHD and specific learning difficulty, some individuals find their learning problems appear to be due to the latter but clinical assessment and formal testing indicates that an attention deficit is the primary problem.

There are three possible explanations for the association between ADHD and specific learning difficulty: (1) attention impairments impede learning; (2) working memory difficulties can affect the ability to unravel complex grammar; and/or (3) both conditions share similar neurobiological underpinnings, particularly those relating to executive dysfunction (e.g. Denkla, 1996). Indeed, frontal lobe systems involving cognitive control are likely to be affected and can result in attentional and information processing difficulties common to both disorders (Duncan *et al.*, 1994).

Individuals with comorbid ADHD and dyslexia may be underrepresented in clinical services because they have difficulty in completing screening questionnaires and this deters them from following through referrals. Such individuals may be helped by having written materials relating to the diagnostic and/or treatment process presented in an appropriate form for their needs, for example, enlarged text using black and white simple characters. Some treatment exercises may be adapted from written form to verbal record using a recording device. Session may be recorded in a similar fashion.

THE TRANSITION FROM ADOLESCENCE TO ADULTHOOD

By the adoption of a lifespan perspective, international guidelines such as those published by NICE (2009) have led practitioners to focus on the needs of young people with persisting or remitting ADHD symptoms in adolescence and how best to support them. These young people are in transition between child services and adult mental health services. However, it should be borne in mind that transition is not simply an administrative healthcare exercise as these young people are also in a personal transition when they mature physically and emotionally (Young, Murphy and Coghill, 2011). During this period young people become increasingly autonomous as they move from a child to adult role and make important and defining decisions about their future, establish key life goals and beliefs and take responsibility for their behaviour. This is paralleled by role experimentation to form their self-concept and develop a personal and social identity. Typical adolescent development is associated with increased risk taking behaviour and mortality, including substance use, accidents and self-harm (Hafner and An Der, 1997). Late adolescence is a risk period for increased mental health problems and greater complexity. It is a time when serious mental disorders such as psychosis and bipolar disorder become more common (Goodwin, 2009; Park *et al.*, 2006). It is also a time of considerable environmental and psychosocial change; moving from school to college/employment, into new relationships and sometimes parenthood and leaving home. It is against this backdrop that young people with persistent ADHD symptoms must make the transition to new clinical services. They are disadvantaged in the process by their underlying mental health condition(s) and from their incomplete development (While *et al.*, 2004). Typically young people with ADHD experience negative feedback from adults from a very young age and they often lack self-efficacy; thus they feel ill-equipped to deal with the challenges and problems they are facing, and attempt to overcome them with an inadequate repertoire of adaptive skills and coping strategies (Young, 2005; Young *et al.*, 2005a). Thus service transfer occurs at a time of increased vulnerability, and when young people with ADHD may require guidance and support from trusted carers, including healthcare professionals.

The quandary is that something is going very wrong at this stage and concerns are growing over the high risk of drop out of ADHD services during adolescence. Late adolescence has been identified as a period of high attrition from ADHD health services with discontinuation of pharmacotherapy by the age of 21 (McCarthy *et al.*, 2009). This cannot reflect rates of spontaneous symptom remission as around two-thirds of ADHD children will continue to suffer impairment of symptoms at age 25 (Faraone, Biederman and Mick, 2006). It is essential that health services maintain engagement with young people; one way may be to target adolescent youths for direct psychological interventions that aim to prevent disengagement, and facilitate transition by the provision of a holistic framework that focuses on the developmental needs of the individual. Yet such interventions are infrequently implemented in spite of these young people being at a developmental stage when they are most likely to be embraced (e.g. older, taking personal responsibility) (Young, Murphy and Coghill, 2011).

The reasons behind a decline in service utilization may be manifold. It may reflect a desire for autonomy; leaving school and perceiving less of a need for medication to control symptoms; a lower perception of need by parents and teachers as the young person matures; and change in environment to one with different cognitive demands (e.g. leaving school and starting unskilled occupations). Young people may reject adult services due to a reluctance to 'start again' with a new team. As young people take on greater responsibility and become less dependent on parental support, they may forget to attend their appointments or make the decision to discontinue with medication. They may also wish to avoid the stigma of referral to adult mental health services. The decline may also reflect the relatively poor service provision for older adolescents and young adults with ADHD, the perception that ADHD needs to be managed by clinicians with specific expertise, or a lack of local shared care arrangements between services. Limited availability of psychoeducational materials for adolescents with ADHD and their families may also contribute to a lack of awareness of the possible change in impact of symptoms with age. A lack of familiarity among child health professionals of the change in presentation of ADHD symptoms with increasing age may lead to underrecognition of symptoms, premature termination of cases and a lack of recognition of the need to assess, triage and transition appropriately (Kooij *et al.*, 2010; McCarthy *et al.*, 2009). Similarly, it may also result in underrecognition of symptoms in adults presenting to community mental health teams (Asherson, 2005).

A COGNITIVE-BEHAVIOURAL MODEL OF ADHD

Based on our research and experience of working therapeutically with people with ADHD, we have devised a cognitive-behavioural model to formulate their presentation (see Figure 1.1). This figure is included on the Companion Website. It may be helpful to work through the figure and 'personalize' the formulation with the client.

Due to their longstanding neuropsychological impairments such as poor concentration, forgetfulness, problem-solving difficulties and a need for immediate gratification, people growing up with ADHD having experienced numerous negative life events. Such experiences include academic underachievement, occupational difficulties, problems in making and maintaining friendships and intimate relationships as well as experiences associated with novelty seeking and risk-taking behaviours.

When faced with certain situations or tasks, such as social encounters, dealing with conflict, or attending a job interview, people with ADHD may find that their neuropsychological impairments hamper their performance. Due to a history of failure, they can be prone to negatively appraise a situation with a pessimistic bias. Failure is likely to impact on their self-esteem; they may begin to doubt their own abilities, and in a self-fulfilling prophecy, expect failure in the future. Following negative appraisal, an individual may engage in negative behaviours such as verbal or physical aggression or they may withdraw or engage in maladaptive coping, such as alcohol or substance misuse. They are likely to have negative thoughts and beliefs about their abilities and focus on weaknesses. The combination of negative behaviour and negative thoughts or beliefs is likely to induce or worsen a negative mood stage such as anxiety, frustration or anger. Being in a negative mood state means that an individual is more likely to appraise a subsequent situation in a negative way, and so the cycle continues.

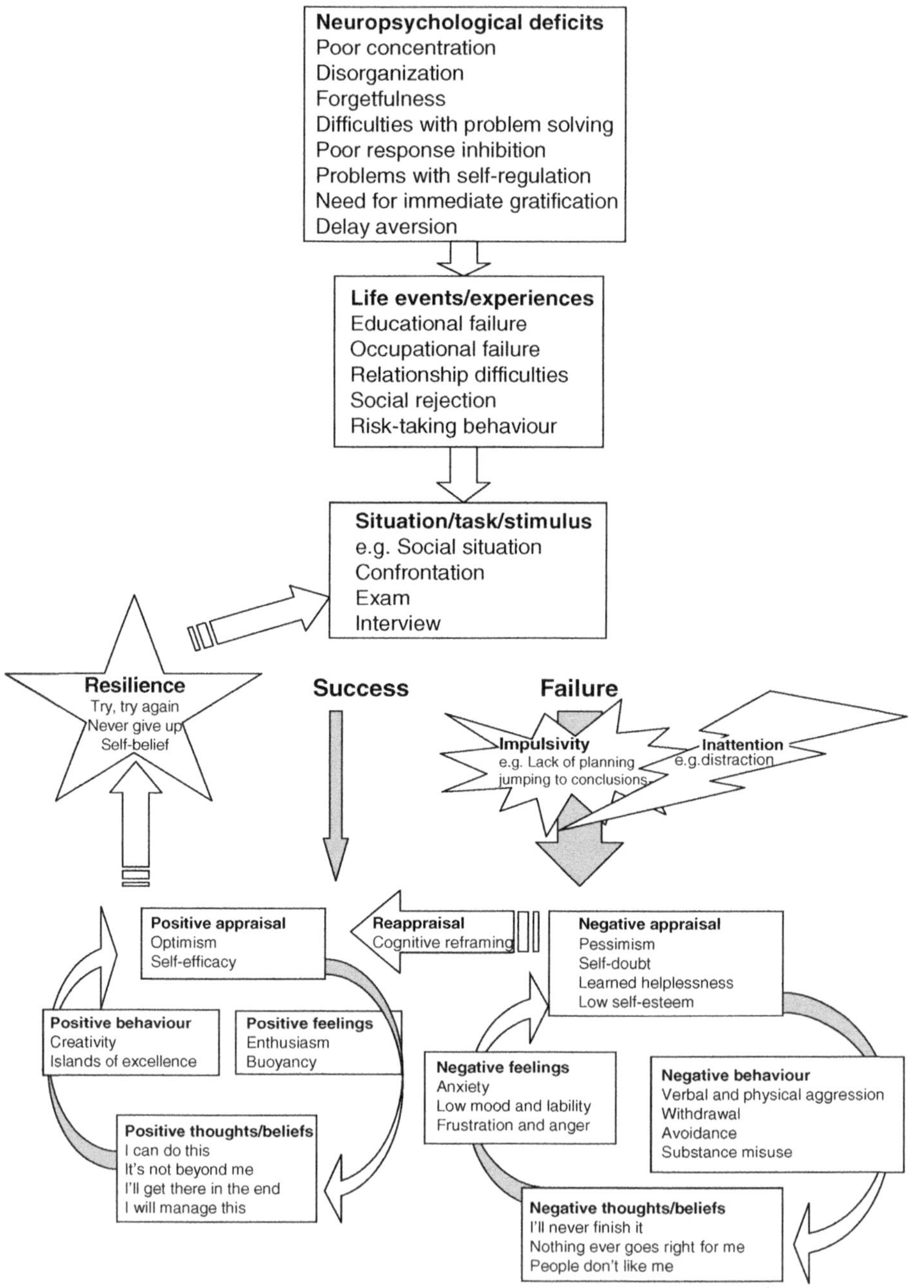

Figure 1.1 A cognitive behavioural model of ADHD in adults

However, there is both anecdotal and research evidence to suggest that adults with ADHD have an aptitude for the reappraisal or cognitive reframing of stressful situations (Young, 2005). It is possible that the negative cycle itself becomes a motivational force that compels change in situation. A 'Drive Theory' was initially proposed by Hull in 1943. According to this theory, humans are driven to reduce arousal or tension in order to maintain a sense of comfort and equilibrium (Hull, 1943). While people with ADHD may engage in a spontaneous process of reappraisal, this is likely to be negatively influenced by their cognitive impairments, resulting in the process being dysfunctional or unsuccessful. Nevertheless, a cycle is re-entered by the ADHD individual positively reframing the negative outcome, causing them to try again in the hope of achieving success. This explains the resilience commonly found in people with ADHD and suggests that this is underpinned by self-efficacy. Therefore the way they interact is associated with their ability to continually compensate and adapt. This adaptive aspect of the syndrome may be expressed creatively in innovative and entrepreneurial endeavours and personality characteristics (Young, 2005).

EVIDENCE FOR PSYCHOLOGICAL INTERVENTIONS

A review of nonpharmacological ADHD treatments across the life-span identified a gap in treatments for adolescents and adults with ADHD. By comparison there was a great deal of guidance, in the form of evidence based practice, for the delivery of psychological interventions for preschoolers and children (Young and Amarasinghe, 2010). This most likely reflects that the indirect psychological interventions typically delivered to children (via parents and teachers) are unsuitable for adolescents and young adults. The review identified two important factors with respect to the provision of psychological interventions as children mature; (1) the agent of implementation must shift from an indirect model in childhood to a direct intervention involving face-to-face contact with the developing adolescent and adult, and (2) the mode of intervention must shift to reflect the developmental needs and circumstance of the young person and adult (Young and Amarasinghe, 2010). Thus the Young-Bramham Programme addresses both of these factors by prescribing direct treatment for adolescents as well as adults and by taking a holistic approach to treatment that incorporates treatment for core symptoms, comorbid and/or developmentally defined associated problems.

Young and Amarasinghe (2010) noted that compared with investigating the effectiveness of psychopharmacological treatments, studies evaluating the effectiveness of psychological interventions in adolescents and adults are meagre. There are more studies using adult than adolescent samples and their findings are that psychological treatment in medicated patients (whether delivered in individual or group format) is effective in treating ADHD symptoms and has an additive effect over and above medication alone (Emilsson *et al.*, 2011; Hirvikoski *et al.*, 2011; Safren *et al.*, 2005b, 2010; Solanto *et al.*, 2010, Stevenson *et al.*, 2002; Virta *et al.*, 2010). The findings for treating comorbid problems however were mixed and most likely reflect that these

CBT interventions primarily targeted core symptoms of attention, impulsivity, planning and organization deficits. The exception being the manualized R&R2 ADHD (Young and Ross, 2007) approach which parallels the Young-Bramham Programme (and shares a co-author) by the provision of a multifaceted treatment programme to address ADHD symptoms and comorbid problems and includes modules on neurocognition, problem-solving, emotional control, prosocial skills and critical reasoning. In their randomized controlled trial, Emilsson *et al.* (2011) found that at 3-month follow-up R&R2 ADHD was highly effective in treating ADHD symptoms, anxiety, depression, antisocial behaviour and social functioning.

Comorbidity in ADHD is so common that interventions that take a holistic and modular approach are more likely to make global improvements in self-efficacy, self-esteem and quality of life. This was investigated in a controlled evaluation of the Young-Bramham Programme when this was delivered as an intensive 3-day intervention (1 day per month for 3 months) to medicated patients drawing on modules of attention, impulsivity, anxiety, anger, interpersonal relationships, time-management, problem-solving and preparing for the future. Clients reported a significant improvement in self-efficacy and self-esteem, together with their knowledge and understanding of the condition arising from the psychoeducational component of the programme (Bramham *et al.*, 2009).

INTRODUCTION TO THE YOUNG-BRAMHAM PROGRAMME

Part 1: Background and Treatment

Box 1.1 outlines how the Young-Bramham Programme is divided into four parts. It commences with a background and introductory section (Part I), followed by core symptom treatment modules (Part II), comorbid and associated problem treatment modules (Part III), and the final module preparing for the future (Part IV). The core symptom treatment modules include topics on attention, memory, organization and time-management, and impulsivity. The comorbid and associated problem modules include topics on problem-solving, interpersonal relationships, anxiety, frustration and anger, low mood and depression, sleep and substance misuse. Issues around individuals' expectations and plans for the future are presented in the concluding chapter.

The primary objective of the Young-Bramham Programme is to impart the psychological treatment that can be combined with or used in preference to pharmacological therapy. The Programme has two primary aims.

1. *Change from the outside in* – to provide clinicians with ways of encouraging young people with ADHD to change their environment and optimize functioning.
2. *Change from the inside out* – to provide clinicians with ways of encouraging the individual to develop psychological strategies for adaptive functioning.

Box 1.1 The Young-Bramham programme structure

Part I: Background and Treatment

Chapter 1	Introduction to ADHD in adolescence and adulthood ADHD, and the Young-Bramham Programme as a cognitive behavioural intervention
Chapter 2	Delivering the Young-Bramham Programme

Part II: Core Symptom Modules

Chapter 3	Attention Module
Chapter 4	Memory Module
Chapter 5	Organization and Time-Management Module
Chapter 6	Impulsivity Module

Part III: Comorbid and Associated Problem Modules

Chapter 7	Problem-Solving Module
Chapter 8	Interpersonal Relationships Module
Chapter 9	Anxiety Module
Chapter 10	Frustration and Anger Module
Chapter 11	Low-Mood and Depression Module
Chapter 12	Sleep Module
Chapter 13	Substance Misuse Module

Part IV: The Future Module

Chapter 14	Preparing for the Future Module

The clinician needs to instil hope and confidence in the client in order that he/she can make progress with appropriate treatment, combined with hard work and support. This perspective needs to be offered in light of the information that there is no 'magic cure' for ADHD. However it is possible to change how the person copes with the disorder and maximize individual strengths.

Chapter 2 sets out the aims and objectives of the Young-Bramham Programme and guidance on its delivery. We describe the intervention style of the programme and describe the strategies employed. This includes: psychoeducation to inform the client about the history, treatment and prognosis of the disorder; motivational interviewing to overcome ambivalence towards treatment; and therapeutic techniques (cognitive behavioural therapy, cognitive remediation, restructuring and reframing, rationalization) to address core symptoms, comorbid and associated problems. It is very important not to skip the psychoeducational component. Throughout their lives, clients may have been told that they are stupid, lazy and unmotivated and it can therefore be extremely therapeutic and can provide a sense of relief for the individual to understand that ADHD has a neurological basis and their problems are not due to a character defect. The chapter concludes with a description of the delivery of the Young-Bramham Programme either in individual or group format.

Part II: Core Symptom Modules

Part II consists of four modules on the topics of attention, memory, organization and time management and impulsivity. Each chapter follows a standard format providing a general introduction to the topic and a description of the functional deficits or problems faced by the developing adolescent and young adult. There follows methods to guide the therapist to assess and treat the problem with the client (and using materials that can be downloaded from the companion website), including specific cognitive behavioural strategies and techniques to address the problems identified. Each chapter concludes with an example template for the module to be delivered in group format.

The *Attention Module* (Chapter 3) addresses what is probably the most disabling symptom as individuals struggle to engage in activities that are long, boring, repetitious or tedious. By contrast, people can concentrate on activities that are interesting and motivating (such as computer games) for long periods of time. Such inconsistencies can be difficult to understand for people around them and can be a source of tension and frustration. In this module we introduce methods to assist clients to recognize tasks that may be problematic. We outline external strategies that can be applied to adapt the environment to minimize distraction, which often involves selecting the most appropriate surroundings suitable for success. We introduce strategies to optimize performance, for example, goal setting, and the introduction of breaks, incentives and rewards.

The *Memory Module* (Chapter 4) addresses a very overt difficulty. It is distressing because it is very noticeable when people with ADHD miss appointments, forget important dates, or turn up late without the things that they need. The most common memory problems are short-term memory problems and these are closely associated with attentional difficulties whereby problems with initial processing lead to later difficulties with remembering. Thus this module follows a similar format as the Attention Module by identifying individual memory problems and applying external strategies (such as use of diaries, electronic devices and alarms) and internal strategies (such as repetition, rehearsal, visual cue and use of mnemonics) to overcome them.

The *Organization and Time-Management Module* (Chapter 5) addresses problems that become more marked as children become adolescents and young adults. The ability to organize and prioritize is particularly challenging for people who tend to flit like butterflies from task to task, especially when an activity is mundane, or when beckoned by a seemingly more important task. Unfinished tasks are a source of frustration and leave the individual with a sense of failure. This module presents ways of applying a methodical approach to make plans by reviewing goals for a set time period (short- and long-term), listing activities, devising a schedule, sequencing and prioritizing activities, and planning breaks and rewards. We also include methods for avoiding pitfalls, such as ways of maintaining attention on a task, ways of adhering to a plan, advice regarding reviewing priorities and avoiding procrastination.

The *Impulsivity Module* (Chapter 6) addresses behaviours that are often closely linked to a low tolerance of boredom, feelings of frustration, a preference for short-term rewards and an inability to delay gratification. People with ADHD find it difficult to wait; they speak out or act without thinking and tend not to engage in a process of consequential thinking. There are obvious social ramifications when individuals present in this manner as they appear to lack consideration for the feelings and needs of others. These behaviours may lead to serious consequences such as delinquency, driving violations and accidental injury. This module introduces self-monitoring techniques to identify situations in which clients are vulnerable to responding in an impulsive way. Stop-and-think techniques are introduced to maximize self-control, including the consideration of personal and social consequences, and the use of self-instructional training and self-statements which are subsequently rehearsed in role-plays.

Part III: Comorbid and Associated Problem Modules

There are several secondary social and emotional sequelae of ADHD. These include: impaired problem-solving skills; poor social skills and interpersonal relationship problems; anxiety; frustration and poor anger control; low mood and depression; sleep difficulties; and substance misuse. We have therefore devised treatment strategies which can be applied to address these areas of comorbid difficulty. Low self-esteem is a problem that is so universal and debilitating for people with ADHD, we have included this as a common thread that is implicitly provided in each of the Young-Bramham Programme modules.

The *Problem-Solving Module* (Chapter 7) examines the reasons that people with ADHD have poor problem-solving skills. This includes impulsive responding, leading to rash decision making and without full evaluation of a situation. They may worry unnecessarily about minor more immediate issues and lose sight of the whole picture. In addition, attention problems may interfere in a functional problem-solving process by them becoming distracted and moving off-task. This module outlines a set procedure to define a problem and distinguish 'problems' from 'worries', generate solutions, evaluate solutions and consider alternatives. A methodology for choosing solutions is introduced through the rehearsal of solutions to evaluate consequences, role-playing appropriate scenarios, and challenging cognitive distortions.

The *Interpersonal Relationships Module* (Chapter 8) addresses disruption to interpersonal relationships. Clients are likely to have experienced a lifetime of adverse interactions with other people and some individuals have underdeveloped social skills. A difficulty maintaining a conversation may be perceived by others as a lack of interest or fickle behaviour. Impulsivity may feature as a difficulty in turn-taking and social reciprocity. Some clients report a long-standing awareness that they are 'different' from others in some way, leading to feelings of rejection and social isolation. In this chapter we focus on the development of micro-skills (both verbal and nonverbal communication skills) and macro-skills that aim to modify and regulate social behaviour in different social settings. We also discuss a common dilemma for people with ADHD relating to the decision of whether to (or when to) disclose to others that they have the condition.

The *Anxiety Module* (Chapter 9) addresses the generalized and social anxiety problems often present in ADHD clients. Social anxiety is commonly reported by clients and due to their uncertainty in social settings because they have difficulty adhering to social norms. Some clients have such little confidence that they avoid them altogether. This seems paradoxical given their often gregarious presentation and it is important to bear in mind that this may mask underlying anxieties and poor self-confidence. In this module, we discuss how to modify behaviour in varying social situations, including controlling the impulse to overcompensate for feelings of inadequacy by 'playing the fool' and attention seeking behaviour. We also introduce methods to re-interpret common responses to anxiety by evaluating thoughts, feelings, behaviours, and bodily reactions. A version of the Clark (1986) cognitive behavioural model of panic is presented and strategies for intervention, including relaxation and breathing exercises. We suggest ways to overcome avoidance and increase confidence by applying techniques of graded exposure, systematic desensitization, and behavioural experiments.

The *Frustration and Anger Module* (Chapter 10) addresses maladaptive ways of coping with feelings of frustration and irritation. This is often expressed as a labile temperament and characterized by emotional outbursts. Indeed, anger is more likely to be expressed outwardly than inwardly suppressed, possibly due to poor impulse control, poor self-regulation and a low boredom threshold. This behaviour may lead to negative outcomes including relationship breakdown, termination of employment and involvement with the police. It is likely to be perceived by others as a negative character trait and clients may be assumed to be unpredictable or in some cases even dangerous. This module examines the stages of anger from a cognitive behavioural perspective with the aim of identifying 'early warning signs' that will enable the client to interrupt the anger process. Anger management strategies are provided such as distraction, self-talk, relaxation and cognitive reframing techniques. In addition we compare assertiveness and anger, address the difference between insults and criticisms and discuss how to accept constructive criticism appropriately.

The *Low-Mood and Depression Module* (Chapter 11) stresses the need for regular monitoring of low mood and depression which may arise due to a history of negative life events including academic failure, relationship difficulties, financial problems, and low self-esteem. The problems mean that many young people have lacked the opportunity to experience a sense of achievement and mastery. Depression in people with ADHD needs to be taken very seriously due to their poor behavioural control, which may cause them to impulsively act on an idea to self-harm. In this chapter we have adapted the Beck (1976) cognitive-behavioural model of depression to incorporate the negative thinking and thinking errors common to people with ADHD. We provide suggestions of how to break the negative cycle and introduce strategies that include activity scheduling, techniques to challenge negative automatic thoughts, reduce the self-talk that perpetuates low mood and develop positive self-statements in line with ADHD strengths.

The *Sleep Module* (Chapter 12) addresses the common complaint of incessant feelings of inner restlessness that are associated with ADHD and prevent people from getting to sleep. Other sleep problems may be more similar to disturbance associated with affective disorders such as early wakening in depression. Sleep problems may also relate to medication for treating ADHD, particularly following withdrawal of stimulant medication, or drug holidays or changes in dose. In this module we review the function of sleep, describe the different stages of sleep, and consider how the core symptoms of ADHD may exacerbate sleep problems such as hypersomnia and insomnia. We detail the management of sleep problems, outlining sleep hygiene programmes and relaxation techniques adapted for individuals with ADHD.

The *Substance Misuse Module* (Chapter 13) covers both alcohol and illicit drug use. People with ADHD may become involved with the latter via two mechanisms. Poor impulse control may lead to increased risk taking behaviour, experimentation with drugs and subsequent addiction. A second route is when individuals with undiagnosed and/or untreated ADHD use illicit substances to self-medicate. This chapter describes the different categories of substance use and their relationship with ADHD. Psychological dependency is addressed by suggesting motivational interviewing techniques to motivate the client to engage in a process of change. We present the vicious cycle of substance misuse and discuss dysfunctional beliefs about substance misuse. The module also outlines techniques to build self-confidence and cope with physical cravings and urges by applying distraction techniques, activity scheduling, and motivating support.

Part IV: The Future Module

We recommend that an episode of therapy is always concluded with a final session (or more) that takes a positive perspective and addresses the future. Many people with ADHD have negative assumptions about themselves and an expectation of failure, and it will be helpful to explore how they perceive their future, and make preparations for how they will deal with perceived obstacles and setbacks.

The *Preparing for the Future Module* (Chapter 14) is therefore a concluding module that summarizes the techniques introduced in previous modules, and reviews those that were helpful. The module follows a relapse-prevention approach whereby plans to identify and manage 'risk' situations are developed that the individual can refer to when they feel vulnerable. This is the time they are most likely to slip back into old habits and the development of these management plans will prepare the client for their eventuality and increase the likelihood that they will respond by applying useful coping strategies and avoid impulsive or dysfunctional responding patterns. It is important that these relapse prevention plans include a variety of options that can be applied to a range of situations, for example, cognitive behavioural techniques, avoidance of troublesome situations/persons, seeking support from family and friends and/or professional advice.

In this module the therapist should also lead the client to examine the positive aspects of their ADHD personality by addressing their functional strengths of creativity, resilience and flexibility. The therapist should draw attention to how the client has applied these characteristics successfully to achieve personal goals. Drawing together these natural adaptive qualities, together with a review of the skills acquired and achievements gained in the course of the therapy, and the preparation for 'going it alone' with the relapse prevention plans will give the client a sense of self-efficacy and purpose. In turn this will enhance the likelihood that the client will succeed in not only addressing the presenting 'here and now' problems that they face in daily life, but will move forward to set and achieve longer term goals.

SUMMARY

The primary intervention for ADHD is pharmacological treatment and this has been reliably shown to provide a reduction in symptoms for many individuals with the condition. However, this may have a 'shelf-life' with benefits limited to short-term (Jensen *et al.*, 2007) and inadequate to address the multiple mental health needs and pervasive impairments associated with growing up with ADHD. Symptom reduction is but one treatment objective for ADHD adolescents and adults, who have accumulated a host of concurrent difficulties and who may require psychological interventions to help them cope with the personal, social and occupational demands that they face in everyday life. The Young-Bramham Programme is a comprehensive cognitive behavioural intervention to address the needs of young people with ADHD and includes treatments for core symptoms of ADHD, comorbid and associated problems.

2

DELIVERING THE YOUNG-BRAMHAM PROGRAMME

The Young-Bramham programme was developed from our years of clinical practice working with adolescents and adults with ADHD. We listened to their stories and their problems and drew on our clinical expertise to help. Over time we learned how to apply cognitive behavioural therapy to support our clients, and we discovered specific techniques and strategies that helped. Thus the Young-Bramham Programme was shaped by the needs of our clients. We researched this by conducting in-depth interviews to ascertain their beliefs and feelings about receiving a diagnosis and being treated with medication (Young *et al.*, 2008). We analyzed these interviews qualitatively in order to gain a rich experiential tapestry of life from their perspective. From these interviews three themes emerged.

1. *Emotional impact of the diagnosis* – on being diagnosed with ADHD, clients often felt a sense of relief and elation that there was an 'explanation' for their problems. This was quickly succeeded by turmoil and confusion as they tried to make sense of past experience in light of the diagnosis. They began to consider what might have been, how their lives may have been more successful if they had been diagnosed with the disorder and received treatment earlier. For example, they may have been able to achieve academically rather than experiencing concentration problems in the classroom, that meant they were unable to gain appropriate qualifications commensurate with their potential. There was also anger that they had not been given appropriate support and advice during their childhood and adolescence. Clients then felt particularly sad and regretful that they had come to expect themselves to fail and underachieve. There was a period of adjustment during which they came to realize that they may have a life-long chronic disorder and this elicited some anxiety. However in the final stages of adjustment, individuals came to accept the diagnosis and the need to take medication.

Cognitive-Behavioural Therapy for ADHD in Adolescents and Adults: A Psychological Guide to Practice, Second Edition. Susan Young and Jessica Bramham.

2. *Review of the past: Feeling different from others* – clients reported that they had always felt different from their peers and family. They had been compared unfavourably with siblings and often told they were stupid, lazy or disruptive. For some individuals, this led them to internalize the negative feedback that in turn had a detrimental impact on their self-esteem. However, other individuals described being relatively resistant to the criticisms of others. This may in part have been due to the protective role of their inattention and impulsivity which prevented them from ruminating about their difficulties. They described not having the ability to dwell on an issue for long enough for it to become distressing or problematic. In addition, some individuals described reviewing their own childhood through observing their children with ADHD and reflecting on how the disorder affected them in their youth.
3. *Consideration of the future* – clients were able to acknowledge how medication had improved their motivation and ability to function in their everyday lives, particularly regarding interpersonal relationships. It also allowed them to recognize the difference between their symptoms when they had taken medication and when it had worn off. However, they were aware that all their difficulties did not disappear with pharmacological treatment and that certain problems required them to makes changes in their behaviour. This distinction was important for clients in understanding the features of their own presentation. Some individuals were worried that others would believe they were using ADHD as an excuse for all their difficulties and hence it was useful for them to understand what was and was not attributable to the disorder. There were also concerns about the stigma attached to ADHD and this influenced their disclosure of the diagnosis.

We also interviewed their partners and analyzed the data in the same way (Young, Bramham and Gray, 2009). Three master themes emerged from the analysis.

1. *Perceptions of inadequacy of the ADHD partner* – prior to the ADHD client receiving their diagnosis, partners perceived them to have global inadequacies. They said they were slow to complete tasks or did not complete them at all. They described their partners as moody, with poor social communication skills, easily frustrated and quick to anger. In addition the ADHD clients had longstanding interpersonal problems and felt misunderstood by their family. These difficulties were associated with low self-esteem, poor self-efficacy and emotional lability. They drowned their sorrows with alcohol.
2. *The emotional impact of the diagnosis* – in parallel with the ADHD client, partners also reported experiencing a psychological process of emotional adjustment to the client receiving diagnosis and treatment. For partners, this process involved initial confusion about being in a relationship with someone who has a 'disorder'. During this period the partners felt uncertain about how to provide support and were apprehensive about what to expect in the longer-term.
3. *Medication is not a panacea* – initially partners said they felt relieved at the ADHD client's response to medication. They noted improvements in the

patients' functioning at a personal level (e.g. improved cognitive abilities, interpersonal style and self-esteem) and interpersonal level (e.g. improved relationships between themselves, the family and a wider social network). This impacted positively on the client's own sense of achievement and family relationships. However the initial honeymoon period was followed by disappointment when they realized that medication was not a 'magic cure'. Many problems persisted, such as low self-esteem, poor self-efficacy, poor time-management, procrastination and motivational problems. Symptoms rapidly returned once the medication wore off and partners speculated that psychological treatment may be needed.

These findings identify a role for psychological treatment in three areas. First it is necessary to help clients through the process of adjustment and make sense of the past. Second, in order to reduce anxiety about the future therapists should emphasize the clients' strengths and positive characteristics that will motivate them to make functional changes in the future. Third, there is a clear need for skills development, particularly in domains that do not improve directly with medication, in order to gain functional improvement. Both clients and their partners' will be assisted by the provision of written psychoeducational materials to facilitate their knowledge and understanding about ADHD and this, in turn, means partners will be better able to support the ADHD client in the longer term.

AIMS AND OBJECTIVES OF THE YOUNG-BRAMHAM PROGRAMME

The Young-Bramham Programme promotes two primary aims of psychological treatment.

1. *Change from the outside in*: whereby it is aimed to provide clinicians with ways to encourage and help the individual to change the environment in order to optimize their personal, occupational and social functioning.
2. *Change from the inside out*: whereby it is aimed to provide clinicians with ways of encouraging the individual to develop psychological strategies for adaptive functioning within different environments. This is achieved by amalgamating aspects of independent evidence-based psychological treatments, drawing on cognitive behavioural, motivational and psychoeducational paradigms and applying techniques to meet the needs of adolescents and adults with ADHD.

However, the neuropsychological presentation of patients with ADHD is not unique to this disorder. Indeed deficits of attentional control underlie many psychological conditions and the Young-Bramham Programme may be helpful more generally for individuals with cognitive deficits of this type (e.g. those suffering with traumatic brain injury, schizophrenia, mild learning disabilities etc.).

The objectives of the Young-Bramham Programme are:

1. to provide information about ADHD; and
2. to provide psychological strategies for coping with symptoms and associated problems.

The Young-Bramham Programme draws on three core psychological techniques: cognitive behavioural therapy, psychoeducation, and motivational interviewing. It is intended to enable the individual to develop self-efficacy and the confidence that change can be achieved, develop strategies to effect positive lifestyle change and cope with obstacles and challenges. This involves education about the disorder by: adopting psychoeducational techniques; overcoming ambivalence by drawing on motivational interviewing decisional balance techniques; cognitive-restructuring and reframing the past by challenging negative automatic thoughts; self-monitoring performance; recognizing errors in thinking; and evaluating cognitive distortions and misattributions. Whenever possible, it will also be important to elicit core beliefs the individual holds about him/herself, other people and the world. Behavioural techniques such as graded task assignments, modelling and role-play are employed to develop and rehearse new skills. Between sessions the client engages in 'behavioural experiments' which are mini experiments (set by the therapist and client within sessions) to test out new strategies and techniques, and identify which ones work well.

Each module follows a similar format outlining the functional deficits of adolescents and adults on the module topic, methods to assess them, and specific interventions to address them. In order to sustain focus and interest in sessions the programme introduces variety in treatment sessions by shifting topics, using visual aids, incorporating role-plays and, if necessary, by taking short breaks. Individuals with ADHD are motivated to satisfy a need for immediate gratification and it is important that treatment is structured to include immediate and delayed reward systems. A feature of the Young-Bramham Programme is the incorporation of practical exercises and specific tools such as worksheets that will maintain motivation and attention. A fast-paced structure incorporating a variety of these cognitive behavioural techniques and practical exercises will be attractive to individuals who have significant cognitive deficits, high intolerance and a low boredom threshold.

THERAPEUTIC ALLIANCE AND ENGAGEMENT IN TREATMENT

A central tenet of the therapeutic programme is collaboration. It is vital to engage and motivate an individual by setting agendas and goals of therapy together. This approach is likely to have face validity for individuals who may feel ambiguity over engaging with a therapist. It is important that the client has confidence in the therapist and perceives that the therapist understands their problems and the prognosis of ADHD.

By adulthood, individuals with ADHD have frequently had many encounters with various education and mental health services (Huntley and Young, submitted; Young, Toone and Tyson, 2003). However, the diagnosis of ADHD has often not been made or the individual may have been given contradictory information. Individuals diagnosed for the first time in late adolescence or adulthood may lack trust in services and feel they have been unfairly treated by a system that has failed to identify their problems. Also, clients with ADHD may have difficulty in coping with waiting for an appointment and become frustrated by any delay before assessment. Once diagnosed, they may feel angry and bitter that their condition had not been recognized sooner. It is important that they develop confidence in what they may perceive as yet another clinician before them. A collaborative and supportive relationship is crucial for the success of therapy; it is important to bear in mind that these young people are likely to have experienced rejection in the past and have difficulty forming healthy relationships.

Nadeau (1995) identifies several roles that the therapist should adopt when treating an individual with ADHD.

1. *Supporter*: this involves supporting the client to convert from being a victim to being empowered.
2. *Interpreter*: here the therapist should facilitate interpretation of the constellation of difficulties making up the individual's ADHD. This information can be communicated to others who are in contact with the client to help them to understand the disorder.
3. *Structurer*: in order to provide a foundation for someone who has difficulty in planning and organizing, the clinician should become active and structured.
4. *Educator*: education may be provided through reading, writing session notes collaboratively, or ongoing (verbally) as part of the therapeutic process.

We propose a fifth additional and perhaps a more primary role:

5. *Trainer*: the predominant function of the therapist is, through guided discovery, to help the individual build a bridge between their internal and external world. Secondly, the individual needs to identify and develop appropriate coping strategies to overcome difficult situations and obstacles to progress.

THE IMPACT OF THE DIAGNOSIS

Treatment for adolescents and adults begins at the time they are diagnosed. Following diagnosis, we found that people engage in a staged process of acceptance: (1) initial relief and elation; (2) confusion and emotional turmoil; (3) anger; (4) sadness and grief; (5) anxiety; and finally (6) accommodation and acceptance (Young *et al.*, 2008). Thus the way that the diagnosis is communicated to the client will influence their future understanding and adjustment to the diagnosis. Our research has supported this proposal as we found that many individuals do not absorb much information at the point of diagnosis. It is not until a second appointment that clients are able to process the experience of having a diagnosis of ADHD, take in relevant information and ask questions. Thus factual information regarding diagnosis and treatment should be presented in written format and reinforced at subsequent appointments.

Many people feel relieved after they have received a diagnosis of ADHD. They say they always knew there was something wrong and it is reassuring to know that it is not their fault. Although people have often thought about ADHD for some time before receiving the diagnosis, hearing the words 'you have ADHD' can still be a shock requiring emotional adjustment. Many people report that, following diagnosis, they experience an emotional reaction such as feelings of regret, guilt, and sadness, which are natural and part of an acceptance process. They then attempt to reframe past events – what can be attributed to ADHD and what cannot? How could things have been different? Following treatment with medication they report a sense of change in identity saying they see themselves as becoming more serious and less 'zany'.

It is therefore important to encourage clients to talk to those who know them well and to reassure themselves that they are still the same person as before. Furthermore helping clients to become more informed about their condition will allow them to understand themselves better and optimize their abilities. Reviewing helpful coping strategies will reassure them. Undoubtedly they will have already developed numerous ways of helping themselves without therapeutic input and this should be explored as it will give clues to what will be helpful to adopt in treatment and what will not.

PSYCHOEDUCATION

Psychoeducation should be applied from the start of the diagnostic process (Jackson and Farrugia, 1997). The aim is to promote knowledge about the disorder, the meaning of the diagnosis, and the impact it has had on the individual (Weiss, Hechtman and Weiss, 1999). The first part of the education process is to provide fundamental information about ADHD, as there is still a surprising amount of erroneous 'lay' information that is misleading and confusing to the client. Murphy (1998) suggests that the therapist should explain the reason why the individual fulfils the criteria for a diagnosis of ADHD to enhance their understanding of the disorder. Education about treatment methods is important at this stage as many individuals may have preconceptions about the impact of stimulant treatment and the utility of psychological approaches. A written handout is helpful.

Following sessions promoting psychoeducation, we have found that there is a greater shift to a biological definition and understanding of the disorder. For example, patients who previously thought ADHD was a 'personality disorder that affects your attention span and thought processes', after psychoeducation described it as a 'condition which affects brain chemistry, and contact mechanisms in the brain'.

Additionally, following psychoeducation sessions individuals recognized how emotional and self-esteem problems are also related to the primary disorder, whereas previously they thought that the disorder was restricted to the core symptoms of inattention, hyperactivity and impulsivity.

We have examined how individuals tend to view treatment for ADHD and found that individuals strongly focus on medication as being the sole treatment available. For example, when asked how ADHD can be overcome, responses included: 'drugs', 'medication' and 'death'. However, after psychoeducation sessions, individuals tended to encompass a greater range of possibilities and recognize a biosocial model, for example, 'medication, psychological strategies, environmental changes to your home/work so it no longer affects your life'.

Through a psychoeducation treatment model, the therapist should inform the individual about the aetiology of ADHD, its prognosis, comorbid problems, cognitive deficits and their expression in daily living. Associated factors of the ADHD syndrome should also be explained such as skills deficits and the likelihood of maladaptive coping strategies. However, this should be put constructively with emphasis on targets for treatment.

Understanding that their problems stem from an underlying neurodevelopmental basis will be an important step in repairing the self-esteem of people who have long believed themselves to be stupid and/or who have been labelled as stupid or lazy by others. Furthermore, by acknowledging and understanding their limitations, individuals can develop realistic expectations for performance. This will be especially important when applied to cognitive behavioural therapy, for example, the rehearsal of new skills requires repetition and patience. These are unlikely characteristics of adolescents and adults who tend to seek novelty and stimulation. Acknowledging that sometimes the Young-Bramham Programme will be challenging and providing information about the disorder will help individuals appreciate that learning new strategies requires ongoing practice until a new skill becomes automatic and routine. Working collaboratively, individuals must be motivated to complete the Young-Bramham Programme and not give up half way through.

MOTIVATIONAL INTERVIEWING

Motivational interviewing techniques, based on Prochaska and DiClemente's (1982) model, are helpful as they draw on a theoretical background where change is regarded as a cycle of stages (see Figure 2.1). The transactional model of change is a paradigm that views change as a dynamic process with the early stages requiring a greater supportive role by others (e.g. therapist, family) and in later stages the individual becomes self-reinforcing and autonomous. Individuals with ADHD may lack confidence in the ability to effect change. Ambivalence and resistance to change can be overcome by introducing motivational interviewing techniques into treatment.

Precontemplation
The client is not considering change

↓

Contemplation
Change is seriously evaluated

↓

Preparation
Planning and committing to change

↓

Action
Making specific behavioural change

↓

Maintenance
Working to sustain change

Figure 2.1 Stages of change

Motivational interviewing is client-centred and therefore focuses on the client's current concerns and perspectives. It is directive, aiming to resolve ambivalence through reinforcement of talk that involves changes and thus diminishing resistance. Rather than imparting a set of techniques, motivational interviewing is a means of communication that facilitates change. Miller and Rollnick (2002) state there are four general principles of motivational interviewing.

1. *Expressing empathy* – that is, using reflective listening techniques to understand the patient's feelings and accepting them, while acknowledging that ambivalence is normal. This will be particularly important when treating people with ADHD, as they may have found themselves rebuffed or ridiculed by others when expressing any interest in trying to make changes in their lives.
2. *Developing discrepancy* – that is, motivating change by highlighting a discrepancy between their current behaviour and important goals or values. For example, helping a client recognize that their disorganization means they have occupational problems, for example, they may be unable to gain or sustain a job, which in turn effects their perception of self-worth.
3. *Rolling with resistance* – that is, not arguing with the client for change and using resistance as a signal to respond differently by inviting new perspectives without imposing them. This is particularly appropriate when working with clients who became defensive and confrontational, as it is less challenging for them to take the perspective of an 'onlooker'.
4. *Supporting self-efficacy* – that is, by imparting the idea that the therapist can facilitate change but cannot change the client. The aim is to promote a client's belief in the possibility for change and enhancing the client's confidence in their capability of coping with obstacles and succeeding.

COGNITIVE BEHAVIOURAL THERAPY (CBT)

Adolescents and adults with ADHD often present with multiple problems and complex histories. Their strengths may be buried under a mountain of negative thoughts and experiences. Thus it is important to identify goals of treatment. These may be:

- *general*, for example, motivation to engage in treatment;
- *modular*, for example, to reduce social anxiety; and
- *specific*, for example, to complete homework tasks.

Individuals with ADHD require structure in terms of personal organization and social boundaries and practical help to cope with everyday problems. They achieve best in an environment where there are clear rules and expectations of behaviour. Therefore a cognitive-behavioural approach is effective for adolescents and adults with ADHD, whether applied on an individual or group basis, because it is structured and has a strong evidence base for mood related disorders. Cognitive behaviour therapy has been successfully applied to this client group even with minimal contact (Bramham *et al.*, 2009, Stevenson *et al.*, 2002; Wilens *et al.*, 1999). CBT emphasizes action as a means of addressing change, thus individuals who adopt a role of a 'passive recipient' are unlikely to be successful and require more intensive motivational interviewing treatment outlined above.

There are a number of challenges in the adaptation of CBT for this client group. These vary from pragmatic difficulties, for example resistance to completing 'homework' tasks, to generic problems such as core symptoms. In the following chapters, specific modules of the Young-Bramham Programme are presented, outlining CBT techniques, which are helpful for treating adolescents and adults with ADHD. More generally the cognitive behavioural treatment aims to provide cognitive remediation, cognitive reframing of the past, cognitive restructuring and cognitive reasoning strategies, rationalization, development of internal/external compensatory strategies as well as drawing on behavioural techniques.

Cognitive Remediation Strategies

Cognitive remediation strategies are an important method for the treatment of core symptoms of ADHD as they may be used to enhance memory, attention, and organization in everyday life. Weinstein (1994) suggests that they are an important active adjunct to other psychological treatment interventions. Learning to apply strategies that directly address and/or compensate for the core symptoms may help individuals feel they have greater self-control and reduce feelings of learned helplessness.

The neuropsychological assessment of clients is useful for establishing a profile of cognitive strengths and weaknesses. For example, individuals who have deficits in selective attention will benefit from learning attentional and memory enhancing strategies. Learning to ignore external distracters and develop techniques to stay on task will be important for individuals who have difficulty sustaining attention. Others may have difficulty with impulse control and require input in this area.

Cognitive Reframing of the Past

Adolescents and adults with ADHD will have experienced a history of failure in many aspects of their life. Often the young person will have been given the message that he/she is stupid, lazy and unmotivated. The cumulative effect of this is often low self-esteem and a belief that the situation can never be changed (Murphy, 1998). Helping the individual to understand that ADHD has a neurological basis and is 'not a character defect or moral weakness' should begin to provide the person with some hope for the future (Murphy, 1995).

Once individuals are diagnosed with ADHD for the first time in adulthood they may go through an adjustment period coming to terms with the diagnosis and the impact of the disorder on their lives. They may reflect on past experiences and ruminate on these from a different perspective. Some individuals may feel relief that there is an explanation for the ways events have unfolded but others may feel resentment and/or regret that their situation could have been different. There is a risk that individuals may become depressed if they ruminate over past underachievements and lost opportunities. The therapist should acknowledge feelings of distress and confusion and normalize these thoughts and feelings. The therapist should then seek to elicit examples of positive aspects of having the disorder and direct the individual to learn from the past and focus on the future and in a constructive manner.

Cognitive Restructuring and Reasoning Strategies

Some people with ADHD are creative and have no difficulty applying helpful CBT strategies, such as thought monitoring, challenging negative thoughts and assumptions, and generating alternative cognitions. Others have specific difficulties in abstract reasoning. In the latter case, clients will require greater support and practice to master techniques. In particular impulsivity may impede the development of reasoning strategies as clients do not think through a course of action or sequentially develop an idea, for example causing them difficulty applying social perspective taking techniques and/or interpersonal problem-solving. These issues are addressed in the Interpersonal Relationships Module (Chapter 8).

Rationalization

Adolescents and adults with ADHD may become overfocused on current thoughts, and hence their preoccupation may mean they have difficulty distancing themselves from distorted cognitions in order to challenge and replace them. This may be the case especially soon after treatment with medication, when individuals (who are less likely to be distracted) may become preoccupied with negative beliefs while reframing the past. It is important that clients are coached using a 'guided discovery' framework to encourage them to reason critically, engage in consequential thinking and rationalize beliefs.

Development of Internal/External Compensatory Strategies

Given that adolescents and adults with ADHD will have experienced ADHD symptoms throughout their life, it is likely that they will have already developed an extensive repertoire of compensatory strategies, both adaptive and maladaptive. Compensatory strategies can be divided into those which:

- require change from within (i.e. internal strategies such as 'stop and think' techniques); and
- involve the adaptation of the environment to suit the individual (i.e. external strategies such as removing potential distractions).

Many problems can be alleviated with a combination of both compensatory approaches. Presenting strategies in this two-pronged format will empower the individual to address future problems by looking for ways of changing themselves and ways of changing aspects of their environment. It is important to emphasize these two methods throughout the Young-Bramham Programme as the adoption of this dual approach will optimize success.

Behavioural Techniques

When treating patients with learning disabilities and ADHD, the therapist will need to draw more heavily on behavioural techniques. While much of the Young-Bramham Programme draws on cognitive techniques, changing behaviour requires the rehearsal of new actions that are modified, applying positive and negative reinforcement and punishment techniques. The individual will be required to observe and record identified behaviours, and monitor change in homework tasks. However, some people may have difficulty organizing themselves to follow a behavioural programme and make observations about themselves. Similarly, some people may find difficulty applying a reward system appropriately. Their impulsivity could mean that they reach for the reward even if they are not entitled to it or become easily frustrated if they feel that they are being deprived of something. It will be important for the therapist to be aware that difficulties may arise in the maintenance of a behavioural programme and to watch out for intermittent reinforcement of maladaptive behaviours. Weiss, Hechtman and Weiss (1999) suggest that all of these difficulties need to be taken into consideration when designing a programme and discussed fully with the individual concerned. See Organization and Time-Management Module

(Chapter 5) for methods regarding organization of time and the introduction of a reward system into a timetable or week schedule.

DELIVERY OF THE YOUNG-BRAMHAM PROGRAMME

The role of the therapist in the early stages is to explain and clarify the therapeutic rules and boundaries. This means asserting that treatment is a collaborative process and displacing potential power struggles. Many individuals with ADHD have personality problems, for example, they may be pedantic, challenging and confrontational in presentation. A tendency to procrastinate will particularly hamper progress. While most clients with ADHD will be motivated, interested and creative, it is important to recognize that others will be therapeutically more demanding.

Concentration problems may mean that individuals have difficulty following a train of thought or developing a theme using cognitive techniques. They may have difficulty keeping to time limits and/or struggle to cope with the duration of a 50-minute session. Adaptations to the therapeutic process will need to take account of these problems by introducing shorter sessions, scheduled breaks, structured changes in topic and/or variety in treatment methods (e.g. switching between visual aids, written exercises and role-plays within sessions).

Cognitive-behavioural therapy is usually time limited ranging between 8 and 12 sessions, sometimes more. However, individuals with ADHD may require longer-term treatment in order to address their multiple problems. It is advisable that sessions are held at a specified time and day each week as making different appointment times can increase the likelihood of nonattendance. Nevertheless, the therapist should expect clients to be late for appointments but try not to accommodate this by extending the session. Instead, techniques should be identified that can prevent this occurring and set homework tasks to address the problem. Telephoning the client the day before their session may improve attendance and time keeping or asking the client to identify a person or method (e.g. telephone alarm) to remind them. Prompting by the therapist should be phased-out during the course of treatment.

As discussed in Chapter 1, the Young-Bramham Programme is modular so specific topics can be selected as appropriate. Alternatively the therapist can work through each module until the Programme is complete (see Chapters 3–14 in Box 1.1).

If modules are to be selected, we recommend these are chosen collaboratively so that the client is empowered by the process. Due to attentional and working memory deficits, it is recommended that sessions allow additional time for consolidation of information and rehearsal of new material. It is recommended that three to four sessions are spent on each module, but this may be shortened or lengthened according to need. However, due to the underlying desire for immediate gratification, we suggest that no more than six sessions are spent on one module at any time. If the material is not fully covered or needs to be repeated, we suggest that this is reintroduced at a later stage and following alternative modules in order to avoid boredom and disengagement. Due to the Young-Bramham Programme's modular design, skills acquisition is cumulative. Thus if clients have difficulty with a module presented early in the programme, this can be revised at a later stage when new skills have been acquired and this may make it seem easier to understand.

Group Therapy

The Young-Bramham Programme may be applied in individual sessions or in a group format. Group work provides normalization, mutual understanding and peer support; these are considered important factors since adolescents and adults with ADHD may feel socially isolated and misunderstood by others. A group forum provides the opportunity to meet people with similar problems and to share strategies for coping with difficulties. Individuals can validate their own experiences by sharing their thoughts with others with ADHD (Bramham *et al.*, 2009). In addition it provides opportunities for acquiring and rehearsing key skills within a supportive noncritical environment.

Each module of the Young-Bramham Programme provides a suggested outline for its delivery in group format over a 6-week period. The advantage of the modular design is that the therapist can select modules that are appropriate to the needs of clients attending the group. In many respects this will 'personalize' the programme for group participants. It also provides flexibility for therapists to determine the duration of their group; it may consist of only one or two modules, or encompass a greater number. Therapists may also determine the intensity of topics by lengthening or shortening the modules; it is up to the therapist whether the group is for 4 weeks or 30 weeks. Whatever the length, however, we strongly recommend that each group ends with session(s) from the Preparing for the Future Module (Chapter 14).

Each module commences with starting activities that form the basis for general discussion, followed by an assessment component. This encourages group participants to think about personal difficulties and problems that they later have the opportunity to work on in individual exercises and/or homework assignments. When applying CBT strategies and techniques in group exercises, therapists should apply these to examples that have arisen from the starting activity discussions as this will also personalize the programme. Group delivery of the programme provides greater opportunity for role-playing and this should be maximized to rehearse potential helpful strategies and obtain feedback. Homework assignments are important because often group participants are asked to test out these strategies in 'behavioural experiments'. This is the best way to discover which are the most helpful.

When putting a group together, it is important that individuals are assigned to age appropriate groups (for example older adolescents, young adults, older adults) and/or by some common denominator such as parenthood, students, transitioning between child and adult services, or unemployment. This is especially important for adolescents who may not have experienced 'direct' therapeutic interventions before, as most childhood interventions are provided 'indirectly' via parent training programmes. In such cases, this is a good topic to address in the first session in order to foster cohesion in the group through shared experiences.

We have successfully delivered the core aspects of the Young-Bramham Programme in one-day 'group foundation workshop' format. In traditional group therapy, patients meet weekly for 1 to 2 hours over a set period, but we have found that a workshop paradigm also works with ADHD individuals as they respond positively to the 'immediacy' of workshops, for example by presenting one topic in the morning and a different topic in the afternoon. It also means that it is possible to provide treatment to individuals who are unable to commit to weekly meetings. However, by delivering the Young-Bramham Programme in an intensive workshop format, it is essential that techniques and teaching aids are introduced in order to shift attention and maintain interest and motivation, for example by the inclusion of group role-plays, working in pairs and/or small groups, and engagement in group discussions. We recommend that frequent breaks are introduced in Programme Workshops (e.g. 10 minutes every 90 minutes) and participants are provided with handouts that contain exercises to complete within the workshop and/or later at home to reinforce the techniques presented.

Whether delivering the Young-Bramham Programme in group or workshop format, it is strongly recommended that therapists prepare for the group well by planning each session. This will involve preparation of handouts and summary materials; in the past we have made up small booklets. Leave plenty of time for discussion and questions, especially when planning starting activities, as in our experience group participants really enjoy meeting other people with ADHD and sharing experiences.

Agendas

Agendas are a method of providing structure within each session and should be drawn up collaboratively. The therapist needs to adhere closely to the agenda and not be distracted by 'crises' which may be presented by the client week by week. This will provide a model for the clients on how to deal with difficult situations in a rational and noncatastrophic manner. For example, an issue arising one week may be put on the agenda for the subsequent session, by which point it may no longer be construed as such a difficult area.

Goal Setting

The therapist must introduce the concept of the modular approach by clarifying with the client that treatment cannot address everything at once. Much as the client may wish to address multiple problems in one disorganized session, this is unhelpful and will leave both the therapist and the client feeling dissatisfied. Clear specific goals need to be established collaboratively at the onset of therapy, which are carefully broken down into stages. The client is likely to require assistance in this latter task, as it may be difficult for the client to see beyond one overarching goal such as 'I want people to like me' or 'I want to succeed'. Goals should be reviewed regularly in order to maintain focus and prevent the temptation to become distracted, for example, by lurching from crisis to crisis. The modular structure of the Young-Bramham Programme will be helpful in this respect.

Rewards

Rewards are important for individuals with ADHD as they find it difficult to delay gratification and tend to opt for a short-term smaller reward rather than wait for longer-term larger reinforcement. This feature of ADHD needs to be incorporated into treatment so that individuals are rewarded regularly for achievement, otherwise they are likely to lose interest in therapy and become distracted.

Homework

Homework tasks are set at the end of each session. It is important that clients learn to take responsibility for rehearsing and endorsing techniques learned in sessions in an applied setting. Resistance to homework tasks needs to be addressed, obstacles identified, anticipated and overcome by planning alternative strategies.

Treatment Termination

Given that ADHD is a chronic disorder, it can be difficult to identify a point at which to end therapy. It is therefore important to clearly specify tangible goals at the beginning of therapy and to regularly review progress. Nevertheless, it may be necessary to offer more sessions than other clients require, as it may take a client longer to acquire skills. This may result in dependence on the therapist and the concept of termination must be introduced early in treatment to avoid a situation in which the client feels isolated, abandoned and without the confidence to apply the structure and techniques learned in the programme. The transition from treatment to autonomy needs to be planned carefully with collaboration, for example reducing the frequency of sessions and/or conducting brief planned follow-ups in person or by telephone.

Relapse Prevention

Adolescents and adults with ADHD have the potential to catastrophize when they encounter future difficulties. Motivational interviewing techniques are therefore useful for reframing problems as slips and lapses. Preplanned booster sessions are a sensible way of supporting a client through termination of therapy and prevent relapse. Treatment needs to incorporate a plan for 'risk' situations and/or times when the client may feel vulnerable. By identifying such times/situations, the client can consider appropriate coping mechanisms and avoid responding impulsively. By forward planning and thinking through the consequences of proposed behaviour, clients may learn to avoid challenging situations and/or cope better when faced with them. Relapse plans need to be multifaceted, for example, including seeking social support and/or advice, applying cognitive techniques, and avoidance of troublesome situations and/or persons.

SUMMARY

ADHD is a disorder that presents with core symptomatology, comorbid problems and skills deficits. Treatment for young adults with ADHD typically follows a pharmacological route, which is helpful to alleviate core symptoms of ADHD and results in clients being better placed to succeed in psychological interventions. The Young-Bramham Programme with its modular cumulative skills acquisition provides treatment according to the needs of the clients.

The Young-Bramham Programme provides an integrated framework for understanding ADHD, adjusting to the diagnosis and developing techniques to cope with symptomatology and associated problems through the provision of psychoeducational information, drawing on motivational interviewing techniques, and the use of cognitive behavioural therapy. The following chapters introduce the Young-Bramham Programme modules and describe these treatment techniques in detail.

PART II

CORE SYMPTOM MODULES

3

ATTENTION MODULE

This module is the first of four modules outlining treatments for the core symptoms of ADHD, beginning with hallmark of ADHD – attentional problems. The human brain has several attentional systems serving different functions in everyday behaviour and impairment in the central executive component of working memory may lead to inefficiency in the allocation of attentional resources (Baddeley, 1986; Baddeley and Wilson, 1988).

Attention is the process that allows us to focus on particular features of our environment such that we are aware of them at a particular moment in time. Attentional control processes determine at any given moment where to prioritize effort and to which stimuli to attend. These control processes are complex 'higher order' cognitive functions that allow attention to be selective to one stimulus, divided between several stimuli, and shifted between stimuli. In some ways, difficulties in attentional control could be regarded as being at the centre of the cognitive deficits underpinning all aspects of attentional impairment in ADHD. If an individual is unable to govern what they will listen to, look at, and focus on, then they have lost attentional control, and they are likely to exhibit the problems presented by people with ADHD. Norman and Shallice (1986) and Shallice and Burgess (1996) theorize that attentional control is achieved through the organization of a 'supervisory attentional system' which is similar to Baddeley's (1986) concept of the 'central executive' (discussed later in this module). These models propose that the supervisory attentional system/central executive is a 'higher order' cognitive function that determines which stimuli in the environment are prioritized with regard to attentional focus, particularly in novel situations. Certain activities make greater demands on the supervisory attentional system than others, for example, forward planning, responding to feedback, and self-monitoring. Conversely problems within the supervisory attentional/central executive system can lead to various attentional deficits and ultimately can affect memory functioning (see Memory Module in Chapter 4).

Cognitive-Behavioural Therapy for ADHD in Adolescents and Adults: A Psychological Guide to Practice, Second Edition. Susan Young and Jessica Bramham.

This module discusses the domains of attention most likely affected by ADHD; the relationship between motivation and attention; the impact of anxiety, stress and restlessness on attention; methods to teach individuals to recognize tasks that are likely to be problematic and strategies to help clients cope more appropriately and adaptively. This includes ways the client may adapt their environment to minimize distraction and thus maximize their ability to concentrate, that is, external strategies that involve the selection of the most appropriate surroundings in which the client is most likely to succeed. Internal strategies to sustain attention and motivation are also suggested and these can be rehearsed in sessions with the therapist.

FUNCTIONAL DEFICITS IN ADOLESCENTS AND ADULTS

People with ADHD have attentional impairments that can disadvantage them in a busy society with its high demand for multitasking. In order to complete a task well, and without making errors, they have to apply all their resources to focusing on that task. This is difficult for three reasons: (1) because they find it difficult to maintain the degree of attentional control; (2) because they are easily distracted from the task; and (3) they give up on the task because they are not reaching their goal (i.e. a lack of positive reinforcement).

Attentional problems are most commonly expressed functionally by poor academic and occupational performance and achievement. It is very common for young people at school, college or other further education establishments to have difficulty organizing their work, leading them to fall behind with course work and/or experience difficulties managing their time during examinations. Teachers/lecturers often complain about late homework assignments that appear messy and rushed. For many young people those difficulties do not disappear when they leave academia but persist into paid employment, for example, missing deadlines, producing work that is disorganized and appearing incomplete. Some people resolve occupational problems by becoming self-employed so they can manage their own time plans or by choosing occupations that will minimize their problems. For example, Andrew worked as an international long-haul lorry driver as this allowed him to avoid nine-to-five work at the same place every day. He liked to be on the move and enjoyed the changing scenery. He had no-one watching over him and clocking him in and out and he could take breaks whenever he wished. Others are less fortunate and they spend their occupational lives trying lots of different occupations, frequently changing direction and career, and experiencing periods of unemployment.

Attentional impairment can lead to many problems in day-to-day functioning including difficulty listening, failure to finish tasks, and being easily distracted. This means that completing tasks simultaneously and to an acceptable and satisfactory standard is difficult for people with ADHD. The attentional impairments associated with ADHD affect different people in different ways. Some examples of reported attentional difficulties are described below.

1. They lose their train of thought. This is especially irritating if they forget what they want to say in the middle of speaking.
2. When there are a lot of people around or a lot of noise in the background they find it difficult to sustain a conversation or complete a piece of work.
3. They find it difficult to sustain an in-depth conversation about a single topic. Other thoughts or ideas come flooding into their mind that they are unable suppress. Friends, family and colleagues get annoyed with them as they see them as fickle as they flit about, talking to different people and/or changing topics of conversation.
4. Their mind wanders and they 'drift off' or start to daydream when they watch television, read a book or study in class.
5. They start lots of tasks but never finish them. They get distracted into doing something different.
6. They find it difficult to do more than one task at a time such as driving a car while having a conversation with a passenger.

The chores that we have to do in our daily lives are by definition routine and many are boring and repetitious. It is not possible to have a daily routine that is consistently full of excitement and high stimulation. When people with ADHD are faced with mundane tasks they respond with irritation, which is a source of frustration for the individual with ADHD as well as those who live or work with them. These feelings, coupled with a lot of unfinished tasks, are likely to leave the individual with a sense of failure and low self-esteem. In contrast, when activities are particularly interesting or motivating and/or involve immediate gratification (such as the rapid feedback and reinforcement introduced in many popular computer games), people with ADHD are generally able to concentrate. Such inconsistency can be difficult for people around them to understand. We have heard many complaints from partners about half finished household do-it-yourself tasks. One of our clients had a half-painted lounge, a half-plumbed washing machine, the shell of a wardrobe built in the bedroom, and tiles for the bathroom had been purchased six months earlier but remained stacked up on the bathroom floor. It can be confusing to observe the individual with ADHD being competent in one domain (e.g. surfing the internet), yet unable to achieve in another that is perceived as more important (e.g. writing a CV).

ASSESSMENT OF ATTENTION PROBLEMS

There are many symptom checklists that are available to screen for ADHD, all of which include items relating to attentional control (e.g. ASRS-v1.1, SNAP-IV, Barkley Childhood and Current Symptoms Scales, Brown Attention Deficit Disorder Scale (1996), Conners' Rating Scales (Conners, 2002; Conners, Erhardt and Sparrow, 1998)). These screens can be used to assess the need for a client to receive specific interventions to improve attention. Aside from providing a baseline score, they can be used as outcome measures by being repeated at intervals to record symptom change following intervention. Most screens can be self-rated or rated by informants. The symptoms

Table 3.1 DSM-IV checklist of symptoms

In the past ***six months****, do you think you:*	*Never* *0*	*Sometimes* *1*	*Often* *2*
Failed to give close attention to details or made careless mistakes in studying, work or other activities?			✓
Had difficulty sustaining attention in tasks or leisure activities?			✓
Have not seemed to listen when spoken to directly?		✓	
Did not follow through on instructions and failed to finish studies, chores or duties in the workplace (not due to oppositional behaviour or failure to understand instructions?)			✓
Had difficulty organizing tasks and activities?			✓
Avoided, disliked or were reluctant to engage in tasks that require sustained mental effort (e.g. studying, homework, leisure activities)?		✓	
Lost things necessary for tasks or activities (e.g. pens, books, tools, study papers)?		✓	
Were easily distracted by outside events and stimuli?			✓
Were forgetful in daily activities?			✓
Fidgeted with hands or feet or squirmed in seat?			✓
Left seat in situations where remaining seated is expected (e.g. in classes, church, movies)?			✓
Experienced feelings of restlessness, especially in situations where it is inappropriate?		✓	
Had difficulty engaging in leisure tasks quietly?			✓
Felt 'on the go' or as if driven by a motor?	✓		
Talked excessively?			✓
Blurted out answers before questions have been completed?	✓		
Had difficulty waiting turn?		✓	
Interrupted or intruded on others (e.g. butting into conversations)?		✓	

listed in the formal classifications such as the US Diagnostic Statistical Manual IV (American Psychiatric Association, 2000) and the International Classification of Disease 10 (World Health Organization, 1992) can also be used in this way by applying numerical values to categories (e.g. 0=never, 1=sometimes, 2=often). Thus scores can be totalled or tallied per subtype (inattention or hyperactive/impulsive). Table 3.1 shows the current DSM-IV-TR checklist of symptoms completed by a client with predominantly inattentive symptoms. The Companion Website includes a version of Table 3.1 for completion by the client (Table 3.1a) and a version for clinicians (Table 3.1b).

While screens provide information about the frequency of experiencing a problem, they lack the richness that qualitative feedback can provide about the level of impairment experienced by the individual and how this affects their self-esteem, self-efficacy and quality of life. Thus we recommend that a comprehensive assessment is conducted that starts with a screen and for each item the therapist asks for detailed examples of how this is expressed or experienced in daily activities. In this way the therapist can identify explicit problems that can be used to generate a list of treatment goals. In turn, treatment goals are outcomes that can be measured to assess the effectiveness of treatment. For example, problems may include: not being able to complete homework; a tendency to write half an essay assignment and then not return to the assignment for several days; going off task when using the computer by interrupting work because the person keeps checking social networking sites; spending too much time wandering around the office talking to colleagues. Improvement in reaching these target activities can be evaluated in several ways including frequency they occur over a set period, record of time (hours/minutes) spent on and/or off task, level of distress (frustration, anxiety, panic) associated with incomplete work and pressing deadlines (e.g. 0–10 none to severe), and/or ratings of the individual's sense of achievement on completion of task (e.g. 0–10 low to high).

COGNITIVE BEHAVIOURAL THERAPY

Psychoeducation

Domains of Attention

There are several domains of attention, the most common being referred to as selective attention, divided attention, attentional shifting and sustained attention. All these domains can be influenced by fluctuations in motivation, by emotional states such as anxiety, and feelings of stress or restlessness.

It is important for clients to understand that there are several domains or types of attention, including selective attention, divided attention, attention shifting and sustained attention, and that their difficulties may vary within these domains. Second, it will be helpful for them to develop an understanding about the relationship between anxiety, stress, motivation and attention so they can develop strategies that maintain motivation as this will support their ability to sustain attention. If clients are able to begin to understand their own motivators and variability in motivation, they can then address many of the attentional problems they face by applying both external and internal cognitive behavioural strategies.

Examples of attentional impairments in each of the domains of attentional functioning are given in Table 3.2 and are provided in handout format on the Companion Website. In our experience people with ADHD want to develop their knowledge and understanding about attentional processes and this explanation will help them to identify, apply and/or adapt strategies to overcome their problems.

Table 3.2 Examples of attentional impairments

Domain of attention	*Associated problems*
Selective	Being unable to see detail Being 'slapdash' Incomplete work (missing items in forms/questionnaires) Making mistakes in reading or filling in forms (errors / corrections)
Divided	Difficulty focusing on a conversation or task when there is background noise Difficulty doing two things at once to an equally acceptable standard
Shifting	Getting stuck on one topic and not being able to change track Always starting tasks but never finishing because it is difficult to resume an original task
Sustained	Losing track of a conversation, film, book etc Being distracted by own thoughts (internal) or anything else going on around (external) Inner feelings of restlessness

Selective attention involves the ability to focus on a specific task in hand. For example, being able to read while travelling on public transport and ignoring all other distractions. However, in some situations it is necessary to be able to attend to two or more sources of information, or 'divide attention'. This is a common demand of everyday life, for example, making conversation while driving. A similar ability is that of 'attention shifting' where there are competing demands on cognitive functions, and attention needs to be shifted from one source to another, for example using a recipe to cook a meal. For adolescents and adults with ADHD, difficulty with sustaining attention is probably the most pronounced and disabling attentional problem as individuals often struggle to engage in activities that are long, especially ones that they find repetitious or tedious. Adolescents, in particular, often present with a low boredom threshold and they are easily distracted from their studies.

There are of course individual differences in everything we do, and this is no different in terms of strengths and weaknesses of attentional control. For example, some people have greater difficulty with sustaining attention whereas others have greater difficulty with dividing attention. Different tasks present different challenges. Some people find that they are more productive with several activities on the go, that is, providing themselves with 'constructive' distraction to reduce the likelihood of them becoming bored with a primary task. Others find this impedes their performance. Mood and motivational processes may also affect performance. The goal of the therapist is to identify specific areas of weakness and help the individual develop compensatory strategies to facilitate achievement. The client should be taught to recognize tasks that are likely to be problematic and respond appropriately and adaptively. This goal will be influenced by what the client wants to achieve and what support they have. In many ways, 'forewarned is forearmed' so recognizing and preparing for tasks that are likely to be problematic is the first major step towards improving attentional difficulties. Once specific tasks have been identified, then these should be targeted for improvement by applying both external strategies and internal strategies. External strategies involve adaptation of the environment and internal strategies involve a process of self-monitoring.

Motivation and Attention

There are two forms of motivation: extrinsic motivation and intrinsic motivation (Deci, Koestner and Ryan, 1999). Both can be affected by ADHD and can fluctuate considerably throughout any given time period.

1. *Extrinsic* motivation refers to rewards or incentives for people for performing well, or avoiding negative consequences.
2. *Intrinsic* motivation is determined by interest in an activity.

With regard to extrinsic motivation, the person must have some expectation that they can achieve the desired goals, otherwise they will feel demotivated regardless of the reward or incentive. However, people with ADHD often feel demotivated as they have experienced years of underachievement. When motivation drops, attention and effort also drop. A status of learned helplessness may develop. A person can change the way they view a task and their ability to achieve it by setting clear goals and rewarding their attention to the task with incentives. External reward systems need to be realistic, appropriate and achievable. Goal setting is a motivational strategy that has been shown to enhance attentional performance when difficult but achievable goals are set (Deci, Koestner and Ryan, 1999). If goals are not achieved then failure will reinforce learned helplessness and the ADHD client will 'switch off'. We describe techniques that will help with goal setting and their achievement in the Organization and Time-Management Module (Chapter 5) and the Problem-Solving Module (Chapter 7).

Feedback is a crucial component of intrinsic motivation as it helps the person determine the discrepancy between desired and actual performance. If a person has a sense of self-efficacy and believes they can do something, they will feel they have control. A sense of control will improve their motivation and optimize their attention for the task. However, if a task is perceived to be out of a person's control, the person may lose interest and stop attending. This means the task will be unfinished thus reinforcing a sense of failure. A negative feedback loop may develop from repeated failures and learned helplessness. Conversely, a sense of self-efficacy will be associated with successful and persistent performance.

Anxiety, Stress and Attention

Attentional control decreases when a person is fatigued, stressed and/or worried. If the person is self-monitoring and thinking 'I can't do this, I'll fail' then their

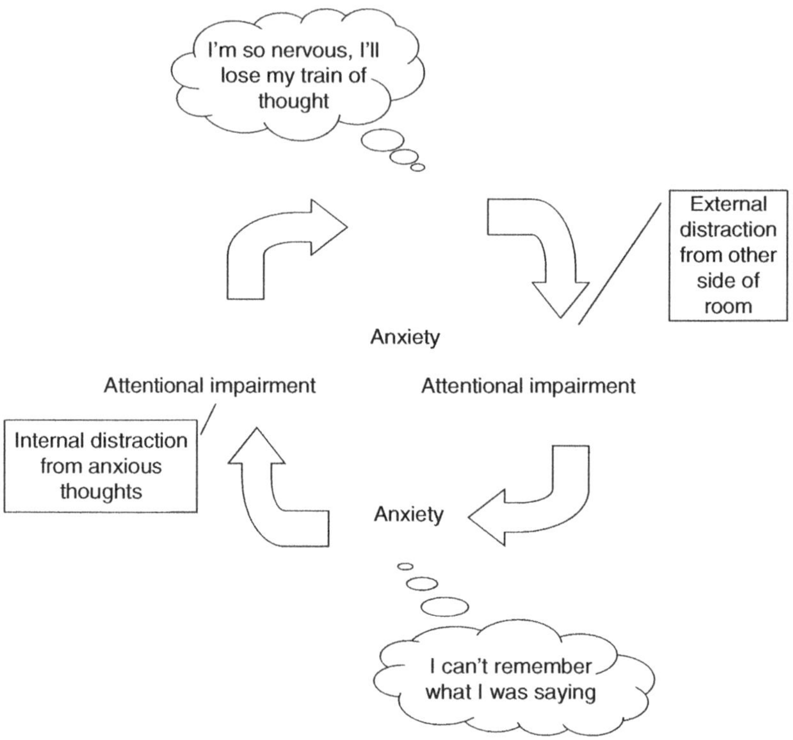

Figure 3.1 The spiral of anxiety and attentional control

attentional ability is likely to be more impaired due to the competing demands of worrying about how well they will do it and their actual performance on the task in hand. The impairment then becomes exacerbated and becomes a function of stress and anxiety. The vicious cycle and self-fulfilling prophecy of stress and anxiety is presented in Figure 3.1 with an example of someone becoming anxious in a social situation (also on the Companion Website in handout form). When this occurs, clients become highly distractible. It is hard enough at the best of times for them to be motivated and remain on task, but if they feel acutely anxious about their performance and/or lose their confidence to do well, they will become even less motivated, have many unfinished tasks (both important and less important) and feel even more stressed and distressed. The Anxiety Module (Chapter 9) outlines specific characteristics of people with ADHD who have comorbid anxiety and techniques to help them.

Restlessness and Attention

A particular problem for people with ADHD is that they are distracted from the task in hand. They find it difficult to stay on task for two reasons:

1. *external* distraction, that is, noticing irrelevant details (e.g. someone walking past the window); and
2. *internal* distraction, that is, feeling restless; having the urge to do something more stimulating (e.g. chatting when they are supposed to be working quietly).

Motoric overactivity is frequently a disabling symptom in childhood, but less so in later adolescence and adulthood. We have not met many ADHD adults running around the therapy room, jumping out of windows, climbing trees, or skateboarding down the hospital corridor. While some of these activities appeal to the younger adolescent, they can usually control the impulse to act them out. Usually by adolescence, young people with ADHD have developed better control over their hyperactive behaviour, but instead they report a feeling of 'internal' restlessness. Of course there remain some people who find it almost impossible to stay seated or have a feeling of being 'driven by a motor'. However, for most, restlessness is most commonly expressed by pacing, tapping fingers, jigging feet, changing posture, fiddling with things, swaying from foot-to-foot, humming, and/or excessive talking. Such difficulties are commonly mistaken or misdiagnosed as generalized anxiety or manic depression.

Attentional Control Strategies

External Strategies

External distraction refers to all outside sensory information (i.e. both auditory and visual), which is being processed at the expense of the required task. Cutting down on irrelevant distraction can help the individual focus on the subject of interest. The application of external strategies requires the individual to make adaptations to their environment in order to maximize the likelihood that they may optimally achieve success. We describe this to clients as making 'change from the outside in' and describe some techniques in Table 3.3 that can be discussed in sessions with the client. The client must be encouraged to set up 'mini-experiments' between sessions in order to test out which techniques are most suitable for them and work best.

There are many possibilities and the client themselves may have ideas to try out or already established strategies that are helpful. When following up the efficacy of a strategy, it is important to determine whether the client applied the strategy correctly and/or appropriately. Sometimes distractions are welcome especially if the client is engaged in a tedious task.

Internal Strategies

The application of internal strategies to optimize performance or 'change from the inside out' requires the individual to learn persistence of effort and the suppression of internal urges. It is important to encourage the client to maximize their ability to sustain attention by increasing interest and motivation. This can be achieved by

Table 3.3 External strategies to improve attentional control

Source of distraction	*Proposed techniques*
Auditory	Listening to low-level music without lyrics can be useful to mask out other more intermittent noises. Music with words should generally be avoided as this can interfere with thoughts and lead to further distraction.
	Although it can be awkward to request that others around them try to reduce their noise, this strategy can be rehearsed in sessions. The client may then work out a way of making this request that is least likely to offend. Often people feel relieved when the environment is quieter, so their efforts may be supported and appreciated.
	The simple strategy of using earplugs can be effective in blocking out all but the loudest of sounds without the individual needing to do their own filtration.
	Telephone calls can interrupt concentration and output. While it is acknowledged that some calls may be essential, this is rarely the case for all calls. Telephones can be switched to silent mode, and checked for messages at a convenient time, regular intervals, or when a task has been completed.
	If a task is portable, it may be helpful for the client to move away from a noisy environment, for example, at home where the television and radio are blaring. If they cannot find a quieter room in their house, then they could negotiate with a friend to use a quiet room somewhere else or work in a library.
Visual	Distracting visual material such as noticeboards, pictures etc. should be positioned out of the line of vision where or when an individual is working.
	Facing a window can be distracting even when nothing is happening outside as it is tempting for people with ADHD to gaze outside and daydream. However, facing a wall can lead to feelings of restlessness. Often facing into a room can provide the best compromise for limiting distractibility and reducing restlessness.
	Using bright colours to attract attention to the task can be helpful. For example using post-it notes, and highlighter pens.
	It can be useful to place a cue card (e.g. a photograph, cut out from magazine, note) in 'risk' places to remind the person to pay attention. For example 'Stop dreaming! Focus!' can be written on notes stuck onto the top of a computer monitor.

setting small achievable goals and introducing an 'immediate' reward system and/or regular breaks. Indeed, a primary difference between treating people with ADHD and other clients is the introduction of systematic reward systems in the treatment as individuals with ADHD are unable to delay gratification and are averse to delay. This means they favour small regular rewards as opposed to having greater rewards that are spread out over a longer period.

Table 3.4 Internal strategies to improve attentional control

Strategy	*Description*
Reward	The development of an incentive and reward programme is a priority. This should be introduced when targeting small goals as well as larger ones as it capitalizes on the need of ADHD people for immediate gratification. Rewards can be simple activities like having a tea break or walking around the block.
Competition	People with ADHD can be encouraged to increase their interest and stimulation in an activity by introducing a competitive element (e.g. let's see if this can be finished in 1 hour) or by incorporating a pre-existing interest (e.g. if a client enjoys using computers, encourage them to pay bills via the internet).
Novelty	People with ADHD may be more motivated in new situations, so they should be encouraged to capitalize on the 'novelty factor' by accepting new tasks in exchange for old, less interesting ones (e.g. taking on new roles with enthusiasm).
Snap!	Encourage clients to wear an elastic band around the wrist. This can be snapped in order to reorient attention at times when it has drifted and increases the overall level of alertness.
Cognitive challenges	Develop strategies to cope with times when a client loses their train of thought, for example, they should not be embarrassed to say to someone 'I'm sorry but I have forgotten what I was saying'. This can be rehearsed in role-play. Dysfunctional thoughts regarding what it means to lose attention and how this may be perceived by others can be cognitively challenged in sessions.
Repetition	In cases when the client has difficulty following and retaining information (e.g. when being given instructions), they should be encouraged to ask for these to be repeated. Again this can be rehearsed in role-play so the client may overcome feelings of embarrassment and/or humiliation.
Goal setting	Help the client to set achievable goals and avoid overarching intangible goals that may be difficult to operationalize. They should be encouraged to reflect on what it feels like to finish a task and gain a sense of achievement. Principles of pleasure and mastery may be incorporated (see Low-Mood and Depression Module in Chapter 11).
Breaks	It is important to break up activities. The client should train themselves to allocate enforced breaks in tasks, especially when these are mundane or tedious. The client should additionally allocate breaks immediately prior to a 'risk period' when they may lose concentration or interest, for example, if they can concentrate for 30 minutes, they should break after 25 minutes.

The client needs to be encouraged to focus on *completion* of a task over a long period so introducing lots of small 'immediate' or regular rewards *and* a larger reward is recommended for completion of the overall goal or task. Clients who feel very restless should be encouraged to capitalize on their energy by performing tasks that involve exertion. If appropriate, this may be introduced as part of the reward system with the day being organized to include regular periods when they are able to move around and dispel pent up restlessness and energy. At the same time, it is helpful to identify situations which the client finds more relaxing and restful and structuring these into their day as part of an activity schedule (see Organization and Time-Management Module in Chapter 5). Such times can be helpfully timetabled following the completion of cognitively challenging and emotionally demanding tasks. Aside from the set reward for finishing a task, completing a task is a reward in itself as it gives the client a sense of achievement. Achievement is a very strong reinforcer. The Organization and Time-Management Module (Chapter 5) provides specific techniques to assist organization skills.

Table 3.4 outlines various suggestions that can be explored in sessions that may help the client improve attentional control. These include the introduction of a reward system, competition with others or themselves, maximization of novelty, physiological arousal, cognitive challenges, repetition, goal setting, and allocating breaks. Of course, not every strategy will suit every client, and some clients will benefit more from some than others, so it is a matter of discussing potential techniques of benefit in the session, setting homework to establish what works by investigating 'mini-experiments' and evaluating the outcome. The client will often have developed their own ideas and strategies. These will be a helpful indicator of what will be most useful to them.

SUMMARY

Attentional difficulties are the most common cognitive deficits for adolescents and adults with ADHD. However, there is much variation in the difficulties that arise due to individual variation in the disorder, motivational factors and state arousal. In addition environmental factors also play a large part in attentional control. This module has explained the ways in which attention is affected in ADHD. It is important for individuals to develop an awareness of specific tasks and situations when their attention becomes impaired. Once these have been recognized and established, the person can then develop strategies to improve attentional control. In treatment, the practitioner adopts a two-pronged approach to overcome attentional problems; by introducing the notion of 'change from the outside in' (external strategies), and 'change from the inside out' (internal strategies).

Group Treatment: Attention Module

It is essential to prepare for group treatment by reading the chapter module. Six group sessions are outlined below, but the number of treatment sessions can be expanded or reduced as required.

Plan

Session 1	Starting activities
Session 2	Psychoeducation – four domains of attention, motivation, anxiety, stress and restlessness
Sessions 3–5	Exercises – external and internal strategies for attentional control (repeat using different examples; identify suitable external and internal strategies)
Session 6	Revision of psychoeducation, techniques and rewards Discussion of homework outcome/experience – what works best? Obstacles and how to overcome them

Starting Activities

What kinds of attention problems do you have?
What do you think causes you to go off-task? (Daydreaming, distraction, boredom).
How do these problems affect you in your daily activities? Guide participants to think about specific events and circumstances. Identify specific goals that have not been achieved due to attentional problems.

Guide participants to think about consequences of poor attention (making mistakes, half finished work/chores, missing deadlines, poor punctuality, social problems, difficulties listening to others).

Have you found strategies to overcome these problems? What works? What doesn't work?
Group discussion (compare individual differences, strengths and weaknesses).

Psychoeducation

Describe the four domains of attention.
Handout Table 3.2 – examples of attentional impairments.
Describe the relationship between motivation and attention.
Explain the difference between intrinsic and extrinsic motivation.
Ask participants to think of situations that increase and decrease their motivation.
Describe the relationship between anxiety, stress and attention.
Handout Figure 3.1 – The spiral of anxiety and attentional control.
Explain the negative relationship between anxiety, stress, and attention.
Discuss how this can become a vicious cycle and self-fulfilling prophecy.

(*Continued*)

Ask participants to complete the handout 3.1 with a personal example, then think of ways that both attention and anxiety can be improved. (NB. This exercise can also be used in the Anxiety Module in Chapter 9.)

Describe the relationship between restlessness and attention – explain the difference between external and internal distractions.

Exercises

Select suitable examples described by participants in Starting Activities or introduce new examples. Using these examples complete exercises in small groups to identify which external and/or internal strategies may be helpful to overcome the difficulty.

Handout Table 3.3 – External strategies to improve attentional control.
Discuss and identify ways in which the problem can be resolved by applying external strategies.
Discuss external strategies participants have used in the past (successfully and unsuccessfully) to improve their attentional control. If unsuccessful – why?
If additional strategies are identified by participants that they have found helpful in the past, add these to the External strategies list.

Handout Table 3.4 – Internal strategies to improve attentional control.
Discuss and identify ways in which the problem can be resolved by applying internal strategies.
Discuss internal strategies participants have used in the past (successfully and unsuccessfully) to improve their attentional control. If unsuccessful – why?
If additional strategies are identified by participants that they have found helpful in the past, add these to the Internal strategies list.
Identify and discuss appropriate motivators/rewards that can be used to help keep them on task (both immediate and longer term rewards).
Discuss obstacles to achievement and methods to overcome them.

Homework

Apply and rehearse techniques between sessions by returning to the specific problems you identified in starting activities, for example, incomplete tasks, working in an area with a lot of distraction (people, noise, activity by a window).

Depending on the task, select a way to measure the problem that can be repeated post-intervention, for example:

- frequency the problem occurs over a set period (day, week);
- time (hours/minutes) spent on and/or off task; and/or
- level of distress (frustration, anxiety, panic) associated with incomplete work (e.g. 0–10 low to high).

(*Continued*)

1. Assess the problem using this measure.
2. Choose one or two external and internal strategies that have been discussed in the session and apply them.
3. Re-evaluate the problem by completing the measure again. If the strategy has not worked, then select a different strategy and start again.
4. Rate your sense of achievement on completion of task (e.g. 0–10 low to high).

Apply and rehearse the techniques between sessions by conducting 'mini-experiments' by applying a strategy and record whether it works (or not). If the strategy does not work, then try a different one until you find what works best for you. It may help to ask a family member/friend to help you.

Once you have identified which strategy/strategies work best for you, continue to measure the behaviour and make a graph to chart improvement. Bear in mind that sometimes change is small. Over time small changes become great changes.

4

MEMORY MODULE

Memory problems are present in many psychiatric disorders, both with and without an organic basis. In people with ADHD, memory problems are often associated with their attentional problems. Indeed, some of the diagnostic inattentive symptoms for ADHD relate more specifically to memory problems, such as 'is often forgetful in daily activities' and 'often loses things needed for tasks and activities'. Memory problems are often the most obvious problem to the person themselves and to those around them. Poor memory is possibly more tangible and exposing than poor attention. For example, it is always noticeable when someone forgets to meet their friend, but it may be less obvious if someone has become distracted when in conversation.

The most common reason for memory problems in all individuals with ADHD is a failure to process information when it is initially presented due to poor attentional abilities (Kaplan *et al.*, 1998). This can lead to failures in short and longer-term storage of memory (Hervey, Epstein and Curry, 2004). The different types of memory systems responsible for memory difficulties are reviewed below. Understanding how memory difficulties arise is the key to intervening and improving memory. This module provides both internal and external strategies for facilitating memory abilities, with a similar principle as described in the Attention Module (Chapter 3), of 'change from the outside in', and 'change from the inside out'.

MEMORY SYSTEMS AFFECTED BY ADHD

There are three major memory systems, which are presented in Figure 4.1: Immediate memory (i.e. very brief storage for all sensations); short-term/working memory

Cognitive-Behavioural Therapy for ADHD in Adolescents and Adults: A Psychological Guide to Practice, Second Edition. Susan Young and Jessica Bramham.

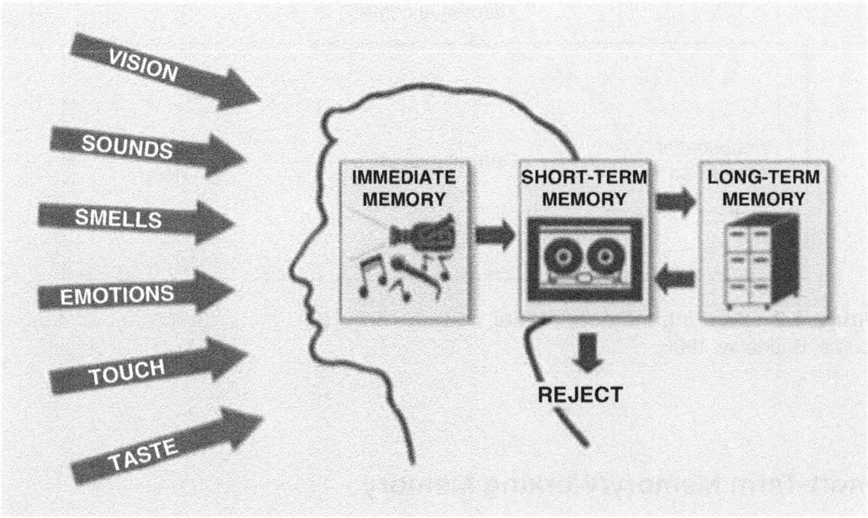

Figure 4.1 Memory systems
Source: Adapted from Head Injury © Trevor Powell, 2004, Speechmark Publishing Ltd, Bicester

(i.e. temporary storage where information can be manipulated); long-term memory (i.e. storage over longer periods).

Both shorter and longer-term memory deficits may be present in clients with ADHD, although 'working memory' or short-term memory deficits are more often identified (Young *et al.*, 2006; MacLean *et al.*, 2004). A figural representation of memory processes shown in Figure 4.1 is presented on the Companion Website, which can be used in sessions to explain the problems commonly experienced by people with ADHD in order to help clients understand their difficulties.

Immediate Memory

Immediate memory is often regarded as a 'sense' memory as it provides brief storage for all the senses including vision, sounds, smells, emotion, touch and taste. It is like a scratchpad or snapshot of information, which is quickly overwritten by new incoming sensations. For some people with ADHD, they may have particular difficulty if their immediate memory becomes overloaded with too much stimulation from too many different sources and this leads them to become extremely distractible. Attentional processes are also likely to determine the quality of information which enters the immediate memory. When information in the immediate memory needs to be used for a purpose it is then transferred into the 'short-term' memory or 'working memory' – here it can be rehearsed or manipulated.

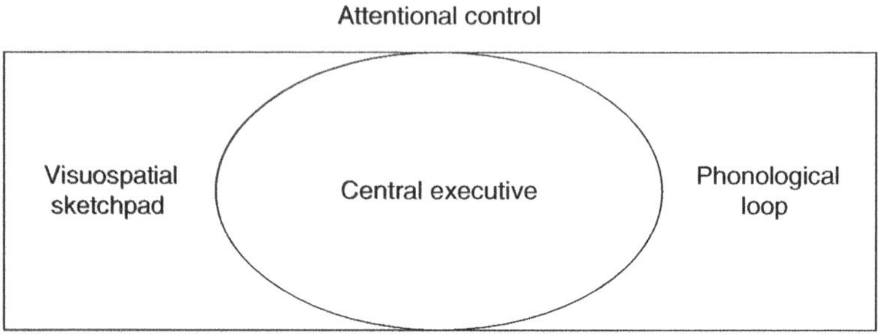

Figure 4.2 Working memory model
Source: Baddeley, 1986

Short-Term Memory/Working Memory

After the information has been received in the immediate memory system, this is then held for a very brief period in a 'short-term' or 'working memory' system. This is a temporary storage for information, like a rewritable cassette or video recording before it enters long-term memory or is 'rejected' and thus becomes unrecoverable. Working memory has been shown to be disrupted in people with ADHD, possibly through poor attention or interference from distraction. Figure 4.2 shows the three components that make up working memory (Baddeley, 1986).

The *central executive* determines what sensory information is attended to or provides an attentional control system as discussed earlier, both for the subsystems of working memory and other cognitive functions. This can be particularly affected in ADHD due to susceptibility to distraction. The *phonological loop* is an auditory memory system, which stores a few seconds' worth of information, like a short circular cassette tape. Information stored on the tape can either be rehearsed after it is recorded or erased by new information overwriting it. The *visuospatial sketch-pad* is a visual analogue, and can be likened to an 'Etch A Sketch' toy where images can be stored then wiped out by further information. In ADHD it is possible that information does not enter working memory adequately and that the same length of material cannot be stored as for people without ADHD. Furthermore, problems with the 'central executive' can lead to difficulties attending to the appropriate material in order for it to be processed by the working memory.

Long-Term Memory

Information is transferred from the working memory to long-term memory, which rather confusingly refers to all information from only a few minutes ago to years since the event. There are three stages of this memory system: encoding, storage and retrieval. *Encoding* involves registering and processing information, and is highly dependent on attentional processes and hence can be affected in people with ADHD. *Storage* of learned information is affected by a large range of factors that interfere with brain functioning and is evidenced by forgetting. *Retrieval* of stored information involves explicit recall or implicit knowledge revealed in later performance.

Retrieval can depend on strategies for accessing information, such as trying to retrace one's steps in order to find a lost possession. In ADHD this process may be more haphazard without a strategy. Retrieval can also be affected by the way information has been encoded. For example, ADHD clients have been shown to exhibit difficulties in organizing information at the encoding stage, for example organizing material into categories, and hence have resulting difficulties in optimal retrieval.

Access and retrieval from long-term memory can also be affected by mood. It has been well established that memories are more available if they are congruent with the current mood state, for example, negative memories are more accessible when someone is feeling low (Teasdale and Fogarty, 1979). This aspect of memory difficulty can be important when working with someone with comorbid low mood or depression as it may be particularly hard for the person to recall instances of more positive situations, such as times when they were able to achieve or had successes.

Prospective Memory

Prospective memory is a further aspect of memory, which is rarely assessed, but possibly the most pronounced cause of functional memory difficulties in many neurological and psychiatric conditions. Prospective memory involves remembering to do something in the future at a particular time, for example, remembering to attend an appointment, submit an assignment, or pay a bill by a certain time. Difficulties with prospective memory in ADHD have been linked to attentional problems, but attentional problems do not completely account for prospective memory deficits (Kerns and Price, 2001). It is possible that broader executive functioning difficulties such as forming strategies and problem-solving skills may also underpin prospective memory difficulties in ADHD. Therefore, it is likely that improving these aspects of functioning using the Organization and Time-Management Module (Chapter 5) and Problem-Solving Module (Chapter 7) will also have a beneficial impact on prospective memory.

FUNCTIONAL DEFICITS IN ADOLESCENTS AND ADULTS

It is often very easy for individuals with ADHD to recognize their memory difficulties as they regularly run into difficulties when they have forgotten what they have been told, to be somewhere or to bring something. The types of memory problem can be categorized according to the memory systems described above. For example, common problems reported by individuals with ADHD include:

1. Misplacing things, for example, forgetting where they have put their glasses, keys (long-term memory).
2. Forgetting appointments, deadlines, and activities that need to be done in the future, such as forgetting to pay the rent (prospective memory).
3. Forgetting instructions, if someone tries to explain how to do a task they have to slow down and repeat it a number of times (short- and long-term memory).
4. Difficulty performing mental processing tasks that require memory of information, for example, mental arithmetic (working memory).

Memory difficulties may be very apparent to those around individuals with ADHD, particularly in education settings and the workplace. People with ADHD have often gained a reputation for being 'scatty' or unreliable. While these traits are often accommodated by others, or seen as a personality feature, sometimes memory difficulties can be interpreted as showing a lack of respect or courtesy, such as arriving late to meetings or submitting assignments after the deadline. Recognition of this impact on others can sometimes provide the motivation to change. People with ADHD may also want to improve their memory so as not to seem different or inadequate.

ASSESSMENT OF MEMORY PROBLEMS

Clients should be asked to record their memory problems during a set period. There may be specific weaknesses in certain areas that the client can readily identify as causing them frequent difficulties. Performing a review of these difficulties and then making sense of where the memory failures have arisen is a helpful way of educating the client about their memory difficulties. Table 4.1 provides an example of a log of memory problems with an analysis of the type of problem and reasons as to why it occurred. A blank version of Table 4.1 is available on the website.

Psychoeducation

Given the generic and therefore confusing nature of the concept of 'memory', it is important to begin with psychoeducation about the fundamentals of how memory works (i.e. by using the material in the introductory section of this module). In particular, understanding the link between memory and attention is crucial for identifying ways to change. Describing the process by which information is acquired, processed and stored in memory can be very useful for someone to understand as often individuals have adopted the notion that memories form a big black box in their brain and sometimes the information they need is there and sometimes it is not.

Table 4.1 Memory problems log

Date and time	*What happened*	*Type of memory problem*	*Possible reasons*
Monday 11a.m.	Forgot name of new colleagues	Long-term storage	Didn't pay attention when I was told first time
Tuesday 3p.m.	Being told how to operate new equipment, forgot what was said at beginning about how to start	Working memory	Was thinking about what to have for lunch and then noticed someone leaving the room
Thursday 3p.m.	Forgot to go to daughter's sports day	Prospective memory	Didn't write it down when she brought letter home then lost letter
Friday 5p.m.	Forgot to sort out repeat prescription for medication and now don't have any for weekend	Prospective memory	Didn't notice that was running out

External Memory Strategies

There are several strategies that the client may adopt to try to help them improve their memory. These commonly include the introduction of external aids, that is, using support systems to minimize problems arising from poor memory, such as the use of diaries, planners and so forth. Specific strategies are listed in Table 4.2. Electronic organizers are invaluable. However as we increasingly move towards advanced information technology, it is important for clients to ensure that electronic organizers are the servant of the individual and do not become the master and provide an opportunity for distraction and time-wasting. Moreover, there are also internal strategies that can be applied; for optimal results the client should be encouraged to develop both internal and external methods to enhance memory. As discussed previously for developing attentional control, the therapist should investigate what the client has successfully applied in the past, identify new possibilities, set homework tasks to evaluate their efficacy and review with the client the best and most appropriate techniques.

Internal Memory Strategies

Aside from the plethora of external strategies, internal memory strategies may also be used in conjunction with external memory strategies in order to enhance encoding and retrieval memory processes. Specific strategies are outlined in Table 4.3. If the client develops internal strategies for improving their memory then this will improve their confidence and self-efficacy, rather than relying entirely on external aids.

Table 4.2 External strategies to improve memory

Strategy	*Description*
Diary	A diary is helpful for short-term planning. A 'page-a-day' diary is most useful as appointments can be recorded as well as additional notes, for example, tasks to complete, items needed,. Having this information presented in a day format serves as a cue and reminder of tasks (or steps) that need to be completed to achieve longer-term goals.
Weekly calendar	A weekly calendar allows family members to write reminders and instructions that may be helpful for the individual. For example, for a family birthday party, another family member may devise an action plan dividing up the responsibilities by noting 'book a taxi', 'buy a cake', 'book the restaurant' and so on. It is additionally helpful for the person with ADHD see how their activities integrate with those of their family.
Annual wall planner	This can be used for longer-term plans and forward planning, for example, by marking up school holidays, family vacations, birthdays and anniversaries.
Portable Dictaphone/ recorder	These can be used to make verbal lists and reminders for information that may quickly go out of mind. Some people find it helpful to carry a Dictaphone around with them so they can quickly record ideas and reminders. The list of tasks or reminders can then be worked through systematically at a later point in time.
Answerphone messages	Some telephone systems, including mobile phones, give the opportunity for individuals to leave themselves answerphone messages. This can help to reduce the need to remember information in the future.
Lists	It will be helpful to get the person with ADHD into the habit of making lists. These will include daily lists of 'things to do', shopping lists, household chores. Organizing ideas into lists and categories can also help someone with ADHD to develop a sense of control. Ticking off completed items serves as feedback and can be a motivator through positive reinforcement.
Help cards	Summarized forms of information such as 'help cards' can be useful for activities that are not performed regularly such as setting the video, or filling in tax return forms.
Watches and clocks.	Clocks can be positioned in obvious places, even in every room in the house, in order to remind the person with ADHD of the passage of time. Clocks with chimes or watches that beep can be useful for orienting someone to time when they have become distracted.
Alarms and/or computerized reminders	These can serve as reminders over varying time periods ranging from a three hourly alarm to take medication to setting an annual reminder to prompt an individual about a friend's birthday.
Personal organizers and mobile phones	Personal organizers and mobile phones can perform many of the above tasks. However, if their organizational functions are new to the client then these should be introduced and developed gradually into a routine, with goal setting agreed with the therapist to make sure that this is not yet another strategy that has been started and quickly abandoned. The aim is that these items are functional and not distracters. The organizer should only be kept in certain places and backed-up, as it may be even more disabling for a person with ADHD to lose the organizer and/or memory system in the organizer.

Table 4.3 Internal strategies to improve memory

Strategy	*Description*
Repetition and rehearsal	Repeating and practising recall of information (for example, through self-talk) can improve the likelihood of information being successfully processed by working memory and then encoded for longer-term recall.
Create a visual cue	Pairing a verbal task with a visual image can improve verbal retention as it allows information to be encoded in both a visual and verbal form. This enhances the memory trace and increases the likelihood of later retrieval. The more bizarre and exaggerated the image, the easier it will be to remember. For example, if remembering to pay a water bill, think of white-water rafting to the bank!
Mnemonics	Learning cues or mnemonics can be a useful method of condensing information for later recall and can appear less overwhelming for someone with ADHD. For example, S.T.O.P. = sausages, tomatoes, oranges, potatoes.
Spaced retrieval	Memory research has shown that gradually increasing the time span between retrieval times increases the likelihood of it being retrieved in the future, and thus improves storage through reinforcement of a memory trace (Ebbinghaus, 1885). Information should be rehearsed with increasingly longer gaps, for example, 5 minutes, 30 minutes, an hour, next day. Performing this exercise throughout a session and beyond can allow the ADHD to improve their self-efficacy.
Problem-solving	A good method for finding lost or mislaid possessions is to mentally retrace steps in a systematic way. This can be done by asking a sequence of questions such as 'when did I last have my keys?' 'where did I go when I got in?' or 'where would I put that key now?'
Keeping calm	High emotional arousal and feelings of stress can exacerbate both attention and memory functioning. Therefore it is important to encourage the client to reduce anxiety and anger before attempting any recall. See the Anxiety Module (Chapter 9) and Frustration and Anger Module (Chapter 10) for specific strategies, including relaxation techniques.

SUMMARY

Memory difficulties can be the source of great distress for many adolescents and adults with ADHD, possibly because they are the most observable aspects of the disorder. Memory problems can be attributed to failures in several aspects of memory functioning but seem often to stem from initial attentional difficulties, whereby problems with initial processing leads to later difficulties with remembering. Through learning when, where and how memory problems are likely to arise, clients can begin to anticipate and pre-empt these difficulties. They can benefit from external strategies, which provide an external memory prompt, or internal strategies, which increase the likelihood of them remembering. Memory can also often be improved through targeting skills as addressed in the Organization and Time-Management Module (Chapter 5).

Group Treatment: Memory Module

It is essential to prepare for group treatment by reading the chapter module. Six group sessions are outlined below, but the number of treatment sessions can be expanded or reduced as required.

Plan

Session 1	Starting activities and complete individual memory log
Session 2	Psychoeducation – different memory systems; immediate, short-term, long-term and prospective memory
Sessions 3–5	Exercises (review individual memory log, present external and internal strategies)
Session 6	Revision of psychoeducation and strategies Discussion of homework outcome/experience – what works best? Obstacles and how to overcome them

Starting Activities

What kinds of memory problems do you have?
What do you think causes you to forget?
How do these problems affect you in your daily activities?
Guide participants to think about specific events and circumstances. Identify specific times when memory problems have caused difficulties.
Guide participants to think about consequences of having a poor memory (missed deadlines, not turning up for meetings, others thinking they are unreliable).
Group discussion
Complete the Memory Problems log. Handont Table 4.1 – first two columns only.
Group discussion on individual differences that can be identified from the completed assessments (i.e. people have different types of problems).

Psychoeducation

Memory systems affected by ADHD – immediate memory, short-term/working memory, long-term memory, prospective memory. Handout Figure 4.1 Memory systems.

Exercises

Understanding memory problems. Handout Table 4.1 – return to Memory Problems Log and complete last two columns.

(*Continued*)

Examine and discuss individual logs in order to categorize the type of memory problems and suggest possible reasons.

External strategies to improve memory. Handout Table 4.2.
Identify potentially useful methods and add to this handout any additional successful methods identified by participants.

Internal strategies to improve memory. Handout Table 4.3.
Identify potentially useful methods and add to this handout any additional successful methods identified by participants.

Homework

Identify one or two external strategies to use for specific memory activities and review to see whether they helped.
Identify one or two internal strategies to use for specific memory activities and review to see whether they helped.

5

ORGANIZATION AND TIME-MANAGEMENT MODULE

'Time management' is the Achilles heel of people with ADHD. People with ADHD achieve more when a time structure is organized for them. Their difficulty is setting and managing this for themselves. Thus the goal of the organization and time management sessions is to train an individual to structure their time appropriately, prioritize tasks and reward themselves for success. The best way of doing this is to use a methodical approach that teaches clients to structure their own time and help them feel that they are taking control of their life. This reinforces a sense of purpose and desire for achievement. The module also provides methods to reconceptualize time and set a time plan. Potential hurdles to success such as 'time-wasting traps' are also discussed.

FUNCTIONAL DEFICITS IN ADOLESCENTS AND ADULTS

People with ADHD find it more difficult than others to manage their time due to their attentional problems inducing them to lack focus on the task in hand. They become easily distracted by other seemingly more important or interesting activities. Prioritization is particularly difficult as people with ADHD tend to flit from task to task irrespective of its importance. They often have many projects on the go, all at various stages of completion. An analogy is that they try to keep too many balls in the air at once but end up dropping most of them. People with ADHD are very spontaneous and they initiate lots of projects with good intentions, but their disorganized chaotic personal style means that they do not see these through. This causes particular problems in their occupational activities whether they be in school, further education or employment because they have difficulty meeting deadlines and maintaining interest in order to complete a project.

Cognitive-Behavioural Therapy for ADHD in Adolescents and Adults: A Psychological Guide to Practice, Second Edition. Susan Young and Jessica Bramham.

Time-Wasting Traps

A major problem is that they start multiple projects and have them at various stages of incompletion. It is a particular problem for mundane tasks which are necessary but boring as people with ADHD have a low threshold for becoming bored. Often such activities are left until the last minute leaving insufficient time to present work at a standard reflecting their true capabilities. This affects both the content and presentation of their work as it is rushed. They don't have enough time to check for errors and the presentation of their work may appear messy and disorganized. Others may attempt to start work in advance but they fall behind due to 'time-wasting traps' that cause them to switch attention from one task (often an uncompleted task) to another. Other time-wasting traps include an aversion to delay, which means they favour immediate gratification over long-term plans and goals. Sensation seeking behaviour may also be a time-wasting trap as young people may favour 'interesting' activities (and possibly reckless or thrilling activities that involve risk-taking) over mundane routines that we all have to do. Another very common time-wasting trap is procrastination. In people with ADHD this usually takes the form of a disproportionate amount of time engaged in means of avoiding engagement or re-engagement in a task. For example, it may take the form of intellectualizing a problem or activity which leads to an inability to make a decision (e.g. the focus becomes the debate over 'how to' or 'why should' rather than task completion).

Time Perception

To people with ADHD, time can seem like it is always against them. It is either going too slowly when they feel bored and frustrated, or can disappear quickly when they become engrossed in something interesting or immediately gratifying. Time passes quickly when their attention slips – this means they become easily distracted and may start to daydream. The end result is that they are often late, do not achieve or complete tasks and miss opportunities. It is therefore important for the therapist to establish a shared understanding with the client about how they perceive time. Time should be seen as a 'resource' that is applied to achieve set goals. Time is a tool. If clients are satisfied or happy with how they spend their time, and what they achieve in that time, then this will reinforce the need for structure. Thus, it is important to encourage clients to find something they enjoy in whatever they do. This may involve 'freeing up time' to integrate pleasurable activities with mundane tasks.

Memory Problems

Some of our clients describe how, even when they have carefully made their plans regarding their aims for a day, they still have great difficulty in achieving this as they forget what they are supposed to be doing and end up being late for appointments and miss tasks. Some individuals overcompensate and arrive unnecessarily early for important events in order to make sure they do not miss out. In such cases they inevitably waste time waiting for the appointment that could have been used more productively.

These problems with time management are due to prospective memory difficulties, in other words, the ability to remember to do something in the future. This can be regarded as a deficit in executive functioning as it is closely linked to planning ability, which has been shown to be impaired in people with ADHD (e.g. Young *et al.*, 2007). Once a mental plan has been made, certain points in time are 'tagged' or marked by an executive functioning process such that the person is alerted at approximately the right moment that they should be performing a certain activity, such as turning down the boiling milk (e.g. Burgess *et al.*, 2000). For people with ADHD, this 'alerting system' could be seen to be working suboptimally such that they are either reminded at the wrong time that they are supposed to be doing something, which then becomes a distraction, or they are not internally reminded until it is too late and they have missed the event.

ASSESSMENT OF TIME-MANAGEMENT PROBLEMS

There are three measures that will assist the therapist in determining time-management problems in their clients: the time-management evaluation, the importance of punctuality evaluation, and the diary activity log. All are available on the Companion Website.

Time-Management Evaluation

Table 5.1 outlines the time-management evaluation and provides an example of a client's perception of their time management by measuring the frequency they experience time-management problems. This individual was particularly concerned about their memory problems. This measure can be repeated at various stages during treatment to evaluate change in the client's time-management skills and demonstrate improvement. In the table the scores range from '0' representing the absence of a problem to '4' representing experiencing the problem with high frequency. However, the numerical scores shown in Table 5.1 are not presented in the questionnaire given to the client and the Companion Website provides this table in an appropriate format for therapeutic use. Nevertheless, the scoring system illustrated in Table 5.1 can be applied to measure baseline difficulty as well as progress in treatment. (Note that scores on items 4, 5, 6 and 9 are reversed). Thus, a reducing total score indicates improvement. (A blank copy is provided on the Companion Website).

Importance of Punctuality Evaluation

Often, people with ADHD develop a sense of 'learned helplessness' regarding their timekeeping such that they assume they will always be late and others come to expect very little of them. A motivating method for improving time-keeping is by asking the individual to rate the importance of punctuality and evaluate the impact of their lateness for different situations. An example is given in Table 5.2 for Chloe, a mother of

Table 5.1 Time-management evaluation

	How often ...	*Never*	*Rarely*	*Sometimes*	*Often*	*Always*
1	Do you make plans for your time?	4	3	2	(1)	0
2	Do you write down your plans?	4	3	(2)	1	0
3	Do you complete everything you had planned to do for a day?	(4)	3	2	1	0
4	Is your time interrupted by seemingly urgent tasks?	0	1	2	(3)	4
5	Do you leave things unfinished?	0	1	2	3	(4)
6	Do you forget what you were supposed to be doing?	0	1	2	3	(4)
7	Do you arrive on time and prepared for appointments?	4	(3)	2	1	0
8	Do you know roughly what time it is?	4	(3)	2	1	0
9	Do you feel that you have wasted your time?	0	1	2	3	(4)
Total Score = 26						

two boys who also have ADHD (a blank form is included on the Companion Website for use in sessions).

By performing the evaluation in Table 5.2, Chloe was able to determine which events were absolutely crucial for her to be on time in order to avoid disadvantaging her children and damaging her reputation. Previously, she had shrugged off the implications of regularly being late, and assumed that others would just think she was 'scatty'. However, she was more motivated to prioritize events and be on time when she had explicitly thought through the consequences of poor punctuality.

Time Plans and the Diary Activity Log

In addition to the time-management evaluation outlined in Table 5.1, it will be helpful to determine *how* the person actually spends their time before they begin learning time-management strategies. This is achieved by keeping a log of activities using a weekly diary record (see Table 5.3). This should be introduced by asking the client to map in the session what they have done in the recent past, for example, in the previous 2 days. The client is then asked to complete the rest of the week prior to the next session and bring this to the next appointment. This will help determine how much time is usefully and constructively spent on tasks and highlight problem times when the client is vulnerable to time-wasting traps, for example, reading junk mail, chatting

Table 5.2 Importance of punctuality evaluation

Situation	*Importance of punctuality (0–10)*	*Potential impact/outcome of being late*
Arriving late at work	8	Looks unprofessional People may think I'm uncommitted Other people have to cover for me until I arrive Would get more work done and not have to stay late
Late for parents' evening	9	Might miss out on hearing what teachers recommend Teachers may assume I'm a bad mother Sons' education may be affected
Late to pick up the boys from school	7	The boys may become unnecessarily worried that I won't come The boys need routine too Other mothers may think I'm neglectful
Late for hairdressers appointment	4	It may delay every appointment that follows mine They might turn me away and then I'd have to rebook
Late for lunch at parents' house	2	The food may be ruined It's not fair on mum who likes to be organized about when we eat. She may be upset They might worry I've had a car crash on the way
Late for doctors appointment for repeat prescription	6	I may miss the appointment and have to wait until the end of surgery Other more ill people might have less time at the end of the day because all the appointments will become delayed I might not get the prescription, so run out of medication and then I'd be even less able to manage my time
Late to meet a friend for a drink	3	My friend may feel anxious or embarrassed about waiting alone It may look like my friend has been stood up It's wasting their time My friend may be in a bad mood by the time I get there. It may spoil the evening

Table 5.3 Diary activity log

Time	Mon	Tues	Wed	Thurs	Fri	Sat	Sun
7–8	Sleeping	Sleeping	Sleeping	Sleeping	Sleeping	Sleeping	Sleeping
8–9	Sleeping	Get up	Get up	Sleeping	sleeping	Sleeping	Sleeping
9–10	Felt too tired to go to work Had breakfast	TAKE MEDICATION No food in house, buy breakfast on way to work	Breakfast and set off early for work	Overslept	Hungover so go to local café for big breakfast	Lie-in	Lie-in
10–11	TAKE MEDICATION Watched daytime TV	Arrive late at job	TAKE MEDICATION Go to cafe for coffee and read papers	Go to warehouse for more paint	Arrive at work but no-one is there to open up	Lie-in	Lie-in
11–12	Watched daytime TV	Start preparing walls	Painting	TAKE MEDICATION Intensive painting as need to get it finished by end of day	Wait for owners to come	Lie-in	Lie-in
12–1	Rang mum	Have bought wrong paint	Painting	Painting	Owners arrive and say they will dock pay – tell them to stuff it and resign from job	Lie-in	Lie-in

(continued)

Table 5.3 *(cont'd)*

Time	Mon	Tues	Wed	Thurs	Fri	Sat	Sun
1–2	Started looking for car tax form	Go to warehouse for more paint	Arrive late for meeting for new piece of work	Painting	Go to pub	Watch TV	Panic because supposed to be at parents for lunch
2–3	Found magazine had been looking for	Bump into old workmate and go for coffee	Supposed to have another meeting but miss it to have lunch	Painting	Go to bookmakers for a flutter	Watch TV	Arrive late at parents – they have finished meal
3–4	Surfing internet for things in magazine	Back to work	Catch up with a few tasks	Lunch	Lose £50 on horses	Watch TV	Sit around chatting
4–5	Feeling hungry – no food in house so go to shops	Stripping walls	Run out of paint	Try to finish by cutting corners	Go to pub	Watch TV	Sit around chatting
5–6	Notice new CD has been released – look around shops	Get distracted and strip too much off	Go home early	Realise it is impossible to finish so give up and leave work early to go to gym	Friends arrive	Make a meal	Miss the bus home so dad drives me
6–7	Bump into friend and go for drink	Just catch super-market before it closes	Watch soap operas	Arrive at gym but have forgotten kit	Out with friends	Late to meet friend	No food in house so get a takeaway

7–8	Stay out drinking	Microwave meal then watch TV	Start cooking food but forget it is in oven because watching a film	Go out with friend from gym	Out with friends	Cinema	Watch TV
8–9	Stay out drinking	Watch TV	Have to start cooking again	Out at pub	Out with friends	Cinema	Watch TV
9–10	Stay out drinking	Watch TV	Watch DVD	Go to restaurant for food	Out with friends	Cinema bar	Watch TV
10–11	Stay out drinking	Phone call from sister	Watch DVD	Restaurant	Out with friends	Get something to eat then go home	Watch TV
11–12	Stay out drinking	Still on the phone	Bed	Miss last train home so have to get taxi	Out with friends	Watch TV	Watch TV
1–2	Get home and watch TV	Go to bed	Sleep	Watch TV	Out with friends	Watch TV	Fall asleep on sofa
2–3	Sleep	Lie awake	Sleep	Sleep	Fall asleep at friends	Bed	Sleep
3–4	Sleep	Sleep	Sleep	Sleep	Sleep	Sleep	Sleep
4–5	Sleep	Sleep	Sleep	Sleep	Wake up and walk home	Sleep	Sleep
5–6	Sleep	Sleep	Sleep	Sleep	Sleep	Sleep	Sleep
6–7	Sleep	Sleep	Sleep	Sleep	Sleep	Sleep	Sleep

at length on the phone, looking for items that have been lost, missing the train, surfing the internet. The time that the client usually takes their medication should also be recorded as it is important to establish the relationship between taking the medication and its effect on concentration; that is the ability to focus and periods of 'lost' or wasted time. Table 5.3 shows the completed diary activity log of David, a painter and decorator, who was taking slow-release stimulant medication in the morning.

The diary activity log will guide you as to how your client actually spends their time and this should be used as a basis for discussion. The client may be surprised to see how much time they spend off-task. It is easy to forget how much time is spent reading junk mail, looking for items that have been lost, missing the train and so on. From examining his diary activity log, David could see that he was rather chaotic in his organization of time. He had not been prompt or reliable in his attendance at work, and when he was criticized for this, he had reacted impulsively by walking out and losing the money for the job. He noticed he was distracted for large amounts of time and not using time efficiently. He was spending large amounts of time in the pub, getting home late and not having sufficient sleep. His meal organization was haphazard and he frequently went for long periods without food. With regard to timing of medication, David realized that he was rather irregular as to when he took his medication. This meant that the optimal hours for him to concentrate varied from day to day. The day he walked out of his job in anger, he had forgotten to take his medication.

COGNITIVE BEHAVIOURAL THERAPY

Psychoeducation

In many respects psychoeducation about the deleterious effects of a disorganized interpersonal style will naturally occur in the discussion about the client's problems and the evaluations outlined in the section on assessment. The best method for people with ADHD to keep time is to rely on external aids such as alarm clocks, digital watches and mobile phone alarms, for example. These alarms can be set at a regular time every day, for example, the night before, and be integrated into a routine. Some personal organizer systems or mobile phones can be programmed to make different tones according to the activity. Clients should be encouraged not just to set an alarm for an event beginning, such as a driving lesson beginning at 1.00 p.m., but they should work out the time they need to begin getting ready for the lesson, for example: start packing their bag at 12.00, catch the bus at 12.30. Such an 'early warning system' can also improve attention as it can increase arousal, which is an interrelated system (see Attention Module in Chapter 3).

Organization and Time Management Strategies

In order to manage time more effectively, the client should be helped to plan their time in advance by making up a time plan. This entails following the six steps outlined in Box 5.1.

Box 5.1 Six steps to making a time plan

1. Set goals
2. Make lists
3. Prioritize activities
4. Estimate time to complete tasks
5. Schedule tasks
6. Incorporate a reward system

The client must be encouraged to determine *set goals* within a time period. In the session, they should *list activities* that they are required to do for the week as well as activities that they would like to do. The next step is to prioritize the tasks. *Prioritizing activities* is likely to require assistance from a therapist initially, until the client develops or improves these skills. This can be achieved by asking the client to allocate an importance rating, for example, how vital is it to get a bill paid this week from 0 – 'not at all' through to 4 – 'essential'. Then the client must *estimate the amount of time* each task will take. This may take some practise as you will need to determine together whether the client has a tendency to consistently overestimate or underestimate time. At this stage, the client should be ready to create a *schedule of tasks* to complete within a determined time period. When making a time plan, it will be important to explore 'contingency plans' as some important tasks may overrun. A final step is to incorporate a *reward system* for successful completion of chunks of time. This may be taking a break from a challenging task or switching to a more enjoyable, lower priority task, for a set period. Thus, there are six stages to designing and achieving an effective Time Plan and these techniques are described in more detail in the following sections.

Step 1: Setting Goals

The therapist must encourage the client to set and review goals routinely, as this will help the client to achieve where they want to go in life. Clients should consider their large-scale and longer-term goals. These include career, educational, family, financial, physical, and pleasure-related goals. However, the client must learn to break these general goals down into smaller achievable 'mini-goals' that represent stepping stones to reaching the overall aim (see Figure 5.1). This will provide short-term focus and motivation in addition to encouraging the client to retain an eye on the longer term outlook. It is important to focus on *specific* tasks as this will help the client to organize their resources. For example, Figure 5.1 describes David, the painter and decorator, who wanted to replace his van.

A blank version of this figure is available on the Companion Website, where the client can complete their own general goals and then break them down. Once goals and

Figure 5.1 Example of breaking down goals into steps

steps have been established, the client should be encouraged to make a time plan for the week to organize achievement of the first steps. At this time, the focus is on the steps, working from the bottom upwards.

David wanted to replace his van which he used for work. Previously he would have gone to a garage and bought one the next day on credit. However, he was aware that this impulsive behaviour would lead him to spend far more in the longer term. He therefore needed to work out a financial strategy that would allow him to save. He also needed to determine how much money he would be able to make by selling his old van. Finally, rather than buying the first van he saw, he needed to spend some time researching his options and finding a good deal.

It is important that tasks are defined *precisely* so that it is clear when they have been achieved. For example, 'save £1000', can be measured but 'spend less' is less obvious when it has been completed. Wherever possible, tasks should be performance-related rather than outcome-related, particularly for activities in which the client may not have absolute control. For example, 'find five possible vans to choose between' is a preferable (and more achievable) goal rather than 'buy a van'. Tasks that seem very large or overwhelming need to be broken down into several stages. If they still seem large, then break them down further. Achievement of realistic expectations is the key. It is easier and quicker to achieve a small step than a great step.

Step 2: Making Lists

Next the client and therapist must make a comprehensive list of what needs to be achieved, for example in the coming week. This must include all the components outlined in Box 5.2.

The Companion Website includes this table in a format that can be used in sessions with the client. However, although clients may think that they will be able to remember

Box 5.2 List components

a Things that the client needs to do to achieve the step(s) they are focusing on
b Things that the client really wants to do
c Things that they have to do
d Things that they might do if they have time
e Things that they hate doing but are necessary at some point soon

the list, they probably will not. Lists should be written down whenever possible to avoid expending valuable mental energy in rehearsing and reminding themselves of tasks. This in itself can be a distraction. Second, it is much more powerful to produce a written document to which the client is 'signed-up'. This is much more motivating as it can be used both within the sessions and applied on their own outside the sessions.

It is really important to include, in the list, activities that the client enjoys. Lists need not be chores! Listing mundane or uninteresting tasks that *have* to be completed will be boring and unappealing. The client will be unmotivated and not achieve their overall objective.

Making a 'to-do list' serves the additional purpose of inducing a sense of control and satisfaction as activities are coordinated in one place. This avoids a sense of feeling overwhelmed or that there are endless demands on the client's time. It is also particularly useful for looking at several commitments together. By imposing structure and order, the client can logically associate tasks, see how they contribute to an overarching goal, and integrate these with desired activities. This will reduce feelings of panic and anxiety.

For example, if the aim is to apply for a job, the steps may include:

1. Monday – go to the Job Centre;
2. Tuesday – obtain relevant application forms by telephone or by writing;
3. Wednesday – fill in personal details on application forms;
4. Thursday – fill in previous employment history on application forms;
5. Friday – fill in reasons why you want the respective job on application forms;
6. Saturday – ask a friend or family member to look through the application forms and give feedback. Find an envelope and stamp; and
7. Sunday – make changes to application forms, re-read them and post them.

Step 3: Prioritizing Activities

It is unlikely that *everything* on a comprehensive 'wish-list' of activities will be achieved in the allocated time. Therefore it is important to *prioritize* as it is very easy

How important is it to go to the Job Centre the next day?

```
0                1                2                3                4
|----------------|----------------|----------------|----------------|
Not at all                                                  Essential
```

How important is it to play football on sunday?

```
0                1                2                3                4
|----------------|----------------|----------------|----------------|
Not at all                                                  Essential
```

Figure 5.2 Prioritization methods

to spend a long time doing a little job that does not actually progress the client towards a goal or affect the quality of their life. Prioritizing involves the client asking the following four questions.

1. What *must* be done this week?
2. What can wait, and for how long?
3. What do I *want* done this week?
4. What will happen if I don't do it?

Use of a Likert scale will help the client determine the importance of tasks (see below). Go through each task and ask the client to evaluate how vital it is to achieve this task within the set period (i.e. day, week, month). For example, if your client's goal is to get a job as quickly as possible because s/he is unemployed, they should ask the questions in Figure 5.2.

For clients who find that a Likert Scale lacks sensitivity to help identify subtle prioritizations, it may be more helpful for them to allocate a percentage rating (ranging from 0 per cent 'not at all', to 100 per cent 'essential'). We have included both methods of measurement on the Companion Website.

The characteristics identified and learned from the diary activity log in Table 5.3 obtained at the beginning of these sessions and prior to intervention should be kept in mind. This will give helpful clues to how the clients naturally apply themselves; that is, the best time of the day to conduct work requiring concentration, physical activity, rest periods. It will also give clues to likely distracters and obstacles to achieving tasks. Forewarned is forearmed and the sessions should be spent preparing for distracters and obstacles and working out a plan to avoid temptations. Once items have been prioritized, they should be ranked in order of importance. These activities can then be scheduled for times when the individual is able to perform at their optimal level. For example, David took his medication in the middle of the morning, which meant that he was best able to concentrate in the middle of the day.

Learning to prioritize is a skill that the client needs to develop. It should be modelled and rehearsed in sessions, for example, by using an agenda and prioritizing work in progress. Clients may be reluctant to prioritize tasks and consider this activity to be a waste of time as they prefer to deal with issues as they present themselves. This reticence or lack of impulse control needs to be acknowledged and discussed in the sessions. It is not until the client engages in the process that they learn that engaging in a process of prioritization takes time, but is a good use of time. It serves a valuable function and leads to positive results. Like all new skills, the process needs to be practised until it becomes habitual.

For example, take the case of David. In the immediate term, David needed to find new employment. Additionally, he thought that if he learned plastering skills, this would improve his potential for gaining regular employment as a painter and decorator. He also enjoyed playing football and going to the pub with his friends. David was running out of ADHD medication. Before walking out of his job, David had intended to sell his old van and purchase a new van, but as he was no longer employed, his priorities changed. Before engaging in the process of prioritization, David was keen to go ahead and take a loan to buy a van that he saw one day when driving past a garage. However, in the session we generated a list of goals and priorities using the techniques described and it became clear that this was now a relatively low priority. Bearing in mind his new goals of getting a job and to learn plastering, David rated the importance of the tasks to be achieved and determined his priority task list as follows (see Box 5.3).

Priorities are dynamic factors, thus it is important to teach clients to review them in a regular and planned way. If a priority task list is not regularly revisited, then the client may waste time on tasks which have been superseded by more important activities. They also become distracted and lose sight of their main priorities.

Box 5.3 Priority task list

0 1 2 3 4
|----------|----------|----------|----------|
least important most important

Request a repeat prescription from his GP	4
Determine and organize financial situation	4
Go to job centre	4
Complete application forms	4
Find lists of courses from local college	3
Enrol on a course	3
Play football on Saturday	3
Go to pub after football	2
Buy a new van	1
Play football on Sunday	0

Box 5.4 Organizing a repeat prescription

a Telephone the GP receptionist and place the request	5 minutes
b Drive to the GP surgery and park	20 minutes
d Wait in reception	10 minutes
e Drive home	15 minutes

Step 4: Estimating Times to Complete Tasks

Next the client must estimate how long they think it will take to perform each task. In David's case, his most urgent priority involved incorporating several steps to schedule him to organize a repeat prescription from the GP, as shown in Box 5.4.

When making his time plan, David also needed to schedule time for 'unpredictable' circumstances such as heavy traffic, difficulty finding a parking space, being late and the surgery being closed. It is better to overestimate and succeed than underestimate and fail.

Perception of time can be distorted for people with ADHD (Young, Channon and Toone, 2000). Usually time passes quickly for a person with ADHD, for example 10 minutes can feel like 2 minutes, so it is difficult to schedule a time plan that accurately reflects all that has to be done within a limited amount of time. Almost certainly this will guarantee failure, leaving a distressed client feeling disinterested, disenchanted and despondent about unfinished tasks and without the motivation to recommence them another day. In order to avoid this negative reinforcement, it is very important to accurately estimate how long it will take to complete a task. So first, determine the client's general time perception by asking them to complete a set of exercises such as those outlined in Table 5.4. These are illustrated as completed by David, but are presented in the Companion Website in a format for use in treatment. Of course, these exercises may be modified as appropriate. What is important is that they are relevant to your client's way of life. First, David estimated how long it would take him to complete a task, and then he timed himself to see how accurately he had estimated the time (as his homework assignment). This behavioural experiment can be further extended by the client timing others performing certain tasks.

This exercise will help the client realize the extent to which they consistently distort periods of time and find out how long regular activities really take, such as shopping, ironing, cleaning. What you need to identify is the client's general trait in time-estimation (i.e. whether they tend to overestimate or underestimate – it is most likely to be the latter) so you can make appropriate adjustments to the time plan.

Table 5.4 Time-estimation exercise

Activity: How long does it take ...	*David's estimated time (minutes)*	*David's actual time (minutes)*
To have a shower and dry off	2	8
To get dressed in the morning	3	5
To make a cup of tea	1	3
To go to the hairdressers/barbers	20	30
To buy a week's shopping	30	60
To change the bed linen	5	15
To clean the kitchen floor	5	15
To read a newspaper	20	40

When constructing a time plan, however, some tasks will obviously be new, in which case clients should always be encouraged to allocate additional time to complete them. Unscheduled gaps in time, that is, 'free time', are viewed as additional rewards for successful completion of tasks.

Step 5: Scheduling Tasks

By this stage, steps or tasks have been identified to achieve goals, a list has been determined to integrate these with tasks for the week, they have been prioritized and the time to complete them has been estimated. The next stage is to sequence the tasks or activities by setting out and organizing the time plan. Ironically it is crucial to schedule time to create a plan and organize time. Depending on individual preference, priority tasks may be organized according to particular inclinations. Some people prefer to do the worst task first to get it out of the way, others would rather ease themselves in gently. The time of day may also be a factor. Most people have a post-lunch dip in their energy levels, therefore it is advisable to avoid scheduling an activity that requires particular mental exertion during this period. The pretreatment diary activity log will be helpful in this respect. Ensure the medication regimes of the individual are noted, as a good time to schedule tasks that require concentration may be within the hours following taking medication. Additionally, when scheduling the time plan, it is important to balance the day evenly with pleasant and unpleasant activities.

Some activities will be difficult to accurately schedule (particularly novel activities for which completion times are difficult to estimate). 'Contingency time' needs to be scheduled in to account for tasks which overrun and/or for unexpected tasks that arise in the course of the day. However when these occur, it is important to distinguish between a genuine 'unexpected item' that is a priority and an idea that springs to mind which functions as a distracter from a mundane task. Irrelevant distracters must be discussed in sessions, so the client can recognize them when they arise and can reject them as time-wasting traps representing obstacles to the client reaching their weekly goal(s). Ideas and initiatives, however, should not be discarded but temporarily put on ice by noting them for scheduling into a future set of activities and/or time plan. Creativity is not a resource to be stifled.

Table 5.5 shows the time plan devised in a session with David (4 denotes the most important). David's specific goals for the week were to organize his finances, get a job, obtain a repeat prescription and enrol on a plastering course. In the week, David also wanted to play football on Saturday, visit his parents, and look into the cost of replacing his van.

David then generated a weekly diary activity plan (See Table 5.6) in order for him to schedule his time so he would complete all of his essential priority tasks as well as the lower priority activities that he wanted to achieve. Thus, David scheduled his week to meet his target goals and his desired goals, for example playing football and exploring the possibility of buying a new van. Desired goals may be incorporated into a reward system to positively reward achievement.

Step 6: Incorporating Breaks and Rewards

Planning breaks and rewards are a vital part of time management for people with ADHD and these are most likely to be omitted from a scheduled time plan. It is crucial to plan breaks and rewards as carefully as planning time on tasks as they provide time to relax and refresh in order to refocus attention. An additional function is that they provide the client with positive reinforcement by engagement in a pleasurable activity. A common problem for people with ADHD is that they do not take sufficient scheduled breaks, especially when tasks are interesting, resulting in them becoming fatigued. Attention dwindles when people become tired, and novel frivolous tasks may seem more attractive and rewarding. In such circumstances, people with ADHD often become engrossed in the distracter task resulting in it becoming impossible to return to the original (now boring) task.

The length of time for which the client can concentrate needs to be evaluated. This will vary between individuals. As a rule of thumb, breaks should be scheduled *at least* hourly but this needs to be tried out, evaluated and adjusted accordingly. It is better for clients to break off at a 'cliff-hanging' moment in the middle of a task, as this raises interest and motivation and makes it easier to return to the task later.

A 'reward' may simply involve a break chatting to a colleague or wandering around the office (local shops, or going for a walk) for 5 minutes. Obviously it is more difficult to do this in a more structured educational establishment, but lectures are often broken up with short breaks. It may also be prearranged with educational staff

Table 5.5 Time plan

Stage	*Activity*	
Set goals	Organize finances	
	Get a job	
	Repeat prescription from GP	
	Enrol on plastering course	
Make lists	Work out budget for next 3 months	
	Pay outstanding bills	
	Visit bank manager	
	Find out value of old van	
	Visit garages to look at vans	
	Go to job centre	
	Look in newspapers at job adverts	
	Telephone an old friend who may have work	
	Complete application forms	
	Ask sister to check application forms	
	Go to post office to buy stamps	
	Book GP appointment	
	Go to GP practice to collect prescription	
	Go to pharmacy	
	Find out about plastering courses	
	Enrol on plastering course	
	Visit Mum and Dad	
	Watch football	
	Out with friends	
Prioritize activities	Work out budget for next 3 months	4
	Pay outstanding bills	4
	Go to job centre	4
	Book GP appointment	4
	Look in newspapers at job adverts	4
	Telephone an old friend who may have work	3
	Complete application forms	3
	Ask sister to check application forms	3
	Go to post office to buy stamps	3
	Go to GP practice to collect prescription	3
	Go to pharmacy	3
	Visit bank manager	3
	Find out about plastering courses	3
	Enrol on plastering course	3
	Visit Mum and Dad	2
	Play football	2
	Find out value of old van	1
	Out with friends	1
	Visit garages to look at vans	1

(*continued*)

Table 5.5 *(cont'd)*

Stage	*Activity*	
Estimate time to complete tasks	Work out budget for next 3 months	3 hr
	Pay outstanding bills	3 hr
	Visit bank manager	1 hr
	Find out value of old van	5–6 hrs
	Visit garages to look at vans	4 hrs
	Go to job centre	4 hrs
	Look in newspapers at job adverts	6 hrs
	Telephone an old friend who may have work	30 mins
	Complete application forms	5 hours
	Ask sister to check application forms	2 hrs
	Go to post office to buy stamps	30 mins
	Book GP appointment	5 mins
	Go to GP practice to collect prescription	45 mins
	Go to pharmacy	5 mins
	Find out about plastering courses	1 hr
	Enrol on plastering course	1 hr
	Visit Mum and Dad	3 hrs
	Play football	3 hrs
	Out with friends	5 hrs

that a young person may need to do this in circumstances that require them to sit for lengthy periods. The point is the individual must be 'off task'. More tangible rewards may be making a cup of tea/ coffee, chocolate biscuits, watching TV, telephoning a friend, going on shopping trips and so forth. The reward must be *desired* and enjoyed or it becomes an aversive stimulus and one to be avoided, thus having a contraindicative effect. People with ADHD require *immediate* short-term rewards rather than making themselves wait for a big reward on completion of a long project. For example, some would rather self-reward with left-over pizza than celebrate the completion of a project by going out to a great restaurant. Once small rewards have been incorporated in the time plan, then a system can be introduced whereby small rewards count towards obtaining a greater reward in the long term. The client needs to learn to organize a system whereby several small rewards count towards a bigger one in the long term, for example, completion of all tasks during the day (including pleasurable reward tasks) results in a 'larger' reward that evening such as giving themselves a 'self-indulgent' hour that evening.

In sessions, David identified his short-term rewards as telephoning a friend, organizing an evening out, coffee breaks and listening to music. His longer term rewards were to look at vans, and play football. He therefore organized his days so that there were regular short-term rewards and more intermittent longer-term rewards when he had achieved certain key tasks.

Table 5.6 Example of diary activity plan

Time	Mon	Tues	Wed	Thurs	Fri	Sat	Sun
7–8	Sleeping	Sleeping	Sleeping	Sleeping	Sleeping	Sleeping	Sleeping
8–9	Get up Shower Breakfast	Get up Shower Breakfast	Get up Shower Breakfast	Get up Shower Breakfast	Get up Shower Breakfast	Sleeping	Sleeping
9–10	TAKE MEDICATION Go to job centre	TAKE MEDICATION Work on budget	TAKE MEDICATION Go to GP to collect prescription and go to pharmacy	TAKE MEDICATION Go to library	TAKE MEDICATION	Get up Shower Breakfast	Get up Shower Breakfast
10–11	Have cup of coffee Back to job centre	Have cup of coffee Work on budget	Pay outstanding bills	Research plastering courses	Go to college to enroll	TAKE MEDICATION Go to visit sister	TAKE MEDICATION
11–12	Contact GP Contingency time	Phone friend about work	Application forms – personal details	Find out how to enroll – contact colleges	Visit bank manager	Go through application forms with sister	Tidy flat
12–1	Buy newspapers Go home	Get application forms	Application forms	Contingency time	Contingency time	Go through application forms with sister	Drive to parents
1–2	Lunch	Lunch	Lunch	Lunch	Lunch	Lunch	Lunch
2–3	Look in newspaper	Drive van to local garage	Buy stamps from post office Contingency time	Application forms – employment history	Application forms – extra information	Meet friends to play football	Stay to chat

(continued)

Table 5.6 *(cont'd)*

Time	Mon	Tues	Wed	Thurs	Fri	Sat	Sun
3–4	Phone friend Contingency time	Visit another garage	Look in newspaper	Application forms – employment history	Application forms – extra information	Football	Go home
4–5	Look in newspaper	Go to supermarket	Look in newspaper	Look in newspaper	Go to garage to investigate vans	Football	Make changes to forms
5–6	Look in newspaper	Drive home and unpack shopping	Look in newspaper	Go to gym	Free time	Football	Make changes to forms
6–7	Prepare meal	Prepare meal	Prepare meal	Gym	Out with friends	Out to pub	Watch DVD
7–8	Watch TV	Phone friend	Watch TV	Go home for food	Out with friends	Out to pub	Make food
8–9	Watch TV	Free time	Watch TV	Prepare meal	Out with friends	Out to pub	Free time
9–10	Watch TV	Free time	Watch TV	Meet friend	Out with friends	Out to pub	Free time
10–11	Watch TV	Free time	Watch TV	Quick drink	Out with friends	Out to pub	Free time
11–12	Get ready for bed	Get ready for bed	Get ready for bed	Get ready for bed	Get ready for bed	Out to pub	Get ready for bed
12–1	Go to bed	Go to bed	Go to bed	Go to bed	Go to bed	Go to bed	Go to bed
1–2	Sleep	Sleep	Sleep	Sleep	Sleep	Sleep	Sleep
2–3	Sleep	Sleep	Sleep	Sleep	Sleep	Sleep	Sleep
3–4	Sleep	Sleep	Sleep	Sleep	Sleep	Sleep	Sleep
4–5	Sleep	Sleep	Sleep	Sleep	Sleep	Sleep	Sleep
5–6	Sleep	Sleep	Sleep	Sleep	Sleep	Sleep	Sleep
6–7	Sleep	Sleep	Sleep	Sleep	Sleep	Sleep	Sleep

Review and Evaluation

It is imperative that sessions include regular reviews of progress and evaluation of success. This can be achieved by re-administering the diary activity log, the time-estimation exercise and reviewing the progress made towards obtaining goals. It is important to give clients positive feedback to encourage them, and improve self-efficacy and confidence. Clients should be encouraged to self-reward by crossing off tasks on their lists as this additionally provides a visual reinforcement system.

Time-Wasting Traps

There are many time-wasting traps in which the client may become involved and these include the switching/diversion of attention, engagement in sensation-seeking behaviour, procrastination and 'false busyness'.

1. Switching attention

Time-wasting traps are not just excuses to avoid completing certain tasks. These may also be due to a momentary loss of concentration or distraction, causing the individual to lose focus and become preoccupied either externally (i.e. with a different task) or internally (i.e. by daydreaming). This often causes people with ADHD to jump from one task to another before they have finished the current one and means that tasks will take longer to complete. The task may never be revisited and is often left unfinished. Incomplete tasks will remain on the client's mind and can cause feelings of anger, anxiety and frustration. For this reason, they are likely to interfere with their concentration on the novel task.

In order to prevent this dysfunctional set, when individuals have intrusive thoughts or ideas, they must be encouraged to make a note of these so they can return to them at a later time rather than acting immediately and embarking on a new set of activities. Usually the idea can wait and be accommodated in future schedules.

2. Delay aversion

As mentioned previously and related to attention switching and distractibility is the issue of delay aversion (e.g. Sonuga-Barke *et al.*, 1992). People with ADHD have been shown to have difficulty in delaying gratification in order to achieve a longer-term goal. This means that they are more likely to opt for a shorter term, sometimes smaller reward, than be motivated to wait for a long-term reward. This systematic bias in the relationship between reward value and time can lead to time management difficulties as the individual is easily tempted to deviate from their original plan by the lure of an immediate reward albeit at the expense of achieving a longer-term goal.

For this reason, people with ADHD may be more likely to give up on a task such as completing a longer piece of work that takes 10 hours for which they will be paid £100 and become distracted by a more immediate reward such as being paid £10 for 3 hours worth of work.

In order to circumvent delay aversion, the therapist needs to determine whether the reward is highly motivating as well as being proportionate to the amount of time spent on a task. For example, they need to check whether a coffee break is an appropriate reward for an hour's work and whether it is sufficiently motivating for the client to continue working for the rest of the day. For some individuals, a coffee break may be an excuse to stay off-task by becoming distracted. The reward of taking a short walk may motivate them better.

3. Sensation-seeking behaviour

Some clients complain that scheduling activities causes their day to lack spontaneity and excitement. In such cases, there is even greater need to plan constructive time breaks (for either planned rewards or free time for 'spontaneous' activities) into the time plan. Goals are the client's servant, not their master. Rewards must therefore meet the client's physical and psychological needs. This means incorporating exceptionally creative and stimulating predetermined prosocial rewards in the time plan. Do not be concerned about this, as the rewards are usually determined by the client relatively easily. Longer-term rewards of this type may include competitive sports and/or constructive venturesome activities (e.g. bungee jumping, go-karting, visiting fun fairs).

4. Procrastination

People with ADHD are extremely adept at procrastination. They are skilled at rationalizing dysfunctional beliefs, intellectualizing and playing 'devil's advocate'. This usually fulfils a functional role as it wastes time and serves to avoid an undesired task. However, it may also be due to a lack of confidence because individuals have set themselves too high a standard or have been unrealistic about what they can achieve. This is a particular problem for perfectionistic individuals who can never attain their own expectations. In such cases, perspective taking can help as individuals rarely expect the same standards in others that they apply to themselves. Individuals need to 'let themselves off the hook' and recognize that by setting stringent standards of achievement, they set themselves up to fail. Avoidance of routine (but often necessary) tasks can also become a problem as these are perceived as boring. The client should consider whether seemingly insurmountable dull tasks need to be done all in one go or whether it is possible to break such tasks down into smaller parts to make them less of a chore.

5. False busyness

A primary time-wasting trap is what can be termed 'false busyness'. This is when a person flutters about usually looking very occupied (and preoccupied) when in fact this 'busy bee' is wasting a lot of time by engaging in nonconstructive activities. Entire day can be filled up by chatting at the coffee machine, making phone calls, surfing the internet, responding to junk email, window shopping and so on. False busyness can be determined by examining the diary activity log recorded prior to the time-management interventions outlined in this module. This needs to be addressed and discussed in sessions and a 'relapse prevention plan' agreed to avoid falling into this trap by recognizing when they engage in these behaviours and the (dys)function they serve.

SUMMARY

Time passes quickly for people with ADHD resulting in them having difficulties with time estimation. This often means they are late for appointments and do not achieve objectives and goals. By encouraging individuals with ADHD to make a time plan of progressive steps towards set goals, they will learn what it feels like to complete and achieve tasks. This in itself is positively reinforcing but, additionally, a reward system must be incorporated into the time plan process.

Time wasting activities trap the individual into engaging in distracting activities that serve as obstacles to achievement. Sticking to a time management plan can be further hampered by timekeeping difficulties and poor punctuality. By developing external strategies to compensate for prospective memory problems and examining the consequences of lateness in more detail, the individual can learn to improve their time keeping.

For the therapist, the goal is to help the individual learn that life is not an obstacle course but to teach the client to navigate their way through a pathway of the difficulties and challenges they are bound to encounter. Apart from the time management and organizational skills outlined in this module, this will also involve the skills discussed in the Problem-Solving Module (Chapter 7).

Group Treatment: Organization and Time-Management Module

It is essential to prepare for group treatment by reading the chapter module. Six group sessions are outlined below, but the number of treatment sessions can be expanded or reduced as required.

Plan

Session 1	Starting activities
Session 2	Psychoeducation – six steps; estimating time; time-wasting traps; rewards
Sessions 3–5	Exercises (repeat using examples; move from short terms goals to longer term goals and apply a more extended time frame using a diary to schedule)
Session 6	Revision of psychoeducation, techniques and rewards Discussion of homework outcome/experience – what works best? Obstacles and how to overcome them

Starting Activities

What kinds of time management problems do you have?
What do you think causes you to go off-task?
How do these problems affect you in your daily activities?
Guide participants to think about specific events and circumstances. Identify specific goals that have not been achieved due to disorganization and time-management problems.
Guide participants to think about consequences of being disorganized (missed deadlines, trouble at school/work, not achieving goals, self-esteem, perception of others).
Have you found strategies to overcome these problems? What works? What doesn't work?
Assess using Time-Management Evaluation and Importance of Punctuality Evaluation – Handout Tables 5.1 and 5.2.
Discuss what can be learned from these assessments.
Group discussion on individual differences that can be identified from the completed assessments (i.e. people have different types of problems).

Psychoeducation

Six steps to making a time plan
Set goals, make lists, prioritize activities, estimate time to complete tasks, schedule tasks, incorporate a reward system.

(Continued)

Estimating Time: Handout Table 5.4
Ask participants to complete 'estimated time' section of the time-estimation exercise (Handout Table 5.4). Amend/adjust items as appropriate and wherever possible drawing on topics/problems raised as being a difficulty during the starting activities. Participants will complete this exercise for homework by comparing the time estimated with the actual time.

Time-wasting traps-switching attention, delay aversion, sensation seeking behaviour, procrastination and false busyness:

Discuss how rewards can be used to motivate task completion.

Exercises

Select suitable examples of goals that have not been met and described by participants in the starting activities or introduce new examples (e.g. You are arranging a surprise birthday party for your mother next month; when you leave school next year you want to go to college/go travelling/get a job). These examples should be goals that can be broken down into a set of tasks that they could do within a week (e.g. finding out about local colleges, classes that are available, visiting the college, obtaining an application form and sending it off). Using these examples complete the exercises either in small groups or as a whole group together.

Breaking down goals into steps
Identify the goal and break this down into smaller steps (Handout Figure 5.1).
Can these be broken down further into more steps?
Make a list of what needs to be done.
Make a list of what else they have to do that week.

Prioritize activities
Look at the list and prioritize activities (see Box 5.3).
Order the items on the list starting with those with greatest priority and add them to Handout 5.7: Time Plan.

Estimate times to complete tasks
Add time-estimations to the Handout 5.5: Time plan.
How accurately did participants estimate time? Discuss results of assessment exercise completed as homework (Table 5.4: Time-estimation exercise). Remind participants to factor in what they have learned from this exercise when estimating times in their time plan.

Make up a diary activity plan
Using handout of Table 5.6 schedule the week so you will achieve your steps and goal(s).

(*Continued*)

Incorporate breaks and rewards
Identify rewards and add these to the schedule.
Discuss obstacles to achievement and methods to overcome them.

Homework

Complete Table 5.4: Time-estimation exercise by testing out and completing the 'actual' time column.
Identify some personal goals and practice the six steps. Try this with short-term goals to be achieved within the next few days but also try this with medium-term goals for things you wish to achieve in the coming weeks/months. Use a diary to schedule the plan.
Apply and rehearse techniques between sessions.

6

IMPULSIVITY MODULE

Impulsivity, both behavioural and cognitive, is a characteristic of ADHD that is associated with an inability to self-regulate and control behaviour, speech or certain thought processes. This means that someone with ADHD is likely to say the first thing that comes into their head, such as expressing feelings, thoughts and opinions without weighing up the consequences. They may also act without considering the consequences of their behaviour. In a way, they do not have an internal 'brake' that allows them to sift out inappropriate responses or behaviours. This is sometimes referred to as having poor 'response inhibition', in other words they are unable to inhibit a prepotent response. Poor impulse control can cause problems for ADHD individuals in their social interactions. They may blurt out inappropriate comments and inadvertently offend people. Nevertheless in some circumstances the tendency to act on the 'spur-of-the-moment' can be advantageous as it means individuals are willing to take risks which may pay off, whereas someone without ADHD is likely to be more cautious and perhaps miss out on opportunities. Impulsivity or a lack of inhibition can also lead to an increase in divergent or lateral thinking that allows people with ADHD to be creative. Indeed, there are several successful entrepreneurs and celebrities in the arts, music and sports industries who have disclosed their ADHD and attribute their success in part to having the disorder.

However, the tendency to act and think in an impulsive way can also bring great disadvantages. People with ADHD tend not to engage in a systematic decision making process or consider alternative perspectives. The need for immediate gratification may make individuals seem demanding, exhausting and tactless and they may be perceived as antisocial and irritating company. They may also be viewed as inconsiderate and fickle as they can become impulsively enthusiastic about doing

Cognitive-Behavioural Therapy for ADHD in Adolescents and Adults: A Psychological Guide to Practice, Second Edition. Susan Young and Jessica Bramham.

something but then quickly lose interest in favour of something new. They may be misinterpreted by some people as self-centred individuals who lack consideration for the feelings and needs of others. This presentation is likely to have negative social consequences resulting in the clients themselves feeling misunderstood and socially isolated.

This module examines the nature of the deficit that underpins impulsive behaviour in young people with ADHD; for many young people this is associated with antisocial behaviour, delinquency and crime. The current theoretical explanations are discussed along with a description of the typical impulse control problems which may be exhibited. Methods are provided for assisting individuals to identifying situations in which they may be vulnerable to responding in an impulsive way and determine appropriate control and coping strategies. Various cognitive-behavioural self-monitoring and self-restraint strategies are presented within the module. These include techniques to improve control including the use of self-talk, distraction and self-instructional training.

FUNCTIONAL DEFICITS IN ADOLESCENTS AND ADULTS

There are several ways in which impulsivity is manifested in people with ADHD. People can seem to be too 'quick off the mark', for example, they respond before instructions have been completed or before they have acquired all the information necessary for starting a task. There are also difficulties when people with ADHD 'act without thinking', where individuals respond without first considering all the possible response options and their implications. Alternatively, a person may verbally or physically lash out at someone who has upset them without considering the social and/or legal implications. They focus on short-term rewards as opposed to long-term rewards, for example, students may have difficulty resisting a readily available reward, such as an evening out, which may prevent them from achieving a longer term goal, such as submitting their coursework on time.

Table 6.1 provides a summary of typical impulse control behaviours (and associated problems) commonly reported by people with ADHD or their friends and family.

The common theme for all these behaviours is that such individuals do not think ahead or consider the consequences of their actions. It is not that they are unaware of the difference between appropriate and inappropriate behaviour or that one solution/response to a problem is better than another. The difficulty arises because they do not think or consider every option. Their decision-making processes may be impulse driven, resulting in a tendency to make important choices rapidly and without careful consideration or planning (also see Problem-Solving Module in Chapter 7). A model of therapy should therefore aim to teach self-monitoring and self-regulation skills (e.g. 'to stop and think'), train the individual to consider consequences of action and generate appropriate and constructive alternatives.

Table 6.1 Typical impulse control problems experienced by people with ADHD

Control problem	*Effect*
Consequence 'blindness'	People with ADHD find it difficult to consider the consequences of their behaviour before acting. For example, the social consequence of blurting out gossip or interrupting people.
Difficulty waiting	ADHD can greatly affect someone's ability to queue or wait for their turn. This is particularly prominent in queues when there is a delay.
Motivation for immediate gratification	People with ADHD are more prone to opt for a short-term reward that involves less effort than working for longer periods and applying more effort for a larger reward.
Taking short-cuts	Individuals with ADHD are notorious for taking 'short-cuts', which may lead to reduced accuracy or a lower quality of outcome.
Demanding behaviour	People with ADHD may seem demanding and self-centred if someone else controls access to what they desire.
Lack of insight	Situations in which they are likely to be impulsive may not be immediately obvious to someone with ADHD.
Abrupt movements	Motor movements can be affected by impulsivity such as getting up out of a chair suddenly, or snatching items from another person.
Reckless driving	Driving can cause problems for an individual with ADHD who has difficulty waiting at traffic lights, or driving patiently behind slower drivers. Poor impulse control on the road can lead to driving violations, commonly including speeding, jumping lights, but also may be more serious when greater risks are taken, such as overtaking when it is unsafe to do so.
Rule-breaking	Behavioural impulsivity may often present as disobedience or deliberate violation of instructions.
Recklessness	Impulsivity can also manifest itself as recklessness due to the tendency to engage in dangerous activities without considering possible consequences.
Jumping to conclusions	Jumping to conclusions is a general problem for individuals with ADHD. They may be more likely to misinterpret ambiguous situations, make assumptions based on very little information and also catastrophize.
Incurring debts	Impulsive spending may lead individuals to buy items without considering whether they can afford them or whether they are necessary.
Novelty seeking behaviour	A search for thrills and novelty may stem from an excessive attraction to immediate reward.
Anxiety	Anxiety may lead to impulsive avoidance of aversive situations or exacerbate impulse control difficulties.

Antisocial, Delinquent and Criminal Behaviour

Childhood ADHD is frequently associated with conduct problems and just as the developmental trajectory of ADHD symptomatology is heterogeneous, so is the developmental trajectory of children with ADHD and conduct disorder. Moffit (1993) has theorized that there are two fundamentally divergent categories of delinquent adolescents. The 'adolescence-limited' group is characterized by noteworthy criminal activity that arises for the first time in early to mid-adolescence and features nonaggressive behaviour that typically desists by late adolescence. The 'life-course persistent' antisocial group is characterized by overt aggression in adolescence, typified by marked defiant and aggressive behaviour from a young age. Moffit suggests that the delinquency of this group is associated with pre-existing cognitive and/or behavioural deficits, including neuropsychological dysfunction, family disharmony and attention deficits/hyperactivity. Indeed, a longitudinal epidemiological study of young hyperactive boys into young adulthood showed that hyperactivity was a risk factor in young men for later antisocial problems including violence, even after the coexistence of initial conduct problems was taken into account (Taylor *et al.*, 1996). This may reflect that young children grow up with a 'double dose' of risk characterized by both cognitive and conduct problems. Indeed there is some evidence that co-occurring ADHD and conduct disorder is a clinically and genetically more severe variant of their independent disorders (Thapar, Harrington and McGuffin, 2001).

Court records suggest that juveniles with ADHD are at greater risk for contact with the criminal justice system (Satterfield *et al.*, 1994) and prison studies have shown that around 45 per cent of offenders detained in youth offending institutions have ADHD (Rosler *et al.*, 2004; Young *et al.*, 2010). The rates of up to 30 per cent are somewhat lower in adult prisons and this may relate to symptom remission. ADHD and offending has been associated with younger age at first criminal conviction, greater recidivism, greater comorbidity including substance misuse, and aggressive behaviour within the institutions (for a review see Young *et al.*, 2011). Many young people will experience symptom remission as they mature, however this may occur too late for young people to break out of indoctrination into an antisocial peer group and culture, reject antisocial attitudes and/or purposefully break out of established antisocial patterns of behaviour.

It is important that ADHD offenders receive specific interventions focussing not only on symptom improvement and emotional control, but also on criminogenic needs including antisocial attitudes and behaviours and labile temperament. This will involve a psychological intervention to complement pharmacotherapy, and to date the only intervention designed for this purpose in this client group (ADHD youths, juvenile delinquents and adult offenders) is the R&R2 for ADHD Youths and Adults, (Young and Ross, 2007). This programme not only teaches symptom control, skills development and prosocial attitudes, but also includes the training of cognitive processes involved in problem-solving. Evidence from a randomized controlled trial has indicated that the programme is highly effective for treating ADHD symptoms and comorbid problems of antisocial behaviour, emotional control, anxiety and depression (Emilsson *et al.*, 2011) in medicated adults. Additionally, this group programme provides the opportunity to assess whether an individual has specific skills deficits or needs that will benefit from individual attention such as interventions outlined in the Young-Bramham Programme modules.

ASSESSMENT OF IMPULSIVITY

Impulsivity can be conceptualized in two ways: 'behavioural impulsivity' and 'cognitive impulsivity'.

1. *Behavioural impulsivity* refers to the inability to inhibit physical or verbal actions due to premature and/or over-rapid responsiveness. This is manifested as an inability to resist doing or saying inappropriate things, for example, ADHD individuals may hit out at someone or something in a fit of temper and/or make hurtful comments. Behavioural impulsivity is associated with excessive attraction to immediate reward.
2. *Cognitive impulsivity* relates to disorganized behaviour associated with problems of executive function. This underpins forgetfulness, poor planning and poor time management. For example, clients may misappraise a situation or the intentions of others and make rash important decisions based on inadequate information.

Neuropsychological measures are available that distinguish between the two concepts. Behavioural impulsivity is commonly measured using tasks assessing response inhibition; that is, the ability to inhibit a salient response when it is inappropriate. People with ADHD have been shown to exhibit impaired performance on such tasks, for example, 'stop' tasks and 'go-no-go' tasks (Rubia *et al.*, 1998, 1999, 2000). 'Stop' tasks typically involve responding according to certain contingencies, for example, pressing a key on a computer in response to identifying cued target items. For example, the individual is required to press a button every time they see an aeroplane on the screen. However, on occasions the testee is instructed to do the opposite, in other words, to stop responding in this way (by withholding their response), and this can be challenging for a person with ADHD who is likely to respond in the cued way and make lots of errors. Similarly, for 'go-no-go' tasks, the individual is typically required to respond to certain targets (i.e. 'go') but not respond if they are preceded or followed by another 'no-go' target. For example, the individual is required to press a button every time they see an aeroplane on the screen, but if the aeroplane is presented with a second aural or visual cue (e.g. a 'bleep' or the aeroplane is a different colour), then the individual is required to withhold their response. In such cases, individuals with ADHD have particular difficulty coordinating their response pattern and make errors by 'misfiring' at the wrong time (i.e. they have difficulty withholding their response). However, performance may improve if individuals are provided with an increase in time between stimuli as this gives them more time in which to respond.

Behavioural impulsivity can also be assessed using a task called the Matching Familiar Figures Test (Cairnes and Cammock, 1978) that assesses impulsiveness versus reflectiveness in cognitive style. The test involves identifying target pictures among five distracters with both speed and accuracy. It is similar to playing 'spot the difference' between pictures. Compared to people without ADHD, individuals with ADHD tend to respond rapidly and make an increased number of errors by selecting incorrect responses. This means that they tend to favour speed over accuracy and adopt a 'trial and error' approach to problem-solving.

Cognitive impulsivity can be assessed neuropsychologically with various executive functioning paradigms as well as through careful observations and anecdotal reports of behaviour. The ability to coordinate a series of tasks and form a strategy can be assessed using the Modified Six Elements subtest of the Behavioural Assessment of Dysexecutive Syndrome (Wilson *et al.*, 1996). Individuals with ADHD are more likely to break rules by impulsively changing task without planning a sequence. Another test from the same battery, which can be used to assess planning skills, is the Zoo Map task. This task requires the individual to assimilate information from rules and instructions about how they should organize a visit to the zoo and form a plan before plotting their route on a map. People with ADHD typically do not take the time to plan and impulsively begin the route without formulating an effective sequence. This difficulty with planning was also found by Young *et al.* (2007) where ADHD participants were less likely to adjust their planning time according to task difficulty on the Tower of London, a test of problem-solving.

It is important to bear in mind that while deficits of cognitive impulsivity may be exhibited on some neuropsychological measures, they are most likely to be extremely debilitating in everyday life. Thus it is very important to question the client carefully about how he/she copes with completing chores and tasks on a daily basis, especially those which require sustained effort and concentration, or those in which the client lacks interest or motivation to complete. Indeed, one advantage of the Behavioural Assessment of Dysexecutive Syndrome (Wilson *et al.*, 1996) is that it is an ecologically valid battery of executive functioning tests that translate relatively well from the artificial testing room into real life. Nevertheless, some individuals are still able to perform in an assessment setting, in other words control their cognitive impulsivity when effectively forced to do so, but have extreme difficulty in doing this on a day-to-day basis.

The IMPULSE Method for Identifying and Monitoring Behaviours

Clients will readily relate to behavioural impulsivity as this is what they perceive as impeding their performance on a day-to-day basis, for example, going 'off-task' and never finishing anything, jumping to the wrong conclusions, losing their temper. The therapist should direct the client to identify *specific* situations when they are likely to respond in an impulsive manner. This should not present a great problem but if it seems difficult, start by getting the client to look back at times or behaviours that they regret in retrospect. In particular, identify problems that have occurred on a regular basis as these may be used to monitor progress in treatment. Through discussion, exploration and socratic questioning regarding these situations (as well as observation of the client's behaviour in sessions), target behaviours may be determined that are suitable for treatment. As with all behavioural measurements however, the target behaviour must be specific and clearly defined by the client and therapist. The frequency of the target behaviour can then be measured either in the course of a session (e.g. number of interruptions) or outside the session by the client, friend, partner or family member (e.g. shouting at motorists while driving), or by using an objective measure (e.g. a record of weekly shopping purchases).

The ultimate aim is for the client to take responsibility for monitoring their own impulsive behaviour. As individuals develop greater self-awareness of their behaviour, learning to self-monitor in this way may, in itself, act as a reduction strategy. Specific interventions should be discussed collaboratively, selected strategies implemented, reviewed and evaluated. This process is called the IMPULSE method of self-monitoring and regulating poor impulse control. Table 6.2 describes the IMPULSE method applied to the problem a client had with making shopping purchases on impulse. This happened so frequently that the client was getting into debt. A version of Table 6.2 which is suitable for use in sessions is provided on the Companion Website. Once clients have successfully mastered the IMPULSE system they should be encouraged to apply it to a range of problem behaviours (including those identified by others).

COGNITIVE BEHAVIOURAL THERAPY

Psychoeducation

There are two explanations for why impulsivity arises in the disorder of ADHD. One is that there is a primary executive functioning deficit in inhibitory control mechanisms (e.g. Barkley and Biederman, 1997), such as the mechanisms that stop a person from running out across a busy road, or stop someone from blurting out a tactless comment. The probability of successful inhibition seems to directly relate to the length of the 'stopping' interval; that is, when people with ADHD are under pressure to inhibit a response in a short space of time, they are more likely to make mistakes. However, if they are given longer to inhibit a response, they are more accurate and hence less 'impulsive'. This concept has strong implications for intervention, as ADHD clients must learn to schedule time and be encouraged to 'stop and think' in order to reduce failures through impulsive mistakes.

An alternative theory is that the disinhibition or impulsivity associated with ADHD is due to aversion to delay (e.g. Sonuga-Barke *et al.*, 1992). According to this perspective, impulsive behaviour is due to a choice to avoid delay, which people with ADHD find aversive. The theory considers that impulsivity is underpinned by a

Table 6.2 The IMPULSE method for identifying and monitoring behaviours

Letter	*Representation*	*Details*
I	Identify the behaviour For example: *Impulsive spending on credit cards*	The target behaviour should be chosen by the client. Not all impulsivity is problematic to the individual. It is important that they identify and target areas that they are motivated to change. For example, interrupting others and not taking turns appropriately in conversation may lead to problems with relationships and isolation.
M	Make the behaviour explicit For example: *Buying CDs and clothes when I do not have the money*	Developing a clear definition of the problem is crucial if change is to be usefully measured. Vague targets such as 'stop being impulsive' are both difficult to measure and difficult to achieve. It is more sensible to use operationalized behaviours such as 'driving over the speed limit' or 'interrupting others'.
P	Peer/partner monitoring For example: *Credit card bills brought to the session. Partner can monitor new purchases being brought into house*	It may be possible for the therapist to monitor some behaviours such as interruptions in a therapy session. However, other behaviours may be less easy to assess. Video cameras might be usefully employed to monitor some behaviours. In some situations it may be possible to enrol the help of a partner, friend or family member, who can count behaviours such as changing the television channel or staying seated at mealtimes.
U	Understanding and self monitoring For example: *For all items purchased, evaluation of whether they were planned and whether the client could afford them*	If the IMPULSE method has been monitored by a person other than the client, the responsibility for monitoring should next be passed to the client. It may be helpful to compare reports of behaviour in order to check that the client is able to recognize the target behaviours appropriately. Self-monitoring can serve as an intervention in itself as it may encourage recognition of triggers or antecedents to behaviour.
L	List plans to tackle the problem For example: *Planning a weekly budget*	Once the behaviour has been monitored and a baseline rate has been established, the client and the therapist collaborate to form an intervention plan (see strategies section).
S	Strategy implementation For example: *Carrying out budget*	The client applies the agreed strategy.
E	Evaluation of strategy For example: *1. Feedback from client, particularly regarding times when they have resisted temptation* *2. Count of number of unplanned purchases*	Evaluation of the strategy success is performed via two methods: (1) The client should be invited to give feedback about the strategy – what has been helpful/ unhelpful etc. (2) There is a repeat monitoring period in order to establish the frequency of target behaviours. This is compared to the original baseline measure.

preference for immediate or short-term rewards and an inability to delay gratification in the longer term. This means that individuals are more motivated to receive a current reward even if it is less valuable than a more valuable longer-term reward. This has implications for everyday functioning where much of our behaviour, particularly in adult life, is governed by the principle of 'good things come to he/she who waits'. For example, most people find that the prospect of a salary at the end of the week or month is sufficient to keep them adequately motivated at work each day. However, for someone with ADHD, if they have become dissatisfied and/or irritated at work for some reason (e.g. bored with the work; annoyed with a colleague), they may be inclined to quit their job, feeling that the short-term reward of getting out of a situation is worth more to them than the long-term reward of being paid. Unfortunately the prospect of immediate reward and temptation may lure some individuals into delinquent and/or criminal behaviour. The implications for treatment strategies are to work with the need for immediate gratification by breaking down tasks into smaller stages and providing short-term goals which can be rewarded.

Impulse Control Strategies

The primary objective of treatment is for the client to develop and *maintain* a behavioural management plan to control impulsive responding in order that in time this may become second nature; in other words it becomes generalized. This involves learning techniques to monitor and control impulsive behaviour. There are several techniques, all of which encourage the individual to 'stop and think'. These include learning to apply cognitive strategies such as self-talk, self-instructional training, double-checks and distraction techniques. Not all strategies will be helpful but it is likely that the client will find some of these methods of benefit. This can only be determined by trying them out and evaluating progress.

Wherever possible, appropriate behaviour should be modelled. In addition, some individuals may benefit from watching recordings of themselves acting in role-plays that require them to behave in an appropriate manner as well as in an inappropriate manner. When playing back the recording, the client should be encouraged to take a different perspective of their behaviour by imagining a friend or family member observing them. What would be going through their mind? Alternatively the client could be asked to imagine that they are observing the behaviour of a friend or family member. What would they make of it? Would they view the interaction differently? Role-plays are particularly helpful in perspective-taking as this gives the client the opportunity of considering the personal and social consequences of behaviour.

Be wary of cognitive avoidance, which may present as a lack of motivation. It may well be distressing for the individual to develop better insight into their own behaviour and its impact on others. This may cause clients to avoid facing up to past mistakes, which have been financially and/or emotionally costly, and/or painful memories. If this occurs, it may hamper progress in treatment. In some cases individuals may deliberately attempt to sabotage treatment by disengagement (this representing a 'secondary gain' as it provides the short-term reward of removing themselves from anxiety-provoking treatment). Being sensitive to the client's feelings and acknowledging their difficulty by taking a nonjudgmental and open approach is likely to be helpful.

Self-talk

Self-talk is essentially proactive thinking. To a certain extent everyone engages in self-talk, sometimes even out loud. People often think through plans in their heads for various situational outcomes and rehearse potential responses. The client can be taught to apply self-talk as a cognitive technique to interrupt an automatic dysfunctional thinking process by saying words like 'STOP', 'CONTROL', 'Look before you leap', 'Think before you speak'. If the client is in a state of high emotional arousal then this will exacerbate cognitive deficits resulting in them feeling overwhelmed and confused. Self-talk such as 'stay calm', 'I can do this' at the same time as visualizing (predetermined) calming images is likely to help the individual feel more in control. Potential calming images should be discussed and tried out in sessions in order that the client may develop a repertoire of helpful and restful visual images that can be accessed and cued as necessary (e.g. a Caribbean beach, sitting on top of a mountain, an English garden, an evening sunset). Once thinking has been interrupted in this way, the client should be encouraged to stand back and take a different perspective, for example, 'Is there another way I can think about this and resolve this problem?', 'What would my mother, brother, friends say?'.

Self-talk must be tailored to individual needs by identifying what the client finds helpful. This needs to be achieved collaboratively in sessions and tested out and evaluated in 'real life' settings, for example, by setting up 'mini-experiments'. Once useful self-talk has been identified, this should be practised. For example, self-talk can be rehearsed when driving on a clear road. The more exposure an individual has using self-talk, the more likely s/he will apply it in the heat of the moment.

Self-instructional training

A second step towards 'taking the heat out of an impulse' is self-instructional training. Self-talk interrupts a dysfunctional thinking process and, once this has been achieved, the individual must then learn to direct themselves towards more positive functional thinking. Self-instructional training helps the client to stand back from a situation, appraise it from different perspectives, evaluate possible responses and outcomes, re-appraise and select an appropriate response. This is achieved by teaching the client to engage in self-directed purposeful instructions. Until the client becomes used to this process it should be enacted out-loud in sessions. For example,

Julie, a client with ADHD, has difficulty waiting in line to pay for groceries in a supermarket. If the line is very long she invariably gets irritated and restless and walks out of the shop leaving her shopping behind. In this case the therapist and client devised the following management plan:

1. whenever possible Julie did her shopping at more quiet periods during the day;
2. when she had to wait in line and began to feel restless and irritated and had thoughts that she should leave the shop, she employed self-talk by saying to herself 'stop', 'calm down';
3. Julie evaluated her options in a self-directed thought process, for example, 'if I walk out of the shop I will not have achieved my goal of getting the shopping done; that means that I will have to make time to come back to the shop at a later time and I will have to change my plans for this evening; the shop may still be busy later on and I may not get my shopping today; I have run out of cereal so I will have to go to work without eating breakfast. If I stay I can cope with feelings of irritation by occupying my thoughts using a distraction technique; I will have my shopping and can have what I want for breakfast; I can meet my friends this evening;'
4. Julie then applied selected distraction techniques (see below);
5. once the shopping had been completed, Julie rewarded herself for achieving her goal, for example, by having a chocolate bar when she left the supermarket.

The most common obstacle to success is the ADHD individual's desire and motivation for immediate gratification. An immediate or short-term reward, such as leaving the shop to avoid feelings of irritability and restlessness, is preferred over the longer-term reward of purchasing the shopping. Thus consequential thinking (i.e. evaluating potential outcomes, their merits and disadvantages) is an important component to any management plan. This may be introduced to the client by encouraging them to rehearse a strategy in sessions called CONTROL (see Table 6.3). CONTROL is a process in which the client engages in self-talk to stop dysfunctional thinking, makes self-directed statements and/or instructions and considers options and alternatives. The CONTROL process is achieved by teaching the client to interrupt their dysfunctional thoughts (which triggers them to go 'off-line') and engage in a sequential thinking process whereby they employ techniques to lessen emotional arousal, generate alternative options and evaluate these options before going back 'on-line' to carry out a solution. Consequential thinking is a particularly powerful tool if the client is able to write down the advantages and disadvantages of potential outcomes, although in some situations this will not be possible. The most important aspect of this technique, however, is that the client learns to introduce an additional feedback loop or circuit in their thinking process, that is, the 'off-line' stage. In order to facilitate the introduction of the process of CONTROL to the client, the client could be provided with cue cards to carry in their wallet or purse that can be used to prompt the individual components of the process. This information has been included on the Companion Website in a format that could be used for this purpose. The CONTROL process has also been provided on the Companion Website in a format for use in sessions whereby the client can write out and test methods to interrupt

Table 6.3 The process of CONTROL

Letter	*Representation*	*Details*
C	Control	In order to interrupt a dysfunctional thinking process, the person should say (either aloud or to themselves) 'CONTROL' as a thought-stopping technique. In addition, they may benefit from temporarily removing themselves from the situation.
O	'Off-line' processing	Self-talk and self-instructions are applied to anchor attention to calmer images and an emotionally neutral state.
N	New solutions	Alternative solutions are generated by using self-directed statements. Rationalization and problem-solving techniques will additionally be helpful (see Problem-Solving Module in Chapter 7).
T	Test solutions	Solutions can be tested through mental rehearsal, and predicting outcomes, for example, I can (a) buy the new TV now on credit but have less money each month for a year, (b) save to buy the TV and have it in six month's time, (c) buy a cheaper one.
R	Re-evaluation	Once the options have been considered, the most preferable can be chosen by reviewing the client's goals.
O	'On-line' processing	Once a decision has been made, this should be carried out, that is, the solution becomes 'on-line'. Determine and include a reward for successful engagement of the CONTROL process.
L	Look for benefits	In order to further positively reinforce the CONTROL process, evaluate outcome by examining advantages and positive outcome.

dysfunctional thoughts (see Table 6.3b on Companion Website). With practice the client will be able to successfully engage in this process without prompting.

Double checks

As self-talk and self-instructional training techniques become a more automatic process the client should be encouraged to incorporate a system of 'double checking' information, assumptions, beliefs on so forth. This involves a decision-making process whereby clients can be encouraged to 'double-check' or review decisions by asking themselves the five questions in Box 6.1.

It is important that the individual keeps in mind the objective or goal to be achieved. For example, a common problem for people with ADHD is that they make impulse purchases. This inclination is not helped by the practice of stores to actively encourage impulse purchases by displaying small relatively cheap 'luxury' products by checkout cash registers. However, many clients have additionally made relatively

Box 6.1 'Double-check' questions

1. Is this what I really want to happen?
2. For how long have I wanted to do this?
3. What will happen if I do this?
4. What will happen if I don't do this?
5. What are the longer term consequences?

large purchases on impulse, many of which are costly mistakes. It is not uncommon for people with ADHD to report the presence of numerous unworn unsuitable clothes and/or unused DIY accessories in their homes!

Learning to postpone decision making, albeit briefly, is thus a good 'safety guard' for people with ADHD. Treatment should focus on getting the person to 'stop and think' and engage in a process of consequential thinking. Individuals should go through the 'double-check' system outlined above and it may be helpful for them to have these questions written down on a small card that they carry around in their purse or wallet. (These are presented in the Companion Website in a suitable format). The client should also determine a management plan in sessions that they then apply 'in vivo', for example, leave the shop without making the purchase; walk about for 5 minutes and go through the questions on a card, before deciding whether to return to the shop to make the purchase or not. It is important to measure and evaluate outcome in order to demonstrate success. In this case, keeping a record of purchases and 'near purchases' would reinforce success by highlighting potential savings from the latter over a set period of time.

Distraction techniques

One of the most common times that impulsive behaviour is expressed by people with ADHD is in situations that require a person to wait or queue. An aversion to delay and lack of tolerance causes individuals to feel bored, frustrated and/or irritated. Every minute seems like ten and individuals will often favour the short-term reward of giving up and leaving the queue altogether, or deciding not to wait any longer but demand instant attention instead. The problem with the former scenario is that this means they will not achieve their objective. The problem with the latter scenario is that they are very likely to provoke a confrontation. In such situations, the individual could apply distraction techniques to develop better self-control (by distracting themselves from ruminating over their negative thoughts and feelings about the situation). These techniques can be practised either in advance of difficult situations that are anticipated, or practised in the imagination. Table 6.4 outlines a variety of distraction techniques which may be helpful. This table is also provided in handout form on the Companion Website.

Table 6.4 Distraction techniques

Technique	*Details*
Object focus	Focus on an object and describe it in detail.
Person focus	Look at the person in front of you in the queue – imagine what they might be called, what they do for a living, where they live, what sort of character they might play in a film and so on. (Be careful not to stare as this may be perceived as confrontational or provocative).
Sensory awareness	Focus on each sense in turn and make a mental list using sight, hearing, taste, touch and smell.
Counting	Complicated counting tasks, such as backwards in 7s, can provide good distraction.
Word generation	Try to think of as many animals/countries/towns/girls names/boys names being with each letter of the alphabet.
Fantasies	Imagining where you would rather be – on a beach, in the mountains, swimming ...
Winning the lottery	How would you spend a million pounds?
Puzzles	Crosswords, wordsearches and so on can assist with waiting, although attentional problems may lead to distractibility.

External strategies

It may be helpful if the client invites parents, partners and/or a good friend to attend some of the sessions (if appropriate) as this provides an opportunity for techniques to be observed and reinforced outside of the session. Friends or family can support the client by reminding them of techniques learned in the session, rehearsing the techniques and providing cues when appropriate for these to be applied 'in vivo', for example, by cueing the client to engage in a process of CONTROL, and/or monitor progress and change in behaviour. Positive feedback by others may also be an important component of a 'reward system' as praise will reinforce successful and/or appropriate behaviour. Inappropriate or unacceptable behaviour should never be reinforced. Exceptions or making allowances such as, 'oh that's our Steve, he's a bit crazy' must be avoided. It is very important that feedback is consistent and constructive and the individual does not feel personally criticized.

SUMMARY

Learning to develop better impulse control involves the recognition of situations in which a person is vulnerable to acting without thinking, applying various cognitive behaviour techniques to cope with that situation, obtaining and rewarding successful outcomes. Once a dysfunctional thinking process has been interrupted, other more positive or neutral beliefs can be recruited and reviewed to develop a more balanced view of a situation and the potential methods for dealing with it. Situations can be rehearsed in order for the client to become accustomed to utilizing self-control techniques and potential outcomes evaluated.

Group Treatment: Impulsivity Module

It is essential to prepare for group treatment by reading the chapter module. Six group sessions are outlined below, but the number of treatment sessions can be expanded or reduced as required.

Plan

Session 1	Starting activities
Session 2	Psychoeducation – executive deficit in inhibitory control mechanisms; aversion to delay; treatment strategies (self-talk, self-instructional training, double checks, distraction)
Sessions 3–5	Exercises
Session 6	Revision of psychoeducation, techniques and rewards Discussion of homework outcome/experience – what works best? Obstacles and how to overcome them

Starting Activities

What are the situations/times when you have poor impulse control? Guide participants to identify specific situations (e.g. when shopping, driving a vehicle, waiting in line).

What makes this better/worse? Guide participants to identify mood states that impact on their ability to control their behaviour (e.g. feeling tired, anxious, angry).

What are the consequences of impulsive behaviour? How has this affected your life? Guide participants to identify negative outcomes (e.g. accidents, driving offences, police attention, conflict and confrontation with others, loss of friends, distress to family etc).

How has this affected your relationships with family, friends, partners?

Have you identified strategies that have helped in the past? Guide participants to consider functional vs. dysfunctional strategies.

Group discussion, handout Table 6.1 for discussion.

Psychoeducation

Describe the two explanations for ADHD and impulsivity and how this provides two opportunities for treatment targets. (Executive deficit in inhibitory control mechanisms, aversion to delay).

Executive deficit in inhibitory control mechanisms

If you have to do something quickly, you make mistakes, so you need to give yourself time and take longer to do tasks. This leads to greater accuracy and less impulsivity.

Treatment opportunity: learn to stop and think and engage in a process of consequential thinking.

(Continued)

Aversion to delay
You chose to avoid delay as it's aversive, that is, you don't like it.
Inability to delay gratification in the long term. Preference for immediate or short term rewards.
Treatment opportunity: break tasks into smaller stages and set short-term goals that can be rewarded.

Describe CBT strategies
Self-talk and self-instructional training, handout Table 6.3.
'Double checks', handout Box 6.1.
Distraction, handout Table 6.4.

Exercises

Select suitable examples of situations/experiences described by participants in starting activities or introduce new examples (e.g. impulsive spending on credit cards described in the chapter). Using these examples complete and repeat exercises (either in small groups or as a whole group together). Note: some situations/experiences may work better with one technique or another.

Executive function techniques – stop, think and engage in a consequential thinking process.
As a practical exercise, work through each step of the CONTROL thought stopping technique.

Delay aversion techniques
Identify goals, break them into smaller steps. Can they be broken into short-term goals that can be rewarded? Identify and discuss appropriate rewards (immediate and longer term that can be introduced successfully to stay on task).
Discuss CBT strategies that may help – discuss each (self-talk, self-instructional training, double checks, distraction).
Write out specific techniques that may help.
Rehearse techniques in role-plays (if appropriate). Obtain group feedback on role-plays (what was good/better, how was interaction perceived, obtain additional suggestions etc).
Discuss obstacles to achievement and methods to overcome them.

Homework

Identify a behaviour that you want to improve that is caused by poor impulse control (e.g. shouting at family, spending money). Make a chart to measure this behaviour, (e.g. by recording how frequently each day you shout at family, or how much you have spent that day).

Select one or two of the four strategies (self-talk, self-instructional training, double checks, distraction) that you think will work the best to help you control

(Continued)

this behaviour. Conduct 'mini-experiments' by applying a strategy and record whether it works (or not). If the strategy does not work, then try a different one until you find what works best for you. It may help to ask a family member/friend to help you.

Once you have identified which strategy/strategies work best for you, continue to measure the behaviour and make a graph to chart improvement. Bear in mind that sometimes change is small. Over time small changes become great changes.

Apply and rehearse techniques between sessions.

PART III

COMORBID AND ASSOCIATED PROBLEM MODULES

7

PROBLEM-SOLVING MODULE

Growing up involves learning to become independent and this means that young people must make important decisions about their future and take increasing responsibility for their behaviour. Inevitably this means that young people will make mistakes. What is important is that they learn from their mistakes and learn how to solve problems. A key problem for some adolescents is that they have not been exposed to problems or methods to resolve them. This is because they have been buffered from facing up to difficulties due to a protective scaffolding erected around them by family and/or teachers. For example, some children attend private schools with smaller class sizes and greater individual attention and feedback, others receive individual tuition for subjects in which they are weak. Parents or older siblings structure time for homework and sit down with the child to help them. They may do things for the child such as packing and unpacking school bags and sports bags or set up systems to help the child become better organized and prepared themselves, for example, by using wall charts. They may facilitate friendships by inviting children to play after school and they may organize structured leisure activities (trips to the zoo, games in the park) as opposed to leaving children to occupy themselves unsupervised.

As young people mature these supportive structures become more difficult to uphold, for example, homework is not set for the next day but a week later and children choose their own friends. Furthermore, while these strategies have helped and supported the child to function better in their daily lives, they are counterproductive in supporting them to meet a key task of adolescence – independence. This becomes apparent once the adolescent begins to break away from the cocoon. For the first time they have personal responsibility but as they embrace this new status, they find that this means there are problems they will need to face and resolve themselves – leaving home, independent study, job applications and interviews, social gatherings, managing money and sexual relationships to name a few. Suddenly the buffering of

Cognitive-Behavioural Therapy for ADHD in Adolescents and Adults: A Psychological Guide to Practice, Second Edition. Susan Young and Jessica Bramham.

the past becomes a disadvantage as they find themselves inexperienced in anticipating or recognizing problems, and at a loss as to how to effectively resolve them.

Thus a primary task of treatment is to determine the client's past experience of resolving problems (to what extent have they been buffered from having to do this themselves?), to find out how they usually solve problems, establish whether a haphazard or directed strategy is applied, and determine whether this is functional or not. Importantly the therapist must reassure the client that problem-solving is a process that can be learned and a skill that can be acquired. By learning to adopt a methodical approach to solving problems, more optimal outcomes can be reached.

This module examines the problem-solving difficulties commonly reported by people with ADHD, what is known about their adaptive functioning and coping mechanisms and the stages involved in successful problem-solving. The model presented is a five stage process that involves identifying and defining the problem, generating solutions, evaluating solutions, implementing the chosen solution and evaluating success.

FUNCTIONAL DEFICITS IN ADOLESCENTS AND ADULTS

Adolescents and adults with ADHD have difficulty applying problem-solving techniques for many reasons. Solving their own problems may not be something they have had to do in the past. They may not be good at recognizing that a problem is approaching. Once they do, they may respond impulsively rather than think through a solution and its potential outcomes. They may worry unnecessarily about minor, more immediate issues and lose sight of the whole picture, in other words 'they can't see the wood for the trees'. This means that they may find it hard to generate solution options. Past experience means they may tend to focus on negative outcomes as these are what they have come to expect.

For individuals with ADHD, problem-solving abilities are hindered by core cognitive impairments, such as deficits in response inhibition, working memory and/or attention. Specific deficits have been investigated using neuropsychological measures in order to establish their cognitive basis in ADHD (e.g. the Tower of Hanoi and Tower of London tasks; Riccio *et al.*, 2004; Young *et al.*, 2007). There are several relevant areas of difficulty including response inhibition, working memory and attention (See Part II Core Symptom Modules for CBT methods to treat these areas).

Failure in inhibitory control when confronted with a problem may lead an individual with ADHD to respond before the optimal solution has been generated. A difficulty in delaying gratification may also lead ADHD clients to opt for a 'short-cut'; that is, an immediately rewarding solution, rather than implementing a longer term solution which requires waiting and more effort but with a greater reward. Young *et al.* (2007) explored these concepts using a Three Dimensional Computerized Tower of London task where 'discs' and 'rods' are presented on a computer screen. The participant is required to solve problems of varying difficulty by rearranging a set of discs in order to make them match a goal arrangement. It was found that people with ADHD did not increase their planning time and were less accurate as task difficulty increased. Failure to increase planning time with increasing problem difficulty was associated with elevated levels of impulsivity. This suggests that impairment in response inhibition or a tendency to act with less prior thought, can lead to problem-solving failure.

Working memory difficulties and attentional impairments can affect problem-solving at several stages for individuals with ADHD. There can be difficulties in generating solutions, as the individual may be liable to lose sight of previously suggested ideas and/or become distracted. They may find it difficult to hold in mind the advantages and disadvantages of solutions in order to weigh up which is most likely to be successful. In addition, working memory impairments may cause difficulties for individuals with ADHD implementing solutions as they may miss out crucial components or muddle up a sequence of events. For example, they may be unsuccessful in renewing a vehicle licence or getting their own passport because they missed out important information on the forms or forgot to enclose a document.

Young *et al.* (2006) used an ecologically valid measure of spatial working memory which involved a computerized simulated golf task – 'The Executive Golf' (Morris *et al.*, 1988). This involves the participant predicting into which hole the 'golfer' will putt a ball. The participant is given feedback as to whether their selection is correct or not. The aim is to avoid returning to any holes previously selected. Performance can be improved by the participant developing a search sequence, however ADHD participants tended not to adopt any strategy at all, resulting in a significantly impaired performance. Furthermore, the deficit became more evident with task difficulty; that is, when their spatial working memory was required to process a larger number of holes.

These specific cognitive difficulties should be borne in mind when developing a problem-solving intervention for a client with ADHD. Their strengths and weaknesses may guide the therapist regarding the areas that may require more attention. For example, for more impulsive individuals, it may be necessary to focus on strategies that involve the generation of multiple solutions in order to avoid them lunging at the first idea that comes to mind to resolve a situation. Alternatively, inattentive individuals may require more assistance in devising strategies for carrying out solutions without deviating from their planned and desired course.

Coping Strategies

It is important to assess the coping styles of clients, both adaptive and maladaptive, as these will determine appropriate problem-solving techniques, the hurdles they will face implementing them and their potential success.

Young adults with ADHD have been shown to use maladaptive coping strategies such as confrontational, escape-avoidance, and less-planned problem-solving than individuals without ADHD (Young, 2005). This study also found that the way young adults coped with stressful situations was determined by their cognitive ability. Indeed, impairment in executive function may lead an individual to lack flexibility in their ability to access and utilize a repertoire of appropriate coping strategies. For example, difficulties with impulse control may lead clients to cope with problems by responding rapidly and without thinking; this may mean they react in an aggressive or defensive way. They may find it difficult to employ problem-focused strategies if they feel emotionally overwhelmed by anger or anxiety, which in turn drives them to act on their feelings. Alternatively, due to previous adverse experiences and attentional difficulties, some individuals with ADHD may respond to stress or problems by not acknowledging the problem or actively avoiding dealing with it.

The coping strategies employed by people with ADHD may also be affected by a lack of intimate, confiding, relationships as social support can act as a stress-buffer. Close, supportive interpersonal relationships provide the opportunity to consult about problems, gain helpful advice, benefit from the experience of others, and learn from the modelling of successful and unsuccessful coping mechanisms. However, 'words of wisdom' and the observation of adaptive functioning may be less accessible to individuals who experience multiple short-term interpersonal relationships, find it difficult to sustain relationships with acquaintances and old friends, and may have strained relations with family members.

The individual's style of adaptive functioning will determine the outcome of a problem-solution, that is, its success and viability. A functional coping style provides the context for the generation and implementation of optimal solutions. A dysfunctional coping style can negatively affect the quality and suitability of solutions generated and may lead to inappropriate decision making. According to the Lazarus and Folkman's (1984) model of coping, stress depends on a person's cognitive appraisal of a situation and their perceptions of their resources to deal with it. They suggest that feelings of stress can be relieved through both emotion-focused coping and instrumental problem-solving. Emotion-focused coping is used when the aim is to manage the emotions that are generated by a situation, for example, a death in the family or the end of a relationship. Problem-solving is used as a general coping strategy in situations that are perceived as changeable or controllable. Problem-solving can affect a person's sense of control and change their negative appraisal of situations. A functional response to stress involves the ability to use emotion-focused coping and problem-solving in the appropriate situations.

There are gender differences in the likelihood of whether emotion-focused or problem-focused coping strategies are employed. Females are more likely to engage in emotion-focused coping, whereas men are more likely to use problem-focused coping. When people have ADHD, it seems that these are the exact areas in which the individuals of different genders need the most help. Females with ADHD often have emotion-related difficulties such as anxiety and mood lability, which can impact on their ability to cope with stressful situations. Additionally, adolescent females have been shown to be less likely to confide in peers and use social support which is a common resource used by young people (Young *et al.*, 2005a). On the other hand, males with ADHD are more likely to externalize their distress and respond impulsively with aggressive or antisocial behaviour, rather than engaging in adaptive problem-solving. For these reasons it is important to begin treatment with psychoeducation regarding when each type of coping may be more appropriate, and follow this through with teaching effective skills and techniques.

If a client is in a situation entirely beyond their control (and the therapist needs to check whether this perception is prone to cognitive distortion, such as catastrophizing the problem), then emotion-focused strategies may be most suitable to help the client manage their feelings. These may include simple counselling or sharing of a difficulty with a friend but may extend to mood-focused strategies such as those provided in the Anxiety Module (Chapter 9), the Frustration and Anger Module (Chapter 10), and the Low-Mood and Depression Module (Chapter 11). However situations which are within the control of the individual can be addressed using the five stage model of problem-solving provided below.

ASSESSMENT AND COGNITIVE BEHAVIOURAL THERAPY

Five Stages of Problem-Solving

Individuals of both genders can benefit from learning to apply an instrumental and structured method of analyzing and resolving their problems. A 'problem' can be defined as any life situation or task that requires something to be changed or resolved. This allows the person to function adaptively. The problem may be explicit (for example, needing accommodation) or intrinsic (for example, feeling unattractive). Obstacles such as novelty, ambiguity, conflicts of interest or lack of resources may prevent an immediate response or solution from being effective. Sometimes people may only begin to realize that a problem exists when they have failed to achieve a desired goal on several occasions, for example getting a job.

A 'solution' is a response or pattern of responses that can be cognitive or behavioural. A solution arises through the problem-solving process and achieves a problem-solving goal (D'Zurilla and Nezu, 1999). Implementation of a solution is an important part of the problem-solving process as this involves carrying out the solution in specific situations. Finally, solutions need to be evaluated as to their level of success in reaching the set goals. Thus problem-solving involves a five stage process.

1. Identifying and defining the specific problem.
2. Generating various solutions to the problem.

3. Evaluating each solution.
4. Implementing the chosen solution.
5. Evaluating success.

Despite the many pitfalls experienced by people with ADHD in solving problems, they have an important strength – they have a tendency to reappraise stressful situations in a positive way (Young, 2005). The trait was found to be positively associated with impulsivity, thus impulsive individuals may be less prone to dwell on their problems but focus instead on their future with optimism. This can be hugely advantageous and may underpin the creative and entrepreneurial personality characteristics often present in people with ADHD. It is therefore important that the therapist emphasizes this strength in treatment and introduces cognitive reappraisal techniques at every opportunity (by asking, for example, how the client could look at it differently, how would their partner/friend/sibling look at it, what other explanations are there for someone's behaviour, have they made an assumption, determine facts versus opinions etc.).

Stage 1: Identifying and Defining the Problem

Problems may creep up on individuals with ADHD or suddenly occur unexpectedly. They may be external obstacles to a goal that arise as part of a natural process (e.g. being unable to purchase materials to complete a task as the shop is out of stock); they may be the result of actions or interference by others, both positive and negative, (e.g. a work colleague is off sick for a week and the client has to cover his work-load); they may also be self-generated and build up through worry (.e.g. 'my boss hates me', 'I'm hopeless at parties'). Common areas for problems for people with ADHD are given in Table 7.1.

However, the client may need some prompting and assistance in teasing out the presenting problem. This can be achieved by asking four main questions in order to determine whether the individual has a 'solvable' problem or more general worries and anxieties. These questions have been included in exercise format on the Companion Website (Box 7.1). The questions will help determine whether the problem really needs tackling. If the problem derives more from a client's general attitude or anxious response-style, then the techniques outlined in the Anxiety Module (Chapter 9) on coping with anxiety will be of help.

Box 7.1: Define the Problem

1. *Why* it is a problem?
2. *How* does it affect the client?
3. Does the situation have *potential for change*?
4. What could happen if it is *not solved*?

For example, take the case of Alex, a client with ADHD. Alex started a new relationship and was unsure whether to tell his girlfriend, Joanne, that he had ADHD.

Table 7.1 Common domains of problems in ADHD

Domain	*Problems*
Education	Missing deadlines, messy work, poor revision skills
Work	Poor CV, underachievement at work, being passed over for promotion, not meeting sales targets
Transport	Missing trains, buses, being late, taxing, insuring and organizing MOT for a car
Financial	Debts due to not paying bills on time, impulsive spending
Lack of Support	Gaining appropriate support, e.g. setting up childcare arrangements, not accessing appropriate benefits
Household Chores	Incomplete DIY tasks, putting off cleaning and laundry
Relationships	Difficulty making or maintaining relationships, argumentative with friends
Low self-esteem	Feeling like a failure, expectancy of failure
Sleep	Restlessness, insomnia, can't get out of bed on time
Disorganization	Disorganization of time, time-wasting traps, day lacking structure, poor work–leisure time balance
Substance misuse	Drug and alcohol addictions, use of substances as a maladaptive coping strategy
Trouble with police	Opportunistic crime, aggressive outbursts, damage to property

1. *Why was it a problem?* Alex often had to take medication when he was with Joanne and did this in secret. If they were together when his medication wore off, he sometimes felt a bit 'ragged' and irritable.
2. *How did it affect the client?* Alex was worried about how Joanne would react if she knew. He didn't want to lie to her but he was worried that she would think he was crazy and/or be embarrassed by him taking medication.
3. *Did the situation have potential for change?* If Joanna knew about Alex having ADHD and was alright about it, Alex would feel very relieved. Alex believed they would have a firmer, more honest foundation on which to build their relationship. The downside was that they might split up if Joanna wasn't happy with it.
4. *What could happen if the problem was not solved?* The relationship would not have an open and honest foundation. If Joanna found out by someone else telling her, she might feel angry with Alex and feel that he can't be trusted.

This example illustrates that problems are often complex. They are not straightforward or simple to resolve. If they were, they would not be a problem! Thus part of the problem-solving process is investigation. Finding out as much as possible about the problem and how it has arisen will provide the client with the knowledge to find the appropriate solution and give them the self-confidence to implement it. This involves not only gathering facts related to the task itself but also examination of personal information, for example, self-expectations and demands. Hence, if a person sets unrealistic, unachievable goals, then the problem is not the failure to achieve set

Table 7.2 Understanding the problem

	Problem list			
	I am unsure whether to tell girlfriend about ADHD	*I am often late for school/work*	*I have been given notice to move out of my flat*	*I have fallen out with a friend*
1. What is the problem/ situation?	Whether or not to disclose	Usually 20–30 minutes late	Need to find somewhere to live within 1 month	My friend has stopped contacting me since I blurted out a confidence
2. What do I want?	That she knows and feels comfortable/ accepts my diagnosis	On time or 10 minutes early	Find new accommodation in next fortnight	Being in touch with my friend again
3. What are the obstacles to getting what I want?	Finding the right moment Finding the right way to say it She may reject me	Difficulty getting up early Time to pack bag in morning Transport delays	Going away for weekend next week Raising deposit Worries about having to live with strangers	Pride Fear of rejection,

goals, but the inability to realistically acknowledge their capabilities and skills, time management problems, perfectionist attitude and so on.

Three questions can be asked in order to assist with understanding the problem;

1. What is the problem or situation?
2. What do I want?
3. What are the obstacles to getting what I want?

An example is provided in Table 7.2 which demonstrates how, by adopting this systematic methodology, problems may become more clearly defined and easier to understand. A blank version is on the Companion Website.

Stage 2: Generating Solutions

The best way of generating solutions is to brainstorm all the possible ways of solving the problem. There are three basic rules for generating alternative solutions through brainstorming (D'Zurilla and Nezu, 1999).

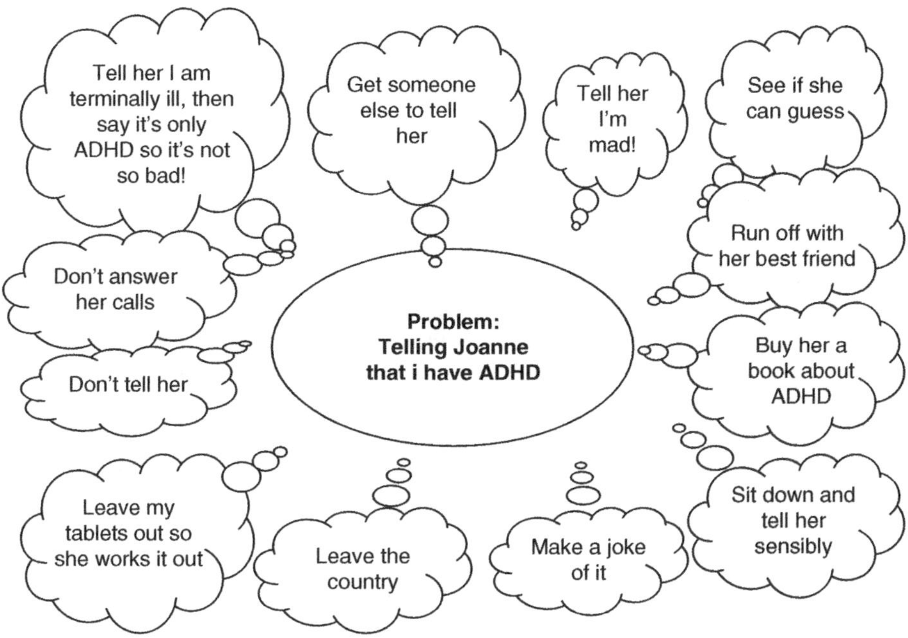

Figure 7.1 Example of brainstorming solutions

1. Quantity leads to quality – the more solutions that are produced, the more good quality ideas there will be.
2. Deferment of judgment – that the person needs to wait to choose a solution in order to generate better quality solutions at this stage.
3. Variety – the greater the range of solutions, the more likely a good solution will be generated. Thinking more laterally may prevent the person from choosing a well-tried but unsuccessful approach.

Thus, the client should be encouraged to produce ideas including extreme solutions ranging from the sublime to the ridiculous. Figure 7.1 shows the solutions generated by Alex when he was brainstorming ideas regarding whether to tell his girlfriend that he has ADHD. A common obstacle to generating creative solutions is 'habits' (Parnes, Noller and Biondi, 1977). Habits hinder problem-solving by causing clients to respond automatically and in a way to which they have become accustomed. Individuals with ADHD may well have a history of habitual and impulsive responding resulting in the development of 'maladaptive habits'. These become maladaptive coping strategies. For example, a client may habitually respond to a situation that is perceived to be threatening in some way by storming out and failing to address the problem.

Whenever Alex prepared himself to tell his girlfriend he had ADHD, he would become anxious and start an argument. The argument distracted him from following through his intention to disclose to her his ADHD status. Such habits may be helpfully identified collaboratively in sessions so that the client may recognize them when they occur and resist the impulse to automatically respond in a predetermined pattern of thinking or behaving.

One of the most helpful methods in solving problems and, one which is often overlooked by people with ADHD, is simply reviewing the previous solutions they have applied to similar problems. The client should be encouraged to think about how they usually tackle problems and what has worked (or not worked) in the past. They should also evaluate the methods by which they have successfully avoided problems in the past. This will involve engaging the client in a cost-benefit analysis of previous decision-making processes. Clients should be encouraged to think not only about what and who helped in the past, but also what made things worse. They need to identify the *process*, how they arrived at the decision, and whether this had a positive or negative outcome. They may also seek the advice of someone who has known them encounter similar situations in the past who may be more objective regarding what worked and what was less helpful.

For example, Alex was asked to consider what had happened in the past when he had told friends and girlfriends that he has ADHD. When he told his first girlfriend, she had laughed it off and helped him do some research on the internet. His best friend asked if there was anything he could do to help. His friend asked him a lot of questions about the disorder. A few weeks later he and his girlfriend split up as she went travelling for a year before going to university. Alex's mother had also told some family and friends that he had ADHD. This was less successful and an aunt sent him a 'Get Well Soon' card! From this experience, Alex decided that it would be better if he provided his own explanation of his condition.

Stage 3: Evaluating Solutions

So far the client will have learnt to identify and define problems and generate multiple alternative solutions. Once several solutions have been generated, these should be assessed according to the degree of satisfaction the client would feel with the outcome of each solution. Several methods are recommended to assist with this process, including evaluating effort, examining alternatives, rehearsal of the solution, role-play and challenging cognitive distortions.

Evaluating effort

People with ADHD may avoid adaptive problem-solving when the effort involved in carrying out a solution is perceived to be too great. A desire for immediate gratification means that a short cut may be more rewarding than the alternative of expending more effort to achieve a greater goal. Motivational interviewing techniques will help the individual focus on the goal or task to be achieved and motivate them to stay on task, avoid distracters and achieve it.

For example, in order for Alex to achieve a successful relationship, effort needed to be expended in planning how to explain to Joanne about having ADHD. The alternative short-cut, which did not require effort, was to not tell her and continue the relationship on the basis of dishonesty. The latter course may have provided immediate relief from the anxiety aroused in Alex whenever he contemplated disclosure to Joanne, but the problem remained unresolved. Indeed it may even have become worse if someone else had told Joanna, or if Joanna had observed Alex surreptitiously taking tablets and assumed that he was taking illicit drugs. Alex examined his motivation to change the situation and achieve a better relationship by discussing his readiness to engage in change by formulating his position in the 'Stages of Change' model (Prochaska and DiClemente, 1982; see Figure 2.1). Alex identified that he had been oscillating between the precontemplation and contemplation state. His ambivalence was expressed by him attempting to find some 'middle ground' by arguing that he should wait to tell Joanne about his ADHD ('I'll do it next week'). In Alex's case, this was a delaying tactic that was challenged in the sessions. However in some cases it may be sensible for clients to be encouraged to avoid premature disclosure in new relationships or less close relationships (e.g. acquaintances, working associates). It is all about doing what is right for the client and getting the balance right. This will inevitably involve encouraging the client to plan ahead and think about the consequences of their actions. As a therapist, the primary task is to help the client to learn to think before they speak and act, or react impulsively on the spur of the moment. Blurting out his medication history at a party is unlikely to be helpful in resolving Alex's problem. Alex determined to progress onto a stage of preparation by examining alternative solutions, rehearsal and role-play of favoured solutions in preparation for the action stage.

Examining alternatives

After eliminating all the ridiculous and least likely options, the client will usually be left with two or three possible 'realistic' solutions. These often have very different courses of action. This is the time to make a 'pros and cons' list for each – often the advantages of one solution are the disadvantages of another. Weightings can be given according to how important each 'pro' or 'con' is for the client. These may depend on the likelihood of achieving the goal, emotional well-being, time and effort.

Alex decided that he should choose between telling Joanne himself ('sit down and tell her sensibly') and not telling her, but continuing the relationship. Alex's pros and cons for telling Joanne that he had ADHD are given in Table 7.3. A blank version can be found on the Companion Website for use with clients.

Table 7.3 Example of a pros and cons list

Pros of telling	*Cons of telling*
It's being honest	It might freak her out
She may not mind	She may leave me
She could find out anyway, and might be cross that I didn't tell her	I don't want to worry her
It would help her understand why I am the way I am	The relationship may not last
The longer I leave it, the harder it will be to tell her	She may laugh at me and tell other people

Next Alex was asked to rank the five most important issues identified in the pros and cons list. He chose:

1. it would help Joanne understand why I am the way I am (pro);
2. it's being honest (pro);
3. it might freak her out (con);
4. she could find out anyway, and might be angry that I didn't tell her (pro); and
5. she may leave me (con).

It then became clearer to Alex that, not only did he choose more Pros than Cons in his importance list, but he also ranked them higher. Therefore, he decided to tell Joanne that he had ADHD. The next stage for him was to work out exactly how best to do this.

Rehearsal

Rehearsal is an effective way of preparing for a difficult conversation or situation. The client should be taken into an imaginal mode by asking them to imagine the anticipated situation and see themselves acting out the chosen solution. The client can be oriented to the situation by being cued to imagine and describe the surroundings in detail, for example, colour of curtains, type of flooring, cooking smells. At first some clients may have difficulty engaging in an imaginal mode but with practice this will become easier. In such cases, it may be helpful for the therapist to initially talk the client through the specific steps that may be taken to solve the problem while the client is in the imaginal mode. However, it is important that the client progresses to rehearsal of the solution unaided. In addition they should try to identify possible pitfalls to success that were not immediately obvious and determine collaboratively how these may be overcome and/or constructively managed. The client should also consider how they feel during the process and at the outcome.

For example, Alex was asked to imagine the situation carefully. He thought it would be better to tell Joanne at her house, when they were relaxing watching television.

However, when this was rehearsed in the imaginal mode Alex discovered that the TV distracted him. Alex then decided to tell Joanne in the kitchen over a cup of coffee. Alex rehearsed what he would say to Joanne and by using this technique, he felt more confident in his ability to see the task through to fruition and to achieve the outcome he desired.

Prior to working in imaginal mode it is very important to determine a calm, happy imaginal state that the client relates to positively. Sometimes the client may become distressed when working in imaginal mode and they may imagine alternative consequences which may be negative. In such an event, the client should signal feelings of distress to the therapist using a predetermined code (e.g. by lifting a finger in the air) and the therapist then verbally directs the client to imagine a neutral, calm scene and focus on breathing exercises (see Anxiety Module in Chapter 9).

Perspective-taking role-play

The next stage involved Alex role-playing the scenario with his therapist. A role-play method is particularly useful for rehearsing problem-solutions involving other people such as job interviews, giving notice at work and ending a relationship. In the case of Alex, the role-play was reversed so that the therapist pretended to be Alex (the client), and Alex role played his girlfriend Joanne (the person receiving the information). This helped Alex think about the likely impact of his problem solution on Joanne and amend his plans accordingly as appropriate, for example, by using more sensitive wording to explain about ADHD, having some written information to hand to her that would help dispel any inaccurate stereotypical lay beliefs she may have. Alex was able to think about the questions that Joanne may ask (for which he could then prepare answers and rehearse either in imaginal mode and/or by further role-play in sessions).

Practising such situations in this way will make individuals feel less nervous when the situation actually happens and they will feel more prepared. This will improve their sense of self-efficacy and belief that problems are solvable and change is possible.

Challenging cognitive distortions

It is likely that at some stage during treatment distorted thinking will handicap the problem-solving process, particularly when maladaptive habitual responses are favoured ('I'm no good at it'; 'I'll fail'; 'I'm stupid'; 'They don't like me'). The client needs to learn how to check that their ideas about various solutions are productive and viable. Cognitive distorted thinking is likely to sabotage helpful solutions in favour of ones that add little to resolving the problem, and/or may make it worse (for more help with cognitive distortions, see Low-Mood and Depression Module in Chapter 11). In such circumstances, potentially helpful solutions may be discarded erroneously due to 'faulty thinking' processes resulting in:

- overgeneralization – 'everything I do always goes wrong, so why bother trying';
- black-and-white thinking – 'if I can't get it 100 per cent right, there's no point in doing it at all'; and
- jumping to conclusions – 'I only just managed to complete Part 1, so I'll never get Part 4 finished'.

Alex tended to jump to conclusions and overgeneralize. In fact his first girlfriend had ended their relationship because she went travelling around Europe with a friend. She was going to be away for a year and she didn't think it was fair to expect Alex to wait. This occurred just after he had disclosed to her that he had ADHD. It may have been a matter of bad timing. Alex had formed the belief that future relationships would end if he told people he had ADHD. He felt very anxious about it. However, Alex had never considered alternative possibilities, such as his ex-girlfriend had planned the gap year travelling before going to university, he had known about this for a long time and it had nothing to do with him disclosing to her that he had the disorder. In fact Alex had ignored evidence to the contrary, as his ex-girlfriend had said that she wanted to stay friends. She had stayed in touch and had sent him postcards from various countries. Additionally, Alex disregarded the fact that his friends had not rejected him. They went out regularly and his best friend had been reading up about ADHD.

Stage 4: Implementing the Chosen Solution

By this stage the client should have become motivated to effect change and resolve problems; they will have generated multiple solutions to their problem and chosen the best. The client will have been prepared by rehearsal in sessions and role played potential outcomes. The next stage is to plan and implement the solution. Once an appropriate solution has been determined and rehearsed, the client is encouraged to implement this, taking care to avoid procrastination and time-wasting traps. For example, say the problem is debt and the target is to pay off £200 of a credit card bill by the end of the year. The solution implemented is putting aside £5 each week. This illustrates how steps to achieve the target should be planned by breaking down the goal into smaller achievable steps.

However, the process is often more complex, especially when problem-solving difficulties involve interpersonal relationships. This involves thinking about the best time and situation in which to address the problem, and if possible 'set the scene'. Depending on the problem, the time management principles set out in the Organization and Time-Management Module (Chapter 5) may also be helpful if ultimate resolution and goal achievement requires the individual to create small achievable steps or tasks that lead to success. Tasks must be clearly defined and goals realistic. In the case of Alex, he was encouraged to work out a specific evening and place most suited to disclosing his ADHD status to his new girlfriend. This was then reviewed in the following session.

Step 5: Evaluating Success

Following the implementation of a solution, the client should evaluate their success. Did they achieve the desired result? If so, congratulate them. Positive feedback by the therapist is a powerful reward! It is important that the client feels proud of their achievement and focuses on the benefits of success. They should reflect on the impact of success on their self-confidence, their mood and also their understanding of the original presenting problem (was it as life-threatening as they first thought?) Positive feedback will increase the likelihood of the client engaging in a problem-solving process without delay (or procrastination) in the future and motivate them to pursue further goals.

For example, Alex told his girlfriend and she was very pleased that he had trusted her and told her. Joanne told Alex that she had diabetes and had to inject insulin every day. She had been worried about how to tell him. In future Alex adopted a similar model of disclosure to friends at the appropriate time. Both Alex and Joanne felt more confident about their relationship.

In case of partial or no success, the therapist must systematically evaluate all the obstacles and difficulties that arose and recommence the problem-solving process to explore how these may be better dealt with. Useful areas to explore include the client's feelings about successful resolution, for example, fearing the consequences, anxiety about change or uncertainty. It may be that the problem needs to be re-evaluated and resolved in a different way. For example, if Alex had been unable to raise the issue of ADHD with Joanne, the therapist could examine where the obstacles lay. Had there been an external distraction that prevented him (e.g. other people nearby) or had Alex been thinking negatively about his solution plan?

Rewards are crucial to encourage the client and provide motivation. The reward system should include rewards for attempting resolution of the problem and one greater reward for successful resolution of the problem. Alex and Joanne went out for dinner to a romantic restaurant.

SUMMARY

People with ADHD are often faced with multiple problems that require solving. Their difficulty is that they may never have learned how to effectively deal with problems because as children other people have done this for them and/or because they have developed maladaptive coping strategies. All too often, people with ADHD respond to the problems in their daily lives in a disadvantageous way, for example, putting off targets, avoiding situations or people, responding in an irrational or impulsive manner. This is likely to be due to cognitive deficits and maladaptive coping styles which can hinder their problem-solving abilities. When small problems mount up these become great problems and sometimes clinical problems such as depression and anxiety will develop if individuals feel overwhelmed by multiple and/or long-term stressful problematic situations. It is therefore important that the individual with ADHD learns to encounter and resolve problems in a methodological, timely and appropriate way. The therapist will be assisted by the natural optimism of young adults with ADHD and their tendency to reappraise stressful situations more positively. This is a real therapeutic opportunity and one that needs to be exploited fully by the therapist as with encouragement clients will learn how to become resilient to disappointments and 'bounce back' from difficulties.

This module has reviewed the main stages involved in solving problems. These include identifying and defining problems, and generating alternative solutions. The implementation of a solution must always be followed by analysis and evaluation of success and reward for success. This provides a constructive feedback loop to inform earlier stages of the future problem-solving process.

Group Treatment: Problem-Solving Module

It is essential to prepare for group treatment by reading the chapter module. Six group sessions are outlined below, but the number of treatment sessions can be expanded or reduced as required.

Plan

Sessions 1–2	Starting activities
Sessions 3	Psychoeducation and exercise (e.g. You are broke and you need to raise £1,000) Set homework
Sessions 4–5	Exercises (including clients' own) Check homework is being done
Session 6	Group discussion of homework (for those who are comfortable to disclose) Obstacles and how to overcome them Revision of psychoeducation

Starting Activities

What is a problem?

Ask the group to provide a definition (situation or task that requires something to be changed).

Ask the group to provide examples of problems and write on flipchart. Highlight that the problems can be:

Explicit – finding somewhere to live, learning better revision techniques; or

Intrinsic – feeling unattractive.

(*Continued*)

Ask the group how they resolved the problems (ask for good and bad ways, was it the best way, did new problems arise, did it take longer than necessary to resolve).
Group discussion.

What is a solution?
Ask the group to provide a definition (an *effective* response or pattern of responses that can be cognitive or behavioural; what is 'effective'?).
What makes it difficult to find solutions to problems? (too much or too little effort, avoidance, emotional reactivity, not enough time).

What are the consequences of poor problem-solving skills?
Brainstorm – problems at school/work, bad decisions, debts, frustration, irritation, distress, stress.
Highlight that consequences can be practical and/or emotional.

How do you know a problem is coming?
What are the warning signs or signals?
Highlight that these may be external (what people say to you, how they look at you) and internal (how you feel inside).
Group discussion.

Psychoeducation

Problem-solving is a process and a skill that you can learn. Introduce the five stages of problem-solving and techniques.

1. Identify and define the problem.
2. Generate solutions to the problem.
3. Evaluate each solution.
4. Implement the chosen solution.
5. Evaluate success.

Give handouts from the Companion Website.

Exercises

Select suitable examples of situations/experiences described by participants in starting activities or from suggested scenarios (see below). Using these examples complete and repeat exercises (either in small group or as a whole group together). Each exercise should be worked through by applying stages 1-3 of the five stage process and using handouts.

Identify and define the problem (see Box 7.1 and Table 7.2).
Generate solutions to the problem (brainstorm Figure 7.1).
Evaluate each solution (pros and cons Table 7.3).
What is the best solution? Why is it the best solution?

(*Continued*)

Scenarios:
You are broke and you need to raise £1,000.
You forgot your sister's birthday and your family are angry with you.
You are applying for lots of jobs but you are never offered an interview.
Should you tell your boss that you have ADHD?

Identify and discuss obstacles to solving problems and how to overcome them. Follow with group feedback and discussion.

Homework

Using the handouts to assist you, work through a problem that you currently have. Using the five-stage process determine the best solution. Implement the solution and evaluate whether it worked or not. If it did not, chose another solution.

If homework is complete and successful, work on a different problem or work with someone else to resolve their problem (not another group participant, but a family member or friend).

8

INTERPERSONAL RELATIONSHIPS MODULE

It is common for people with ADHD to feel they have difficulties in their interpersonal relationships, whether these are friendships, romantic relationships, working relationships or family relationships. Negotiating social relationships can be just as difficult with people whom they know well, with close acquaintances and with strangers. Most teenagers form and develop social relationships from their immediate environment, such as at school and college. However, young people with ADHD tend to develop relationships from the local neighbourhood; through parental associates, or by 'hanging out' in the street. This perhaps reflects a need for individuals to draw upon wider social networks and sometimes make friends with peers who are excluded from school or unemployed (Young *et al.*, 2005a).

This module describes methods to help the therapist facilitate identification of social skills deficits in adolescents and adults with ADHD and outlines techniques for improvement. Sessions have a skills development focus and include aspects of: verbal communication (e.g. conversation and listening skills); nonverbal communication (e.g. body language, gestures and posture); emotion recognition; and the modification and regulation of social behaviour in different social settings (e.g. at work, at parties). The module pays particular attention to difficult situations that individuals may face. This includes coping with rejection, as many individuals with ADHD experience rejection more than most. This is encountered early in school when children report feeling socially isolated and recall times when they played alone in the playground, being the last to be picked for team activities, not having anyone to sit next to on school trips and not being invited to tea. These early experiences mean that as they grow up and can exercise greater choice and control over how and with whom they spend their time, they may avoid social situations. However, individuals with ADHD are not naturally reclusive as they are enthusiastic, social and friendly people. Thus, the paradox is that they desire and strive for social acceptance but feel anxious when

Cognitive-Behavioural Therapy for ADHD in Adolescents and Adults: A Psychological Guide to Practice, Second Edition. Susan Young and Jessica Bramham.

in company or in social situations, and uncertain about how to behave. They sometimes overcompensate by engaging in highly extraverted, outrageous behaviour. It may also mean they are unsure and nervous about disclosing their ADHD status in new relationships. Some people overdisclose. The issue of disclosure is one of the most hotly debated topics in group treatment sessions.

FUNCTIONAL DEFICITS IN ADOLESCENTS AND ADULTS

Children with ADHD often grow up believing that they are misunderstood or that they are 'different' from others in some way. No matter how much they try, relationships go wrong, and they do not develop as intended or expected. Anger management and impulse control problems may lead people with ADHD to have volatile relationships which break down easily. In the end they stop trying and lack the confidence to initiate friendships and more general social behaviour. Self-awareness of their social difficulties causes distress and, at times, a defensive attitude. Sometimes these feelings are taken out on loved ones, such as parents or partners. They may respond in an 'unnatural' way or attempt to overcompensate. For example, often young people with ADHD will report feeling that they need to 'play the clown' in social situations in order to mask anxiety or attentional problems. Being the centre of attention reduces the need for them to focus attention on others. They may also feel that by being funny and amusing they will be more attractive to others. However, despite being the 'life and soul' of the party, many people with ADHD report feeling very isolated generally. They find it difficult to form meaningful and lasting relationships because of low self-esteem and a history of being rejected or let down by others. They may find others are intolerant of their ADHD symptoms. Some individuals may be vulnerable to exploitation by others because of their motivation to be liked and ingratiate themselves in a peer group. They may become part of a 'bad crowd' believing that bad friends are better than no friends. Others may be encouraged to engage in antisocial behaviours for the benefit of others, for example by delivering drugs, or theft from shops. Females, in particular, may try to compensate by engaging in promiscuous behaviour in an attempt to develop meaningful relationships. Some people are vulnerable to inappropriate self-disclosure in an attempt to 'fast-track' friendships. Sadly, disruption to social relationships is an experience often acquired at a young age.

It is important for individuals with ADHD to recognize that the way they present themselves to others can influence the way others interact with them. This includes the way they talk to others and express themselves (verbal communication), their nonverbal posture and actions (body language) and the general impression they give of themselves (emotional expressions; ADHD features). This involves raising awareness of social behaviour and examining the effect that some or all of these behaviours have on influencing other people's perceptions. For example, inattention in ADHD may be perceived by another person as the individual lacking interest in what they are saying. A person with ADHD may be perceived as fickle because they flit from one person to another or from one topic of conversation to another. This may be perceived by others as lacking sincerity. Due to impulsivity, individuals with

ADHD may also be prone to making snap decisions and jumping to conclusions. This means they may take things at face value, based on first impressions and stereotyped influences. For example, if an acquaintance walks down a corridor and does not acknowledge them, they may immediately assume that that person does not like them and behave in a way which reflects this, thus leading to a self-fulfilled prophecy. They may not consider other explanations for the lack of acknowledgement, for example, the person is in a hurry and preoccupied with an urgent matter.

The skills covered in this module refer to 'appropriate' behaviours as determined by prosocial rules and norms. These should be selected and adapted in a 'pick and mix' fashion according to the needs of the client. However, it is worth noting that different cultures have different social rules. For example, loud and boisterous behaviour may be viewed as a sign of being social/friendly/happy in some cultures, while in others it may be viewed as rude and obnoxious. Therefore, it is necessary for the therapist to consider cultural issues. Similarly the client must think about the social circumstances and the expectations of those around them as this will guide them as to how they should behave. Different social situations have a range of expectations regarding how individuals should present themselves. For example, the social demands of an interview are very different from the requirements of being with a group of friends at a party. It may be more difficult for people with ADHD to be adaptive to the changing social demands of situations and they may rely on a social repertoire that has worked well in one setting, but is totally inadequate or inappropriate for another.

Treatment sessions should be structured to include aspects important for the development of both micro-skills and macro-skills. Micro-skills include the adoption of specific social skills training techniques to encourage skills such as appropriate eye contact, voice volume and tone, and body positioning. Macro-skills encompass more complex interactions such as giving compliments, constructive feedback, turn-taking and listening skills.

ASSESSMENT OF SOCIAL PROBLEMS

Some clients may report 'hundreds' of good friends but on closer questioning these turn out to be casual acquaintances and the other 'friend' probably holding an entirely different perspective of the relationship. It is extremely important to overcome defensiveness and embarrassment about social relationship difficulties as it is clearly difficult for the therapist to help unless the client recognizes and acknowledges the problem. Thus, the first step to improving social relationships is through self-evaluation and identification of target areas for treatment that the client may wish to build on to give more confidence and proficiency when interacting with others. Table 8.1 presents a Social Skills Questionnaire completed by a client who lacked confidence socializing in large groups, for example, at parties. The questionnaire may be self-rated or completed by friends/family. The aim is for clients to identify their areas of weakness that become treatment targets for skills development. If the client rates a high number of 'I don't know' responses then it may be helpful for clients to ask fam-

Table 8.1 Social skills questionnaire

How good are you at:	*Never good*	*Rarely good*	*Sometimes good*	*Mostly good*	*Always good*	*I don't know*
1. Interacting with friends					✓	
2. Interacting with strangers		✓				
3. Talking to strangers at parties	✓					
4. Going to parties		✓				
5. Meeting a friend in the pub				✓		
6. Listening to people				✓		
7. Starting a conversation			✓			
8. Asking questions			✓			
9. Answering questions			✓			
10. Admitting if something has not been understood		✓				
11. Looking at people when talking to them			✓			
12. Not fidgeting			✓			
13. Speaking clearly		✓				
14. Recognising how others are feeling		✓				
15. Explaining to others about your ADHD diagnosis	✓					

ily and/or friends to complete a questionnaire. For those who lack insight into their social problems, the comparison of their own perspective with that of others will be a useful exercise to compare their own perspective with that of others. Discrepancies can be used as a basis for further discussion and treatment to help them develop a more accurate interpretation of intentions and emotions signalled by others.

COGNITIVE BEHAVIOURAL THERAPY FOR VERBAL COMMUNICATION SKILLS

Psychoeducation

The way we present ourselves verbally (aspects of our voice, speech and conversation) informs others of how pleasant or easy it is to interact with us. Too little or too much can cause difficulties in how well others are able to listen to or understand us. People with ADHD often interrupt or butt into other people's conversations. They may switch topics of conversation or 'go off at a tangent' and this can be difficult for the listener to understand or follow what they are saying. People with ADHD often report a feeling of ceaseless mental activity, this can be exhausting for both the individual themselves and the people with whom they communicate. They can be particularly excited by novelty and high stimulation, and may have a tendency to speak rapidly, too loudly and too much when they get excited. At such times they may experience a 'flood' of ideas and thoughts which, although enthusiastically expressed, are hard for the listener to follow. The listener may be overwhelmed or bored if they do not share the same interest. Thus, it is important for individuals with ADHD to increase their awareness of times when they are speaking too quickly and make people feel pressured or rushed. At such times, the response of the listener may be to withdraw.

Verbal Communication Strategies

Rate of Speech

Clients may benefit from using self-talk to encourage themselves to 'slow down'. By practising this skill, they can appear more calm, collected, confident and in control when talking to others. Clients should also learn to attend to physiological changes in the body; as they become excited and aroused about a subject, they may feel hot, notice their heart beating faster. Identifying physical changes will allow them to consider that they may be speaking too fast or overly-passionately about a topic. Rehearsal is another useful method of improving rate and volume of verbal communication and this may be done initially through reading passages or repeating what the therapist says. The client should then move on to role-playing situations and it is especially helpful if this can be recorded and discussed in sessions. During the playback of the recording, the client becomes the observer or listener in the interaction and is better able to take an alternative perspective. Performance may be self-rated (or informant-rated) according to each of the items in Tables 8.2, 8.3 and 8.4 (see Companion Website).

Conversational Skills

People with ADHD have a tendency to dominate and monopolize conversation, with little recognition of turn-taking or the level of interest the listener has in a topic. They also have difficulty attending to what others are saying, drift off, and lose the thread of the conversation. This may lead them to butt in and make inappropriate comments. Conversations may appear very 'one-sided' and the client must learn to balance talking and listening. Putting questions to another person indicates interest in that person and their life, and in what they have to say and contribute to a conversation.

Recording sessions and/or role-play interactions are helpful techniques to demonstrate appropriate and inappropriate skills. These should be discussed from the perspective of each person in the dyad. Improvements in some of the common problem areas outlined in Table 8.3 can be rated on a Likert scale (See Companion Website) – either by self-evaluation of progress, self-ratings of observed recordings, or informant-evaluation of progress.

Table 8.2 Characteristics of ADHD speech and suggestions for improvement

Feature	*ADHD Characteristic*	*Perceived by others*	*Skill development*
Rate	Speaking too quickly and others are unable to keep up	Intense personality, a person who is 'hard work'	Slowing down and taking breaths between sentences
Clarity	Mumbling	Lacking in confidence	Speaking clearly, articulating each word
Intonation	Speaking at a high pitch	Overexcitable personality, irrational, histrionic	Lowering the tone of the voice
Fluency	Becoming distracted and going off at a tangent	Disinterested in others and lacking in sincerity	Keeping track and structuring what is being said
Volume	Speaking loudly	Aggressive and intimidating	Quieten down to a moderate volume
Amount	Talking to much	Superficial and narcissistic	Being more succinct, learning to summarise information or get to the point more quickly

Table 8.3 Conversational skills

Feature	*ADHD characteristic*	*Skill development*
Turn-taking	Not giving the other person the opportunity to talk	Allowing equal talking times
Interruptions	Butting into conversations	Timing speech appropriately i.e. waiting for others to finish
Multiple Questioning	Interrogating other people	Asking questions to stimulate conversation
Latency	Delaying after someone has asked a question	Giving a prompt response
Being relevant	Wandering off the topic and confusing people	Keeping the conversation relevant and to the point
Interesting content	Conversation is motivated by ADHD individual's interest	Making it of interest to other people, to maintain their attention
Repairing	Being offended by mistakes, e.g. if other person calls you by the wrong name	Correcting them politely
Overenthusiasm	Dominating the conversation. Not asking questions or opinion of others. Talking about yourself all the time.	Develop listening skills. Ask questions.

Table 8.4 Listing skills

Feature	*ADHD characteristic*	*Skill development*
Attending	Not maintaining focus on what is being said	See Attention Module (Chapter 3)
Acknowledgement	Seeming to not listen	Responding as though you have heard what has been said e.g. 'mm', 'yes' or nodding head
Responding	Not noticing a question, or saying I don't know	Acknowledgments, e.g. nodding, saying 'oh right'. Sharing your opinion or giving question-type feedback, e.g. 'did you really?'
Personal self-disclosure	Fear of people prying into their private life	Sharing selective information can put others at ease
Reflecting	Forgetting what someone has said	Summarising the conversion means that they have more chance of remembering and makes the other person feel that you are listening to what they are saying.

Listening Skills

It is clear from the foregoing that listening skills are a big problem for people with ADHD and a primary target for intervention. Clients may not have adequate listening skills for two reasons. First, they do not give the person an opportunity to speak, thus appearing disinterested in their point of view. This occurs when they become overly aroused (either by anxiety or enthusiasm) and they are motivated to fill the gap by talking, or their thoughts tumble out in an incoherent jumbled manner. Second, they do not adequately attend to what the person is saying, perhaps because they are distracted by noise or activities going on around them or because they are focusing on what they are going to say next (or perhaps internally distracted by lots of thoughts and ideas springing to mind). Specific listening skills are outlined in Table 8.4 (see Companion Website for this in a format suitable for use in sessions).

COGNITIVE BEHAVIOURAL THERAPY FOR NONVERBAL COMMUNICATION SKILLS

Psychoeducation

Nonverbal communication can express thoughts and feelings without the use of spoken language. A great deal of information is conveyed nonverbally. A useful exercise is to watch a television programme without sound and ask the client what they think is being said and how the speaker/recipient feels. Ask the client why they have come to their interpretation and guide them to think about body language's subtle indicators. This will increase awareness of how individuals with ADHD communicate nonverbally and how they are perceived by others. It will also improve their ability to correctly 'read' the nonverbal cues of behaviour.

ADHD symptoms themselves may convey inaccurate information about the individual, for example, attentional deficits may be interpreted as lack of interest. A tapping foot may be misinterpreted as impatience and rudeness rather than as a restless symptom of ADHD or anxiety. Impulsive interruptions or gestures may seem discourteous or abrupt by listeners and perceived by the listeners to be insulting.

Nonverbal cues serve a very important function in social interaction and by explaining the rationale of certain nonverbal cues to clients they will be more inclined to use these more frequently in their social interactions.

Nonverbal Communication Strategies

Making Eye Contact

This informs others they are being listened to and are interesting. Clients should try to look people in the eye intermittently, as avoiding eye contact may be interpreted as them feeling bored with the conversation, lacking interest in the conversation and/or not listening. Staring people straight in the eye without looking away may be interpreted as aggression and/or intimidation.

Facial Expressions

Facial expressions inform others of feelings; smiling when happy, scowling when dissatisfied. Some facial expressions may evoke undesirable responses from others; failing to smile when greeted may be interpreted as being unfriendly. It may be helpful to look at magazine photographs together and using the list of possible feelings, outlined in Table 8.5, see how well the client and therapist agree about facial expressions and the feelings of the person in the picture. Emotions can be role played using facial expressions only. The subsequent introduction of body posture and language in the role-plays will help the client build up a repertoire of social cues. Table 8.5 provides a suggested 'emotion list' from which the therapist and/or client may select an emotion to act out a situation or guess the emotion portrayed (for example the therapist may role-play eating a meal and act out a feeling of satisfaction and the client has to guess the feeling 'satisfaction').

Posture

This informs others of attitude; slouching may be interpreted as laziness/disinterest. An upright body posture can inform others that attention is being paid. Magazine photographs can also be discussed from this perspective.

Table 8.5 Emotions and facial expressions

Positive emotions	*Negative emotions*
Calm	Disappointed
Happy	Frustrated
Excited	Ashamed
Satisfied	Bored
Relaxed	Restless
Sexy	Tired
Loving	Sad
Proud	Angry
Attentive	Frightened
Important	Confused

Body Movements

Body movements add emphasis to what is being said. However, excessive use may be annoying to others, for example, fiddling/fidgeting. Pointing a finger at someone may be perceived as intimidating or provocative. Nodding your head when someone is talking shows that they have been understood, and that you are in agreement with them and supportive.

Physical Proximity

This informs others of familiarity as well as intention. Distance and 'personal space' will be different with different people; you stand closer to a friend than to a stranger. Personal boundaries are usually invaded when a person behaves in an aggressive and provocative manner.

Figure 8.1 summarizes some useful 'do's' and 'don'ts' with regard to social communication (see Companion Website for the figure in handout format).

Emotion Recognition

Misappraisal of social situations may arise from misinterpretation of social cues. These basic social perception skills are crucial for recognizing and engaging in appropriate social behaviour. These can be rehearsed in role-play and modelling an appropriate response. In particular, people with ADHD may be less able to recognize emotional cues due to poor attentional control. This means they are disadvantaged through an inability to adapt their behaviour appropriately in response to another's mood state. Social information that draws on verbal and nonverbal cues

Figure 8.1 How to communicate effectively

constantly requires reading and integration. It is important that responses can be shifted according to changing cues and emotion recognition is an important aspect of the process. To be able to better understand others, clients with ADHD need to be encouraged to look out for 'clues' or indicators (some of which may be subtle) about how that person may be feeling, for example, what kind of mood they may be in. Emotional cues can be perceived from several sources and are presented on the Companion Website in a format which can be used as a source for discussion in treatment, including facial expressions, posture, gesture and voice quality (see Table 8.5 in Companion Website).

Facial Expressions

The key is to focus on the different movements and patterns of a person's *eyebrows*, *eyes* and *mouth* for cues on how someone is feeling. It is possible that some individuals with ADHD mistake a happy face, with eyes slightly scrunched up and teeth showing, for an angry face. They can also miss facial cues due to poor attention and thus not pick up on someone's altered mood state. Examples of typical emotion states include:

- Happy = eyebrows neutral, eyes screwed up, mouth elongated and corners up
- Sad = eyebrows down, eyes lower, corners of mouth down
- Angry = eyebrows lowered, eyes wide open, mouth tense, nostrils flaring

Posture

Positioning of different *parts of the body* produces an overall pattern, which can convey emotions to others. People with ADHD can often forget that their posture can be read, and enter situations with an anxious and tense posture, which can override all their efforts to make appropriate conversation. They can also misinterpret others' postures as aggressive if someone is standing in an assertive way. Examples of postural emotion expressions include:

- Happy = hands in the air, waving, hands outspread – 'open' presentation
- Sad = body bent up, head down, hands to face – 'closed' presentation
- Angry = fist up and clenched, leaning forward

Gestures

The pattern of movements of a person's *hands*, *arms* and *shoulders* can reveal a great deal about how they are feeling. Since people with ADHD tend to fidget and make rapid movements, this can be misinterpreted by others as threatening or distracting.

Furthermore, fidgeting can make others feel irritable and annoyed, wishing that the person would stop fiddling, and lead them to terminate the conversation early. People with ADHD can also misperceive emotional gestures or find sudden movements unsettling when they have lost attention in a conversation, leading them to react inappropriately.

For example:

- Happy = waving arms about, clapping hands together
- Sad = restricted, hands in pocket, shoulders slumped
- Angry = fist shaking, finger wagging, pointing, foot stamping

A fun way of learning to display and read social behaviour and emotions is to role-play feelings in the session with the client. The client and therapist take it in turns to select emotions listed in Table 8.5 and instead of just relying on facial expressions as previously outlined, the speaker and the observer have to guess the emotion expressed drawing on gestures as well as facial expressions.

Voice Quality

The pattern of *tone*, *speed* and *loudness* of speech usually varies with emotions. Someone's mood state can be clear from the quality of someone's voice without any recognition for the content. If people with ADHD have become distracted, a route back into a conversation can be for them to establish the tone of the topic before interrupting inappropriately, for example, with a cheery flippant remark when someone is explaining how unhappy they have become. Other examples of the way voice quality can express emotions are:

- Happy = loud, high and variable pitch, fast
- Sad = soft, slow, low
- Angry = loud, high, harsh

A useful exercise with clients is to watch video recordings of social behaviour (TV soap operas are particularly good for this purpose) and analyze the emotions presented together. Through positive reinforcement of the client's judgments, they will develop greater confidence about interpreting social situations correctly. It may also be helpful to develop the theme further by pausing the video and discussing the consequences of the behaviour/interaction – how they think the other person will respond. This will encourage the ADHD person to think about the consequences of behaviour and consider alternative possibilities rather than jumping in with both feet and making snap decisions or incorrect assumptions based on inadequate information.

MODIFICATION AND REGULATION OF SOCIAL BEHAVIOUR IN DIFFERENT SOCIAL SETTINGS

So far social skills training techniques have been discussed, which the individual may employ to improve verbal and nonverbal methods of communication. However social interaction is a dynamic process that usually involves rapid shifts in the appraisal of a situation and the ability to respond in an appropriate way. A particular difficulty of individuals with ADHD is self-regulation. This means they may not be good at modifying their behaviour in complex social situations just as they may have difficulty determining subtle shifts in the attitude of others. Responding to the variable demands in social situations becomes a problem as they develop a set way of behaving, such as being jovial, which works in one setting but may not be portable. It can therefore be helpful to role-play changing social demands and look for shifts in behaviour patterns.

The type of social situations that can be problematic for young people with ADHD include making and maintaining friends, friendships with the opposite sex and sexual behaviour, parenting, unfamiliar social situations, important and/or formal conversations, peer pressure, dealing with criticism, admitting mistakes and disclosure of ADHD status.

Making and Maintaining Friends

Although some people with ADHD may appear to be the centre of attention and the 'life of the party', they may actually lack many meaningful relationships or true friendships. Recognizing that interpersonal relationships require mutual effort and input is a good starting point. However, as children move into their adolescent and young adult years it becomes much more difficult for them to make and maintain friendships. This is because social interactions become more selective and open to individual preference, and more general co-operative social opportunities are reduced, for example, school playtimes are removed. While they are at school or in further education, young people will at least have a peer set to refer to for reinforcement (both positive and negative) of their social behaviours. Others do not continue in further education and go out to work where they have to negotiate very different relationships and occupational hierarchical structures. For those who are unemployed, the social world may become considerably smaller.

Making friends and maintaining friends is a long-standing problem. The fights and arguments of childhood become peer rejection in adolescence and, for some, social isolation in adulthood. Sometimes a young adult may report to have many friendships but closer questioning reveals that these are superficial acquaintances. One problem is that people are not considerate or diplomatic and blurt out what they are thinking or betray confidences. Others may lack patience and tolerance; they get into arguments and lose their temper (see Frustration and Anger Module in Chapter 10). They have a propensity to impulsively curtail relationships, for example, if they feel let down or misunderstood. It is therefore important to reinforce the idea that relationships require tolerance, persistence, compromise and flexibility. They need to learn to read social situations accurately. Attentional problems may mean that individuals forget arrangements or fail to keep in touch. Time management strategies (see Organization and Time-Management Module in Chapter 5) will help individuals make plans to meet up with friends, remind them of the appointment and remember important dates such as birthdays. Telephone and computer technology is becoming increasingly sophisticated in helping us plan and organize our time and individuals should be encouraged to incorporate social networking techniques, text messages and emails in their daily routine.

Friendships with the Opposite Sex and Sexual Behaviour

Individuals with ADHD have a natural enthusiasm but this may result in them becoming excited and overaroused when meeting someone to whom they are attracted. This may be perceived as boisterousness or 'showing off'. Their eagerness may lead them to push limits and seek to escalate intimate relationships at a faster pace than is anticipated or acceptable to the other party. Role-plays designed to encourage the individuals to note the behaviour and body language of the person of interest, and then match and mirror this can be a useful exercise for the individual with ADHD. It teaches them to focus their attention and inhibit impulsive responses and/or assumptions. Role-play can also help young people who need to learn to assert themselves to say 'no' and explain that things are moving too fast (see peer pressure below; also assertiveness techniques in Frustration and Anger Module in Chapter 10).

It is important that adolescents learn the importance of responsible sexual behaviour and matters relating to sexual health. It is not the role of the therapist to give specific advice on these matters, but it is important to be aware that a tendency to act without thinking may mean that young people put themselves, and their partners, at risk of having unprotected sex which in turn may lead to sexually transmitted diseases and/or pregnancy. When such cases are present, the therapist should engage the individual in a process of consequential thinking and develop strategies with the young person that will reduce the likelihood of putting themselves at risk (e.g. forward thinking and planning; set up a peer 'buddy' system). They should of course be directed to appropriate services that can help them more precisely with advice about contraception and other important topics. Some females engage in promiscuous behaviour as they perceive sex to be a 'currency' for friendship. They attract boys' attention by making themselves sexually available in an attempt to gain a 'loving' relationship. This behaviour is born out of low self-esteem and social isolation and girls who engage in promiscuous behaviour need to learn more functional ways of making and maintaining friends, and develop self-confidence. People with ADHD are often very creative and the key is finding something that they are good at and encouraging them to channel their energy into developing it (e.g. sport, art, music). A sense of achievement will raise self-esteem.

Parenting

Most young people will become a parent at some stage and this brings additional challenges and responsibilities for the ADHD adult. Numerous studies of children with ADHD have reported high rates of parenting stress and negative cycles of interaction between parent and child (irrespective of whether their child has ADHD or not). As these children mature and have children of their own, they bring to the relationship an experience of negative cycles of interaction between parent and child. They have difficulty optimizing the home environment for their children because they have inconsistent parenting skills; a difficulty organizing childcare, setting boundaries, applying structure and routine, and difficulty dealing with oppositional behaviour and interpersonal conflict. ADHD parents often lack patience with their children. They are intolerant of challenging or attention seeking behaviours and may respond with overreactive, angry outbursts. Marital dissatisfaction and distress is common in ADHD adults and the therapist needs to assess for discord and conflict and make referrals for additional support as appropriate.

It is important that the therapist recognizes the increased risk of ADHD and related disorders in the offspring of adults with ADHD. There is 50 per cent likelihood that the offspring of an ADHD parent will also have ADHD. Thus, ADHD children become ADHD parents who, in turn, may have to cope with ADHD children. In such cases parental and marital stress are magnified manifold and comorbid disorders (e.g. anxiety, depression, substance misuse) and psychological problems are likely to require separate evaluation and management (specific techniques are provided in relevant modules). ADHD parents will also struggle in their endeavours to learn techniques to manage their ADHD children, for example, they are likely to do less well in behavioural parent training programmes (Sonuga-Barke, Daley and Thompson, 2002), suggesting that they should learn to manage their own ADHD symptoms first.

Unfamiliar Social Situations

While most people experience some anxiety about entering social situations in which they do not know anyone or very few people, people with ADHD are often acutely anxious about their ability to cope in such social settings. This is because they have often received negative feedback in the past when they have said the wrong thing, drawn unwanted attention to themselves, felt foolish or perceived disinterest or rejection by others (see Anxiety Module in Chapter 9 for further information). Social events can be intimidating and the client may be helped by carefully planning and rehearsing appropriate social behaviour beforehand. The therapist should review strategies that the client has found helpful in the past, along with techniques that they have successfully used to resolve problems in previous sessions that may be adapted for this purpose, for example, distracting or challenging negative thoughts. In sessions, rehearse conversations on topical news which are of interest to the client (e.g. from newspapers or magazine articles). The client should be guided to observe the 'rules' of interaction, such as turn-taking and body posture. In advance of a social event, the client could prepare topics for conversation from current news items and/or an interesting personal experience. This will 'arm' the client with something to talk about if they are worried they may run out of things to say and/or blurt out something inappropriate and look stupid. While this preparatory work in sessions may increase the client's confidence in social settings, he/she should be discouraged from talking about themselves all the time or monopolizing the conversation. An important technique to teach the client is to get the other person to talk about themselves by encouraging the client to ask questions and *listen* to the answers. The target person should not feel they are under interrogation but that the person they are talking to is really interested in what they have to say. Role-plays in sessions will be helpful for the client to get the balance right.

Important and/or Formal Conversations

People with ADHD can sometimes appear overfamiliar due to a lack of formality, poor impulse control and/or anxiety. This is very likely to be perceived by others as them not taking the matter or situation seriously. They may be viewed as superficial, uncaring and/or irresponsible. It is extremely important that individuals respond appropriately to the formality of a situation. For example, when interacting with individuals in authority, such as in a police interview, people with ADHD should be advised that being overly formal is better received than informality. Using titles can increase the sense of respect, so in some situation clients should be discouraged from using first names. In the workplace, they need to adopt a level of professionalism when interacting with colleagues and line management. The client may need to develop various impression management techniques such as the manner of addressing authority figures (e.g. the police or occupational managers); to review the use of slang and swear words commonly used by the client for acceptability as some words are unsuitable for formal occasions and may even cause offence; and pace speech differently as serious and important conversations are more likely to be paced more slowly.

One of the most frequently experienced 'formal settings' is that of the job interview. People with ADHD are often disadvantaged at interview by their ADHD symptoms which are exacerbated in this situation by anxiety causing them to become distracted, to not listen fully to questions, give impulsive responses and fidget in their seat. It is particularly important for people with ADHD to prepare well for such events. The first step is to work out a route to the destination with a time plan. Arriving late, hot and flushed is not a good start and will unnecessarily increase anxiety! Practising asking for questions to be repeated or rephrased can be a useful skill to develop and rehearse in therapy. The introduction of anxiety management techniques may also help empower the individual (see Anxiety Module in Chapter 9).

Peer Pressure

People with ADHD are often motivated to forge interpersonal relationships by a need to be liked, as they have difficulty getting along with others for any length of time. This means they may at times accede to unreasonable demands as they are eager to please others. Some individuals may be vulnerable to exploitation by others. This may mean they put pressure on themselves to fulfil certain roles or functions to a standard that they cannot achieve and they let down the person they are seeking to ingratiate or impress. They may behave in a way that is hurtful to other people who love them. The client needs to recognize this pattern of interaction, acknowledge it and resolve it. Sessions that focus on social perspective taking (by challenging negative thoughts and assumptions; identifying dysfunctional assumptions about weakness and failure; and acting out different roles of a dyad), rehearsing situations that acknowledge mistakes and apologizing for them will prepare the client to put this into practice 'in vivo'. Some individuals may be asked to comply with illegal requests, for example, to steal items or deliver drugs. They may come under peer pressure to take risks and engage in dangerous or reckless behaviour, for example, driving a car while drunk. Challenging negative thoughts about what it means to be a 'dissenter' may be a useful exercise.

Assertiveness techniques, described in Frustration and Anger Module in Chapter 10, will be helpful for the client to improve their ability to assert themselves with confidence, reduce feelings of inadequacy and choose a course of prosocial behaviour. The therapist can teach the client to evaluate the feasibility of requests by creating a list of advantages and disadvantages of complying with a request. It is recommended that initially these are set out in writing. Of course this is not possible *during* a social interaction and strategies for postponing decisions should be role played with the therapist; the client may be helped by rehearsing making a statement such as 'OK, I'll give it some thought and come back to you' or 'I can't talk about this right now as I have to go, but I'll phone you about it later'. Once the client become familiar with applying the technique, they should be encouraged to learn to apply it as a cognitive process so they can respond immediately. The written word however is powerful and should not be underestimated. Important choices should *always* be made by writing down advantages and disadvantages of options. Strategies for refusing to take on additional responsibilities or demands may be developed by the client and therapist role-playing scenarios in which the client rehearses saying 'no' and refusing to comply with a request.

Dealing with Criticism

People with ADHD are used to being criticized. They've been criticized by their parents at home, by teachers at school, and by youth workers in social settings.

To name a few, they may have been labelled obstinate, hyperactive, unruly, disruptive, oppositional, aggressive, rude, disobedient, unhelpful or lazy. Adults are taught that criticism should always be constructive but this technique of delivering criticism is not always applied. Even when it is, what the child or young person with ADHD hears is only the criticism. ADHD children have tried to do better, they have tried to improve and please their mother, teacher, youth worker, neighbours and friends but it never quite comes out right. Their intentions are good but are often not achieved because something gets in the way or distracts them from their course of action. However, just because they have always been criticized and are used to it does not mean that it no longer hurts. As time passes, individuals learn to put up a 'front' that defends them from critical onslaughts. This may be perceived as a lack of interest on the impact of their behaviour or attitude towards family and friends. The more criticism they receive, the more they protect themselves by disregarding it. This means that helpful feedback may be ignored. Clients will know about criticism as they have grown up with it. What they need to learn is the cycle of negativity outlined above, and how a negative attitude – which is their protective mechanism – provides a feedback loop that induces negative behaviour and critical attitudes from others. They need to learn to *listen* to the 'constructive' part of feedback, as this may provide important advice, and to become less hypersensitive to just one part of the message. Specific techniques for dealing with criticism are outlined in the Frustration and Anger Module in Chapter 10.

Apologizing and/or Admitting Mistakes

Saying sorry is a difficult skill as it involves admitting an error. This makes some people feel exposed. As children, people with ADHD have often felt blamed or held responsible for things for which they should not have been. They have often apologized for misdemeanours they have not fully understood, for example they cannot think through the outcome of a given situation and this has not been explicitly explained to them, such as drawing their attention to the potential dangers of playing with matches, playing 'chicken' across roads and railway tracks. In young adulthood, some individuals become pedantic and argumentative. They are more motivated to explain their point and be 'right' than think about an issue from a different perspective. It is not possible to be right all the time and the ability to compromise is important in negotiating interpersonal relationships. The therapist must help the client to find common ground and compromise, even if this means agreeing that a difference of opinion exists. However, because some people with ADHD have a defensive attitude and are intolerant of attitudes that are not similar to their own, they may behave in a way that is hurtful towards others. This means they need to recognize this pattern of interaction, acknowledge it and resolve it. Sessions that focus on social perspective taking (e.g. by challenging negative thoughts and assumptions that may identify dysfunctional assumptions about weakness and failure; acting out different roles of a dyad), rehearsing situations that acknowledge mistakes and apologizing for them will make it easier for the client to put this into practice 'in vivo'. Possibilities will probably present themselves that can be modelled in treatment sessions. For example, if a client forgets to do their homework or arrives late for a session, the therapist should express their own thoughts and feelings, for example, by saying that they felt annoyed that the client had arrived late for the session; that this had made them feel the treatment was a low priority. If a client misses a session the therapist should express deep concern about the welfare of the client, for example they may have had an accident. It is important that the therapist expresses their concern and/or distress *and* goes on to explicitly outline what the client may have done to reduce this, such as by telephoning to say he/she was late because of traffic.

Disclosure of ADHD Status

One of the most challenging social issues for people with ADHD is whether to reveal that they have the disorder to acquaintances, colleagues, friends and family. If they decide to make this disclosure, they need to evaluate at what stage in their relationship to do so and/or the most appropriate time. This is a very important issue for people with ADHD and a great source of anxiety. This topic has therefore been expanded in the Problem-Solving Module (Chapter 7). Some individuals resolve the issue by telling everyone they meet, irrespective of the anticipated outcome. Other people are very circumspect and do not even tell close members of their family.

A primary concern seems to be related to anxiety about how other people will respond/react to them if they know they have the disorder. They worry about possible stigma or inaccurate understanding about the disorder and believe this will affect them in the future, for example, through discrimination in the workplace. This was a particular concern for one client who worked as a manager in a supermarket and was terrified that his boss would find out that he had ADHD and that he took medication. Although he did well in his job and had been promoted, he thought this would prevent future promotions as he would be perceived as an individual unable to cope with greater managerial responsibility. This client was also very concerned that the staff he managed would discover that he had ADHD, as he believed he would become a source of ridicule and be defined as a 'nut' who needed psychiatric medication. This caused him to feel anxious and stressed as it took effort to 'hide' the disorder. The client felt he could not be himself and he felt isolated, which reinforced childhood feelings of being misunderstood, alone and differentiated from others.

Other people with ADHD respond in quite a different way. They act indiscriminately by being overtly open towards people they do not know very well and by giving them a lot of personal information and unnecessary detail about themselves, including their ADHD status. This causes people to feel uncomfortable and withdraw, which is perceived by the individual with ADHD as rejection. Alternatively other people may take advantage of the person with ADHD by viewing their social insecurities as an opportunity to exploit them (e.g. encouraging them to become involved in antisocial or criminal activities).

ADHD individuals report that they spend a lot of time trying to tease apart 'what is me' and 'what is ADHD', but very few come to any conclusions. This process is most likely to occur following diagnosis and treatment with medication. Indeed this process may become a source of distress as people feel that their personality is only associated with the ADHD disorder and not 'owned' by them as individuals. Following treatment, this preoccupation seems to become more marked and it is helpful to improve self-awareness by outlining a story or description of 'what I am like as a person'. Of course this will include characteristics that are generally associated with ADHD but will also include case-specific characteristics that relate personally to the individual. When completing this task the client should be encouraged to include as many positive aspects about themselves as possible. They should then imagine that they spend 6 months on a desert island and consider what other people (friends, family, work colleagues, partners) would miss about them during this period. By increasing an awareness of self – both the positive and negative – the client will be more able to improve the way he/she interacts with others. This means he/she will have greater confidence about how to explain to others about their ADHD condition and how it affects them personally, to whom they give their explanation and when.

Many members of the public have misconceptions about ADHD. The client themselves is often the best source of information about what it is like to have ADHD. Once the client has decided to disclose to someone that they have ADHD, it will be helpful if they can give that person some written information about ADHD and/or explain first-hand ways in which they can be helped and/or changes that can be made to the environment that will optimize performance – for example by being precise and succinct in instructions and in their interactions, by feeding back (constructively) if they are: getting over enthusiastic; interrupting others; standing too close or talking too loud. Instead of being expected to remember lots of information, they can write it down, for example having a 'things to do' list, shopping lists. Nevertheless some people prefer not to disclose their ADHD to anyone at all and hold their diagnosis as a safely guarded secret. Seeking social support is a constructive coping strategy and if individuals do not wish to 'come out' publicly they may find it helpful to link with ADHD support services. Often these groups have internet chat rooms that are an important source of practical information and emotional support, and which can be accessed anonymously.

Once they have disclosed having ADHD, some people will undoubtedly feel that they are being judged in some way and possibly experience rejection (real or perceived). This perception is likely to be stable in spite of the fact that several factors may have influenced the disclosure. The therapist can help the client examine whether this is an accurate perception and determine the dysfunctional assumptions that arise from (or result from) their thoughts.

SUMMARY

Social relationship difficulties can be the source of many problems associated with ADHD, including anxiety, depression, low self-esteem and substance misuse. Moreover, these comorbid difficulties, in addition to the core symptoms of ADHD themselves, can impact on social behaviour, through inattention, poor impulse control and restlessness or fidgeting. A common theme for individuals with ADHD is feeling isolated and misunderstood, despite paradoxically often seeming gregarious and self-assured in social situations. Clients' confidence in their social abilities can be improved thorough psychoeducation techniques regarding verbal and nonverbal communication. Several exercises have been suggested in the module to help individuals to determine their own social strengths and weaknesses, with strategies to develop both self-awareness and recognition of others' social intent. In particular, the module introduces techniques to improve the ability to recognize emotion by accurately identifying facial expressions, posture and gestures. Social situations are often transitory and variable in nature requiring swift responses and rapid change in social discourse. This is a considerable challenge for individuals who have developed a set of maladaptive social repertoires.

Group Treatment: Interpersonal Relationships Module

It is essential to prepare for group treatment by reading the chapter module. Six group sessions are outlined below, but the number of treatment sessions can be expanded or reduced as required.

Plan

Sessions 1 & 2	Starting activities Social Skills Questionnaire
Session 3	Psychoeducation
Sessions 4 & 5	Exercises (including clients' own)
Session 6	Group discussion of homework (for those who are comfortable to disclose) Obstacles and how to overcome them (role-play if necessary) Revision of psychoeducation

Starting Activities

With whom do we have interpersonal relationships? (parents, partner, friends, teachers/tutors, line-managers/supervisors, neighbours, in-laws, therapist). Ask the group to think about how often they have to interact with these people.

Are all relationships easy? Which relationships are more difficult and why? Highlight that difficulties can arise from specific circumstances, from personal characteristics, and from misunderstandings.

(*Continued*)

Is there something that you do that causes difficulties in relationships? (behaviours they have, behaviours they don't have, temperament/reactivity).
What are the consequences of dysfunctional interpersonal relationships?
Group discussion.
Hand out Social Skills Questionnaire (Table 8.1) and complete individually.
Group Discussion (compare individual differences, strengths/weaknesses).

Psychoeducation

How we present ourselves influences the impressions people have of us.
Verbal communication and nonverbal communication.

How will other people perceive the following behaviours?

Verbal communication (Perceived as…).
Speaking too quickly (intense, muddled, confused).
Mumbling (lacking confidence).
High pitch (over excitable).
Going off on tangents (disinterested).
Speaking too loudly (aggressive, intimidating).
Speaking too much (superficial, narcissistic).
Interrupting others (rude).
Nonverbal communication (Perceived as …).
Poor eye contact (disinterested, bored).
Slouching (lazy, disinterested).
Fidgeting (rude, disinterested, wanting to leave).
Pointing (provocative, intimidating).
Standing too close (provocative, intimidating).
It is important that we correctly recognize how other people are feeling.
How do we know how other people are feeling?
Have you ever got it wrong in the past?
What happened?
What were the consequences?
Group discussion: In what circumstances/settings do we need to adapt our social behaviour?
How do you do this? (Differences in how we behave with our family, friends, acquaintances, tutors, at home, in public places, at parties, in job interviews).
Have you got it wrong in the past?
What happened?
What were the consequences?
Group discussion: Disclosure of ADHD status.
Worry of rejection – don't disclose.
Providing information indiscriminately can make people feel uncomfortable.
Ask for people to provide constructive feedback on your behaviour.

(Continued)

Exercises

Role-play scenarios: discuss what happened, discuss how it made actors feel and what they were thinking during the role-play, point out things that you notice (e.g. positive verbal and nonverbal behaviours, things that could be done better, how emotions were displayed), discuss how the scenario could be improved, give specific indicators (e.g. stand further away, prepare what to say and make notes, be assertive, speak slower), repeat role-play but with actors introducing new material and incorporating suggestions discussed by the group, discuss again how the new role-play felt for the actors, point out positive differences from first action.

Select common problems that have been discussed in the starting activities that can be role played. Alternatively make some up such as the following suggestions:

You are at a party and you do not know anyone and start a conversation with two people but you keep interrupting them.
You are in a job interview.
You tell your new girlfriend/boyfriend that you have got ADHD.
You have upset a good friend as you forgot to meet them in town. They waited over an hour in the rain. Your friend is very angry as this has happened several times before. You are sorry and want to make up.
Someone you admire very much is pressing you to smoke cannabis but you don't want to.
Your boss is telling you off for being late for work again. You don't like him and you are feeling very angry as you feel he picks on you.

Homework

Interactions and behaviour are reciprocal. If I say to you 'hello', you will say (hello). If I hold out my hand and say 'hello' you will respond by reaching out to shake my hand.

Introduce the idea of 'behavioural experiments'. This involves deliberately changing a behaviour in order to see the impact this has on the response of the other person. (The person should not inform the other person that this is an 'exercise'). For example:

1. Give five compliments to someone you like when you next see them (parent, friend, partner).
2. Next time you see someone with whom you have had a 'difficult' relationship, make a point of speaking to them. Do not talk about yourself. Have a conversation about a neutral topic. Ask them about their work, weekend, next holiday.
3. Smile and say hello to people you see every day but pass by in the corridor.
4. Tell a friend and/or partner the things that you really like about them.

(*Continued*)

5. Tell a partner and/or parent how much you appreciate the things that they do for you or have done for you in the past.
6. Start a conversation with someone that you do not know (e.g. at a party) and find out what they like to do in their spare time.
7. Identify three stories of interest in a newspaper (neutral topics that do not involve politics or religion). Discuss these with people you meet.

Discuss outcome of homework set in sessions – if something went wrong, find out why and resolve, possibly incorporating a role-play in the session.

9

ANXIETY MODULE

Anxiety is a common condition in the non-ADHD population but its prevalence is increased in individuals with ADHD with comorbidity rates reported to be around 25 per cent in children (Biederman, Newcorn and Sprich, 1991) and rising to 50 per cent in adults (Biederman *et al.*, 1993). When present as a comorbid condition with ADHD, anxiety exacerbates low self-esteem, stress intolerance and aspects of cognition such as impairment in working memory (Tannock, 2000). In addition to those who meet the criteria for a comorbid anxiety disorder, there are also many individuals who fall short of this classification but who experience mild to moderate anxiety that affects them in certain activities. This usually stems from past experiences, a lack of self-confidence and poor self-efficacy.

It could be argued that comorbidity rates of ADHD and anxiety are artefacts of a similarity between ADHD symptoms and anxiety symptoms (e.g. restlessness, inattention, ceaseless mental energy). However a 25 per cent overlap has been reported in both community and clinic studies (Anderson *et al.*, 1987; Biederman *et al.*, 1991; Millstein *et al.*, 1997), suggesting that it is unlikely that comorbidity rates simply reflect symptoms being 'counted' twice in around one-quarter of cases. In some cases anxiety has been reported as a side-effect of stimulant medication and when this appears to occur following treatment, then it may be helpful to recommend a psychiatric review and possible change of medication to nonstimulant treatment.

Anxiety disorders present in several forms; for example, generalized anxiety, social phobia, simple phobia, agoraphobia, panic disorder, obsessive-compulsive disorder and post-traumatic stress disorder. Our clinical impression is that people with ADHD are more likely to have generalized anxiety, but social phobia, panic disorder and obsessive-compulsive disorder have also been reported by our clients at the clinic. Of course these are not mutually exclusive categories and people with ADHD may have problems associated with one or more of these disorders. Difficulties may be more

Cognitive-Behavioural Therapy for ADHD in Adolescents and Adults: A Psychological Guide to Practice, Second Edition. Susan Young and Jessica Bramham.

prominent according to the social, academic or occupational demands and/or their life course at the time. For example, an individual may have generalized anxiety problems and social phobia depending on the presenting situation, and in times of great stress they may additionally experience symptoms of panic.

Due to the overlap between ADHD symptoms and anxiety symptoms, it is important to conduct a thorough and comprehensive assessment of the anxiety-related presenting problem, and ascertain the relationship between the thoughts, beliefs, feelings and behaviours of the individual about their ability to complete a task or perform competently in a situation. As in the usual cognitive behavioural treatment of anxiety, it is important to provide a psychoeducational component, outlining the anxiety model and the relationship between cognitions and behaviour.

FUNCTIONAL DEFICITS IN ADOLESCENTS AND ADULTS

In today's society, people are evaluated by success, by the job they do, the house they live in, the car they drive. These icons represent achievement. There are multiple demands to fulfil, requiring an ability to multitask and take on multiple responsibilities and roles, such as mother, father, wife, husband, daughter, son, friend, congregation member, youth leader, mentor, manager, employee, executive. These roles have to be juggled and it can feel as though there are many plates in the air that have to be kept spinning. Society is fast and busy, and people with ADHD favour speed over accuracy, so when they work at a rapid pace they make errors and they fail.

Feeling anxious makes everything else that one has to think or do much harder. Anxiety affects cognitive processes by affecting appraisal and evaluation of situations, causing a shift of focus internally and to exaggerated self-monitoring and self-regulation. Anxiety increases attentional difficulties and impulsivity. It can inhibit the ability to reason in a rational way. Thus, ADHD individuals, who already have cognitive vulnerabilities, will become even more vulnerable in an anxiety-provoking situation by performing less competently. For an individual with anxiety, this means that they have a 'double dose' of cognitive impairments due to ADHD symptoms becoming much more pronounced at times when they probably need to focus the most.

This causes a difficulty with the neuropsychological assessment of ADHD symptoms (attention and impulsivity) as clients may become very anxious in the testing environment. In order to evaluate individual differences in strengths and weaknesses, many cognitive tests start with very easy items and become progressively more difficult. This means that an individual will consistently reach a stage when they are unable to answer a question or resolve a problem or puzzle. This highlights their difficulties and the testing procedure may reinforce underlying beliefs that they are 'stupid' and/or remind them of negative school experiences. If individuals become very anxious they are unlikely to do well and give up easily on tasks, causing them to not reach their potential and the tester underestimating potential performance. Children with comorbid anxiety and ADHD have shown greater impairment on tasks that put demand on short-term or working memory (Pliszka, 1989); that is, tasks that involve both active processing and transient storage of information (Baddeley, 1986). It is possible that anxiety diverts some resources away from processing and storage within the working memory system. However, it has also been suggested that anxiety has a motivational function as it increases arousal, which may in turn improve attentional control. This is likely to occur in tasks that do not require retention of information (i.e. memory processing) but require the individual to inhibit a response, for example, continuous performance or stop tasks. On such tasks, children with ADHD and comorbid anxiety may perform better (Pliszka *et al.*, 1993). Unfortunately such studies have not been conducted with adults with comorbid ADHD and anxiety.

Predisposing factors for comorbid ADHD and anxiety are reported to be perinatal complications such as late pregnancy difficulties, delivery problems and the neonatal period, particularly in those without a familial history of ADHD (Sprich-Buchminster *et al.*, 1993). Thus, many individuals enter the world with a predisposition to develop anxious and dysfunctional coping strategies. These usually become expressed following persistent demoralization and criticism from others (both real and perceived), causing individuals to become nervous about performing tasks or entering situations. Disadvantages regarding academic attainment, experience of failure in the workplace and difficulty getting along with others can lead young adults with ADHD to develop 'anticipatory anxiety' regarding events in which they have previously experienced disappointment and/or failure. In addition to worries about future events and interpersonal performance, people with anxiety and ADHD may also become preoccupied with their past behaviours and/or performance. In such cases individuals may re-live negative experiences, for example, when they believe they have performed badly; when they believe that people have judged them to be 'below standard' compared with others; and times of embarrassment regarding errors of judgement and/or inappropriate behaviour in the past.

For ADHD adolescents and adults, anxiety is likely to be expressed in multiple ways. People with ADHD are more likely to suffer from marked self-consciousness or susceptibility to embarrassment or humiliation stemming from childhood (Keller et al., 1992). For most people with ADHD anxiety starts in school as 'performance anxiety', for example, when they have to stand up in class and read out loud. They may make mistakes and miss out words, or even skip whole lines. Their peers can then tease them or bully them; they get laughed at and called names. In such situations, they may either withdraw or impulsively lash out. Either way this has negative social consequences and ADHD children begin to lack the ability to interact confidently with their peers. Some children overcompensate by trying to overly please others, or by bullying other children. Others compensate by 'acting the clown'. They may seek friendships at school from children outside of their peer set, in other words children older or younger than themselves, or by preferring the company of adults. With the passing of time small anxieties become greater anxieties; this is especially exacerbated as they progress through education into young adulthood when greater academic and social demands are required. Before they know where they are, the young anxious ADHD child has developed a way of interacting with the world that is based on uncertainty and insecurity. Anxiety becomes generalized, affecting their beliefs and confidence regarding whether they will achieve in just about anything that they attempt to do. This often results in a preoccupation or overconcern about their level of competence to fulfil various roles and domains of function.

A generally anxious disposition about everything and everyone they encounter may become more specifically focused as social anxiety for people with ADHD. Feeling different from their peers leads some individuals to compare themselves regularly and unfavourably to others, resulting in their selectively attending to their own perceived negative features and the positive characteristics of others. Some people may frequently require reassurance in social situations, for example: 'Did I come across ok? I wasn't tactless, was I?' They worry that they are being observed by others in social gatherings and become self-conscious and clumsy. Some people try to over compensate by acting the fool and being the 'life and soul of the party'. In such cases, a target of anxiety treatments should focus not only on reducing anxious cognitions, feelings and behaviour, but also to aim to calm down the individual so that they do not respond in an overly excited manner, drawing undue attention to themselves by behaving in a bizarre and/or inappropriate manner (sometimes perceived by others as childish). This is not to dampen down the natural creativity and enthusiasm of people with ADHD but to encourage the individual to behave with more control and maturity.

The increased prevalence of obsessive-compulsive disorder (OCD) in individuals with ADHD may be mediated by its links with Tourette's syndrome (Pauls and Leckman, 1986), since the rate of ADHD is higher among those with Tourette's syndrome and the rate of Tourette's is elevated among those with ADHD. OCD symptoms are also likely to worsen attentional difficulties by diverting functional resources to the obsessive thoughts. However, symptoms that appear to be associated with OCD may be strategies developed by people with ADHD to compensate for an attention deficit by regularly checking for errors or things they may have forgotten. Nevertheless as a person becomes increasingly anxious, this checking behaviour may become more ritualistic and obsessive. Clients may be embarrassed by their private obsessions and/or compulsions and this may cause them to avoid mentioning them to clinicians particularly during their assessment. They may hope that by having their ADHD treated, their OCD symptoms may also disappear. Overfocussing in an obsessive or perseverative fashion can lead to failure to complete tasks, due to concentrating on a minor aspect of a task to excess. Some individuals with these difficulties may prefer to not do a task at all, rather than risk doing it incorrectly. Exploration and challenging thoughts are useful treatment strategies, in addition to systematic desensitization to reduce ritualistic checking behaviours.

ASSESSMENT OF ANXIETY

The Companion Website provides a questionnaire, the Anxiety Checklist, that will help the therapist determine and classify the type of anxiety-related problems experienced by the client in the past week. The Anxiety Checklist is presented in Table 9.1 and is designed

Table 9.1 Anxiety checklist

In the past week, rate how often you have experienced the following symptoms:	*Never*	*Occasionally*	*Sometimes*	*Often*	*Very often*	*Always*
Generalized anxiety						
I have worried about money e.g. being able to pay bills, debts					✓	
I have worried about not coping at work, school				✓		
I have worried about my health						✓
I have worried that things will go wrong in the future, anticipating disappointment/failure					✓	
I have worried that I am not a capable of being a good parent, employee, son/daughter						✓
Social anxiety						
I felt self-conscious			✓			
I avoided social events, e.g. parties		✓				
I avoided crowds	✓					
I was concerned about performance				✓		
I was worried about meeting new people		✓				
Panic						
I felt constriction in my chest						✓
I felt heart palpitations						✓
I thought I was having a heart attack						✓
I felt dizzy and faint					✓	
I felt the blood rushing around my head				✓		
Obsessive-compulsive disorder						
I felt uncomfortable if the house was not clean and tidy	✓					
I needed to check everything several times before I was confident that it was right		✓				
I had to do things in routines otherwise I worried	✓					
I had intrusive thoughts	✓					
I tended to overfocus		✓				

around themes that are regularly discussed by our clients at the clinic as sources of anxiety (e.g. generalized anxiety, social anxiety, panic, obsessional-compulsive problems), in order to help the client and therapist to identify the subtype of comorbid presenting problem of anxiety. Table 9.1 gives an example of a completed Anxiety Checklist for a client with generalized anxiety and who had experienced an acute panic attack relating to feeling overwhelmed by pressure to meet a deadline at work. Thus, the Anxiety Checklist provides a helpful guide to identifying whether anxiety problems are general or more specified, and form a basis for discussion and exploration, in order that the therapist may take an adaptive approach to treatment and conceptually plan and frame treatment, although it should be borne in mind that categories of anxiety are not mutually exclusive.

The Anxiety checklist provided on the Companion Website deliberately excludes the names of categories (i.e. generalized anxiety disorder, social anxiety, panic disorder, obsessive-compulsive disorder) in order that the client's responses are not biased. These categories are included in the Table 9.1 for illustrative purposes only.

COGNITIVE BEHAVIOURAL THERAPY

There are two primary differences when treating people with ADHD and comorbid anxiety compared with treating people without ADHD who have anxiety.

1. It is important to acknowledge the overlap in anxiety and ADHD symptoms and attempt to disentangle symptoms that are better addressed by the techniques discussed in the sessions to improve attention, improve memory, and reduce impulsivity (e.g. see Attention Module (Chapter 3), Memory Module (Chapter 4) and Impulsivity Module (Chapter 6).
2. Since ADHD adolescents and adults have difficulty in delaying gratification, it is important to introduce an immediate reward system to positively reinforce success and achievement on a much more frequent basis than that usually applied.

The CBT model of treatment proposed involves four fundamental stages to the treatment process: psychoeducation about the anxiety model from a cognitive behavioural perspective; learning to cope with negative thoughts; the development of self-control; and changing behaviour.

Psychoeducation

Psychoeducation is an important part of the treatment process. It is important to explain to the client what happens to them when they become anxious or worried and apply this to the anxiety-provoking experiences of the client. This includes teaching the client how their anxiety impacts on their thoughts, feelings and behaviour, and explaining that there is an interrelationship between these factors. To a certain extent, this also means normalizing anxiety as a functional process. Everybody becomes anxious or worried at some point in their lives. It is a normal and healthy reaction. Anxiety or worry usually arises during times of stress or danger. It allows preparation for fight or flight, in other words whether to stand one's ground or whether to run away. People understand that if they were to be put into a cage with tigers then they would feel anxious. Their anxiety would cause them to have a sharpened awareness of pending danger, and prepare to protect themselves. Anxiety is dysfunctional if this process is activated when the person is not in the tigers' cage, but when, for example, they have to go to their sister's birthday party. This explanation will usually make perfect sense to the client.

The Companion Website contains an Anxiety Chart called: 'What happens to you when you become anxious?' This introduces the client to the core components that develop and maintain anxiety – thoughts, feelings, physical reactions and behaviour. Encouraging the client to complete the chart by separating out these factors will be helpful when the model of anxiety is introduced as the client will be able to theoretically relate the model to their own experience. An example of a completed Anxiety Chart for a person with anxiety about completing a project on time for work is presented in Box 9.1. A blank copy is provided on the Companion Website.

Box 9.1 Anxiety chart: What happens to you when you become anxious?

Thoughts	*Feelings*
• I can't focus • I'm going to lose concentration • There must be something seriously wrong with me if I can't do this • Everyone else will criticize me • I'm going mad • I can't manage this • I'm useless	• I feel frightened • I feel panicky • I feel like I've lost control • I feel that fear is going to take over • I feel on edge and irritable • I feel uncomfortable
Physical reactions	*Behaviour*
• Increased fidgeting • Sweaty palms • Increased heart rate • Going pale as blood rushes to major organs • Stammering • Restless pacing • 'Butterflies' in stomach	• Not wanting to go out • Avoiding social situations • Making excuses not to do things • Using tobacco, alcohol, drugs, comfort foods etc. to calm nerves • Only going out when someone else is there • Overcompensating by being outgoing and/or overwhelming • Playing the fool or behaving in a reckless manner

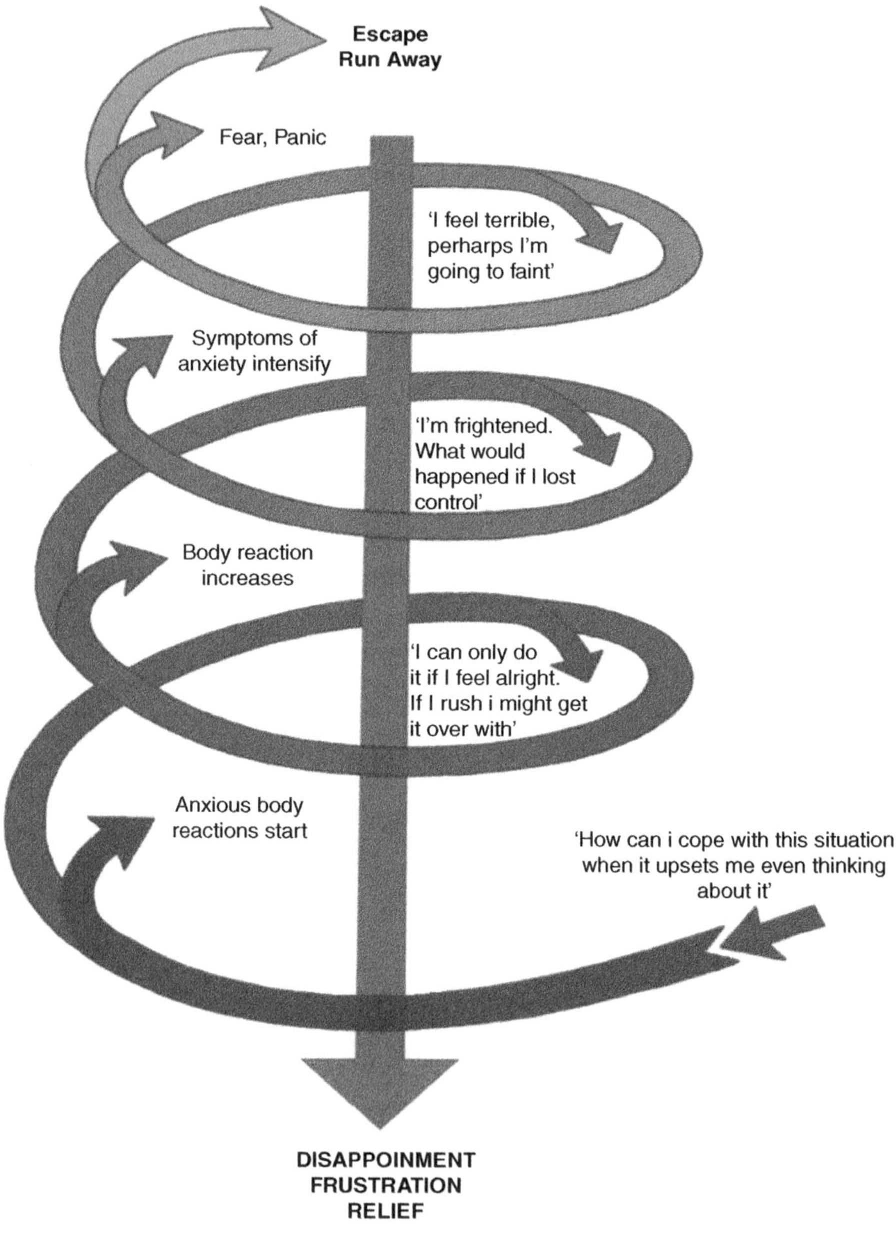

Figure 9.1 Anxiety spiral

Explaining the cognitive-behavioural model of anxiety, that is, the interrelationship between thoughts, feelings and behaviour in the development and maintenance of anxiety, usually makes complete sense to the client on an intellectual level. For example, explaining that feeling anxious about a missing pending deadline set by their manager at work may influence *thoughts* (e.g. by thinking 'I'm useless, I never get it right. I won't get promoted'), which may lead to *physical reactions* of nervousness (e.g. nausea and dry mouth) and *feelings* of irritability and rising panic. This in turn influences *behaviour* (e.g. give up trying, making excuses, avoiding the situation and stay at home).

Alongside learning about the interrelationships between thoughts, feelings and behaviour, the client must also understand how these factors are dynamic and work together to cause deterioration in functioning. This becomes a cycle or a downward negative spiral of increasing anxiety, with thoughts, feelings and behaviours fuelling each other as they become more severe. Figure 9.1 gives a visual representation of the Anxiety Spiral and this is also included on the Companion Website in handout format. Figure 9.2 shows a completed 'Thought bubble anxiety spiral' and a blank version of this is on the Companion Website which may be completed in sessions with the client.

Anxiety can be described as a three-legged table (see Figure 9.3). If one of the legs is knocked out, then the anxiety table will be unstable, fall over and be eliminated. Anxiety exacerbates cognitive deficits and if the client can learn to reduce their anxiety then they are more likely to cope in settings and situations perceived as anxiety-provoking. The 'legs' of the table are thoughts, feelings and behaviour, and these will be discussed in the following sections. Explain to the client that you are going to teach them ways to knock out each of these legs; that is, by using a 'three-pronged attack'.

Anxiety Management Strategies

Coping with Negative Thoughts

Anxiety is associated with unpleasant negative thoughts. These are automatic and flash through the mind in situations that provoke anxiety. For example, if an individual worries about what other people think of him/her, then they may feel anxious when they are talking to people they wish to impress but do not know very well. This may mean that the individual will alter their behaviour in order to reduce feelings of anxiety, such as by not contributing to the conversation in order to avoid being evaluated by others. Common thoughts expressed by our clients follow.

- Thinking there must be something seriously wrong with them.
- Thinking that they are being foolish.
- Thinking that they are being criticized by others.
- Thinking that they are not mentally well.
- Thinking badly about themselves.
- Putting themselves down.
- Thinking that they are a failure.

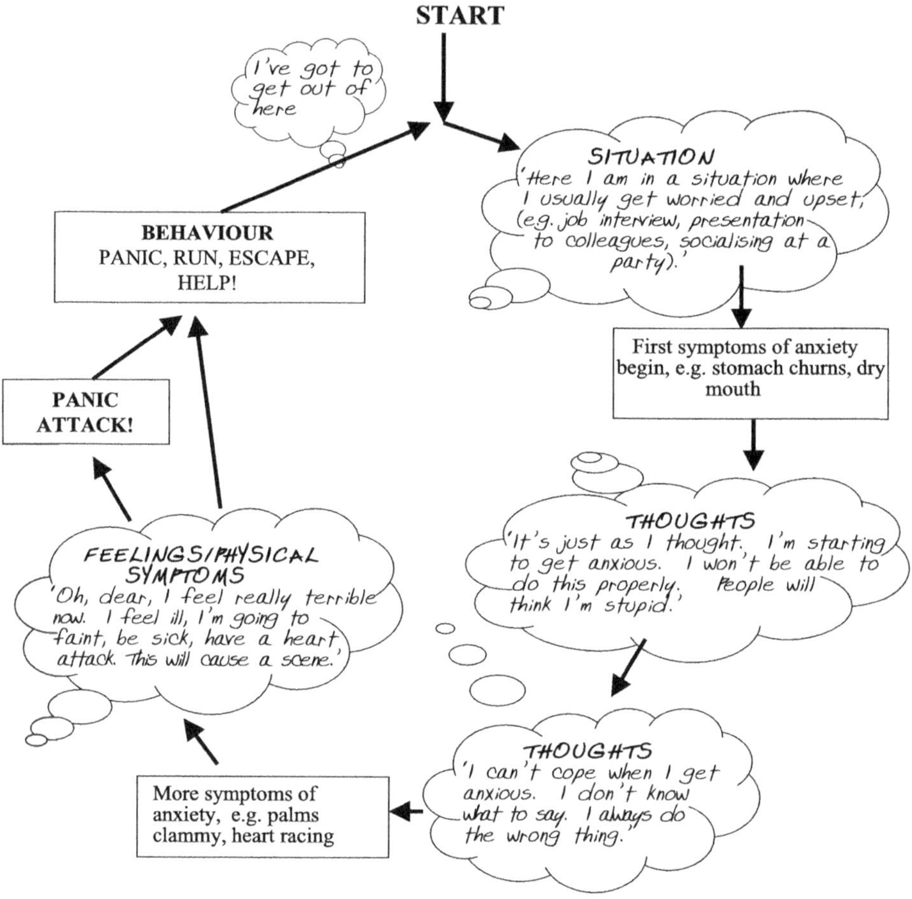

Figure 9.2 Thought bubble anxiety spiral

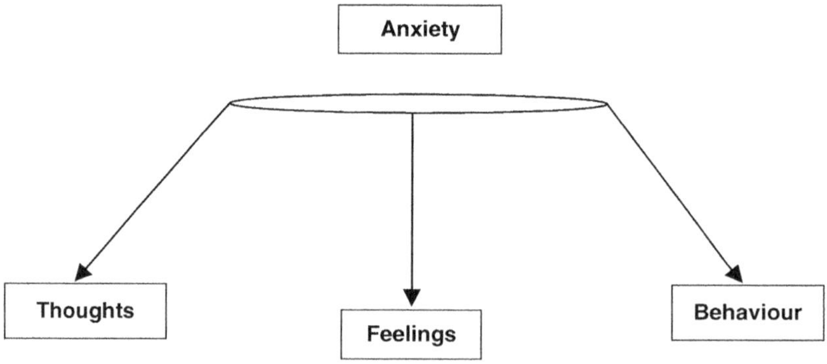

Figure 9.3 The three-legged anxiety table

Clients need to learn how what they think and believe affects their feelings and behaviour. For example, if a person wakes up hearing a crash in the middle of the night and believes this is a burglar they may feel frightened and call the police. If they believe it is because they have left a window open and the wind has blown something over, they may feel less frightened, go and pick up the object and go back to sleep. Thus, different thoughts in the same situation lead one to experience different feelings and to carry out different behaviours.

Negative, anxiety-provoking thoughts are difficult to identify for a number of reasons. They are habitual and flash though everyone's minds without us even realizing. They are automatic and occur without effort, and some thoughts further perpetuate anxiety, for example:

- 'I'm going to make a fool of myself' (anticipation);
- 'I can't cope with this anymore' ('I-can't-stand-it-itis');
- 'I can't breathe, I'm choking' (misinterpretation of body reactions); and
- 'I've got to get out of here' (thoughts of escape);

A common technique that has been shown to be useful to help clients identify negative thoughts is keeping a 'Thought Diary'. This is a record of the situation they were in, what was going though their mind at the time and how they were feeling. These feelings can then be rated for how much they believe in them. An example is provided in Table 9.2 for an individual who was having difficulties at work, who is feeling under pressure from their employer to meet a deadline and also having social anxiety regarding socializing with colleagues. A blank version is provided on the Companion Website.

Once the individual has learned to apply cognitive techniques to challenge negative thoughts, the diary can also be used to record the challenges and then re-rate how much they believe in them. Using this method, the client will be able to evaluate the success of their cognitive challenges demonstrated by a weakening in their belief

Table 9.2 Example of a thought diary

Time and date	*Situation*	*Feelings*	*Thoughts*	*How much do I believe this? (%)*
Mon 4th 8.15am	Getting ready for work	Feeling jittery and a bit sick	I will never survive this week.	40
Mon 4th 10.15am	Boss asks to see me in his office	Terrified	I'm going to be fired.	50
Tues 5th 6.15 p.m.	Going to pub with colleagues	Feeling out of place	I've got nothing to say	70
Wed 6th 12.00 p.m.	Deadline at end of day	Complete panic	I can't do this. It's all over	50

Table 9.3 Example of negative challenges in a thought diary

Time and date	*Situation*	*Feelings*	*Thoughts*	*How much do I believe this? (%)*	*Cognitive Challenge*	*How much do I believe the thought now? (%)*
Mon 4th 8.15am	Getting ready for work	Feeling jittery and a bit sick	I will never survive this week.	40	I felt like this last Monday and got through the week	20
Mon 4th 10.15am	Boss asks to see me in his office	Terrified	I'm going to be fired	50	I don't know for sure I'll be fired. I was called in last Friday when the boss told me that my last project was now implemented and working very well	20
Tues 5th 6.15 p.m.	Going to pub with colleagues	Feeling out of place	I've got nothing to say	70	Of course I have something to say. I'm not mute…all I have to do is ask people about themselves. I'll ask what they are doing at the weekend	40
Wed 6th 12.00 p.m.	Deadline at end of day	Complete panic	I can't do this. It's all over	50	I can do this. I am catastrophizing. I must relax and calm down. I have worked under pressure before.	30

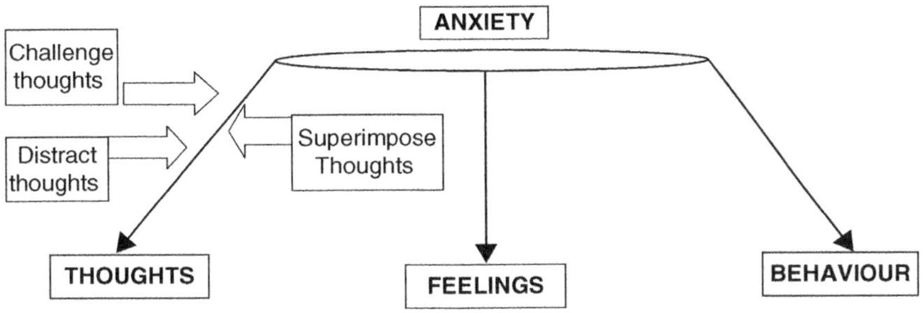

Figure 9.4 The three-legged anxiety table: Coping with negative thoughts

system. Table 9.3 provides an example of negative challenges and a blank version is provided on the Companion Website.

Figure 9.4 shows the three techniques that can be used to cope with negative thoughts: (1) challenge negative thoughts – Tuesday 5th; (2) superimpose negative thoughts with more positive thoughts – Monday 4th; and (3) distraction from thinking negative thoughts – Wednesday 6th. In practice the techniques applied by the client will depend much on the context and their personal preference. Figure 9.4 is included on the Companion Website in handout format.

In sessions, the therapist will need to teach the techniques, rehearse them with the client and determine what works best and when. For example, ruminative thoughts about future performance may be best dealt with by cognitive challenges; superimposing negative thoughts with positive thoughts may be helpful to motivate the client to finish a task; distracting themselves from negative cognitions may be more helpful when coping with social anxiety. Thus, experiencing anxiety is a *process* and techniques will vary in efficacy depending on at what point they are applied in the process. Table 9.4 outlines some suggestions for techniques that are appropriate for the different stages of anxiety.

Table 9.4 Cognitive techniques and the process of anxiety

Onset of anxiety	Identify negative automatic thoughts
	Cognitive challenges
	Identify thinking errors
Midst of anxiety	Coping self-statements
	Self-instructions
	Flashcards
	Distraction techniques
Decreasing anxiety	Self-praise
	Rewards

Challenging negative thoughts

Just as thoughts can increase anxiety and low mood, they can also decrease it. Different thoughts in the same situation lead people to experience different feelings and to carry out different behaviours. This means they can learn to change their behaviour by controlling their thoughts. This is a difficult skill to master. The therapist should begin by explaining to the client that when they feel anxious or distressed, then they are particularly vulnerable to 'thinking errors'. This essentially means that the client is viewing the world through glasses that distort what they see. Common thinking errors for people with ADHD are that an individual catastrophizes and/or jumps to conclusions ('it's all completely hopeless, it will never work and I'll be ruined, no one will ever speak to me again'). Table 9.5 describes some common thinking errors and these are also provided on the Companion Website in Table 9.5a, together with an exercise in a format that can be given to the client and used as a basis of discussion. The most likely categories for thinking errors are provided in Table 9.5 but note that thinking-error categories are not mutually exclusive. Usually, by using these materials and by looking back over the thinking errors they have recorded in their Thought Diaries, the client will recognize the thinking errors common to them.

In order to break the cycle, the client must learn to change old ways of thinking, this means challenging their thoughts and assumptions. Assumptions are 'if ... then ...' statements such as 'if I don't do this report in time for the meeting, then I'm a complete failure'.

One way of encouraging the client to challenge their thinking is to get them to imagine that they are a clever lawyer who is 'cross-examining' a thought. For example, they could ask themselves the following questions.

1. What evidence do I have for thinking in this way?
2. What is the evidence that I can't cope? Think of times when I have successfully coped in the past.
3. Am I overestimating the likelihood of this event happening?
4. What is the worst that could happen?
5. What can I do about it?

These questions are presented in a 'handout' format on the Companion Website (see Table 9.5b), together with the example of cognitive challenges that can be applied to challenge common negative thoughts shown in Table 9.6.

Fortunately, the ADHD personality seems to be predisposed to engage in a 'cognitive challenge process' as young adults with ADHD have a tendency to positively reappraise stressful situations (Young, 2005). This means they seek to cognitively reframe situations and are receptive to thinking about their problems in a different way. This

Table 9.5 Thinking errors

Thinking errors	*Definition*
All or nothing	The client sees everything in black and white and cannot appreciate that there is any middle ground or 'grey areas'. e.g. 'I can never concentrate on anything'
Overgeneralizing	The client draws a general conclusion on the basis of a single event. They often assume that something will always happen even when this has occurred on one occasion. e.g. 'I will mess it up next time'
Catastrophizing	Exaggerating or overestimating the likelihood of events can be due to catastrophizing. The client often thinks that whatever can go wrong will go wrong. e.g. 'Because I didn't pay the gas bill on time, I'm going to be evicted'
Personalizing	The client blames themselves for anything unpleasant. They believe everything people do or say is a reaction to them. They assume everything is their fault. e.g. 'She had left the room because I upset her'
Negative focus	Positive aspects of a situation are ignored or misinterpreted, so that the client tends to look on the 'dark side' and is pessimistic. e.g. 'At my work appraisal, they said I needed to learn a new skill, so I must be useless at my job'.
Jumping to conclusions	The client has an automatic negative interpretation of events, even in absence of facts. This may mean that they tend to predict the future or read minds, when there is little evidence to support these predictions. e.g. 'I have been too slow, she thinks I cannot possibly do this'
Shoulds and Oughts	The client believes they are failing to meet standards or expectations, without considering whether they are reasonable or realistic. They may believe they should always get everything right. e.g. 'I ought to always be on time'.

Exercise

What are the following thinking errors?

1. 'I did that badly. What's the point in doing it again?'
Answer: *Negative focus*

2. 'I upset her by blurting out gossip. I'm a terrible person.'
Answer: *Overgeneralizing*

3. 'I should have finished everything I planned to do.'
Answer: *Shoulds and oughts*

4. 'Everything goes wrong.'
Answer: *Catastrophizing*

Table 9.6 Examples of negative thoughts and challenges

Negative thoughts	*Examples of cognitive challenges*
I am just not good enough.	I am not perfect. Like everybody I am good at some things and not so good at others.
What is the point in trying?	If I don't try, I won't know. Trying in itself will broaden my experience and skill. Nobody is expecting me to do it perfectly.
What if I make a mistake – it would be awful.	Everybody makes mistakes. It is good to make mistakes because that is the best way to learn.
I have nothing to say – I'm boring.	I have opinions, thoughts and feelings. I like reading and going out. Perhaps I need to improve my ability to express myself. I can practice.
Nobody likes me.	There are people who like me. I have had good relationships in the past and will in future.
Everybody else has a better time than I do – they're happy.	I don't know this for a fact. Just because they seem busier doesn't mean they are more satisfied.
It would be best if I stayed away from people, because I'm no good at relationships.	If I stay away I don't give myself a chance. I'll probably be all right if I can just relax.
I might break down emotionally in front of people and feel ridiculous.	I have good reason to be upset. People are a lot more understanding than I think. It would not be the end of the world. What is wrong with showing emotion?
I'm hopeless at everything. I'll never sort myself out like this.	Just take one step at a time. Totally condemning myself is nonsense. I've overcome more difficult problems than this.

characteristic probably leads people with ADHD to face disappointments with resilience, and gives them the determination to try again.

A second way of inducing clients to challenge thoughts is to teach them to take the perspective of another person. Social-perspective taking is a very helpful technique, as often clients expect something of themselves that they would not expect from others. The therapist should invite the client to imagine that a friend came to them with the same problem, what would they tell them? Would they view it in the same way, in other words, believing that there are no solutions and they will fail? Techniques that look at alternative interpretations or alternative outcomes may be helpful, for example replacing thoughts like 'I can't cope' with 'This is difficult, but I can manage if I take it a step at a time'.

Superimposing positive thoughts

A problem for people with ADHD is that they often do not have a plethora of 'successful' experiences to counterbalance life's disappointments. The scales seem tipped against them and every idea they have or every project they start comes to nothing – usually because they do not stick to it and either become distracted by something else that takes their interest and so give up when it becomes more difficult, or it takes longer than anticipated to finish. This means that their negative automatic thoughts may have some evidence base, and this possibility makes it a more difficult task for the individual to challenge these as 'thinking errors'. One solution is to superimpose negative thoughts and assumptions with positive cognitions and beliefs, such as making positive and motivating self-statements.

Identifying and challenging negative thoughts is helpful to reduce the onset and escalation of anxiety. However, once a person is involved in a full-blown anxiety attack, it is not always easy for them to apply cognitive challenges. In such cases, the client should be encouraged to list the cognitive challenges that have been particularly appropriate and efficacious and put these on small 'flashcards' and keep them in a wallet or purse. Then, if they become very anxious and cannot engage themselves in an alternative thinking process, all they have to remember is to look at the card which will jolt them into engaging in the process.

Superimposing positive thoughts rather than challenging negative thoughts may be a more helpful technique for patients with ADHD because of their resilience and tendency not to give up. This may be a more 'natural' way for them to cope with negative thoughts, to identify them and immediately superimpose them with a more positive and motivating thought. For example, if the client thinks 'I can't cope with this situation, I am going to lose control', they replace the thought with 'I can cope, I am in control of this situation'.

'Coping self-talk' in the form of making positive self-statements and giving self-instructions to talk themselves through the anxiety process may be helpful strategies that are more accessible to the individual at a stage of advanced anxiety. However, replacing negative thoughts is also a process that takes practise and patience but with time it becomes easier as it becomes as automatic as 'old ways' of thinking.

Box 9.2 Positive self-statements

Anxiety is not harmful; it is a normal human response.
I can cope with these feelings.
There is no need to escape or avoid this situation, if I just carry on the anxiety will subside.
As I relax the anxiety will begin to ease off.
Relax, breathe gently and try to let go of the tension.

There are many different positive statements that will help to replace negative thoughts. Some examples are shown below in Box 9.2 (and are also on the Companion Website in 'wallet-size' handout form) and the client should note that some cue them to apply other techniques that will help 'knock out' other legs of the anxiety table.

Distraction from negative thoughts

A further cognitive technique that may be applied once the individual is in the midst of feeling acutely anxious, is that of cognitive distractions. This involves teaching the client to distract themselves from thinking negative and damaging thoughts that serve to increase anxiety. To work, this must involve a specific and directed active process, such as making themselves engage in mental arithmetic or counting items, as opposed to reading a newspaper and relaxing. In the latter case the client is likely to find that they have read a whole article but not taken in any of the information. The active process could be either cognitive or physical. If clients distract themselves from negative thinking by engaging in periods of intense physical activity (e.g. running, team sports), this is likely to not only reduce the negative thinking but relieve feelings of agitation and restlessness.

Controlling Feelings of Anxiety

To understand how anxiety affects us, it is necessary to be aware of the physical sensations it can produce. These include breathlessness, nausea, palpitations, dizziness, sweating, and chest pains. Individuals with extreme anxiety may believe, or have believed in the past, that there is something seriously wrong with their health. For example, they may have interpreted these physical symptoms or signs as coronary heart failure and believe that they are having a heart attack. Common feelings expressed by our clients with ADHD include:

- feeling frightened and panicky;
- feeling they are losing control;
- feeling confused and having difficulty focusing on a task or on thoughts;
- 'flooding' of thoughts and ideas;
- ceaseless mental energy;
- feeling irritable and/or aggressive;
- feeling on edge and nervous;
- feeling unhappy; and
- feeling overemotional and labile.

Figure 9.5 can be used to discuss common physical expressions of anxiety. A copy can be found on the Companion Website and it may be helpful for the client to determine the somatic symptoms they have experienced in the past and self-regulate for these early signs of anxiety. If the client can identify early indicators of anxiety, they

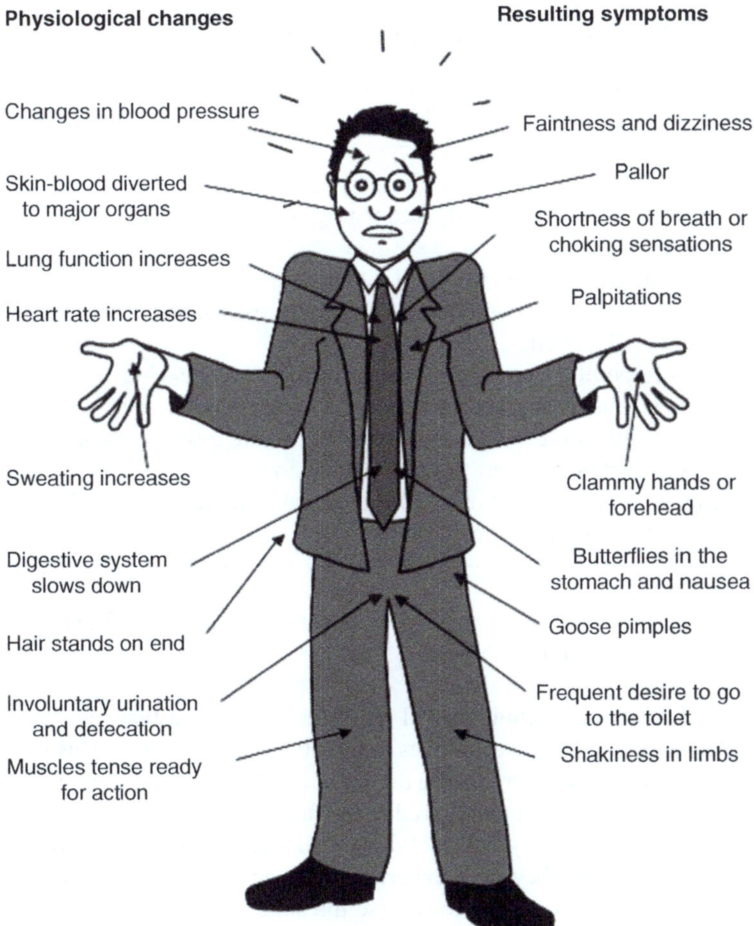

Figure 9.5 Bodily reactions to anxiety

can apply techniques to manage the anxiety at an early stage and increase the likelihood of them managing it successfully.

Body reactions to anxiety may be understood as a physical health problem and not recognized to be symptoms of an underlying psychological problem or disorder. In cases of acute anxiety leading to panic attacks, some clients are even admitted to Accident and Emergency departments, as they believe they are having a heart attack. This may especially occur if the clients' problems are associated with work, stress and performance anxiety (such as not completing tasks on time and missing deadlines). Body reactions to anxiety, or somatic symptoms, are relatively easy to identify and clients should be taught to use somatic indicators to trigger the use of treatment options outlined in the module.

Box 9.3 Ten rules for coping with panic

1. Feelings of panic are an exaggeration of the body's normal reaction to stress.
2. They are unpleasant but not harmful or dangerous. Nothing worse will happen.
3. Stop adding to panic with frightening thoughts about what is going to happen.
4. Concentrate on what is really happening in your body, not what you fear might happen.
5. Wait for the fear to pass. Accept it. Do not fight it or run away from it.
6. Notice that once you stop adding to thinking frightening thoughts, the fear starts to fade by itself.
7. The whole point of practice is to learn how to cope with fear – without avoiding it. This is an opportunity to make progress.
8. Think about the progress you have made. You are moving towards success.
9. When you feel better, start to plan what to do next.
10. When you are ready, start off slowly in an easy and relaxed way. There is no need for effort or hurry.

A method of coping with feelings of panic is presented in Box 9.3 and this is also included on the Companion Website.

A paradoxical treatment technique will help the client learn that they can control feelings of panic by applying techniques to effectively cope with it. This is achieved by inducing hyperventilation by asking the client to take rapid and shallow breathing. After a few minutes the client will go red in the face, feel hot and flushed, their heart will start to palpitate and they will feel dizzy and sweaty. The client will recognize these symptoms as those they have experienced when in a state of panic. Once this has been achieved, it is necessary to reverse the state by asking the client to breath slowly and deeply, to close their eyes and concentrate on their breathing, and on the air filling their lungs. The therapist can then introduce calming self-talk by asking the client to say to themselves coping self-statements identified in earlier sessions; pointing out that if they can induce this state at will, then they can reduce it. This is an important lesson in self-control.

It is important for the client to understand how their body feels when they are relaxed as this means they will better develop an awareness of signs of tension (i.e. that will 'flag-up' changes in the body and indicate the presence of a problem that they can treat). When in a relaxed state the body has a slow heart rate, breathing is slow and regular, tension in muscles is reduced. The client should feel psychologically calm and their body should feel 'quiet' as if they are gently ticking over rather than feeling revved up and active.

Controlling 'feelings' of anxiety means knocking out a 'leg' of the table using techniques that induce a sense of calm and well-being (see Figure 9.6). This can be achieved by relaxation techniques to reduce muscle tension and create a state of

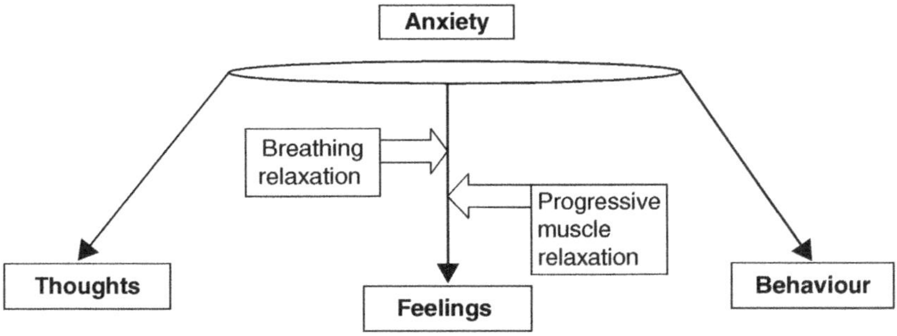

Figure 9.6 The three-legged table: Controlling feelings of anxiety

physical calmness. When clients learn to manage and reduce unpleasant feelings, they can adapt the method to help them feel more relaxed in anxiety provoking situations. This means they will feel more in control. However, relaxation techniques need to be practised until they become an automatic process. In order to do this, the client needs to rehearse the relaxation techniques morning and evening (preferably before they go to bed). It will help if they find a quiet space somewhere, perhaps after a warm bath to maximize the efficacy of the techniques. Gradually, the techniques should be introduced in a briefer form at times during the day when the client feels anxious, if appropriate.

There are different types of relaxation exercise, the most helpful for people with ADHD being breathing exercises and progressive muscle relaxation techniques. Both should be introduced to the client in sessions and practised at home. Initially practise should be set as specific homework tasks but the aim is for clients to make relaxation a part of their visual daily routine. Progressive muscle relaxation techniques are particularly good for 'preventative' relaxation, to help the client induce and maintain a relaxed frame of mind. They are also helpfully applied in anxiety provoking situations, but may be inappropriate in some situations, such as staff meetings, as colleagues may wonder what they are doing. Breathing exercises can be more subtly applied in such situations and are just as effective. The exercises outlined in this module are also presented on the Companion Website for the client to practise outside sessions.

Relaxation strategies: Breathing exercises

These are exercises that can help correct breathing. In order to learn the technique, breathing practice needs to be initially when the client feels reasonably calm and relaxed. Box 9.4 provides two exercises that can be used in treatment sessions and a handout of instructions is provided on the Companion Website for the client to use at home.

The client should be reminded that they are learning a new skill – at first it may feel strange, or difficult to breathe like this. It is important to continue practising, despite these feelings, as gradually they will notice an improvement.

Box 9.4 Breathing exercises

Exercise 1

1. Begin by lying quietly on your back, rest one hand on your stomach and the other on your upper chest.
2. Breathe in gently. Tell yourself to breathe IN and OUT, gently and rhythmically, aiming for 7–8 breaths per minute. Don't hold your breath for too long, just slowly IN and OUT. Concentrate on the breath filling your lungs and being expelled from them.
3. As you breathe out imagine your body relaxing, deeper and deeper. With each exhalation, your body is sinking further and further into a state of relaxation.
4. Practice this for 10 minutes every day and once it feels easy and natural to breathe like this move to Exercise 2.

Exercise 2

Repeat the steps from Exercise 1, but this time in a sitting position, progressing to standing up. For at least 3 weeks, try to be aware of your breathing at different times during the day, and correct it if necessary.

Relaxation strategies: Progressive muscle relaxation

Alternatively, the therapist can teach the client to induce a state of total relaxation of mind and body by teaching progressive muscle relaxation techniques, breathing techniques and mental imagery. Research has shown that, apart from treating anxiety, progressive muscle relaxation techniques reduce tension, headaches, and migraine; lower blood pressure; relieve chronic pain and/or menstrual symptoms; and improve sleep (Roth and Fonagy, 1996).

Box 9.5 (also on the Companion Website) outlines the instructions for progressive muscle relaxation techniques which require the individual to engage in a set of deep muscle relaxation procedures by working through the body's muscle sets. The exercise can be completed in 10 minutes or extended for much longer. The client can lie on a bed or sit up in a straight backed chair. The client may start with the breathing techniques learned in the exercises in Box 9.4, proceed to the Progressive Muscle Relaxation procedure then incorporate mental relaxation whereby the client is asked to focus mentally on different parts of the body and imagine them 'unwinding'. They can also use relaxing visual imagery, for example, by asking them to imagine being in a tranquil place. Clients often imagine being on a beautiful beach with white sand and palm trees. Cue the client to see the colours, hear the wind rustling and see the sun glinting on the water.

It can be difficult at first for clients to practise the progressive muscle relaxation technique on their own as they have to learn a sequence and remember what to do.

Box 9.5 Progressive muscle relaxation

For each exercise, tense your muscles for about 5–7 seconds. Relax for about 30 seconds between each exercise. Practise in a quiet, comfortable environment.

1. Make a tight fist with your right hand, then relax.
2. Push your right elbow down into the chair while at the same time pulling your arm towards your chest. Then relax.
3. Make a fist with your left hand, then relax.
4. Push your left elbow down into the chair while at the same time pulling your arm towards your chest. Then relax.
5. Arch your eyebrows as high as you can, then relax.
6. Squint your eyes tightly together while wrinkling your nose, then relax.
7. Clench your teeth together tightly while pulling back the corners of your mouth in an exaggerated smile, then relax.
8. With your teeth separated, press your lips together while pressing your tongue against the roof of your mouth, then relax.
9. Pull your chin down as if trying to touch it against your chest while at the same time pulling your head backwards, then relax.
10. After taking a deep breath, press your shoulder blades together behind you as if you are trying to touch them together, then relax.
11. After taking a deep breath, make the muscles of your stomach hard and taut (or make the muscles of your stomach tense by pulling them in or pushing them out), then relax.
12. Press your heels into the ground, then relax.
13. Point your toes towards your head, then relax.
14. Point your feet downwards, while turning your feet inwards and curling your toes under, then relax.

This means they stop and start, as they have to read the instructions, which interferes with the relaxation process. It is extremely helpful to make a recording of the process in the session for the client to keep and use at home. This also means that it can be adapted to be personally appropriate, for example by introducing at the end visual imagery to the client that has been previously discussed and applied successfully in sessions.

Changing Behaviour

The third leg of the table involves treating behavioural avoidance (see Figure 9.7). Avoidance is probably the greatest and most negative behavioural implication of anxiety. When we feel anxious we tend to want to avoid what we perceive as psychological threats. Our natural response is to avoid unpleasant situations.

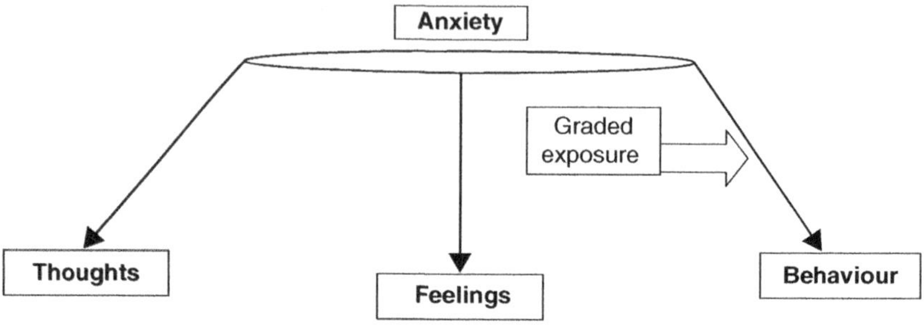

Figure 9.7 The three-legged table: Changing behaviour

Common feelings expressed by our clients include:

- not wanting to go out;
- becoming distracted, losing concentration and going off task;
- avoiding social situations;
- making excuses not to do things;
- not sticking up for themselves when they should;
- calming their nerves by smoking, drinking alcohol, taking drugs, eating;
- only going out when they have someone with them;
- overexertion, overactive, 'high' energy; and
- preoccupation with thoughts, ideas and worries.

On a short-term basis avoidance is useful as it is the quickest way for clients to protect themselves and alleviate their anxiety. Of course this is not functional, however, as this means that the client learns to cope by avoiding anxiety-provoking situations, such as going to work, going to parties, finishing important tasks. This adds to the vicious cycle of negative thoughts (see anxiety spiral in Figure 9.1). Unfortunately, this becomes habitual and the client engages in a process of avoidance whenever they face anxiety-provoking situations, for example, by thinking 'I can't do this; the last time I tried I couldn't do this and I gave up; I gave up and didn't do it'. Thus, this cognitive and behavioural process is self-reinforcing. Instead of facing and resolving the problem, the client avoids it and makes the problem more daunting to face the next time. Fear leads to avoidance, which leads to more fear, which leads to more avoidance and so on. The more the client avoids a situation the worse their anxiety becomes. It becomes gradually worse and the anxiety generalizes to other situations and circumstances. In time, avoidance behaviour reduces confidence and self-esteem. Confidence is developed through achievement and an important part of managing anxiety is to start facing up to fears and to stop avoiding anxiety-provoking situations. This is a very difficult thing to do, so it is important that the client (and the therapist) does not expect too much too soon, or that unrealistic targets are set. The taste of success will involve the therapist structuring a hierarchical schedule of graded exposure to tasks that have become challenging to the client. Using this approach the client will learn to plan a gradual way to develop confidence and

Box 9.6 Overcoming avoidance and increasing confidence

1. Make a *list* of situations you avoid because of your feelings.
2. *Grade* each situation, using a scale of 0–10 (0 = no anxiety, 10 = severe anxiety).
3. List situations in *order* of difficulty – put the least difficult at the top of the list and the most difficult at the bottom.
4. *Take action* – tackle each situation in turn – begin with the least difficult first. Reward yourself for completing each stage. Succeeding in completing the least difficult task on the list will make it easier to face other fears and help prepare you for the most difficult.
5. Keep a *record* of what happens and the progress you make, i.e. use a diary.
6. *Evaluate* how you coped. Congratulate yourself on what you have achieved. Initially, the most important aspect of success will be just 'facing' the situations. Gradually, you will be able to evaluate how well you are managing your feelings.
7. *Reward* with small rewards for each step and a greater reward for completion of the programme.
8. *Practise* – KEEP PRACTISING – the more you tackle a situation the better it will become and the more confident you will grow. By tackling your fears a step at a time you can gradually regain confidence and self-esteem.

Remember: do not expect too much too soon and be proud of whatever progress you do make!

Box 9.7 Example of stage 1: List of situations avoided

Make a *list* of things you avoid because of your feelings:

Entering the supermarket past the security guards
Going around the supermarket with a basket
Paying the cashier
Going to the nearby newsagents
Going to the hairdressers next door
Walking down the road past the supermarket
Going to the chemists

re-introduce activities they have avoided and achieve them. Box 9.6 describes a set of incremental stages for the client to follow to build confidence and achieve tasks. This is also included on the Companion Website, in a format to handout to clients.

For example, one of our clients, Sarah, was extremely anxious about going to the local shops as she had previously absent-mindedly walked out of a supermarket shop with her basket without paying. The security guards had stopped her and brought her in for questioning, but not pressed charges. Sarah was anxious that people would

Box 9.8 Example of stage 2: Grading of list of situations avoided (0–10)

Grade each situation, using a scale of 0–10 (0 = no anxiety, 10 = severe anxiety).

Entering the supermarket past the security guards (because they may grab me, or I might impulsively draw attention to myself)	10
Going around the supermarket with a basket (because they could spot me at any moment)	8
Paying the cashier (because she may recognize me from before and tell other people in the queue)	9
Going to the nearby newsagents (because they may have been told about me, but I know the shopkeeper from the past)	2
Going to the hairdressers next door (because staff from the supermarket may look at me through the window)	6
Walking down the road past the supermarket (because the security guards may think I've stolen something and follow me)	5
Going to the chemists (because they may have a 'wanted' list of potential shoplifters)	3

Box 9.9 Example of stage 3: Ranking list of situations avoided (0–10) and choosing rewards

List situations in *order* of difficulty – put the least difficult at the top of the list and the most difficult at the bottom.	*Grade*	*Reward*
Going to the nearby newsagents	2	chocolate
Going to the chemists	3	shampoo
Walking down the road past the supermarket	5	magazine
Going to the hairdressers next door	6	haircut
Going around the supermarket with a basket	8	long bath
Paying the cashier	9	cake
Entering the supermarket past the security guards	10	CD

recognize her and that they would embarrass her by escorting her off the premises. The situations she avoided are shown in Box 9.7.

Sarah then rated how difficult she thought each situation would be on a scale from 0 to 10 (see Box 9.8).

These were then rearranged into the order of difficulty as shown in Box 9.9.

Sarah and the therapist then planned each step of the hierarchy. They carefully discussed what could go wrong and planned around these difficulties. They role played what Sarah might say to the security guards if they did stop her. She decided that after each stage she would reward herself by having a bar of chocolate from the newsagents, new shampoo from the chemists, a haircut, and a CD from the supermarket. ADHD clients are particularly motivated to work towards short-term rewards and, although anxiety reduction in itself can be an internal reward, motivation can be enhanced using external rewards in addition. Sarah found that she quickly progressed and once she had walked towards the supermarket, her anxiety was not as severe as she had anticipated.

SUMMARY

Many individuals with ADHD present with some anxiety difficulties, even if they do not meet full criteria for a formal diagnosis. Anxiety can develop in many different ways in line with the main categories of disorder including panic disorder, social anxiety, generalized anxiety and obsessive compulsive disorder. However, there may be some overlap in the phenomenology of anxiety symptoms and the core symptoms of ADHD, including feelings of restlessness and distractibility. It is therefore important to carefully assess for such difficulties and intervene as necessary using appropriate techniques. A CBT approach has been provided which begins with psychoeducation regarding the disorder using the 'three-legged table analogy'. In order to tackle anxiety difficulties, the client and therapist can decide to 'knock out' each of the legs (thoughts, feelings, behaviours) in turn. Thoughts are addressed using challenging strategies and superimposing positive thoughts, or developing distraction techniques. Feelings of anxiety can be modified using a range of relaxation techniques and avoidance behaviours can benefit from using graded exposure. While these strategies are well known to therapists who work with individuals with anxiety disorders, it is recommended that they are adapted in order to accommodate the idiosyncrasies of people with ADHD and the examples through the module illustrate how this may be achieved.

Group Treatment: Anxiety Module

It is essential to prepare for group treatment by reading the chapter module. Six group sessions are outlined below, but the number of treatment sessions can be expanded or reduced as required.

Plan

Session 1	Starting activities Anxiety Checklist
Session 2	Psychoeducation – the Anxiety Spiral; the Three-Legged Table; Rewards

(*Continued*)

Session 3	Exercises – Leg 1: Negative thoughts
Session 4	Exercises – Leg 2: Feelings of anxiety
Session 5	Exercises – Leg 3: Avoidance behaviour
Session 6	Revision of psychoeducation, techniques and rewards Discussion of homework outcome/experience – what works best? Obstacles and how to overcome them

Starting Activities

What makes you feel anxious?

Guide participants to think about specific events and circumstances.

Discuss past experiences and lead participants to understand this causes an expectation of future difficulties when in similar circumstances.

What happens to you when you become anxious?

Direct participants to identify thoughts, feelings, physical reactions and behaviour (see Box 9.1 Anxiety chart and Figure 9.5 Bodily reactions to anxiety).

What would be an 'early-warning sign' that they might notice and which would indicate that they need to apply an intervention?

Hand out Anxiety checklist (Table 9.1) and complete individually.

Group discussion (compare individual differences, strengths/weaknesses).

What is a panic attack? Have you experienced this? How does this differ from anxiety?

Group discussion.

Psychoeducation

Describe the cognitive behavioural model of anxiety: Negative thoughts, physical reaction, avoidance behaviour. Describe the link between them.

Handout Figure 9.1 The anxiety spiral.

Describe the three-legged anxiety table.

Anxiety topples over if you knock out one of the legs (thoughts, feelings, behaviour).

Handout Figure 9.3.

Identify appropriate rewards for incremental steps leading to completion of goal, and identify a larger reward for completion.

Leg 1: Negative thoughts.

Handout Figure 9.4 – Coping with negative thoughts.

Three things can be done: challenge thoughts, distract thoughts, superimpose thoughts (describe techniques for each).

Different stages of anxiety – when to do what – See Box 9.4.

Leg 2: Feelings of anxiety

Handout Figure 9.6 – Controlling feelings of anxiety.

Relaxation strategies: breathing exercises and progressive muscle relaxation.

Handout Box 9.3 – Ten rules for coping with panic.

(*Continued*)

Leg 3: Avoidance behaviour
Describe graded exposure techniques. Apply to example.
Handout Box 9.6 Overcoming Avoidance.

Exercises

Select suitable examples of anxiety provoking situations/experiences described by participants in Starting Activities or introduce new examples (e.g. 'Sarah' described in the module). Using these examples complete the exercises.

Leg 1: Negative thoughts
Handout Table 9.5 Thinking errors. Do thinking error exercise.
Using one of the examples, identify negative thoughts that increase and/or maintain anxiety.
Practise challenging negative thoughts – cross-examine thoughts as a skilled lawyer using questions provided in the module – role-play in pairs with one person 'thinking out loud' and the other being the lawyer.
Practise superimposing positive thoughts and making positive self-statements (see Box 9.2) – role-play by 'thinking out loud'.
Discuss distraction techniques that may be helpful.
Leg 2: Feelings of anxiety
Handout Figure 9.5 – Bodily reactions to anxiety and circle body reactions they have experienced.
Panic attack exercise – ask participants to take rapid and shallow breaths. Ask them how this feels (red and hot face, flushed, heart palpitations, feel dizzy, sweaty).
Explain this is what it feels like when you have a panic attack. If you can induce it, you can reverse it by focusing on your breathing and breathing slowly and deeply.
Relaxation strategies: breathing exercises and progressive muscle relaxation (do in session).
Leg 3: Avoidance behaviour
Revise graded exposure techniques using Handout Box 9.6 (Overcoming avoidance).
Make a list of situations avoided, grade anxiety associated with each situation and rank them to create starting point and ultimate goal.
Discuss obstacles to achievement and methods to overcome them.

Homework

Handout Box 4 and Box 5 (relaxation techniques) for homework.
Apply and rehearse techniques between sessions.

10

FRUSTRATION AND ANGER MODULE

Everyone gets angry sometimes, it is a natural emotion. Most people feel angry when they perceive injustice or feel that their rights have been violated. However, due to their symptoms, ADHD individuals may be predisposed to have a labile or explosive temperament. They may have developed maladaptive ways of coping with feelings of anger and express their feelings inappropriately. For people with ADHD, feelings of anger are more likely to be expressed outwardly than inwardly suppressed, due to their inability to inhibit a response, and a low threshold for irritability and boredom. However denial of anger and suppression of angry feelings is not uncommon, especially in compliant individuals.

When anger is expressed overtly, other people are likely to perceive this as a negative character trait, and view the person with ADHD as being unpredictable and, in some cases, frightening and dangerous. Tolerating frustration can be difficult for young people with ADHD and, in particular, they may become annoyed by their lack of achievement and failure to finish tasks. As they grow up they seek to become independent and they feel frustrated and irritated by family who, meaning well, continue to give direction, organize their life for them, or complain about lack of commitment and motivation. This is perceived as 'nagging'. A cycle of negativity is commonly reported between parents and children with ADHD, especially their mothers (Barkley, 1998). Research into ADHD in childhood has shown that negative interactions are a reciprocal process, with ADHD affecting the manner in which the child responds with their parents and, hence, the way in which the parents behave towards the child. These learned cycles of responding may well extend to adult close friendships and intimate relationships. People with ADHD may feel resentment towards other people who do not have ADHD and seem to have fewer difficulties and more successes in life. Thus, anger management difficulties can lead to numerous negative outcomes including breakdown in

Cognitive-Behavioural Therapy for ADHD in Adolescents and Adults: A Psychological Guide to Practice, Second Edition. Susan Young and Jessica Bramham.

relationships, school exclusion, termination of further education and employment, and involvement with the police.

Those who are not diagnosed with ADHD until their adult years often have accumulated feelings of anger towards psychiatric services. This is frequently expressed, following diagnosis and treatment, as dissatisfaction towards services for not meeting their needs. These individuals usually have a long history of presenting to both child and adult psychiatric services (Young, Toone and Tyson, 2003). They feel that their problems have not been taken seriously by clinicians and also may feel misunderstood by partners and friends. Some individuals may blame others for not identifying the disorder in the first place and for not providing appropriate support. They may feel frustrated and angry if they believe that they have been previously misdiagnosed or labelled, or misjudged. It will not be easy for individuals with this type of experience to make a collaborative therapeutic alliance. Clinicians need to be aware of these issues and may need to sensitively introduce anger management techniques early in therapy, in order to develop rapport and gain trust.

This module will explain how, in order to understand their anger, people with ADHD require education regarding anger's function as a normal emotion. Reasons for becoming angry will be reviewed for people with ADHD, such as the need for immediate gratification. Dysfunctional ways of managing anger will be addressed, including having too much control and having too little control. Treatment involves psychoeducation regarding the stages of anger, according to a cognitive behavioural model, focusing in particular on observing the physical signs of anger such as body language. Ways of dealing with insults and criticisms will be addressed, including recognizing the difference, appreciating constructive criticism and learning to accept criticism. Similarly, developing assertive expression in the context of poor impulse control and recognizing the difference between aggressive behaviour and assertive behaviour will be covered.

FUNCTIONAL DEFICITS IN ADOLESCENTS AND ADULTS

Anger is a normal emotion experienced by everyone. The aim of treatment is therefore not to 'stop' anger, but to improve control and use anger adaptively. It can be particularly functional in motivating change. Anger is a healthy emotion that allows individuals to problem solve, to impose control and/or to change a situation. A second aspect of anger is that it has an alerting function. It signals potential danger and protects us from harm. It is not uncommon for anger to be triggered in situations where other emotions are activated, such as fear or sadness. Situations where there is a perceived or actual injustice are likely to trigger anger and it represents an adaptive response to dissatisfaction with the environment. Anger management is about identifying effective ways for the client to show their discontent without causing distress to themselves or others. There are obviously many reasons why people become angry. The following themes seem to be shared by many people with ADHD.

Taking Things Personally

People with ADHD may be more likely to interpret any threat or blame as a personal slight, and become angry as a result of these feelings. For example, if a family member has mislaid a belonging and asks whether other family members have seen it or used it, it might be presumed that they are being accused of something (borrowing it without asking, stealing the item). Because the person feels they are being (unjustifiably) blamed for something, they feel upset and angry.

Losing Control of a Situation

If someone with ADHD feels like they are not succeeding, they tend to give up easily. It is better to give up than plough on with a task, struggle alone with it and feel hopeless and stupid. Their inability to achieve may make them feel angry inside and giving up can compound frustration. It may also make other people annoyed with them and lead to confrontation. Feeling angry in such circumstances has a secondary function, as high emotional arousal is distracting. The individual focuses on their feelings, enabling them to escape or avoid the situation, such as the unfinished task.

Feeling Threatened

Situations where an individual is being directly challenged or threatened can be difficult to manage for anyone. However individuals with ADHD are more likely to catastrophize and over-react to criticism, even when this is constructive, due to their own learned sense of underachievement. If they do find themselves in a provocative situation when someone is bullying or intimidating them, they may act on impulse and respond aggressively without thinking about the consequences of their behaviour.

Learned Behaviour

People with ADHD may have developed maladaptive response patterns over the years for dealing with frustration and anger. It may be that they are not particularly angry, but behave in a way that suggests they are as this is how they have learnt to behave. This will give the wrong impression of themselves to other people who perceive them as being 'prickly' and overly sensitive.

Poor Impulse Control

This core symptom itself can lead to an escalation in feelings of anger, whereby an individual may be more likely to act on their anger either in an aggressive or violent way towards others, themselves or property. Thus, individuals are less likely to walk away from a severe verbal confrontation and more likely to respond with physical aggression. This may mean that they enter into many fights or destroy property. Some people may harm themselves impulsively and abuse substances.

Feeling Resentful

Angry feelings may build up slowly, especially if the person feels that they are being judged or stigmatized by others. They may feel resentful of people who seem to have an easier life.

Frustration with Attentional Difficulties

It can be obvious when assessing someone with ADHD when they become annoyed with themselves for not being able to focus or sustain attention. They become frustrated when they make mistakes, forget instructions, or are slow to finish. They are often observed to give an incorrect response and then later correct themselves realizing their mistake. This indicates insight into their difficulties. However anger can often compound attentional problems as individuals can become distracted by their angry thoughts and lose focus on the task in hand.

Frustration with Lack of Services

Individuals with ADHD are likely to have encountered experienced professionals who either dismiss the ADHD disorder as a clinically valid condition and/or who lack knowledge and understanding about the disorder and their special needs. This occurs in educational services, social services and health services. Often an individual has presented at multiple child and adult services and told their story over and over and over again. This can be a hurdle for a therapist to overcome and can hinder progress.

Anger as an Avoidance Mechanism to Processing other Emotions

Feelings of anger may be expressed in preference to the expression of other emotions, such as distress and crying, in order to avoid the expression of what may be perceived as 'weaker' emotions. This is more likely to occur in males with ADHD.

Stimuli for Excitement

Moving into a state of high arousal provides a state of high stimulus and, for some individuals, excitement. This may satisfy a desire to seek 'thrills' or 'sensation' and relieve feelings of boredom and monotony. For example, an aggressive argument with lots of drama, shouting, gesticulating, slamming doors and banging may provide an individual with an adrenalin rush. This acts as a positive reinforcement of the behaviour, with the adrenalin rush as the 'reward', thus increasing the likelihood of them repeating the behaviour. Anger can also be rewarding if the angry individual is able to avoid an uncomfortable or boring situation.

A Source of Communication

Many individuals have poor social skills and have difficulty communicating and expressing their thoughts and feelings. This may be due to a specific skills deficit and/or to lack of confidence that has been negatively reinforced by a history of dysfunctional social interactions with peers and siblings. Individuals may respond with anger for two reasons, they may misappraise social situations and the intentions of others and respond aggressively (social skills deficit) and/or feel resentment and anger towards people they interact with in a world they perceive as harsh and biased against them.

Establishment of Superiority

People with ADHD commonly develop low self-esteem, and this is probably established early in childhood. It becomes reinforced as they become older and failures become a self-fulfilling prophecy. In order to defend against feelings of vulnerability and in order to hide them, individuals may use aggression to convey the message 'I'm better than you'. As the therapist will demonstrate in treatment, simply engaging in this process (even when feelings of anger are not actually present) will have an iatrogenic effect, resulting in 'real' feelings of anger.

Road Rage

There are many opportunities on our roads for drivers to build up feelings of anger due to people driving too fast, too slow, cutting in, not indicating, not giving way, abruptly stopping, people flashing their lights, tooting their horns or making gestures. Driving on busy roads and at peak times is stressful at the best of times and everyone knows what it is like to be in a driving situation when they feel irritated and frustrated. However, there is an increased risk that people with ADHD will experience road rage and also have road traffic accidents (Barkley, 2002; Barkley *et al.*, 1993). These occur because individuals drive without due care and attention; they may become distracted from their driving by talking to passengers or by scenery; they may drive recklessly. An alternative or additional possibility is that they become wound up in situations that are common to most people, but are unable to self-regulate their feelings of anger and inhibit their responses. People with ADHD are therefore more likely to act in a provocative way on the roads, to jump out of their cars at traffic lights and threaten other drivers.

DYSFUNCTIONAL MANAGEMENT OF ANGER

There are two main ways in which people with ADHD may manage their anger maladaptively. The first is through escalation of a situation by overt expression of aggression and the second by suppression of angry feelings.

Escalation

A person with a predisposition to 'escalation' is likely to explicitly express their feelings of anger and to make them well known to the people around them. Their threshold for revealing annoyance is much lower and they may be labile in temperament. Such individuals are likely to have many impulsive symptoms and their poor behavioural control and emotion regulation difficulties result in them being more likely to respond explosively in stressful and challenging situations. For example, if someone pushes in front of them in a queue, or if someone makes a personal remark, they are unlikely to inhibit the impulse to respond aggressively, by either making a remark verbally or through nonverbal expression (e.g. glaring or standing too close to the person). This can lead to either a subtle escalation of aggression or a rapid escalation, depending on the severity of response, the manner in which their feelings have been communicated and the response of the recipient. Some people feel a sense of power and excitement by deliberately provoking and intimidating other people, which has a reinforcing property by providing an immediate reward. It may also be functional, as it means the individual avoids displaying other emotions, such as their own fear and anxiety, and/or revealing feelings of vulnerability. There may also be positive reinforcement from the recipient backing down. Although this will often be a 'normal' way to respond to overt threat and provocation, the behaviour will be perceived as submissive and reinforce the fact that they can achieve this status through intimidation. Of course, the longer-term impact of this type of behaviour may include expulsion from school and further education, unemployment, losing friendships, destruction of property, physical injury and criminal convictions.

Suppression

This second type of anger is latent or suppressed anger. When asked, individuals often deny feeling angry and do not admit to situations that have made them feel angry or upset. A person with a predisposition to suppress angry feelings expresses these covertly. They may be passive-aggressive and compliant. They may appear to be coping well with stressful situations but all the time feelings of resentment and anger are slowly building up inside. In such cases individuals may suddenly explode, the trigger being seemingly innocent. Their response will be commented on by others as being disproportionate to the trigger. They may have a reputation for being unpredictable – a 'loose cannon'. Another way in which suppressed anger may be released is in circumstances when this has developed from experiences that remain unresolved, in other words that were not dealt with at the time. Anger that has been 'bottled up' may surface in completely unrelated situations that remind the individual of the earlier experience and their feelings about it. It is thus misplaced anger and can cause great confusion to those around. In order to avoid the inappropriate expression of this type of anger, the client needs to develop an understanding about difficult situations they have experienced in their lives, relate these to their feelings and learn to express these appropriately and move on.

ASSESSMENT OF ANGER AND ASSERTION

Anger

Anger can be understood as a three stage 'ABC' process involving antecedents to anger, behaviour during anger (anger expression) and consequences of anger. It is therefore useful to establish a personal pattern or 'blueprint' for the expression of inappropriate anger. For some people, rather than beginning with an examination of the client's own anger behaviour, it may be useful and less threatening for them to think about someone else whose anger they have recently observed, even a confrontation on television. Following this example, they may then feel more comfortable talking about the stages of their own anger.

Antecedents

There are often common triggers of anger, for example, being with certain people in certain places (e.g. family celebrations, job appraisals). Clients should be encouraged to look for commonalities in situations when they become angry. They may then develop strategies for either avoiding such situations or preparing themselves so that they can handle the situation more appropriately. This can include preparing self-statements to keep themselves calm, practising in advance what they could say, and also to determine which compromises they may be willing to make to diffuse the situation.

For example Jonathan, who was an IT programmer, found that he was more likely to become angry when he was concentrating and people interrupted him at work. He had a tendency to be verbally aggressive to people who disturbed him. He often regretted being rude to colleagues immediately afterwards and spent the rest of the day worrying about what they thought of him and not managing to get his work done. Using problem-solving techniques, Jonathan developed a system to convey to colleagues that he could not be disturbed between certain times and was willing to act as a help-desk at certain times of the day.

Behaviour

The client should learn to recognize their physical signs of anger and develop ways of behaving and thinking which allow them to display their anger appropriately, so that they do not lose control. Techniques are discussed in the anger management section to address these issues.

For example, Jonathan learned that an early indicator for him feeling angry was him becoming impatient with the approaches and requests of others. Usually he was very helpful and would take great care to explain a concept. He also noticed that his face started to feel hot and in his mind he started to swear at the people asking for help. By identifying these indicators, Jonathan was able to recognize his own signature early warning signs of anger and avoid losing control and upsetting colleagues.

Consequences

The client should be asked to reflect on how they behaved and coped with that situation. They can examine both the positive and negative consequences. For example, Maria often became angry in traffic jams and, instead of waiting, she responded by driving down side-roads even though she often did not know where they led. This relieved her feelings of tension but she often ended up lost and took longer to arrive at her destination. Having recorded the time it took her to make both journeys (taking alternative options) over a two-week period, Maria discovered that she actually saved more time, and arrived at her destination earlier by sticking to the main route (despite the traffic jams) than driving around back roads to avoid the queues. Sessions focused on establishing methods to support Maria in sticking to the main route, by making the back routes less attractive and finding a way to fill the time while she was in the traffic jam (see Distraction techniques below).

Assertion

It has already been suggested that some people with ADHD suppress their anger. They can be compliant in demeanour and go along with the wishes and/or suggestions of others that they would normally reject (Gudjonsson *et al.*, 2008). This means that over time they may build up strong feelings of resentment inside. For these individuals it will be helpful for them to learn to become more assertive and to express their own wishes and needs rather than going along with an attitude or behaviour with which they disagree and which will make them angry later.

It may seem odd that people who have anger problems may also have difficulty asserting themselves, but the two are not incompatible. Since they have low self-esteem, some people are more likely to accept a situation than complain or try and make changes. Their anger builds up inside because: (a) they feel angry with themselves for not standing up for themselves; and (b) because they feel angry with

Table 10.1 Measure of assertion

How well can you.....	*Never good*	*Rarely good*	*Sometimes good*	*Mostly good*	*Always good*	*Don't know*
1. Stand up for yourself if you feel someone is taking advantage of you	✓					
2. Make alternative suggestions to the ideas of others				✓		
3. Say 'No' to other people		✓				
4. Tell someone you disagree with them			✓			
5. Resist being pressured to going along with something you don't want to	✓					
6. Request an explanation if someone is not being clear			✓			
7. Express your feelings of dissatisfaction		✓				
8. Tell someone they have made a mistake	✓					
9. Face up to difficult or challenging situations		✓				

other people who they perceive as taking advantage of them. These feelings slowly increase until, for some individuals, they explode unpredictably.

Being assertive is different from being aggressive or passive. People who are aggressive tend to be overly forceful when communicating with others, while people who are passive tend to be submissive. Their underlying needs are not met, thus leaving them with feelings of resentment and/or anger. To be assertive is to be able to express how you feel in a direct and honest manner without hurting or putting down others (as in aggression) or feeling hurt or put down yourself (as in passive behaviour).

Table 10.1 provides a list of assertive attributes completed by a man who had difficulty telling people what he really wanted or felt. The table can be reviewed with the client in order to help them identify particular strengths and weaknesses. The chart can be used pretreatment, during treatment and posttreatment to measure progress and outcome. (This is presented on the Companion Website in Table 10.1a for the self-report version and in Table 10.1b which provides an informant report version.)

COGNITIVE BEHAVIOURAL THERAPY

When treating individuals with anger problems, the therapist needs to begin with psychoeducation. This is achieved within a CBT framework of teaching the individual to recognize feelings of anger, physiological responses, thoughts, and behaviours.

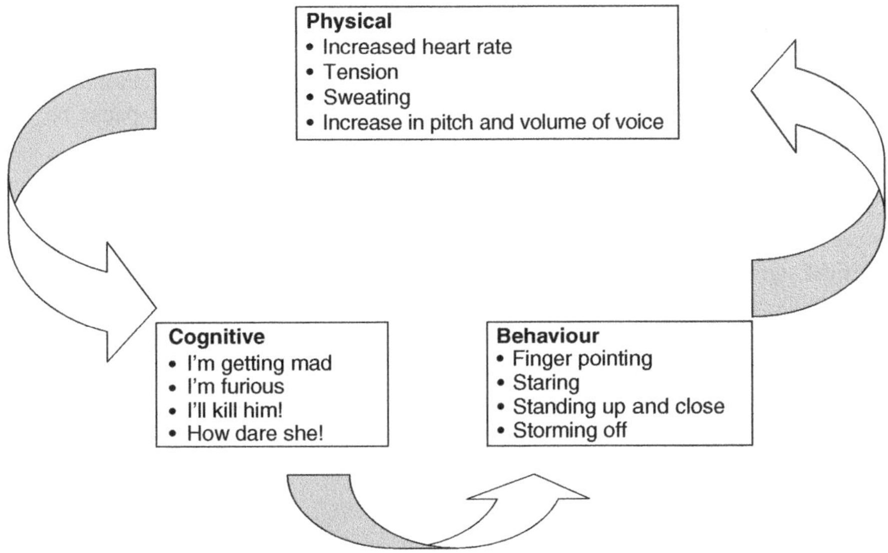

Figure 10.1 Physical, cognitive and behavioural aspects of anger

They are then encouraged to determine the stages of anger, the antecedents, behaviours and consequences of anger. Specific anger management techniques are then introduced, such as distraction techniques, self-talk and relaxation methods.

Psychoeducation

This may sound silly, but clients need to be taught how to recognize anger. The aim is for them to pay attention to signs or signals that they are starting to feel wound up about something and/or that an angry situation is developing. It is no good recognizing this once they are full flow in an angry episode; by then they have limited opportunity to do something constructive to calm the situation. They need to recognize it much earlier in the cycle.

As with other emotions, anger can be conceptualized as having three components which are interrelated: physical, cognitive and behavioural (see Figure 10.1 – also presented on the Companion Website in handout format). Clients should think about the last time they were angry. What parts of the body do they notice change when they are angry? Such changes are caused by increased adrenaline as the body is preparing to face a threat. After the physical symptoms, negative or aggressive thoughts occur automatically and can serve to increase the physical anger symptoms. Negative thoughts may be 'I hate this man', 'I want to kill him'. Negative thoughts can lead to angry behaviour such as clenching fists, squaring up, or invading personal space, which may similarly go unnoticed by the individual. Videoing role-plays may be a useful method to identify behaviours to be the focus of intervention. However, negative thoughts occur so rapidly when anger takes hold, so it may mean that only identification of feelings or initial 'gut reactions' are possible. It is important to encourage the client, in such circumstances, to *stop* and not respond automatically. Simply encouraging the individual to stop and take stock; that is, to pause before acting, may be sufficient to prevent an escalation of anger into violence.

Clients should be encouraged to pay particular attention to body language as it is an important and primary indicator of anger. They should be asked to identify the physical signs of anger, both their own nonverbal signs and those of other people. If individuals are more aware of their own anger signs, they are also more likely to be able to identify them in others. Early identification of a situation getting out of control means that the individual has a longer period to think rationally before high levels of arousal cause them to react. It also provides the opportunity to introduce techniques to de-escalate the situation and walk away.

Anger Management Strategies

It is not easy to learn to manage feelings of anger, especially when individuals are predisposed to impulsive responding, which may mean they make angry outbursts and cannot inhibit themselves from lashing out. It is one thing to practise anger management techniques within sessions and quite another to apply them when the individual feels upset and aroused. Together with a labile temperament, this can mean that individuals have considerable difficulty with anger control.

Role-Play

It is important to move away from the perception that it is the person that is the problem. It is a problem that the person has. Just as an individual can make themselves feel angry inside by thinking about situations and people who have caused them to become upset in the past, it is possible for them to make themselves feel less angry. It is a matter of anger control. The client needs to feel empowered. It may be helpful to actually demonstrate this process in sessions by asking the client to 're-live' and describe an anger provoking scenario in an imaginal mode. When they start to feel angry, the client should be reminded that they have induced themselves to feel this way and that their physical and cognitive state has undergone some fundamental changes. The therapist should point out changes in the body, ask the client to write down what is happening to them (sweating palms, palpitating heart, face feeling hot). The client should also be asked to look in a mirror and describe what they see (red face, furrowed brow).

If the client cannot re-live a previous anger provoking experience or can do so without inducing physical symptoms of anger, then it may be helpful to role-play a scenario that is meaningful and relevant to the client. For example, take the case of

Mick. Mick was getting very upset with his housemate, Dave, who kept 'borrowing' his CD player to take to work each day. Dave was a car mechanic and his CD player at work had broken. On three occasions Dave had brought the CD player back with flat batteries. Mick had put in new batteries but Dave had made no comment. Mick liked to play his CD player when he had a bath in the evening as he found it helped him to relax and unwind. Mick was getting fed up with Dave's lack of consideration and he was feeling taken for granted. In the treatment session, the therapist role played Dave and Mick role played himself becoming extremely angry with Dave and telling him he was inconsiderate and taking advantage of him. The therapist escalated the situation by shouting at Mick saying he was being petty and childish. The therapist used negative body language, by moving closer to Mick and pointing a finger at him. The therapist then called 'STOP' and de-escalated the situation, reminding Mick that this was a role-play and they were in the treatment room. Mick was asked to say how he felt, to think about his own physiological arousal, look in the mirror and describe what he saw. He was asked to describe his thoughts, what was going on in his mind while the therapist shouted back at him. He was asked to think about what he might have done next. Fight or flee? Mick was then taken through a relaxation technique that included him imagining a calming, positive image (see Anxiety Module, Chapter 9).

By engaging in the above process, clients can learn to recognize how they behave when they feel angry and how others perceive their body language. The role-play or 're-living experience' can be gone through frame by frame, like watching a video, and together the client and therapist can discuss the escalating and de-escalating factors. For example, how did the client feel when the therapist pointed their finger at him/her or stood closer to him/her. Did he/she notice facial and/or body changes in the therapist? Most important, however, is the lesson that if anger is induced deliberately within a session, then this is under the control of the client and therefore they also have the ability to control anger outside of the session.

Of course, the therapist needs to exercise their judgment before role-playing anger provoking scenarios within sessions. In some cases it may be wise to agree with the client that a third party is present who can help by participating in the role-play.

Once the client has learned to recognize their feelings of anger, and that they may exercise control over them, the next stage is to teach the client strategies to help them manage their feelings of anger. There are three basic techniques that may be useful; distraction, self-talk and relaxation.

Distraction Techniques

Recognizing that a situation is escalating and becoming confrontational usually means that the individual has an option. The option is to decide to opt out of the situation by walking away. If the individual notices early signs of feeling angry then they can distract themselves by walking away from the situation and occupy themselves in a neutral, unrelated task. However, it does not help to walk away from the situation and then wind themselves up by talking about it to lots of people. Seeking social support and asking friends for a perspective is different from complaining to lots of people and directing their anger at them. For example, if Mick had got into an argument and felt like hitting Dave but instead walked away, this would be a positive response. However if he then went and telephoned all his friends to rant and rave about Dave, he would have continued to become increasingly more angry and distressed. He may have returned and acted provocatively towards Dave and escalated the situation further. Furthermore, he may have upset and irritated his friends. So when walking away, attention should be diverted to a positive or neutral occupation and not one that will fuel the persons anger further or direct it at someone else. This is destructive so the therapist must encourage the individual to be constructive when they have extracted themselves from an anger provoking situation. This is especially so in cases when the individual is unable to walk away from situations indefinitely, for example, in work situations. By distancing themselves from the situation, the physiological response will decrease, and the person will be able to think more rationally and calmly. The client can then devise a constructive response and return to the situation in a better frame of mind.

Self-Talk

Calming self-talk is about developing the ability to speak positively to ourselves. This is achieved by collaboratively devising phrases the client may say to him/herself to help control feelings of anger. Some people call this 'positive thinking' but it is not just about thinking, it is a deliberate cognitive rehearsal of positive self-statements that encourage and reaffirm the individual's ability to get through the situation and exercise self-control. For each person the statements will differ, but they may include statements such as 'I can get through this', 'I am not going to show this person that I am feeling angry', 'I am better than this'. This can be practised by reliving the angry experience or by role-playing it again and including calming self-talk statements. When working in an imaginal mode, the client should imagine a past situation that made them feel angry and then imagine themselves talking to themselves and encouraging themselves to cope better with the situation and have a more positive ending. Self-talk statements may be cued by the therapist, but these should be rehearsed several times until the client is able to apply the technique independently. It is very important that the client can imagine themselves coping constructively with the situation, that they imagine controlling their feelings and determining a positive outcome.

Relaxation

Relaxation techniques are described in detail in the Anxiety Module in Chapter 9. However, these techniques are very helpful for coping with feelings of anger as well as anxiety because the techniques make the individual focus on themselves. This not only means that clients learn to regulate their breathing, but that they concentrate on their internal state and distance themselves from external concerns. This has been practiced for many years by cultures throughout the world in the form of meditation. Of course, relaxation techniques are not very helpful in controlling a reactive response to a provocative situation by a person with a labile temperament in vivo. However these techniques will help people control feelings of resentment that are bubbling under the surface and are being suppressed. By applying the breathing exercises, inducing a state of relaxation, alternating tension and relaxation in the muscles of the body, and engaging in calming mental imagery, the client can manage 'generalized' feelings of anger, such as the feelings of resentment and dissatisfaction that are present most of the time, but they are unsure why or where they come from. The client should be encouraged to practice relaxation techniques regularly and make them part of their daily/weekly routine as appropriate. Whilst doing these exercises, it may be helpful for the client to listen to music they find particularly calming.

Reframing the Situation

The client will begin to learn to recognize feelings of anger in themselves and in others, to identify signs or triggers that indicate a conflict or confrontation is getting out of control, to impose self-control and manage feelings of arousal and de-escalate the situation. A further way of managing conflict and confrontation is to teach the client to reduce the likelihood that a difficult situation will become threatening or anger-provoking. This involves cognitively reframing a situation and controlling the situation by improving the client's mode of communication. This means teaching the individual to apply the 'ADHD Formula' (see Box 10.1).

A = Address the situation

First the client should state the facts of the situation. This is a simple appraisal of the problem stated briefly and neutrally.

> MICK: Dave, this evening when you returned my CD player the batteries were flat.

Box 10.1 The ADHD formula

Address the situation
Describe your feelings
Help them understand
Define the consequence

D = Describe your feelings

Then the client describes how they are feeling. Again this should be factual and the client must only use 'I feel ...' statements rather than 'You made me feel ...' statements, which can antagonize and attribute blame.

MICK: I feel really annoyed about this.

H = Help them understand

The third stage is for the client to help the (target) person understand how they can make the situation better. Again this is explicitly stated by providing a statement of the desired resolution or outcome. This is a very important stage which is often left out of a process of resolution. It is very important to let the target person know what it is that is wanted, they are not 'mind readers'.

MICK: In future I'd appreciate it if you would replace the batteries if they are flat.

D = Define the consequence

Finally the client defines the consequence if the specified behaviour is not met. Again this must be pragmatic and explicit.

MICK: If you can't agree to this, then in future I won't lend you my CD player.

By adopting the ADHD Formula, Dave learned how Mick was feeling, why he was feeling that way, how he could put it right and what would happen if he did not agree. It was simply but explicitly explained. Dave had been very busy at work. He had been very distracted and he had meant to replace the batteries but had forgotten. Dave realized that he had not thought about the situation from Mick's perspective or realized that his behaviour had caused ill-feeling. The position was clear and the situation was defused immediately by Dave apologizing and replacing the batteries. Mick had the outcome he wanted, he did not get worked up inside with building feelings of resentment and thoughts that he was being taken advantage of by his friend.

Dealing with Insults and Criticisms

People with ADHD are particularly susceptible to anger following both insults and criticisms. This is possibly because they are more likely to be defensive due to having received an accumulation of critical comments and feedback throughout their lives from parents, teachers, friends and siblings, and now wish to protect their self-esteem. They are also more likely to respond impulsively to criticism, without hearing the person out or fully understanding what has been said, without accurately appraising the intention of the other person and assuming malicious intent. However, if clients are able to learn to distinguish between insults and criticisms, they are more likely to be able to respond appropriately to both types of statements.

Insults

An insult is something that is said to cause annoyance whereas a criticism is something that is said about a behaviour. Insults are inherently designed to make a person feel bad and/or angry. In order to prepare themselves to deal with insults, a client should be asked to think of the worst insult someone has said to them that has made them feel angry. They should then be asked the following questions:

- Why did this make you feel bad? (e.g. Was it threatening to your family, masculinity.)
- What was it about the statement that made you upset? (e.g. Was it just what was said or did the way it was said cause you to be upset also? Was it the tone of their voice? Was it the demeanour of the person? Was it a specific body language?)
- Why do you think the person said these things?

By taking a step back and being able to review an insult as a comment that was intended to cause upset, the client may be able to learn why it made them angry. However, more importantly, they will be able to speculate on the motivation behind the comment. This will help them to relocate the anger by understanding that this is an emotion within the other person that is being expressed inappropriately and unkindly towards others. This should help clients to see insults for what they are and reject them as a truth about themselves. If a client feels they are being insulted, self-talk in the form of calming statements will help them control their feelings and control the impulse to retort aggressively, for example:

- 'I know he is only saying this to wind me up, I won't give him the pleasure';
- 'What does he/she know about my family anyway'; or
- 'I know that I am a decent person and that is what matters'.

Criticisms

Criticism is a necessary, and often helpful, form of feedback. It is much better if it is presented constructively. However, it can be difficult for anyone to receive, particularly if it is framed negatively. An example of the difference between positive or constructive criticism and negative criticism is:

> Negative: This report is really difficult to read. It is so badly structured that it is difficult to follow what you are trying to say. You need to learn how to structure reports or you will never get a point across.
>
> Constructive: You have written a good report and made lots of interesting points. It could be made better if you structure it more by using sub-headings. Here is an example of really good report which may be helpful for you to look at.

Due to their history of failure and/or underachieving their potential, people with ADHD are used to being criticized and, unfortunately, insulted. This means that they find it hard to acknowledge any feedback that is not positive and rewarding because they are hypersensitive to perceived criticism, even when this is sensitively and constructively delivered. As soon as they perceive any form of critical feedback, they feel threatened and become irritated and/or angry. This means they are likely to disregard what is being said or interpret the comment in an overgeneralized way (usually without hearing it out or discussing the comment fully and appropriately). They may respond to the perceived criticism in one of two ways, both of which involve an overreaction; (1) by becoming angry and aggressive or (2) by feeling excessively hurt and wounded. In the latter case they may internalize the comment as an unchangeable personality flaw, rather than perceiving the criticism as relating to a behaviour that is changeable.

In order to deal with criticism, individuals with ADHD need to *listen* carefully to what is said to them and make sure they fully understand the problem. Attentional deficits may lead them to miss the earlier part of a statement and just catch the end, meaning that their reaction will be based on missing information, an inaccurate appraisal and interpretation of what has been said. Constructive criticism usually begins with a positive comment, and if this has been missed they are more likely to interpret the comment or feedback as a personal insult. By now the client should be self-monitoring their feelings and more able to recognize signs of increasing feelings of irritability and anger that may trigger an inappropriate response and/or one they may regret. They will then be able to recognize 'warning signs' within themselves when they receive feedback, comments and/or criticism that they perceive be negative and/or threatening. At this point they need to be able to interrupt the anger process by asking the person to explain the problem or comment in more detail. Through repetition of the comment they may hear parts that had been previously missed. They will understand the issue better and establish the person's motivation. It may of course become clear that the person was being insulting but equally it may become clear that the person who is criticizing the client is trying to help by offering good advice and constructive feedback. Encourage the client to accept this gracefully even if they are still slightly aroused and irritated. In sessions role-play both aspects; giving constructive criticism to others (avoiding rapid, blunt delivery of information) and receiving it. It is important to role-play both aspects because the giving and receiving of constructive criticism is a mutual process and understanding the dynamics of both sides will help the individual to accept critical feedback better in future.

Giving constructive criticism means phrasing a criticism in a helpful way, through emphasizing positive aspects, offering suggestions for improvements and supporting the individual to make changes or corrections. Receiving constructive criticism appropriately means making a statement of acknowledgement of the problem, clarifying any misunderstandings, outlining a shared understanding and plan for

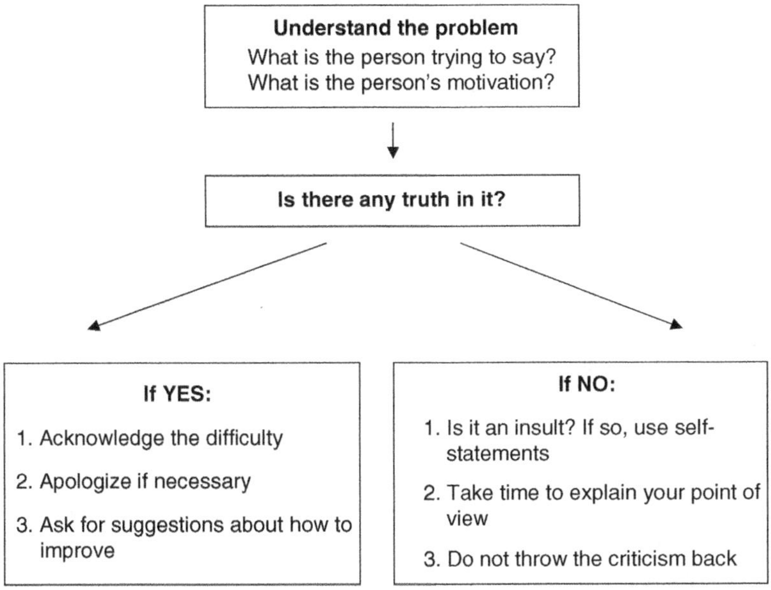

Figure 10.2 Dealing with insults and criticisms

resolving the issue. In some circumstances, it may be appropriate to apologize for errors or mistakes.

Figure 10.2 is a flow chart which summarizes ways of dealing with insults and criticisms. This is presented on the Companion Website in handout format.

ASSERTIVENESS TRAINING

Treatment sessions should initially be psychoeducational and enable the individual to understand the difference between assertiveness and aggression. Assertiveness involves standing up for oneself, but being calm and courteous. It requires acting in one's best interests but without inducing anger or aggression in others. Both assertiveness and aggression can involve feeling angry, but being assertive requires the ability to express anger or distress without hurting or angering others. For example, someone who is being assertive may communicate their anger but without threatening the other person, or insulting them, or being punishing and sarcastic. The way to convey this to the client is to encourage them to think about the outcome they wish to achieve. What do they really want out of the interaction? Then show them the way to get it using the steps outlined earlier in the ADHD formula; that is, tell the person how they feel, tell the person what they want, tell the person the outcome. Express this calmly and state it factually and explicitly. Then ask the client to determine the outcome of not asserting themselves. This means they are unlikely to get what they really want and achieve the desired outcome.

The manner of expression is important. Clients should be encouraged to express themselves using the first person because 'I' messages are assertive and communicate feelings, for example, 'I feel very angry at the moment'. In contrast, 'You' messages are more likely to be perceived as aggressive and punishing, for example, 'You make me feel very angry'.

The tone and manner of expression can be role played in sessions. The therapist should also look out for opportunities during treatment to acknowledge and positively reinforce assertive behaviour. In such situations, and in role-plays, attention should be drawn to functional characteristics of speech and body language that impress assertion as opposed to aggression. These include:

1. Take a step back – do not stand too close as invading another person's personal space could be perceived as threatening and induce a 'fight-or-flight' response. This is likely to escalate a situation and maximize the possibility that it will have a negative outcome, as the recipient is likely to respond in an angry way, which in turn will increase the client's anger.
2. Maintain eye contact and a firm facial expression – this allows the other person to see that the client is serious about what they are saying. Help the client to practice facial expressions and avoid 'menacing looks' by encouraging them to practise in a mirror. Get them to do this in sessions and at home.
3. Maintain voice volume and pace at a steady level – no shouting or whispering. Raising the volume and increasing the speed of speech may feel threatening to the other person, thus increasing the likelihood that they will become angry and the situation may escalate. If the other person is already angry, using a normal volume of voice may also assist them in calming down. In contrast, speaking very quietly or not at all may irritate the other person by appearing 'passive-aggressive' and/or denying the individual the opportunity to be heard and understood.
4. Use the ADHD formula outlined above.

SUMMARY

This module highlights the nature of anger and its adaptive functions. It identifies how people with ADHD may respond to anger and sensitive areas for them. Anger management skills crucially require the ability to identify anger signals within a CBT framework and raising awareness of antecedents, behaviours and consequences of anger. The module also discusses the difference between insults and criticisms and presents techniques for coping with each. Finally, the issue of assertiveness, as distinct from aggression, is explored with strategies for increasing assertive behaviour. It is important for the therapist to be aware of previous anger inducing experiences with services that may block the development of a therapeutic alliance. Furthermore, it is also necessary for the therapist to ensure their own safety when addressing topics which may arouse anger in their client.

Group Treatment: Frustration and Anger Module

It is essential to prepare for group treatment by reading the chapter module. Six group sessions are outlined below, but the number of treatment sessions can be expanded or reduced as required.

Plan

Sessions 1 & 2	Starting activities Measure of assertion
Session 3	Psychoeducation – the cognitive behavioural model, the ABC process, anger management techniques/assertiveness training
Sessions 4 & 5	Exercises
Session 6	Revision of psychoeducation and techniques Discussion of homework outcome/experience – what works best? Obstacles and how to overcome them

Starting Activities

Guide participants to think about specific events and circumstances when answering the questions.

What makes you feel angry?
How do you usually respond when you are feeling frustrated and irritated?
How do you usually respond when you are feeling very angry?
Group discussion.
How to you move from feeling frustrated or irritated to feeling so angry that you have an angry outburst?

Discuss escalation and suppression.

What have been the consequences of your angry outbursts in the past?
What is the worst thing that could happen?
What happens to you when you become angry?

Direct participants to identify thoughts, feelings, physical reactions and behaviour. What would be an 'early warning sign' that they might notice and which would indicate that they need to apply an intervention.

Hand out the Measure of Assertion (Table 10.1) and complete individually.
Group discussion (compare individual differences, strengths/weaknesses).

Psychoeducation

Describe the cognitive behavioural model of anger – angry thoughts, physical reaction, provocative behaviour. Describe the link between them and point out how they escalate behaviour.

(*Continued*)

Handout Figure 10.1: Physical, cognitive and behavioural aspects of anger.

Describe the three-stage ABC process – Antecedents, Behaviour and Consequences.

Describe anger management techniques: distraction techniques to divert away from angry thoughts; calming self-talk; breathing and relaxation techniques (see Anxiety Module, Chapter 9); and reframing the situation.

Discuss when techniques may be helpful, which are better for situations previously identified and discussed?

Exercises

Select suitable examples of anger provoking situations/experiences described by participants in starting activities or introduce new examples (e.g. 'Mick' and 'Dave' described in the module). Using these examples complete exercises.

Recognizing anger and when to intervene.

- Role-play the scene.
- Discuss what was observed by participants (physical/body reactions, tone of voice, physical proximity, etc.).
- Discuss with role-play partner how it felt, what escalated the anger.
- Discuss 'early warning signs' and when to intervene.
- Point out that you can induce 'real' feelings of anger artificially this way. If you can do this, then you can learn ways to reduce feelings of anger.

Agree with the group a way to calm the situation down (what could be said/done etc). Re-run role-play several times using distraction and self-talk techniques. Discuss.

Select a suitable situation/experience described by participants in starting activities or introduce a new example and discuss how the situation could be re-framed.

- Use the ADHD formula.
- Role-play (if appropriate).
- Discuss how to be assertive without becoming angry.

Demonstrate relaxation strategies – breathing exercises and progressive muscle relaxation (do in session).

Select a suitable situation/experience described by participants in starting activities or introduce a new example to demonstrate the difference between insults and criticisms – role-play giving and accepting constructive criticism (cushion it by framing information as positive, negative, positive – like a sandwich; pay attention to tone, body language). Discuss.

Discuss obstacles to achievement and methods to overcome them.

Homework

Handout Boxes 9.4 and 9.5 (relaxation techniques) for homework.

Apply and rehearse techniques between sessions.

11

LOW-MOOD AND DEPRESSION MODULE

A review of the literature on the comorbidity of major depression or mood disorder (dysthymia) found a range between 15 per cent and 75 per cent in childhood ADHD. Up to one-third suffered major depression (Biederman, Newcorn and Sprich, 1991). Similar rates are reported in adults with ADHD suggesting that major depression and dysthymia continue to be common comorbid conditions (Biederman *et al.*, 1993; Murphy and Barkley, 1996). Dysthymia is a milder but persistent form of depression with low mood as a core feature. Thus, dips in mood are very likely to be experienced by adolescents and adults with ADHD and it is important to teach the client techniques to prevent low mood from spiralling into a more permanent depressed mood state.

People with depression have symptoms of low mood, loss of energy and motivation, and a sense of hopelessness about the future. When these symptoms are comorbid with ADHD, the person also has additional symptoms such as greater concentration problems and feelings of lethargy. Although they feel restless inside, their lack of motivation and energy means their natural optimism and creativity is 'trapped' in a negative cycle of depressive rumination.

In a study of individuals diagnosed with ADHD for the first time in adulthood and comparing severity of depression in different age groups by decade (Bramham et al., in press), a positive association was found between age and depression ratings. This means that the later a person received a diagnosis, the greater their severity of depressive symptoms. Thus clinicians need to be sensitive to the possibility of underlying depressive symptoms in adults diagnosed with ADHD, especially when this diagnosis was made well into adulthood. Qualitative research investigating the experience of obtaining a diagnosis of ADHD and treatment found an increased likelihood that following diagnosis, treatment and improvement in ADHD symptoms, people with ADHD are more likely to engage in depressive rumination (Young *et al.*, 2008). Even mild depression should be taken seriously and treated as a priority,

Cognitive-Behavioural Therapy for ADHD in Adolescents and Adults: A Psychological Guide to Practice,
Second Edition. Susan Young and Jessica Bramham.

especially since ADHD individuals are more likely to attempt suicide in the context of a depressive illness (Weiss *et al.*, 1985). If they have thoughts of suicide, they may impulsively act out their ideation.

When clinicians are faced with individuals with comorbid ADHD and severe depression, it is recommended that the depression is treated with antidepressant medication *and* psychological interventions. Traditional psychostimulants (e.g. methylphenidate) have been shown to be of benefit for depression and therefore may act as a dual intervention. However, a side effect of this treatment is that it may induce anxiety (Vance *et al.*, 1999). Norepinephrine reuptake inhibitors such as Atomoxetine, have been shown to treat ADHD (Pliszka, 2003) but these can also be used as an antidepressant and may be a treatment of choice for individuals with both diagnoses.

Suggestions for psychological treatment of people with ADHD and comorbid mood problems are presented in this module. A cognitive model of depression can be adapted for individuals with ADHD with an intervention that addresses depressive and ADHD thinking styles. The module examines common negative thinking and thinking errors of ADHD adults. Cognitive and behavioural interventions are suggested that include challenging negative thoughts and activity scheduling.

FUNCTIONAL DEFICITS IN ADOLESCENTS AND ADULTS

There are several possible explanations for why individuals with ADHD may be at greater risk of depression. First, they are more likely to have experienced adverse events early in childhood. It is likely that parents of ADHD children are not without their problems. It is not easy being a parent at the best of times and parenting an ADHD child who challenges authority, breaks rules and disrupts stable family life is difficult to manage. Additionally many parents have undiagnosed ADHD, meaning that they themselves may be disorganized and chaotic in their parenting style, and unable to provide the appropriate structure and stability for their children. At school as well as home, a child with ADHD is likely to have been overly criticized. Scholastic underachievement is usually not associated with ADHD symptoms but construed by others as 'laziness'. Relationship difficulties seem to be a consistent problem; as children, they may have had difficulty developing supportive relationships and become unpopular with peers; as adults they have difficulty maintaining friendships and lack intimate relationships. They may have low self-esteem. It is no great surprise that these experiences predispose an individual to feel low and develop depression at some period in his/her life.

People with ADHD can find that, along with low mood, they become particularly irritable and intolerant. They may feel guilty about the hurtful things they say and do on impulse to people they love and care for. Attentional deficits can also be exacerbated, leading the person to be even less likely to complete tasks and depriving them from feeling a sense of achievement. People can become distracted from constructive activities and preoccupied by their own internal negative automatic thoughts that characterize depression. This leads to disturbed sleep with insomnia and early waking. The internal conflict between feelings of restlessness and lack of motivation can be a source of discomfort and emotional exhaustion. Seeing the world through dark glasses and observing hopelessness all around leads some people to cope by increasing their alcohol intake or taking drugs. Such coping mechanisms are only temporarily effective. Alcohol 'drowns their sorrows' and drugs give brief relief (and possibly temporary symptom improvement, depending on the substance of preference). However the short-term aftermath is a hangover and symptoms of withdrawal, including low mood. In the longer term these strategies have the expensive price tag of psychological and physical dependence. These issues are discussed in the Substance Misuse Module (Chapter 13).

Mood regulation is a considerable problem for adults with ADHD and their capacity to regulate mood worsens when depressed or low in mood due to an increase in emotional lability. Individuals may find that they become tearful quickly and without apparent reason. They are also much more likely to be 'touchy', or 'snappy'. Indeed in clients with ADHD, low mood is often displayed as anger and understood by others as bad temperament. This may reflect a need to hide their feelings of despair and futility from others.

Emotional lability has been misdiagnosed in people with ADHD as bipolar disorder. Mania is characterized by excitability, overtalkativeness, racing thoughts, euphoria and increased energy. All of these symptoms are exhibited by adults with ADHD and it can sometimes be difficult to tease them apart phenomenologically. One way of differentiating between these disorders is to establish rate of onset of the elated mood and its persistency. Mood swings in ADHD can occur very rapidly and dissipate quickly, for example, within an hour or a day, whereas manic episodes are more likely to have a prodromal stage, increase gradually and be more persistent over time, for example, weeks or months. The age of onset is also a useful indicator as the majority of bipolar illnesses do not emerge until late adolescence or early adulthood, whereas ADHD has onset in early childhood. It is unusual for a 7-year-old to be diagnosed with bipolar disorder.

Beck's (1976) well-established cognitive model of depression can be adapted to describe the experience of adults with ADHD who exhibit depressive symptoms. Individuals with ADHD are likely to be able to elaborate upon multiple early negative life experiences. They have usually a history of being criticized by parents and teachers who have told them that they are lazy, stupid or unable to learn. In comparison with their peers, there may even be objective evidence, for example test marks, which may have made them feel less able than others and lead them to internalize the idea of their reduced status. Through this typical ADHD childhood experience, individuals are likely to have generated schemas about themselves that are related to feelings of inferiority. In our experience a common schema is that the individual is 'different' from others in some unique way and that others are more able, successful, likeable and so forth. Such schemas lead to the formation of dysfunctional assumptions. These are usually 'if ... then' statements and they serve to maintain a sense of self-value and self-worth. For example, 'If I don't play the clown and entertain people, then they won't want to spend time with me'; "If I miss the deadline this week, my boss will think I'm no good and fire me". These assumptions are not available at a conscious level, but are likely to have influenced the manner in which ADHD individuals interact with others and the expectations they place on themselves. These expectations are often unrealistic and overly high, causing them to be perfectionistic and pedantic in their attempts to achieve them. This is stressful and in order to reduce the stress, some people with ADHD choose to settle for undemanding activities in which they are more likely to achieve. However, deep down they know that they are underachieving and lack the confidence to stretch themselves and reach their potential, which causes them to feel unhappy and deeply dissatisfied. For others their schemas mean that they accept criticism uncritically from others and they may become enmeshed in an abusive relationship.

Due to both their inattentive and impulsive symptoms, ADHD individuals are more likely to incur critical life events such as losing their job (either because they walk out on impulse or are fired), getting divorced or being involved in accidents, for example. When such events occur, this precipitates the activation of previously developed dysfunctional schemata and leads to an increase in negative automatic thoughts about themselves (see Figure 11.1 adapted from Beck, 1976; also on the Companion Website in handout format as Figure 11.1a). Unlike earlier, at this stage in the process the individual assumptions are conscious and the individual may be aware of the multiple negative thoughts about themselves racing through their head. These thoughts may be so rapid and so severe that the individual feels completely overwhelmed and metaphorically beaten by them. An inability to modulate cognitions and emotions means the individual may develop symptoms such as: labile mood swings of low mood and anger; hopelessness and a sense of loss of control about the future; distraction and preoccupation; and a loss of the creative resources, interest and energy that are usually readily accessible to the individual. It is not easy for a person with ADHD to stay on task at the best of times, but it is especially difficult when their own thoughts and feelings become 'internal distracters' or an additional hurdle or obstacle to overcome. If low mood spirals further into depression, the person may become withdrawn, indecisive and give up completely. In turn, this will confirm an underlying schema and the dysfunctional assumptions that are held about themselves are activated. This in turn reinforces the behaviour and keeps the person engaged in a vicious cycle of depression.

However, there appears to be a positive aspect to the ADHD personality that may protect individuals from spiralling into clinical depression – this is 'resilience' and the ability to cognitively reframe social problems and disappointments. Indeed, from interviewing individuals with ADHD, it appears that a common characteristic is their ability to bounce back and try again. Lability in mood means their mood state is changing (sometimes rapidly) and these fluctuations may 'kickstart' their creativity and zest for life. An alternative explanation may be that they are unable to resist the

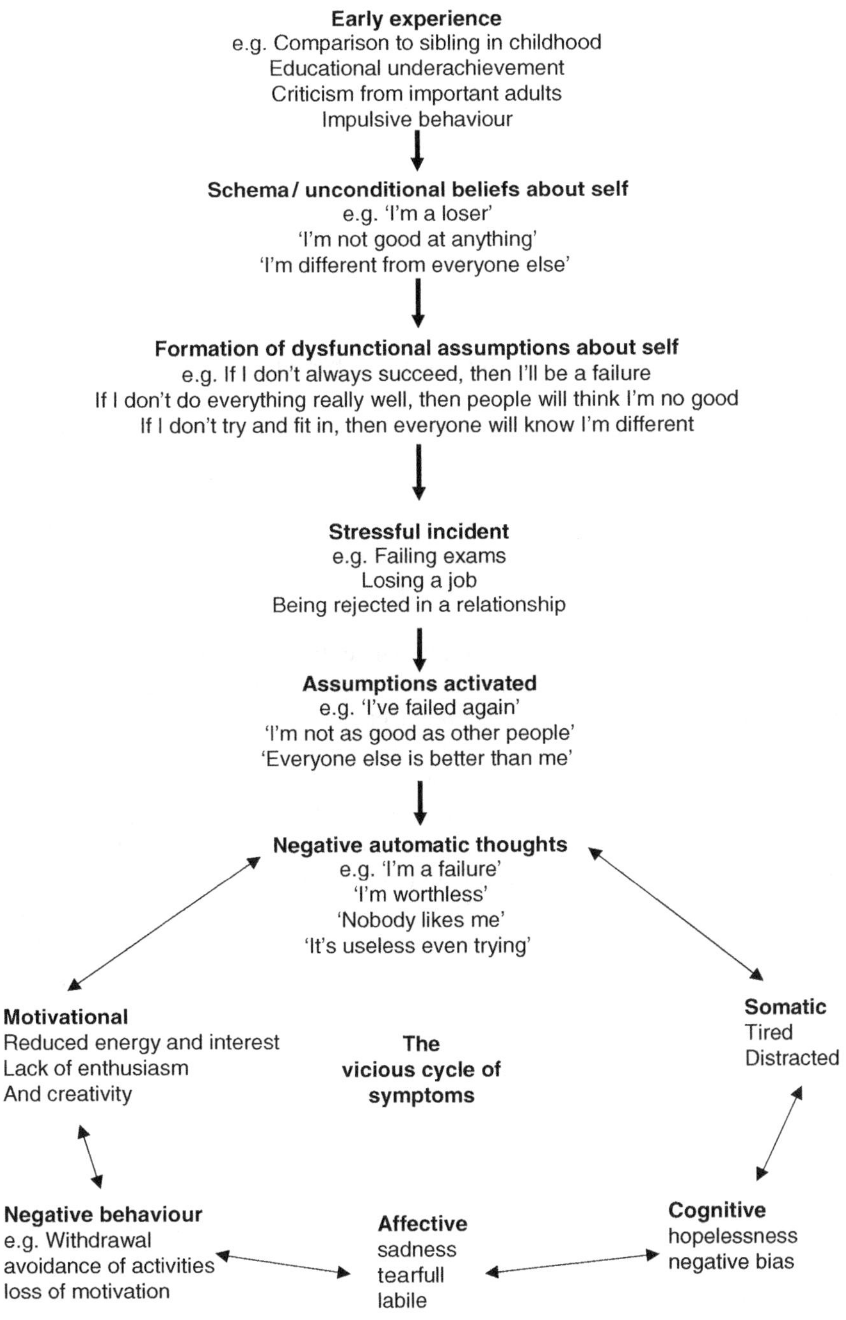

Figure 11.1 Cognitive model of depression in ADHD
Source: Adapted from Beck 1976

impulse to have another go when others may conclude that an option is unviable. Attentional problems may also feed resilience by limiting the ability to reason about the implications of negative consequences and predict or anticipate future problems. A word of warning, however, while in some individuals this characteristic may serve as a protective factor, in others it may predispose to depression as it leads them to experience a higher number of negative events or failures. These may aggregate to reach a critical mass when resilience can no longer spring them back to positivity and they are left with a legacy of failures and regrets that appear insurmountable.

ASSESSMENT OF LOW MOOD AND DEPRESSION

People with ADHD often seek for an explanation of their negative life experiences and problems. The cognitive model is something that they understand and recognize. By seeing the model outlined in Figure 11.1 and completing the categories with their own experience (see Companion Website Figure 11.1b), clients will take important steps towards making sense of any confusion and inner turmoil. Although recognition, insight and understanding of past problems and current needs may seem like 'turning on a light', the problem remains; feelings of inadequacy and anxiety that they will fail to meet their own expectations and those of others. These concerns underpin their self-assumptions and core beliefs that they are inferior human beings. Thinking errors may additionally relate to the tendency of ADHD adults to make rapid erroneous attributions due to their inability to 'stop' and engage in a process of consequential thinking. This haphazard 'hit and miss' approach to life means that ADHD adults do not develop the ability to reason in a rational stage-by-stage process. The most common thinking error for people with ADHD is the tendency to jump to conclusions, which stems from their poor impulse control. For example, Pete, a client with ADHD thought his manager did not like him. One day he was asked to go to speak to his manager, and he jumped to the conclusion that he was going to be fired from his job. Acting on this notion, he went into the general office, shouted at his manager, resigned and walked out. This was in the absence of any information suggesting that he was going to be fired. He later learned that he was about to be promoted. Thinking errors common to people with ADHD are presented in Table 11.1 (also on the Companion Website).

The therapist may jointly perform an exercise (see Box 11.1) with their client in order to teach them how to identify and evaluate thinking errors before going on to encourage them to identify their own (i.e. without the support of the therapist). A blank version is included on the Companion Website (see Table 11.2a). However, the categories are not mutually exclusive and there may be more than one error of thinking present. It does not really matter if the client identifies the categories correctly, the point is to get the client to recognize that they are making thinking errors. If they stop and evaluate their own thoughts, they may not make the same errors.

Table 11.1 Typical thinking errors of people with ADHD

Type of error	*Exposition*
Jumping to conclusions	Negative interpretations in the absence of facts. *Example*: Predicting the future or reading someone's mind.
All or nothing	There seems to be no middle ground and everything can be categorized as 'black' or 'white'. *Example*: I can't concentrate at all.
Overgeneralizing	Drawing extreme conclusions from a single event. *Example*: I am always tactless and offend people when I speak to them.
Catastrophizing	Exaggerating and overestimating outcomes. *Example*: I have missed a deadline and therefore am going to be sacked.
Personalizing	Taking the blame for everything that goes wrong or is unpleasant, believing that everything people do or say is a personal reaction to you. *Example*: It's all my fault.
Negative focus	Ignoring or misinterpreting positive aspects due to learned helplessness. Always assuming the worst. *Example*: The glass is half empty rather than half-full.
'Shoulds' and 'oughts'	A belief of failure to meet standards or expectations, without consideration of whether these are reasonable or realistic. *Example*: I should always get it right.

Box 11.1 Thinking errors exercise

What are the following thinking errors?

1 I did that badly and have completely ruined it all.
Answer: Catastrophizing

2 I upset her by blurting out gossip. I'm a terrible person.
Answer: Personalizing

3 I should have finished everything I planned to do.
Answer: 'Shoulds' and 'oughts'

4 Everything goes wrong.
Answer: All or nothing

5 He didn't shake my hand. I definitely won't get the job.
Answer: Jumping to conclusions

6 She didn't return my call. All women find me unattractive.
Answer: Overgeneralizing

COGNITIVE BEHAVIOURAL THERAPY

Psychoeducation

Negative thinking styles directly relate to mood and lead to social withdrawal, so CBT targets the reduction of negative automatic thoughts (NATS) and increasing activities. When their mood fluctuates, as is common in people with ADHD, their cognitions fluctuate and this can cause the person to feel confused, uncertain and distressed. Additionally, depressed ADHD individuals are more likely to be snappy or irritable, which is likely to increase the frequency of negative social encounters. This may lead to social withdrawal in order to reduce feelings of irritation, by avoiding people or situations they perceive will make them feel this way. However, this may mean they conceptualize themselves as an 'unlikeable' person.

The 'cognitive triad' is a focus on negative aspects of the self, the world and the future (Beck, 1963). It is easy to see how this position may develop when a person has an underlying schema that they are stupid and useless (self), others find them lazy and irritable (the world), and that tomorrow is bleak and unchangeable (the future). Perhaps it is this latter aspect that prevents people with ADHD completely capitulating to clinical depression as fundamentally they see the world as a challenge that may be changeable. They see a better outcome is possible because they sense that they are underachieving their potential. This means that they believe they have potential even if they do not appreciate the full extent of this. Such beliefs are 'food' for cognitive challenges and alternative thinking that can be achieved by developing the ADHD individual's natural interest and curiosity for novel tasks. Their talents must be identified and exploited.

The ADHD thinking style is driven by speed. People with ADHD involuntarily react both behaviourally and cognitively. People describe themselves frequently being distracted by thoughts that 'come from nowhere' and flit from one idea to the next, when they are trying to focus on one thing. When these thoughts are negative, they are particularly distressing. The characteristics of negative thoughts are that they are:

- *automatic* – they just pop into your head and are not generated consciously;
- *distorted* – they only take into account the negative;
- *unhelpful* – they keep the vicious cycle of low mood going;
- *plausible* – they are not questioned, because they seem 'true'; and
- *involuntary* – they do not happen through choice and are hard to switch off.

Individuals with ADHD are more likely to accept the plausibility of NATS because they have difficulty thinking about consequences and evaluating thoughts, so they often erroneously accept negative thoughts as the truth. Psychoeducation regarding the nature of NATS is important in any therapy for depression. However, this will be particularly important for individuals with ADHD as their familiarity with such thoughts may be exceptionally strong. People with ADHD are passionate people and when they feel low they will feel passionately low. It is not easy to learn to identify NATS and this will take practice and guidance in sessions.

Adolescents and adults with ADHD often feel overwhelmed by what are perceived to be insurmountable problems and therefore give up very early or easily. It can be difficult to know where to start, especially if motivation is low and the task is not of particular interest. This can make the client feel worse, because they are even less likely to achieve tasks and more likely to lose attention before they are completed. When this happens, the system needs to be 'kick started'. Activity makes people feel better and more alert and motivates further activity, that is, the more you do, the more you feel like doing. This can be counterintuitive, however, as many people do not perform activities because they 'do not feel like it'. The client should be encouraged to understand the behaviour-motivation lag, whereby starting an activity (even when they do not want to at first) can make them feel like doing it. However an attention deficit means that people have difficulty finishing tasks at the best of times, let alone when they feel low in mood. So tasks need to be broken down into smaller stages, with the client aiming to complete one stage at a time. By learning to apply this methodology, clients who feel unmotivated and are low in mood may find that not only do they complete their target but in the course of time they develop motivation to complete many other parts, and in turn complete the whole task.

Mood Control Strategies

Challenging Negative Thoughts

Individuals with ADHD need greater practise and rehearsal of challenging negative thoughts due to their attentional problems and difficulty in grasping concepts. They are also more likely to give up impulsively and quickly decide that they cannot do it. It is therefore crucial to make homework very manageable. Early failure will reinforce the negative schema and lead to disengagement. Adaptations need to be made to improve the likelihood of clients completing thought records, for example, by getting them to quickly telephone an answerphone to record the thought or by saying it into a recording device (the latter facility is often incorporated into mobile phones or computers providing an easily accessible resource).

Just as thoughts can exacerbate low mood, they can also be exploited to improve moods. Explaining how the vicious spiral can be reversed can be a strong motivator and give a sense of hope. Recognizing that different, more positive thoughts in the same situation can lead to the experience of positive feelings and result in positive behaviours can improve mood. This is a difficult skill to master as the client must learn to impose control over a lability they have long believed they lack control.

The client should be encouraged to look at alternative interpretations or alternative outcomes, for example, replace thoughts like 'I can't cope' with 'this is difficult, but I can manage if I take it a step at a time'. However, people with ADHD are likely to find considering alternatives to original thinking difficult due to their executive functioning problems and inflexibility. This seems ironic given that they often have strong creative talent. The issue here is that they have the ability to generate lots of original ideas but do not do so spontaneously as they either stick rigidly to one aspect for some time and do not consider alternative ideas or solutions at all, or give up and move on to a completely different topic leaving a task incomplete or a problem unresolved. This rigidity needs to be overcome by teaching the client to relax and let new ideas flow. Brainstorming techniques are helpful (see Box 11.2).

Box 11.2 Brainstorming Techniques

1. Think of many different solutions to the problem, even silly ones;
2. Disregard all solutions that are not pragmatic;
3. Consider the remaining solutions and rate how useful they may be on a scale of 0 = useless to 10 = very helpful.
4. Select a solution.

Apart from the brainstorming techniques outlined (and presented for client use on the Companion Website), it can be useful in sessions to develop with the client a set of standard questions that they ask themselves to help them challenge the belief that they cannot cope with their negative thinking, generate alternative thinking or commence a creative thinking process (See Box 11.3 and Box 11.4). Table 11.2 provides examples of challenging the negative thoughts of people with ADHD. (See also the Companion Website.)

One positive aspect of working with people with ADHD is that once they have procured the skills of brainstorming and perspective-taking, they seem to quickly develop these skills and adopt them in their daily lives. This most likely reflects the fact that these techniques tap into their creativity and ingenuity and, once they have learned the skill of alternative thinking, they have no difficulty applying the process. The key is learning to stop their automatic acceptance of an original thought or idea and engage in a process of consequential or alternative thinking. The therapist may have to prompt many times to do this. It may be helpful to encourage the client to write out the prompting questions and carry them on a card. The Companion Website contains this list in a format that can be copied for this purpose. The client could, at a more fundamental level, be encouraged

Box 11.3 Exercise: Challenging negative thinking

1. What is the evidence that you can't cope? Write down the times when you have successfully coped in the past.
2. Imagine your friend came to you with this problem – what would you tell them? Would you view it in the same way, i.e. believing that there are no solutions?
3. What is the worst that could happen? Am I overestimating the likelihood of this happening?

Box 11.4 Replacing negative thoughts

Exercise

Think of a negative thought:
I cannot complete this form – it's too difficult and long
Now counteract it with a positive self-statement:
I have managed to finish many more forms in the past and some were even longer

Table 11.2 Examples of negative thoughts and challenges

Negative thoughts	*Challenges*
I am not as capable as other people.	I am not good at everything. Like everybody I am good at some things and not so good at others.
There is no way I can complete that task. What is the point in trying?	If I don't try, I won't know. If I break it down into smaller sections I will be able to complete it. Trying in itself will broaden my experience and skill. Nobody is expecting me to do it all in one go.
I'm bound to miss something out or make a mistake.	Everybody makes mistakes, even people without ADHD. I know how to check what I have done for mistakes and I can ask others to help me. Sometimes it is good to make mistakes because that is the best way to learn.
I end up talking about rubbish and nobody wants to listen to me.	I have opinions, thoughts and feelings. A lot of people find it very difficult to talk in public and I may put them at their ease. I can make sure I talk about things that interest them.
Everybody hates me and thinks I'm a moody person.	There are people who like me for who I am. Everyone is allowed to have their down moments.
People without ADHD are happier than me.	I don't know this for a fact. Some people may be and others may be very unhappy. Just because somebody seems like they are in control, doesn't mean they are more satisfied.
It would be best if I avoided people, because I end up being rude and offending people.	If I stay away I don't give myself a chance. There are many more occasions when I get on well with people than occasions when I offend them.
My mood swings around so much – I may start crying in front of everyone.	It is acceptable to be upset sometimes. When I see others crying, I am understanding and do not think any worse of the person. It would not be the end of the world. What is wrong with showing emotion?
I'm hopeless at everything and always have been. I've been trying all my life to sort myself out and have got nowhere.	There are many things that I can do very well. I have made great improvements in many areas of my life.

to interrupt automatic responding by linking the process with a visual image, for example, a new idea, red flash, 'stop' sign.

Once negative thoughts have been determined and the thinking process halted, the client may be helped by learning to replace a negative thought with a more positive one. This may be motivating as well as rewarding. It can be helpful to make up a list of possible negative/positive thoughts. This involves dividing a sheet of paper into two columns and writing a list of negative thoughts down one side of the page and then a list of positive self-statements (challenges) on the other. Make sure that items are not 'global' abstract thoughts or schemas but refer to thoughts about that moment in time. With careful prompting, the therapist must ensure that positive thoughts and outcomes far outweigh the negative outcomes. If the page is folded over to only show the positive side, this provides a list of self-generated positive statements that may be usefully applied in treatment. Examples of negative thoughts, positive self-statements and cognitive challenges are presented in Table 11.2.

Activity Scheduling

The first task for the therapist is to engage the client in a process of categorizing what has to be done. The way to do this is to make a list of tasks that are compulsory, important and necessary and finally desirable (see Box 11.5 also on the Companion Website). This will be intuitively interesting to the client as they will see spread before them a frame or plan that structures achievement. People with ADHD are generally active and so activity schedules and plans are unlikely to be rejected. However, because clients can be chaotic and disorganized in their general approach to life, using such plans and outlines will be unusual. If they have tried and failed to use similar techniques, this is probably for one of two reasons: (1) either they have not broken tasks down into sufficiently small steps, or (2) because they have not incorporated a reward system into their schedule.

Box 11.5 Making a task list

1. *Tasks that must be done*
   - collect the children from school
   - go shopping
   - renew bus pass
2. *Tasks that client wants to do*
   - watch new film at cinema
   - go to hairdressers
   - meet friend
3. *Rewards*
   - read magazine
   - go for a run
   - watch television

By definition, a reward is something that is pleasurable to the individual and will lift mood. However, if a person is very depressed, their avoidance of tasks or social withdrawal may represent a 'reward' to the individual and reinforce their depressed state. In such cases the therapist must guide the client to select rewards that will act as positive reinforcers. Of course rewards will vary between individuals. One man's meat is another man's poison! If the client is feeling particularly low it can be hard to think of things that give pleasure so it can be helpful to encourage the client to think about what they would suggest to somebody else. If they find it difficult to define 'rewards' they would like now, that is, in a dysphoric mood, ask the client about activities and or treats that used to give them pleasure. Identify small rewards as well as large rewards. A reward could be taking a bath, watching a television programme, going for a swim, going to the cinema, going to the gym, meeting a friend, going for a walk, making a telephone call to a friend, a piece of cake, listening to music, a holiday ... there are endless possibilities.

Once the tasks and rewards have been established, the client can be guided to plan ahead by making up a Diary activity plan which divides each day into hours (see Table 5.3 on Companion Website). The client should be encouraged to avoid the temptation of doing too much in one go. Activities need to be scheduled in small amounts so that they become manageable. Initially, the planning phase may seem a daunting task for someone with ADHD so the client should be encouraged to reward themselves once the planning is completed. The schedule should include regular breaks, such as stop for a drink or go for a quick walk. The timing of breaks should be determined by their concentration span. This may need to be determined by trial and error, however, they have to ensure that the schedule is not all reward for little achievement. The rest of the time can be filled in, from morning to evening, with the activities identified previously in the Task List. People with ADHD have a difficulty with 'delayed gratification', i.e. they find it difficult to wait for a reward, so long periods should not be scheduled between rewards. Completion of tasks or structured activity must be paired with reward, which may be brief periods of relaxation or alternatively high stimulation. Rewards that involve some form of activity can be particularly stimulating, such as physical exercise, as this will help alleviate feelings of restlessness.

The aim is to create a system whereby frequent rewards are incorporated to reward completion of tasks that have been put off or avoided. Rewards can be matched according to task demand and complexity, for example if the client is working on a task requiring a lot of thought and sustained concentration (such as completing a report) then schedule in frequent short breaks for a drink and/or snack. When the form has been completed, say at the end of the day, a bigger reward can be scheduled such as going out to the cinema or going for a run. The goal is to maximize activity levels and increase the level of satisfaction and feeling of achievement.

Clients should be reminded of the thoughts, feelings and behaviour cycle while completing tasks and increasing productivity. By being more active, the cycle can be

Box 11.6 Example of a task list for activity scheduling

Tasks John must do:

Complete his tax return
Cut the grass
Buy his daughter a birthday present
Grocery shopping for the week
Household chores
Prepare invoices and statements for work
Visit a potential client and prepare an estimate
Finish his current job fitting a water feature
Go to the bank
Return a movie to the hire shop

Tasks John wants to do:

Go to the cinema
Finish reading his book
Find out about joining the local gym
Visit a friend in hospital
Go to the opticians for an eye test
Find out about how to run in the next marathon

Rewards:

Go running
Reading the newspaper
Watch the football on television
Watch a movie he has hired
Meet a friend for a drink
Have a takeaway meal

reversed by using behaviour to improve mood. For the client, this will also increase a sense of control over their life and what they can achieve. The aim is to reduce an insurmountable mass of unstarted or half-finished tasks into a prioritized manageable list – a list that can be completed and has an end. Once tasks are completed, the client should be encouraged to see this visually and increase feelings of satisfaction and achievement by ticking off items on their list or crossing them through. One client has told us that he used to use a highlighter pen to mark completed tasks as he wanted to highlight achievement. He said it was a reward in itself to see a block of tasks in fluorescent yellow ink.

It is important to review what has been achieved at the end of each day and think about the days ahead. The client should be encouraged to focus on what they have managed

Table 11.3 Diary activity plan

Week beginning……………….							
	Monday	Tuesday	Wednesday	Thursday	Friday	Saturday	Sunday
9–10	Work	Work	Tax form	Invoicing And	Cut grass	Sleep	Sleep
10–11	Work	Work	Tax form	Statements	Cut grass	Read book	Vacuuming
	Break	Break	Break	Break	Break	Break	Break
11.15–12	Work	Work	Tax form	Phone calls	Paperwork and correspondence	Travel to shops	Ironing
12–1	Work	Work	Go out for run	Vacuuming	Write and post letters	Shop for present	Ironing
1–2	Lunch	Lunch	Lunch	Lunch	Lunch	Lunch	Lunch
2–3	Work	Work	Tidy up house	Prepare estimate	Travel to shops	Visit gym	Go out for run
3–4	Work	Work	Post tax form and travel to client	Post estimate Travel to hospital	Banking	Travel home	Watch football on TV
	Break	Break	Break	Break	Break	Break	Break
4.15–5	Work	Work	Visit new client	Hospital visit	Opticians	Read book	Watch football on TV
5–6	Travel home	Travel home	Travel home	Travel home	Travel home	Go out for a walk	Read book
6–7	Break	Break	Break	Break	Break	Break	Break
7–12	Takeaway	Football on TV	TV	Watch movie	Cinema	Out with friend	Visit family

to do and not to punish themselves for what they did not achieve – after all, they could have stayed in bed and done nothing. Some adjustments will inevitably need to be made to the plan, depending on how well the client has overestimated or underestimated the time it takes to complete tasks. As mentioned earlier, in the initial stages, it is better to schedule very short tasks into a longer period, in order to maximize the likelihood of success. If the plan has not been adhered to, then try to identify what went wrong and at what time. It will be useful to note this information in the Diary Activity Plan at the appropriate place. It could be, for example, that the client is able to stick to the plan in the morning but not after lunch in which case the therapist should adapt the schedule to start the afternoon with a 'desirable' activity before moving to one from the 'must do' list. It is important to include tasks that give pleasure, and not just a list of chores.

An example of a diary activity plan is given in Table 11.3 (see blank version for use in sessions in Table 5.3 on Companion Website). This is a week's schedule for a client, John, a self-employed landscape gardener who lives on his own.

Before John made his Diary Activity Plan, he made a task list (see Box 11.6). He had to break down some of the items he wished to achieve. For example, in the 'must do' list he wrote 'household chores'. What John had to do was the vacuuming, tidying up, washing and ironing. These tasks needed to be listed out separately. Similarly some tasks required John to make telephone calls, for example finding out about the local gym and the marathon; enquiring about costs of materials required for his next job.

John could work for a 2-hour span before he lost concentration, so his Diary Activity Plan was organized around this time span to optimize completion of tasks. In the regular allotted breaks John either ate lunch or dinner. During the 15 minute breaks he had a cup of tea or coffee or wandered outside. He usually relaxed during the longer breaks and read the newspaper or watched something on television.

An example of John's schedule is provided in Table 11.3. The highlighted areas represent break and reward periods.

SUMMARY

This module discusses the reasons why many individuals with ADHD may also experience comorbid low mood or depression. It elaborates the traditional cognitive model in order to elucidate how particular features of ADHD can exacerbate low mood and/or typical depression. There may be a potential risk period following the diagnosis and treatment of ADHD symptoms, when the individual appears to engage in depressive ruminations and analysis of the past. Examples of thought patterns and thinking errors are provided along with exercises for the client and therapist to perform in sessions. Suggestions for activity scheduling are explained with a particular emphasis on how short-term rewards are crucial in maintaining motivation in depressed individuals with ADHD.

Group Treatment: Low-Mood and Depression Module

It is essential to prepare for group treatment by reading the chapter module. Six group sessions are outlined below, but the number of treatment sessions can be expanded or reduced as required.

Plan

Session 1	Starting activities
Session 2	Psychoeducation – cognitive behavioural model of depression; ADHD negative thinking styles; activity scheduling; rewards
Sessions 3–5	Exercises
Session 6	Revision of psychoeducation, techniques and rewards Discussion of homework outcome/experience – what works best? Obstacles and how to overcome them

Starting Activities

What is the difference between low mood and depression?

What makes you feel low in mood? What makes you feel depressed? Guide participants to think about specific events and circumstances.

Group discussion.

What happens to you when you become depressed? Direct participants to identify negative thinking styles and behaviours (avoidance). What would be an 'early warning sign' that they might notice and which would indicate that they need to apply an intervention.

When you feel this way, what makes you feel better? What can you do yourself? What can others do?

Identify potential reward to lift mood and/or motivate activity.

Group discussion

Psychoeducation

Describe the cognitive behavioural model of depression.

Negative thinking styles and behaviour (avoidance).

Describe the link between them.

Handout Figure 11.1: Cognitive model of depression in ADHD.

ADHD negative thinking styles.

The cognitive triad – negative focus on self, the world and the future.

Characteristics of negative thoughts.

Thinking errors, handout Table 11.1.

Challenging negative thoughts, handout Table 11.2 and Box 11.3.

Replacing negative thoughts, handout Box 11.4.

(*Continued*)

Activity scheduling.
- Making a task list, handout Box 11.5.
- Make an activity plan, handout Table 11.3.
- Rewards and breaks.

Exercises

Complete the Thinking Errors Exercise (Handout Box 11.1).
- Can participants identify with any of these thinking errors?
- Ask them to describe their experiences and discuss (important to relate the thinking errors to the experience).

Using examples from these experiences, challenge negative thinking.
- Practice challenging negative thoughts (Handout Table 11.2 and Box 11.3). Discuss.
- Cross-examine thoughts as a skilled lawyer using questions provided in the module – role-play in pairs with one person 'thinking out loud' and the other being the lawyer.
- Discuss replacing negative thoughts with positive thoughts and generate a list of replacements (see Box 9.2 and Box 11.4).
- Practise superimposing positive thoughts and making positive self-statements – role-play by 'thinking out loud'.

Activity scheduling
- Select a volunteer who agrees to work with the group for this exercise.
- Make a task list for the week (see Box 11.5).
- Identify rewards.
- Add things the participant would like to do.
- Discuss length and frequency of breaks.
- Make up a Diary Activity Plan for the week (Handout Table 11.3).
- Repeat with other volunteers.
- Set homework and check in following sessions what was achieved. If not, why not?

Discuss obstacles to achievement and methods to overcome them.

Homework

Personalize Figure 11.1 Cognitive model of depression in ADHD.

Make a task list and prioritize tasks for the week. Include things they would like to do. Put into a Diary Activity Plan and do it!

Apply and rehearse techniques between sessions.

12

SLEEP MODULE

Many people with ADHD report difficulties with their sleep and research suggests that people with combined subtype sleep less while people with the inattentive subtype have a greater need for sleeping, especially during the day (Gau *et al.*, 2007; Mayes *et al.*, 2008; van Veen *et al.*, 2010). However, the nature of the relationship between ADHD and sleep disorders is unclear. Sleep disorders themselves can cause underfunctioning of the prefrontal cortex and lead to symptoms such as short attention span and impulsivity in people without ADHD. It is therefore likely that sleep problems can exacerbate existing ADHD cognitive deficits. Sleep difficulties may arise from a comorbid disorder that coincides with ADHD such as depression, anxiety or substance misuse. It is also possible that some sleep problems are experienced as a symptom of the ADHD syndrome, as ADHD is characterized by poor regulation of the arousal system, leading to attentional difficulties and overactivity. Some individuals report feeling as though they are constantly 'on the go' and cannot relax and therefore, too restless to fall asleep. These sleep problems may be related to disturbances of the arousal system, so the neurobiological basis of ADHD is also responsible for producing disturbances in sleep.

There is evidence to suggest that there is a specific relationship between attentional problems and sleep disorders due to the close linkage between brain systems involved in the regulation of the domains of sleep/arousal and those involved in the regulation of attention and affect (Owens, 2005). Sleep (during the night) and attention/alertness (during the day) can be conceptualized as being opposite extremes of the same continuum. Disturbance in attention and alertness in the daytime may impact on sleep at night, and vice versa. It may be that a problem with regulating the arousal system renders individuals with ADHD unable to achieve both full alertness and deep sleep, and only allows them to function in grades of semi-alertness throughout the day and night.

Cognitive-Behavioural Therapy for ADHD in Adolescents and Adults: A Psychological Guide to Practice,
Second Edition. Susan Young and Jessica Bramham.

Restlessness is one of the core symptoms of ADHD and this may prevent individuals from relaxing and/or achieving adequate sleep. Children with ADHD have been shown to exhibit higher levels of nocturnal activity (as measured by upper and lower limb movements at night) than controls (Konofal *et al.*, 2001). However, this activity was not shown to affect sleep continuity in a significant way, in other words, it did not cause them to wake up. Nevertheless, when children mature into young adults, they commonly report experiencing difficulties with ceaseless mental activity and this problem may well persist into the night and prevent them from sleeping. This can have a knock-on effect on their ability to attend in the day when they may be more prone to 'day-dream' due to sleep deprivation. In addition, ADHD individuals' difficulties with organization and prioritization can often leave them trying to complete tasks very late at night, which encroaches on their sleep time. When they do go to bed, they may be preoccupied with their unfinished tasks. A further explanation may relate to sleep problems being a side-effect of medication that is used to treat ADHD symptoms, as this is often a cerebral stimulant that may cause the individual to have difficulty falling asleep.

This module will describe the sleep disorders that are commonly experienced by people with ADHD including insomnia, sleep apnoea, nightmares, narcolepsy and restless legs. In order to treat sleep problems, it is necessary to provide clients with psychoeducational information regarding the process and function of sleep, and the ways in which this can be disrupted. Strategies for monitoring and managing sleep problems are outlined in the module. The relationship between mood and sleep is also considered, as affective disturbances may be maintaining difficulties getting to sleep and staying asleep.

FUNCTIONAL DEFICITS IN ADOLESCENTS AND ADULTS

There is evidence from studies of ADHD in children that they are more likely to suffer from insomnia, snoring, restless legs and daytime sleepiness than children without ADHD (Owens, 2005). It is not yet clear to what extent these problems persist into adulthood as very little research has been conducted. This section will describe how sleep difficulties may affect people with ADHD and the characteristics of each of the following disorders: insomnia, apnoea, nightmares, narcolepsy, restless legs syndrome.

Insomnia

Clients with ADHD usually report sleep problems that fall in to one or more of three categories (Brown and McMullen, 2001):

1. Difficulty getting to sleep – not being able to fall asleep and lying awake for several hours.

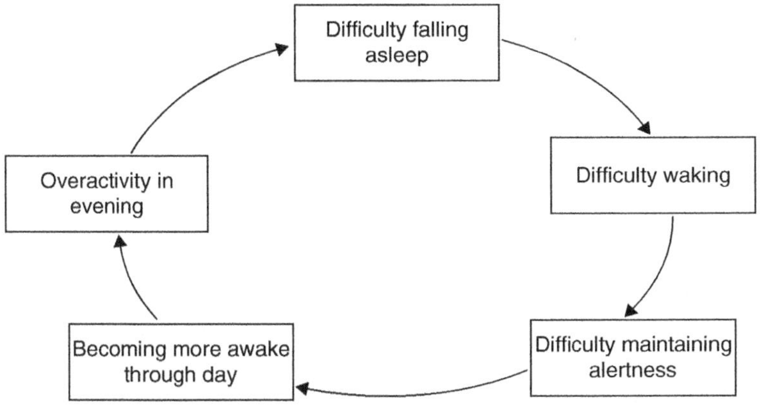

Figure 12.1 Dysfunctional sleep cycle

2. Not being able to wake up in the morning – finding it impossible to gain enough momentum to get themselves out of bed.
3. Maintaining alertness during the day – feeling sleepy, particularly when there is little stimulation.

Many individuals with ADHD experience all three sleep problems (getting to sleep, waking up, maintaining alertness) because these are interrelated. They have difficulty in getting to sleep because they are wide awake in the evenings and tend to do stimulating activities such as studying, working or socializing intensively. They may find it difficult getting to sleep, eventually sleep fitfully then find it hard to wake up in the morning as they are still tired. Since they have not had enough sleep during the night, they feel drowsy and find it difficult to remain alert during the day. However, as the day wears on they gradually feel more awake and are ready to become more active. The achievements made in the evening when they believe they are more alert seem to negatively reinforce this schedule. In time this cycle of negative reinforcement becomes a dysfunctional pattern, in other words, a sleep disorder (see Figure 12.1, which is also provided on the Companion Website in handout format).

People with ADHD often describe difficulties in falling asleep and staying asleep. Their problems can include any one or more of the following: delay in falling asleep, insufficient duration of sleep, frequent awakenings, early final awakening. However, most clients who complain of insomnia will *overestimate* how long it takes them to fall asleep and *underestimate* how long they have actually been asleep.

Some people with ADHD may find that they become more restless later in the day and as a result find themselves becoming involved in activities in the evening that are incompatible with sleep such as sport, playing computer games or surfing the internet. Overactivity in the evenings for other people with ADHD can be related to their finding it easier to concentrate in the evening perhaps because it is quieter and the opportunity for distraction is minimized, for example, when their children have gone to bed. Also some evening activity can become necessary for individuals with ADHD as their tendency to procrastinate throughout the day means that they have to make up time and complete tasks by working late at night. Others describe gradually feeling sluggish in the morning but become increasingly alert and energized as the day progresses. For example, Jane, a student, felt that she only had the motivation to get her assignments completed the day before a deadline and usually ended up staying up extremely late to finish her work.

Problems waking up in the morning are often related to not getting enough sleep earlier in the night. Many individuals with ADHD describe finding it extremely difficult to settle to sleep until well past midnight, even when they need to get up early for work or college. This problem therefore may be a delayed reaction to a late onset of sleep. Some 'night owls' can adapt their schedule to their sleep-wake cycle and may, if necessary, be in a position to organize themselves so their day begins later than most. This will work particularly well for self-employed individuals, although this could feed into a lack of structure and cause more time management difficulties through the day. Those who cannot be so flexible find themselves trying to function on insufficient sleep. They end up feeling 'groggy' and irritable, particularly in the morning. This can lead to an exacerbation of ADHD-related cognitive deficits due to tiredness. Of course, lateness and fatigue will negatively influence an individual's progress in education and work. This sleep problem can also cause problems for families if morning responsibilities are not being shared appropriately, for example, partners of clients have reported feeling very resentful if they are left to get the children up and ready for school while the ADHD partner continues to sleep through the morning. For example, James was a self-employed carpet layer and he had always had a problem with getting up in the morning. As a consequence, he often only scheduled his first appointment of the day at 12.00 noon, and in order to get jobs finished, would have to work until 8.00 p.m. or beyond. This meant that he spent very little time with his young children as they were usually in bed when he arrived home and he was in bed when they were getting ready in the morning. The majority of the childcare was left to his partner.

Most people with ADHD have difficulty with sustaining attention, however, some people with ADHD also have difficulty in maintaining a sufficient level of arousal or alertness when they are not performing stimulating mental tasks or physical activity. They may feel drowsy and find themselves yawning persistently. They may fall asleep in lectures or meetings, in some cases despite having an adequate night's sleep. Again, this can have a huge impact on their education, career and social relationships. For example, Simon was made redundant when his firm went bankrupt. He quickly ran out of money and was extremely worried about being able to last until his next social security cheque. He often lay awake at night thinking about what might happen to him in the future. As a result, he was unable to sleep and during the day found himself feeling sleepy and yawning all the time. He managed to get several interviews but was never offered the posts because he was told he seemed disinterested and lethargic.

Sleep Apnoea

Sleep apnoea is a disorder of interrupted breathing during sleep. A common form is *obstructive* sleep apnoea where the windpipe collapses during breathing when the muscles relax during sleep. The brain responds by awakening the person to open the windpipe, usually resulting in a snort or gasp. This can happen hundreds of times a night. Sleep apnoea is associated with obesity or loss of muscle tone and can result in loud snoring. It is often associated with excessive daytime sleepiness, fatigue and altered attention, particularly vigilance (Mazza *et al.*, 2005).

In a study of children with sleep disorders and/or ADHD, Chervin *et al.* (1997) found that habitual snoring was more common among children with ADHD and that in general snoring was associated with higher levels of inattention and hyperactivity. They suggest that sleep related breathing disorders could be a cause of ADHD symptoms and that these difficulties would improve if their sleep disorder was treated. Improvements in ADHD symptoms have been reported for three adults with ADHD who had their sleep apnoea treated (Naseem, Chaudhary and Collop, 2001).

Nightmares and Night Terrors

Night terrors are extreme and animated versions of nightmares. The sleeper experiences a sense of terrible danger and may physically and vocally appear distressed and try to defend themselves. Terrors can differ from nightmares in that they are less likely to be remembered. This can be particularly frightening for the individual as they may wake in the night with palpitations and other symptoms similar to a panic attack, and yet not recognize the triggers. This may lead to a catastrophic interpretation in terms of their health, for example, that they are having a heart attack. For children, it has been noted that some medications, particularly dexamphetamine-based preparations, can increase the frequency of nightmares (Efron, Jarman and Barker, 1997). For adult clients, nightmares seem to be more likely in the context of daytime anxieties where distress or preoccupations can adversely affect their sleep and content of their dreams.

Narcolepsy

People with narcolepsy fall asleep at various times of the day, even if they have had a normal amount of night-time sleep. Narcoleptics skip the first four stages of sleep and plunge straight into REM sleep (REM sleep is explained in the following section on psychoeducation). These attacks last from several seconds to more than 20 minutes.

People with narcolepsy may also experience cataplexy (loss of muscle control during emotional situations), hallucinations and temporary paralysis when they awaken.

Adults and children with ADHD have been shown to be significantly sleepier during the day. However it is unclear to what extent individuals with ADHD suffer from true narcolepsy or whether their attentional difficulties may lead them to day-dream and drift into a sleep-like state.

Restless Legs Syndrome

Restless Legs Syndrome (RLS) is a disorder causing unpleasant crawling, prickling, or tingling sensations in the legs and feet and an urge to move them for relief. RLS can lead to constant leg movement during the day and repeated awakening during the night. Children with ADHD have been reported to be more mobile and restless during sleep than control group children (Cortese *et al.*, 2005; Sadeh, Pergamin and Bar-Hamin, 2006). In a study of adults with RLS, Wagner, Walters and Fisher (2004) found that over a quarter exhibited ADHD symptoms. It is not clear whether discomfort from RLS leads to poor sleep quality which then affects concentration and hyperactivity, or alternatively whether RLS and ADHD are part of a symptom complex with dopaminergic deficiency being involved in both disorders.

ASSESSMENT OF SLEEP PROBLEMS

Intervention with sleep disorders initially requires close monitoring of the problem in order to obtain a baseline from which to measure change. This should include consideration of multiple factors which may affect sleep such as activity levels, diet, caffeine, alcohol, medication and so on. It is also important to fully explore the person's expectations of sleep, for example, by determining how much they believe they need and what happens to them when they do not achieve this: for example, assuming that if they do not have eight hours of sleep, then they will be unable to perform the next day. Much of the literature regarding insomnia suggests that people with sleep difficulties expect more sleep than is necessary. Sleep needs vary between individuals and also reduce with age. It may be that a 40-year-old client believes that they should aim to sleep as much as they did when they were 18 years old. The therapist can therefore educate the client about this issue and assist them in establishing their optimal amount of sleep.

Methods of managing sleep difficulties can be practically based by monitoring sleep problems and changing behavioural patterns and/or include a more cognitive focus, the latter technique being more effective if mood factors are influencing the quality of sleep. Both of these approaches are described in the following sections.

The first stage in treating sleep problems is to carefully monitor sleep in order to identify features which may be contributing to sleep difficulties. The sleep diary shown in Table 12.1 (and also on the Companion Website in a format for use in sessions) provides a strategy for recording the features of sleep that are necessary to

Table 12.1 Sleep diary

Night of week	Did you sleep during the day? If so, for how long?	How much caffeine did you drink and when?	How much alcohol did you drink and when?	What was the last thing you ate and when?	What time did you take your medication?	How were you feeling before you went to bed?	What were you doing before you went to bed?	Time you went to bed	Time you went to sleep approx	Times you woke up in the night and for how long	Time you woke up in the morning	Total hours of sleep	Quality of sleep (0–10)
Mon	No sleep	Coffee at 10.30 p.m.	Whisky at 1.15 before bed	Pasta at 1.00 a.m.	Tablet at 6 p.m.	Stressed	Finishing assignment	1.30 a.m.	3.45 a.m.	5.10–5.55 a.m.	8.15 a.m.	4 1/2	4
Tues	Nap at 2.00–3.30 p.m.	Tea at 6.00 p.m.	Bottle of wine, brandy	Curry at 10.30 p.m.	Forgot	Agitated	Out with friends	1.00 a.m.	2.45 a.m.	4.30 a.m., 5.10 a.m., 6.00 a.m.	9.30 a.m.	6	3
Wed	No sleep	Coffee at 11.00 p.m.	None	Toasted sandwich 10 p.m.	Tablet at 9 p.m.	Worried about course	Trying to read for seminar tomorrow	11.45 p.m.	3.00 a.m.	4.00 a.m., 4.30 a.m., 5.00 a.m.	6.30 a.m.	3 1/2	2
Thurs	No sleep	Tea at 4.30 p.m.	None	Shepherds pie at 6.30 p.m.	Tablet at 4 p.m.	Tired	Watching soap operas	10.15 p.m.	10.30 p.m.	None	10.30 a.m.	12	8
Fri	Nap at 3.00 in lecture	Coffee at 4 p.m.	2 bottles of wine	Takeaway pizza at 1 a.m.	Forgot	Drunk	Chatting to friends	3.00 a.m.	3.05 a.m.	6.00 a.m.	6.00 a.m.	3	2
Sat	Napping all afternoon	None	None	Soup at 6 p.m.	Tablet at 5 p.m.	Low	Watching DVD	11.00 p.m.	2.00 a.m.	3.15–4.30 a.m.	10.00 a.m.	6	4
Sun	None	Coffee at 1 a.m.	Bottle of wine	Sandwich at 1 a.m.	Tablet at 11 p.m.	Stressed	Preparing presentation for Mon	3.20 a.m.	6.30 a.m.	None	7.00 a.m.	30 mins	0

investigate prior to intervention. Ironically, the process of monitoring may exacerbate sleep difficulties as they are the subject of focus. Therefore, the monitoring process must be applied over a period of several days or weeks in order to obtain a reliable baseline. Table 12.1 shows the sleep diary of Jane, a student at university. Jane had deadlines for course work and exams pending. She was having problems organizing her work. Some nights she worked late into the night and she was feeling very anxious about passing her exams.

The sleep diary records information relating to 13 areas of interest following.

1. *Sleep during the day*: extra sleep during the day can affect sleep during the night and disrupt circadian rhythms. Therefore napping during the day should be avoided wherever possible.
2. *Caffeine intake*: caffeine stimulates the central nervous system, and leads to increased heart rate and alertness. Most people who consume caffeine experience a temporary increase in energy and elevation in mood. Sensitivity to caffeine can vary and depends to some extent on body mass (i.e. a smaller person would require less caffeine to produce the same effect as a larger person). However, caffeine sensitivity is particularly affected by caffeine use, so people who drink caffeine regularly develop reduced sensitivity to caffeine. Nevertheless, caffeine has a long half-life and remains in someone's system for up to 16 hours after consumption before being passed through urine. Therefore, even drinking a cup of coffee in the afternoon can affect sleep patterns later in the evening when the noticeable effects have worn off. People who are experiencing sleep difficulties may increase their caffeine intake during the day to keep them alert. This in turn has a delayed effect on their sleep.
3. *Alcohol intake*: although alcohol can be used by some individuals as a 'nightcap' to help them go to sleep, this can actually perpetuate sleep difficulties. Alcohol can induce drowsiness, but paradoxically prevents the individual from entering the deeper more restorative stages of sleep. Thus, people who have been drinking alcohol and then slept all night may still complain of being tired in the morning as the majority of their sleep may have been in sleep stages 1 and 2 where brain waves are slowing down, rather than the more restorative stages 3 and 4 (see Table 12.2).
4. *Food intake*: different types of food can affect sleep in various ways. Heavy food which is protein-rich or high sugar can lead to increases in overall level of alertness and also activate the digestive system for longer. However, food which is high in carbohydrates but low in protein and sugar (e.g. cereals and pasta) can stimulate the release of neurotransmitters, which induce relaxation, such as serotonin and melatonin.
5. *Medication*: both prescribed and non-prescribed drugs can have side-effects that affect sleep. Cerebral stimulants are the mainstay treatment for ADHD and they work on the 'recticular activation system', which is involved in arousal. Sometimes people with ADHD find that if they have taken their medication later in the day, they have difficulty getting to sleep, possibly because the drug is still acting on their level of arousal.

6. *Affective state*: happiness, excitement, sadness, stress, anxiety can all play a role in preventing sleep. The individual should try to record their feelings and associated thoughts in order to identify what might be keeping them awake, such as recurrent worries. This issue is dealt with later in this module.
7. *Activity before bed*: it is important for the body to be cued that it is time to slow down and then sleep. Activities which counteract this process should be avoided, such as exercise, mentally stimulating work or stress-inducing conversations. People with ADHD are likely to be active throughout the day and the evening is no exception. If they are busy performing last minute tasks right up until their bedtime, this may affect their sleep. It is preferable to use activities to 'wind down' such as listening to relaxing music, having a caffeine-free drink and reading a magazine.
8. *Time in bed*: the basic boundaries of sleep are important to record as an ADHD individual may lack routine and their bedtime may vary according to the day's activities and whether they suddenly remember to do something just before they go to bed. Having a fixed bedtime helps to induce a regular pattern of sleep and can reduce difficulties falling asleep. For example, if someone frequently does not go to bed until after 2 a.m. and then tries to 'catch-up' on some sleep by going to bed at 9.30 p.m., they may find it difficult to fall asleep.
9. *Time fallen asleep*: although this is difficult to record directly, people generally have a sense of roughly when they have fallen asleep because they do not remember seeing their alarm clock after a certain time.
10. *Waking times during night*: people with ADHD may be more likely to get out of bed due to feelings of restlessness, and (impulsively) engage in activities such as watching television and playing computer games. These provide stimulation and make it more difficult to naturally return back to sleep. However, other people may lie awake and have restless thoughts that stop them from going back to sleep.
11. *Waking time in morning*: the individual may not have a consistent pattern of when to sleep and when to wake, so this can lead to them oversleeping or waking too early. Early morning waking and then lying awake ruminating can be associated with low mood and depression. However, sometimes individuals feel that if they have been awake for a great deal of the night, they are too tired to get up in the morning so lie in bed.
12. *Total hours of sleep*: this is a useful quantitative way of measuring any improvement (or deterioration) in sleep. It will also allow the therapist to explore any expectations of the number of hours of sleep an individual believes they should be getting per night. As described above, sometimes expectations can be too high and some normalization of what is usual can help an individual realize that they are maybe even sleeping too much.
13. *Quality of sleep*: the client should rate the quality of each night's sleep on a Likert scale from 0 (worst possible night's sleep) to 10 (fully relaxed and refreshed in the morning). This area is where clients may have most complaints. Conversely, this is the area where the client is most likely to see improvements during therapy.

The example provided in Table 12.1 illustrates how Jane's napping during the day affected how late she went to bed in the evening and the amount of time she slept at night. Caffeine and alcohol consumption also affected the time she was able to fall asleep and the quality of sleep she gained. For example, on Friday when she was out late drinking wine with friends, she only managed 3 hours of very poor quality sleep. Eating late at night also seemed to affect her sleep. However, her sleep quantity and quality were strongly related to her activity before going to bed, such as last-minute preparation of coursework, and the anxieties this caused. The night when she had the best quality of sleep was Thursday when she went to bed early but then she overslept. This shows how important it can be to have regular times to go to bed and get up in the morning so that a sleep-wake rhythm can be achieved.

COGNITIVE BEHAVIOURAL THERAPY

Psychoeducation

It is important for individuals to gain an understanding about the process and functions of sleep in order for them to identify where their sleep problems arise, and consequently how to improve their sleep. The sleep cycle is a good starting point as it allows the client to recognize that sleep is not just one steady state but goes through phases and actually that sometimes it is normal to wake through the night. Reviewing the functions of sleep with a client can be a useful exercise in order to identify any misconceptions about what happens if they do not obtain sufficient sleep or their sleep lacks quality. In addition, the causes of sleep problems should be explained to a client as they may quickly recognize a pattern to their sleep difficulties and be able to help generate suitable strategies for improving their sleep.

The sleep cycle

In order to improve sleep disorders, it can be useful for people with ADHD to understand the characteristics and cycles of normal sleep. It was once thought that sleep was a passive process, in which the brain 'shuts down' and nothing happened, but it is now established that sleep is a highly active state. Sleep goes in cycles moving quickly into deep restorative sleep, then coming back up towards wakefulness, then back down again. This cyclical pattern is thought to exist for evolutionary reasons, as it can be dangerous because of increased vulnerability to 'shut down' completely. The intermittent return to a state from which it is easy to wake therefore serves an important function that enables the individual to enter a state of semi-vigilance from which they may wake if they perceive danger.

There are two different states of sleep: non-REM sleep and REM sleep. REM stands for Rapid Eye Movement as the eyes move rapidly during this stage of sleep, but not during non-REM sleep. During sleep, an individual passes down through four phases of non REM-sleep then back through them in reverse order before entering REM sleep

Table 12.2 Stages of sleep

Stage	*Description*
1	This stage is characterized by drowsiness and 'half sleep' with a pattern of moderately alert but relaxed brain waves. This is when drifting in and out of sleep occurs for about 5 to 10 minutes but it is possible to be woken up easily.
2	Brain waves slow down from about 8 per second to 5 per second and eye movements stop. The heart rate slows down and body temperature drops.
3	Extremely slow *delta* waves begin to appear, interspersed with some small quicker waves.
4	During this stage the brain produces delta waves almost exclusively. It is very difficult to wake someone during stages 3 and 4, which together are called *deep sleep*. There is no eye movement or muscle activity.
REM	REM sleep is associated with shorter brain waves. This occurs after the sleeper has moved back through a reversal of stages 4 to 3, to 2, to 1. In REM sleep breathing, pulse rate and eye muscles fluctuate erratically and the muscles of the body, apart from those involved in breathing, become paralyzed.

(see Table 12.2, also on the Companion Website in handout format). Each stage can be characterized by different patterns of brain activity as measured by EEG recordings.

Non-REM sleep is associated with slower electrophysiological waves than during waking; that is, the electrical activity of the brain becomes less pronounced. As the muscles of the body become relaxed, the person enters a deep sleep from which it is difficult to be roused. If someone is woken during this time, they may report fragmented and/or static visual images. It is during non-REM sleep that sleepwalking and night terrors are most likely to occur.

After stage four, the sleeper goes back through stages three and two until they reach stage one again. This phase is sometimes referred to as 'stage one emergent' but more commonly called 'REM' sleep. When the sleeper switches to REM sleep from non-REM sleep, their breathing becomes more rapid, irregular and shallow, their eyes jerk rapidly in various directions and limb muscles become temporarily paralyzed. Heart rate and blood pressure rise. REM sleep is also associated with shorter electrophysiological waves. The respiratory system, pulse and eye muscles fluctuate erratically. In addition, the muscles of the body, apart from those involved in breathing, become paralyzed. A sleeper woken during REM sleep will have an 80 per cent chance of recalling a dream.

These sleep stages progress in a cycle down to deep sleep and back up to stage one and into REM sleep, then the cycle starts over again going back into a deeper sleep (see Figure 12.2, which is also presented on the Companion Website in handout format).

As we get older we spend more time in REM sleep. Adults typically go through four or five cycles of sleep, each taking about 90 minutes. Each cycle becomes gradually

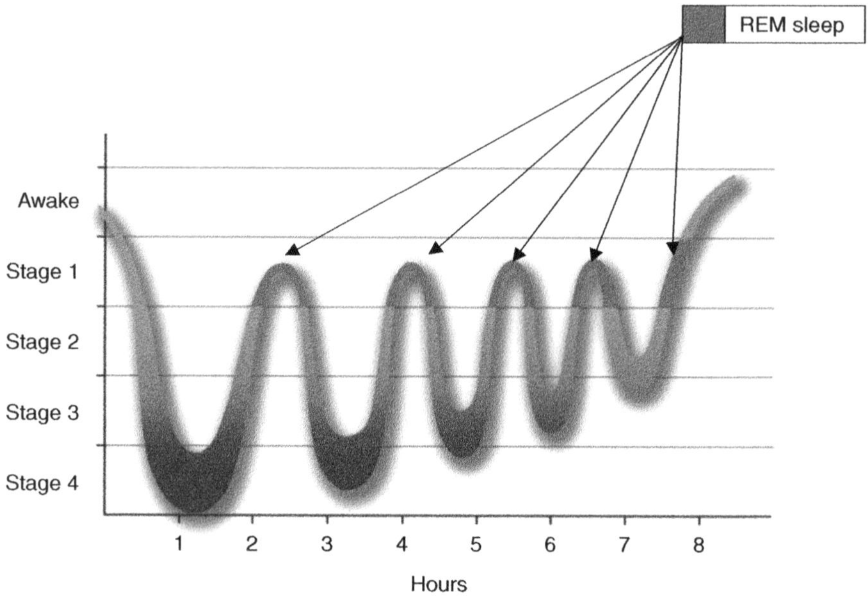

Figure 12.2 The sleep cycle

less deep, such that most of the deeper stage four sleep occurs in the earlier half of the night. Almost 50 per cent of total sleep time is spent in Stage 2 sleep, about 20 per cent in REM sleep and the remaining 30 per cent in the other stages. Infants spend about half their sleep time in REM sleep and typically sleep for 16 hours a day. Sleep requirements decrease through childhood although adolescents still need over 9 hours per night. This is because considerable growth occurs during this period. Most adults need approximately 7 to 8 hours of sleep per night, although this varies from individual to individual. People who sleep more or less than this amount may be at increased risk of illnesses, as sleep is unable to carry out its usual functions such as restoration of the immune system.

Functions of sleep

Sleeping takes up such a significant proportion of our lives and yet it is still not clear why it is so necessary. The functions of sleep can be surmised from what is affected when someone has not had adequate sleep. Sleep deprivation has an effect on the nervous system, the immune system and cell growth and repair. Without sleep, neurons may become depleted in energy or over polluted with the by-products of normal cellular activity. They need sleep to repair themselves in order to perform effectively during the day. In addition, sleep may allow the brain to encode and store new information. Deep sleep coincides with the release of growth hormone in children and young adults. There is also an increased production and reduced breakdown of proteins during sleep. These are the body's building blocks needed for cell growth and repair. Sleep deprivation can impair judgement, reaction times and can magnify the effects of alcohol. In extreme cases it can lead to hallucinations and mood swings.

Sleep may have increased importance in ADHD because many individuals have heightened activity levels during the day, and hence may require even more sleep than non-ADHD people to fully recover their energy expended during the day.

Causes of sleep problems

Many different factors can influence sleep, including psychological, behavioural, environmental or biological factors. Psychological factors include ADHD related symptoms such as restlessness, as well as other mood disorders. Behavioural difficulties, particularly maladaptive sleeping patterns, can affect sleep during the night. Although they are often very obvious, external triggers from the environmental can be causal in sleep difficulties because they wake the individual up. Biological factors may be particularly relevant for people with ADHD as not only can their medication influence their quality of sleep but also other lifestyle characteristics may play a role. The different factors are explained in Table 12.3 (also provided on the Companion Website in handout format).

SLEEP STRATEGIES

If the client takes longer than 30 minutes to fall asleep on most nights, then the first step is to review bedtime routines. 'Sleep hygiene' refers to arranging environmental and behavioural factors that are conducive to sleep. For people with insomnia, the bed and its surroundings can become a signal for being unable to fall asleep and for the worry and frustration associated with that state. It is possible to 'undo' this association so that the body learns to sleep in bed and view sleep as rewarding.

In order to achieve this, all activities in the bedroom should be stopped except sleep and intimacy. Visual or physical contact with the bed should be avoided except when going to sleep. For example, people should avoid activities in the bedroom such as working, reading, watching television, or playing computer games. Sometimes rearranging the furniture can help by creating a new 'environment' that is not associated with insomnia.

Paradoxically, sleep difficulties can often best be managed by making adjustments during the day to activities and consumption of food, cigarettes and alcohol. Preparing for going to bed is also crucial for the individual to develop a routine so that their body is expecting sleep from regular cues. While in bed, the client should aim to be relaxed even if they are awake, and they should get out of bed if they feel uncomfortable or unable to sleep. Strategies to cue waking up can complete an intervention as sometimes the individual may be anxious about going to sleep in case they do not wake-up on time. Table 12.4 provides a selection of behavioural strategies which

Table 12.3 Factors which may affect sleep in people with ADHD

Psychological/behavioural
Restlessness/ceaseless mental activity This core ADHD symptom may affect normal sleep patterns because the individual still feels 'on the go' at bedtime and finds it very difficult to settle and relax.
Worrying specifically about sleep Worries about getting enough sleep or being tired in the morning if sleep is not achieved may adversely affect the likelihood of falling asleep.
Incompatible bedtime activities For example, playing computer games while sitting in bed can make the individual more alert and less likely to go to sleep easily. Working in the bedroom can also have a similar effect – it distracts the individual from the function of the room which is to sleep and rest.
Chronic anxiety and/or depression Ruminating about issues, such as the day's events or low self-worth, may keep individuals awake as they become more alert due to an increase in mental activity.
Disturbance of activity-rest cycles Irregular sleep patterns may arise from irregular bedtimes and waking times. For people with ADHD, this may occur as a result of disorganization causing them to leave tasks until the last minute and stay up late to complete them. Other influences include changing from night to day shifts, or jet-lag.
Oversleeping during the daytime A common problem for individuals with ADHD is not getting up in the morning and lying in bed until lunchtime or beyond. This has an effect on their ability to sleep at night. Similarly napping during the day may provide a short-term fix but does not facilitate a good night's sleep.
Nocturnal panics People with ADHD often procrastinate and leave things until the last minute. This can leave them panicking late at night about the tasks they have not achieved for the deadline the following day. They may then either choose to stay up all night working on the activity, or decide to flout the deadline, which may then affect their sleep through worry or nightmares.
Environmental
Unpredictable sensory stimulation (noise, light, etc) Given their distractibility, people with ADHD are more sensitive to external noises when they are trying to get to sleep. For example, voices outside their window, noise from the traffic, other people switching lights on and off outside their room or even when they have fallen asleep with the television on.
Significant signals Again, due to their distractibility, ADHD individuals may be more sensitive to predictable significant signals such as daylight in the morning, or children waking. Children with ADHD are more likely to have sleep disorders which obviously affect their parents' sleep quality.
Intense sensory stimulation High or low temperatures may unduly affect sleep, as can humidity.

Table 12.3 *(cont'd)*

Biological
Stimulant medication For some people with ADHD cerebral stimulant medications such as methylphenidate (Ritalin, Concerta) may improve ADHD symptoms and reverse restlessness. However for many individuals, stimulant medication may also keep them awake.
Side effects of medication for health problems or psychiatric disorders Other treatments, such as antidepressants, may affect sleep.
Excessive caffeine intake Some ADHD individuals choose to consume large amounts of caffeine during the day either to self-medicate their ADHD symptoms or to stay awake or more alert. Given that caffeine has a long half-life (i.e. it remains in the system for several hours), intake of caffeine in the late afternoon or early evening may disrupt sleep.
Heavy meals shortly before bedtime Digesting food is not conducive for sleep as the body is more active. Many people with ADHD find that they forget to eat during the day, possibly due to their medication suppressing their appetite, and then feel incredibly hungry in the evening and eat just before they go to bed.
Vigorous physical exercise shortly before bedtime Due to their hyperactivity, some people with ADHD find that at the end of the day they need to 'burn off' excess energy, for example by going for a run or playing squash. Such physical activity serves to wake the body up and may make it less possible for them to sleep adequately immediately afterwards. Nevertheless, exercise earlier in the day is often beneficial for sleep.
Physical health problems Comorbid health problems, particularly pain, may prevent individuals with ADHD falling asleep and maintaining sleep. For example, they may suffer from chronic toothache because they have not organized to go to the dentist for several weeks.
Need for urination Late night drinking may lead to an individual waking up with a need to urinate during the night.
Respiratory difficulties Problems such as obstructive sleep apnoea can lead to disturbed sleep and cognitive deficits which may masquerade as ADHD-like symptoms, or exacerbate pre-existing attentional difficulties.

may be tried at appropriate times. The Companion Website includes a version of the strategies which clients may find helpful.

In order to improve, the mature student, Jane's sleep (see Table 12.1) the therapist suggested avoiding all sleeping during the day. She also developed a routine whereby she did not drink any tea or coffee after 4 p.m., she ate her evening meal at 7 p.m. and did not drink any alcohol during the week. At 11 p.m., she changed into her

Table 12.4 Behavioural sleep strategies

During the day
Avoid taking naps and do not lie down When the client is feeling tired, it can be tempting for them to 'cat nap'. While this is a quick fix with a short-term gain (and therefore appealing to individuals with ADHD), it is likely to disrupt sleep in the night. If the client feels particularly tired during the day, they may take rests without lying down, or alternatively try to distract themselves by becoming involved in a more energizing task.
Relax by reading/listening to music if necessary Instead of sleeping during the day, the client should be encouraged to read or listen to music (but not in the bedroom). If they perform these activities when feeling tired, they may become conditionally paired with this feeling, and thus induce this state in the evening when the individual needs to sleep.
Make a list of the activities for the following day This prevents mental rehearsal at night when the client is attempting to get to sleep but trying not to forget certain things they need to do the next day.
Eating and drinking The client should avoid heavy meals just before going to bed as this can cause increased alertness. Spicy and acidic foods may cause indigestion which will affect sleep. However, light snacks which are high in carbohydrates but low in sugar can be helpful before going to bed. Also drinking too much liquid in the few hours before bed may mean that sleep is disturbed by a need to go the toilet in the night, so clients should limit their liquid intake in the later part of the evening.
Smoking Nicotine is a stimulant, which acts in a similar way as caffeine and stimulant medication, and therefore should be avoided just before bedtime. Smokers may therefore have reduced REM sleep and only sleep very lightly. Some heavy smokers may wake up a few hours after going to sleep due to nicotine withdrawal. It is advisable for people to avoid smoking if they wake up in the night.
Alcohol The effects of alcohol on sleep are counterintuitive. Although alcohol can make drinkers feel drowsy, it actually prevents people from achieving REM and deeper sleep. Alcohol induces only a light sleep and therefore the restorative processes cannot occur, and individuals may be woken up more easily. Alcohol consumption should be avoided or kept to a minimum when treating a sleep disorder.
Before sleep
Maintain a consistent bedtime Irregularities in bedtimes for people with ADHD are often determined by what is happening around them. For example, starting to watch a film late at night, being invited to go for late-night drinks. This should be minimized where possible during the sleep intervention as having a consistent bedtime allows a routine to develop where sleep is expected at a certain time.
Changing bedtime to when normally get to sleep. For example, if a client is only getting 4 hours of sleep per night, then they should only be allowed 4 hours in bed but this can be gradually increased by 15–30 minutes per night.

Table 12.4 *(cont'd)*

Follow a routine An hour or more before going to bed, the client should allow a 'winding down' period which can be organized into a routine. For example, reading enjoyable magazines or books, listening to music, having a bath. *Get ready for bed* This should be done before the client gets tired or commences the winding down routine in order to avoid waking themselves up by the routine. For example, brushing teeth and washing or showering can wake up the individual as these activities are also associated with the morning. *Only get into bed when tired* The aim is to associate the bedroom with rapid onset of sleep
In bed
Avoid activities incompatible with sleeping For example, watching TV or listening to the radio, eating, reading in bed should all be avoided. The bed must be associated with sleep and intimacy, and nothing else. *Do not lie awake for long periods* If the client is unable to fall asleep within 30 minutes, they should get out of bed, move to another room and only return to bed when they are ready to fall asleep. They should make sure the room is not at a noticeably different temperature from that of the bedroom. If they return to bed and still cannot sleep, this stages should be repeated. The goal is to minimize the amount of time spent in bed ruminating about lack of sleep.
Awakening
Regular alarm The client should be encouraged to try and wake with an alarm and rise at the same time each day, even at weekends. *Two alarm clocks* It may be helpful to set two alarm clocks. The client can take their medication when woken by the first clock in order to improve their concentration and focus for their morning routine. The client should also set a second alarm clock at a time when their medication is likely to have begun acting. This could be positioned at a distance that requires them to leave the bed to turn it off. *Hide alarm clock* Exposure to bright light or sunshine soon after waking can help the client wake naturally and feel more refreshed from their sleep. This could be done using lamps which are on timers. A partner who wakes earlier than the individual can help by throwing open the curtains. This can help regulate the body's natural clock.

nightclothes, brushed her teeth then sat for 30 minutes in the living room listening to relaxing music and reading a magazine. Then she went to bed at 11.30 p.m. For the first few nights, Jane found that she still could not sleep, so she was advised to return to the living room and continue reading or just sit still, before returning to bed. She set her alarm for 7.30 a.m. every morning, took her medication and listened to the radio before a second alarm roused her at 8.00 a.m. when she got out of bed. The total number of hours asleep gradually increased to a more regular 7–8 hours per night and her quality of sleep improved. She also reported feeling less worried about the amount of sleep she was getting as this had been preoccupying her thoughts during the day.

Sleep and Rumination

Ironically people with ADHD often report lying awake restlessly worrying about not being able to sleep. Worry and chronic anxiety can affect the amount and quality of sleep at all stages of the process.

1. Before falling asleep – worrying thoughts can cause and maintain insomnia.
2. During sleep – day time stress and chronic anxiety can be associated with restless 'tossing and turning' or even nightmares.
3. After awakening – worrying thoughts and anxiety can occur after nightmare/night terrors and prevent sleep. Also when individuals with ADHD experience low mood, their sleep may be affected and this can lead to reduced quality of sleep through the night accompanied by early waking. However, they may also find it extremely difficult to get up and face the day.

For individuals with ADHD, mood disturbance can also be exacerbated by a lack of sleep whereby irritability, 'frayed nerves' and snappiness can lead to social problems. These difficulties can be self-perpetuating if others begin responding in a negative way towards the individual and cause them to feel more negative about themselves. The sleep hygiene techniques described above can be particularly useful for treating comorbid low mood and anxiety.

As for other affective symptoms, a cycle between thoughts, feelings and behaviours can maintain sleep difficulties. For example, a client who is unable to fall asleep may start thinking that they will not be able to perform the following day because they will be too tired, they then become anxious and frustrated about not being able to sleep, which means that they are less likely to sleep. They may then get up and try to carry out tasks that they hope will help them from underachieving during the following day, but this makes them more alert and even less likely to be able to sleep during the night.

Examples of the thoughts, feelings and behaviours that mediate sleeplessness are provided in Box 12.1. In practice Jane, the student, reported that when she woke up in the morning, she was already planning how she could fit extra sleep into her day in order to catch-up on sleep missed during the night. Before she got into bed in the evening, she would be concerned that she would not fall asleep and then would

Box 12.1 Examples of the thoughts, feelings and behaviours that mediate sleeplessness

Thoughts
If I don't get seven or eight hours sleep, I haven't had enough sleep
If I don't sleep, I won't be able to get up
I won't be able to concentrate tomorrow and will forget things
Lying in bed with eyes closed is more restful than sitting up

Feelings
Anxiety; Frustration; Worry

Behaviours
Unable to fall asleep
Surfing the net
Have a night cap
Get up and pace around
Get up and do activities in case by tomorrow they have been forgotten
Get up and look for something that may have been lost

frequently check her alarm clock and calculate the maximum number of hours more she could sleep before she had to get up.

Behavioural strategies to overcome sleep problems were outlined previously in Table 12.4. If these problems are associated with ruminative thinking, then it may also be helpful for the client to engage in anxiety reduction techniques provided in the Anxiety Module (Chapter 9). They may also be low in mood and benefit from work focusing on this issue as suggested in the Low-Mood and Depression Module (Chapter 11). However, there are also several simple techniques which can be useful when working with clients who have specific concerns about their ability to sleep, which target thoughts, feelings and behaviours (see Box 12.2, which is also presented on the Companion Website).

SUMMARY

This modules describes techniques that can be helpful for people with ADHD, regardless of whether sleep is their main complaint or their sleep problems are associated with other symptoms. Gaining an understanding of the nature of a sleep disorder and careful monitoring of the difficulties using a Sleep Diary will provide useful clues as to how best to intervene. Strategies can be implemented through the day,

Box 12.2 Mood-related sleep strategies

Thoughts

Have designated 'worry time' well before winding down. Worries can be written down so they do not need to be rehearsed or remembered until the following day. Calming self-talk may also be useful by rehearsing statements such as 'A few hours sleep is better than no hours sleep'.

Feelings

Relaxation techniques can help to reduce anxious feelings. For example, the client could imagine having their thoughts switched off or perform one of several simple techniques:

1. Counting from 1 to 10 steadily but pausing after one of the numbers, e.g.
   1 (pause) 2 - 3 - 4 - 5 - 6 - 7 - 8 - 9 - 10
   1 - 2 (pause) 3 - 4 - 5 - 6 - 7 - 8 - 9 - 10
2. Progressive muscle relaxation (see Anxiety Module in Chapter 9)
3. Deep breathing
4. Guided imagery/distraction – Imagine a pleasant scene: what can you see?; what can you hear?; what can you smell?; what can you feel?

Behaviour

Behavioural strategies have been outlined previously in Table 12.4. If anxiety is driving the sleep problem, then the 'thought' and 'feeling' components described above should additionally be targeted.

before bedtime, through the night and in the morning. Routines may be particularly useful for people with ADHD, who are often very active late at night by trying to catch-up with tasks they have not completed during the day. Change is usually monitored by the client spontaneously who will quickly notice any improvement in the quantity and quality of sleep. However, it is also useful to repeat the exercise of monitoring sleep shown in Table 12.1 in order to objectively demonstrate improvements and the changes which underpin them.

Group Treatment: Sleep Module

It is essential to prepare for group treatment by reading the chapter module. Six group sessions are outlined below, but the number of treatment sessions can be expanded or reduced as required.

Plan

Session 1	Starting activities
Sessions 2 & 3	Psychoeducation – sleep disorders, sleep cycle, factors that affect sleep, behavioural strategies Instruction for completing the Sleep Diary
Sessions 4 & 5	Exercises – set up 'behavioural experiments' for homework and discuss outcome
Session 6	Revision of psychoeducation and strategies Discussion of homework outcome/experience – what works best? Obstacles and how to overcome them

Starting activities

Describe the sleep problems that you experience (difficulty getting to sleep at night, interrupted sleep, early waking, sleepy during the day etc).

What makes it better or worse? (emotions, mental activity, physical activities, things you eat or drink).

What are the consequences of sleep problems on your daily life? (interpersonal relationships, lack of achievement, poor study skills, impact on occupation, thinking errors, impact on temperament).

Have you found any techniques or strategies that help resolve the problem?

What is the worst thing that could happen?

Group discussion (compare individual differences, strengths/weaknesses).

Psychoeducation

Describe the different types of sleep disorders and their relationship with ADHD.
- Insomnia, sleep apnoea, nightmares, narcolepsy, restless legs syndrome, and sleep and rumination.

Describe the sleep cycle.
- Handout Figure 12.1 Dysfunctional sleep cycle.
- Handout Table 12.2 Stages of sleep.
- Handout Figure 12.2 The sleep cycle.

Describe the functions of sleep.
- Impact of sleep deprivation.

Describe factors that affect sleep in people with ADHD.
- Psychological and behavioural factors.

(*Continued*)

Environmental factors.
Biological factors.
Handout Table 12.3.

Discuss which factors are easier to change.

Describe behavioural strategies to manage sleep problems.
During the day, before going to sleep, once in bed, and waking up.
Handout Table 12.4: Behavioural sleep strategies.
Handout Box 12.2: Mood-related sleep strategies.

Exercises

Handout Sleep Diary (Table 12.1) and discuss how to use this to identify patterns of behaviour and monitor sleep.

Discuss information to note in the sleep diary (sleep in day; caffeine, alcohol and food intake; medication; affective state; activity prior to bedtime; time in bed; time fallen asleep; waking times during the night; waking time in morning; total hours of sleep).

Rate quality of sleep 0 (worst possible) – 10 (fully refreshed).

Demonstrate relaxation strategies.
Breathing exercises and progressive muscle relaxation (do in session).

Discuss completed sleep diaries in sessions and identify what may be contributing to sleep problems and how these may be changed.

Set up 'behavioural experiments' for clients to see if they can improve the quantity and/or quality of their sleep by identifying problems and suggesting changes using Tables 12.4 and Box 12.2. Continue to monitor sleep pattern using Sleep Diary (Table 12.1).

Compare and contrast Sleep Diaries (pre/post) following implementation of chosen intervention(s).

Select alternative interventions and continue to apply 'behavioural experiments' to determine what works most effectively.

Discuss obstacles to achievement and methods to overcome them.

Homework

Monitor quantity and quality of sleep by completing Sleep Diary (Table 12.1).
Apply selected intervention(s) as 'behavioural experiments' and re-monitor.
Handout Boxes 9.4 and 9.5 (relaxation techniques) for homework.

13

SUBSTANCE MISUSE MODULE

Substance use disorders are common comorbidities associated with ADHD, especially alcohol and cannabis (Faraone *et al.*, 2007) followed by cocaine and amphetamines (Sullivan and Rudnik-Levin, 2001). The lifetime risk of people with ADHD having a substance misuse disorder is very high at 58 per cent (Sizoo *et al.*, 2010); increased rates of substance use disorder have been reported within ADHD populations and increased rates of ADHD have been reported within substance use disorder populations (Sobanski, 2006; Staller and Faraone, 2007; Upadhyaya, 2008). Furthermore, the likelihood of polysubstance use is much higher for adolescents with ADHD (Gudjonsson *et al.*, forthcoming).

Thus, when people with ADHD are being assessed by clinicians for the first time, it is important to include a screen for past and current history of substance misuse. In cases of serious drug misuse and/or dependency, the client should be treated by the appropriate service, (e.g. drug rehabilitation service) prior to treatment for their ADHD. For some individuals, serious substance misuse may mask the underlying condition of ADHD. A study conducted in a substance misuse disorder clinic in South London and using a comprehensive screening and diagnostic protocol based on DSM-IV criteria found high rates (12 per cent) of unidentified and untreated ADHD. Those individuals with substance misuse disorders and ADHD had significantly greater levels of impairment across several domains of daily life; and higher rates of substance abuse and alcohol consumption, suicide attempts, and depression recorded in their case records (Huntley *et al.*, submitted).

Substance misuse most commonly arises via conduct disorder and antisocial behaviours. However, young people with ADHD often experience a different route into substance misuse than others as it develops through a need to self-medicate with stimulants, alcohol, cannabis or other sedatives (Nutt *et al.*, 2007). Often people with

Cognitive-Behavioural Therapy for ADHD in Adolescents and Adults: A Psychological Guide to Practice, Second Edition. Susan Young and Jessica Bramham.

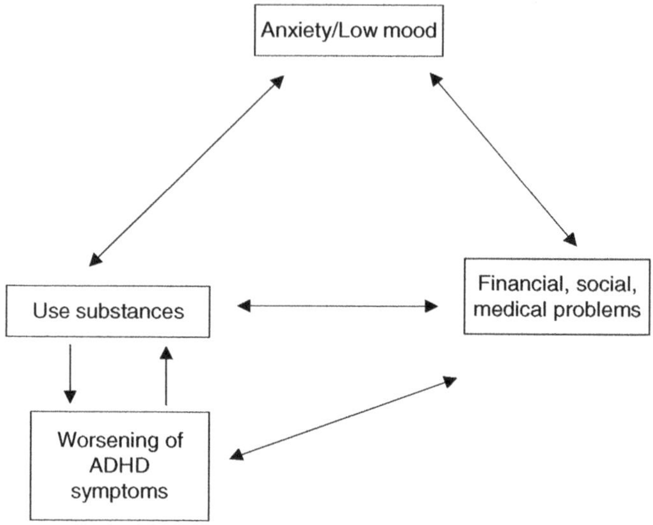

Figure 13.1 Context of substance misuse for people with ADHD

ADHD report a contraindicative effect, for example, when taking amphetamines they may find that they do not experience the same hyped-up excitement as other people and report that they are better able to focus and concentrate. They may smoke a considerably greater number of cigarettes as nicotine, like amphetamine, is a dopamine agonist, which induces secretion of dopamine in the brain. This can have a similar effect as psychostimulant medication and can reduce their ADHD symptoms. Other substances such as alcohol and cannabis tend not to have the same reinforcement in terms of symptom reduction but are used by young people with ADHD in order to dampen down feelings of agitation to help them feel calmer.

When health professionals work with ADHD clients who have addictions they often voice concern about the prescription of psychostimulant medication to treat ADHD. This causes anxiety regarding the potential for abuse, for example: that it will be taken irregularly and in large doses; crushing, snorting and injecting it intravenously for its euphoric properties; taking it to stay awake for long periods of time; to lose weight; or sold for the recreational need of others. While it is obviously difficult to generalize and caution must be taken, studies have suggested that treatment with stimulant medication for childhood ADHD does not increase the likelihood that young people will misuse substances in later life (Brasset-Grundy and Butler, 2004; Wilens *et al.*, 2003).

Substance misuse rarely occurs in isolation from other difficulties or stress affecting the individual. Figure 13.1 shows how many of the features often associated with ADHD that have been discussed in previous modules can play a role in substance misuse.

People who become addicted to substances find themselves trapped a vicious cycle, wherein emotional lability and/or low mood exacerbates ADHD symptoms and vice versa. Both problems may independently or cumulatively increase the risk that a person will use substances to bring (temporary) relief of their symptoms and/or fluctuating emotions. In turn, and with increasing use of substances, this may lead to financial and social problems, and/or medical complications. Such problems may overwhelm an individual who does not necessarily have adaptive coping strategies, causing them to feel anxious and /or low in mood. This state can exacerbate symptoms causing the individual to seek relief for their discomfort and engage in the cycle again.

This module will review each potential substance of abuse likely to be favoured by people with ADHD. Ways in which the therapist can best support and treat the ADHD client who is engaging in substance misuse will be introduced, drawing strongly on psychoeducation and motivational interviewing techniques to encourage the individual to engage in a process of change. Specific psychological management techniques are proposed for treatment and inclusion in a relapse prevention plan. A comprehensive treatment plan that would be required for individuals who have chronic and long-term substance misuse problems is not outlined comprehensively here as this would require specialist rehabilitation. However, the module does provide a brief intervention to motivate change in individuals who engage in intermittent use of drugs and alcohol.

SUBSTANCES USED BY ADHD INDIVIDUALS

The substances of preference are likely to vary across individuals and also depend on local availability as well as cost. However, in a large study of adolescents, the main substances used that distinguished between participants with ADHD and those without were nonprescribed sedatives, cannabis and sniffing substances (Gudjonsson *et al.*, forthcoming). The following review covers the main groups of substances, their impact on individuals with ADHD and their associated difficulties.

Nicotine

Nicotine is primarily derived from smoking cigarettes and tobacco, although some individuals use nicotine patches or gum when they are trying to quit smoking. Many individuals with ADHD smoke over 20 cigarettes per day and find it extremely difficult to give up. Nicotine is one of the most addictive substances of misuse. It is a cerebral stimulant drug and hence provides some effect in reducing ADHD symptoms through its impact on the dopamine system. For individuals without ADHD, it has been shown to enhance sustained, divided and focused attention (Kassel, 1997). Indeed, there has even been research that suggests that nicotine patches may be an effective treatment of symptomatic ADHD (Levin *et al.*, 1996). The health risks incurred from the long-term consequences of smoking are now well established in medical research and include cancer, lung and heart disease. However, ADHD smokers may be exposed to greater risk than their non-ADHD peers due to their inattentive problems. This is not from a health perspective, but from a risk perspective, for example, ADHD clients are easily distracted and/or forgetful; they may not fully extinguish a cigarette, they may put their cigarette near flammable material or leave matches within the reach of small curious children.

Alcohol

Alcohol is the most commonly misused drug in the world and yet it is frequently not acknowledged as a potential substance of misuse, most likely reflecting its social acceptance in many cultures. However, alcohol has a sedative effect and people with ADHD report using alcohol to calm them down, which reduces feelings of agitation and restlessness. In social situations, they may use alcohol to overcome social inhibitions or social anxiety, arising from a history of social gaffs and/or poor impulse control. However, due to their poor impulse control, people with ADHD may find it difficult to regulate their alcohol intake; they may drink quickly and to excess. When intoxicated, individuals with ADHD will be even less likely than usual to regulate their mood, increasing the risk that they will become reckless and engage in risk-taking behaviour such as dangerous driving or criminal acts. While the sensation of intoxication can provide initial rewards in terms of apparent symptom relief, a contraindicative side effect is that it may exacerbate underlying cognitive deficits associated with ADHD. Heavy alcohol use has been associated with executive dysfunction and poor short-term learning and memory, particularly in the visual domain, in a general population study (Powell, 2004a). Other health risks include chronic liver failure, kidney disease and gastrointestinal problems in addition to acute alcohol poisoning leading to accidental death.

Tranquilizers

As with alcohol, tranquilizers are often used for their sedative effects in order to calm the individual. Benzodiazepines, which are prescribed for anxiety, are readily available in many homes and Tamazepam has been reported to be the most frequently abused. Barbiturates are now rarely used in the United Kingdom. ADHD individuals with sleep difficulties may be prescribed tranquilizing medication which is highly addictive (see the Sleep Module in Chapter 12 for psychological treatment to help reduce sleep problems).

Solvents

Solvent use (e.g. butane gas, lighter fluid, glue) is more common in young children and adolescents, possibly due to their relative availability to these age groups (Uzun and Kendirli, 2005). Matsumoto *et al.* (2005) found that inhalant abusers have a higher incidence of childhood ADHD than methamphetamine abusers. Inhalation initially gives rise to a pleasurable reaction, but frequent use leads to problems such as poor coordination, confusion and hallucinations. Adolescents who use inhalants are more likely to go on to develop substance abuse problems with alcohol and opiates (Wu, Pilowsky and Schlenger, 2005). The long-term health implications include neurotoxicity, in addition to alterations in gastrointestinal, respiratory and cardiovascular functioning.

Cannabis

If young people are going to use illegal drugs, then cannabis seems to be the drug of choice. Anecdotal reports from clients suggest that they started to use cannabis as teenagers and have continued to use it into their middle years and beyond. They report that it 'takes the edge' off their ADHD symptoms; particularly their feelings of restlessness and inability to relax. They report feeling that cannabis induces a sense of control and well-being by smoking small amounts of cannabis throughout the day to reduce symptoms yet maintain an adequate degree of day-to-day functioning. This is in contrast to alcohol misuse, which may impair functioning. The major disadvantage of cannabis for people with ADHD is that it exacerbates existing cognitive deficits associated with ADHD, for example, it has an adverse effect on attention, working memory and time estimation. Excessive use may induce feelings of paranoia and deterioration in mental state.

Stimulants

Psychostimulant use (i.e. amphetamines, cocaine, crack etc.) in individuals without ADHD can produce an elevation of mood and a sense of increased energy with reduction in appetite and sleep. However, lower doses may 'normalize' the behaviour of people with ADHD as this group of drugs impact on the dopaminergic system, leading to improved attention and a reduction in impulse control difficulties. Some individuals with ADHD report having used amphetamines regularly for years prior to their diagnosis and receiving prescribed treatment with psychostimulants. Nevertheless, notwithstanding the huge variability in quality and purity of the substance, the disadvantages of self-medicating (either consciously or unconsciously) by using recreational drugs, are that high doses of stimulants can make people feel anxious or irritable. In addition, stimulants can be highly addictive and people can develop dependency very quickly. Withdrawal and cravings can lead to changes in their behaviour, such that they may change from being talkative and overly-friendly to agitated and irritable. In some cases, clients have reported feeling deeply disturbed by feelings of paranoia, for example, visual or auditory hallucinations in the context of heavy stimulant use. In such cases, individuals will require close and regular monitoring if they are to be prescribed psychostimulant medication, possibly on an inpatient basis.

Hallucinogens

Hallucinogens include ecstasy and LSD. These drugs may be used by people with ADHD in their quest for stimulation and sensation seeking. Ecstasy is associated with a sense of euphoria, well-being, increased activity and a reduced need for sleep. Dehydration is a very common side effect and it is extremely important that users consistently drink fluids such as water. However, ecstasy is commonly used recreationally at 'raves' or clubs; where fluid intake may be excessive alcohol. High doses can result in paranoid psychosis, depression, anxiety and suicidal ideas. Ecstasy is also associated with rapid development of tolerance.

LSD is a second hallucinogen. This drug creates the effect of visual distortion, disturbance in sense of time and increased sensitivities to colours and sound. These sensations may be attractive to people with ADHD, who are experimental in nature and not afraid to take risks. However, users are particularly sensitive to their environment and a threatening atmosphere can create a 'bad trip'. Adverse effects include later flashbacks and panic attacks.

Opiates

For some people, drug use will develop to the use of harder drugs such as, heroin, methadone and codeine. Regular use of such drugs results in a higher tolerance to opiates leading to dependency and addiction. Dependence withdrawal occurs 8 to 12 hours after the last dose, leading to symptoms of intense craving for the drug, restlessness, irritability, increased bowel activity, nausea and vomiting. Withdrawal and craving, combined with an impulsive temperament, may increase the likelihood that individuals will commit opportunistic theft and violence to fund their habit. The prescription of oral methadone is the commonest approach to the management of opiate withdrawal. If individuals present with this level of dependency, then it is strongly recommended that the person is referred for detoxification. Only after this has been successfully completed and the person has been drug free for a period of at least 6 months should psychological treatment for ADHD be commenced. Prior to this, it would be difficult to determine whether symptoms relate to drug misuse or ADHD.

ASSESSMENT AND MOTIVATIONAL INTERVIEWING

Psychoeducation is a vital component of the process of change. It is important that clients make informed decisions and are empowered to make choices. This is achieved by the therapist outlining the model of the stages of substance misuse (see Table 13.1), assessing the position of the client within the model and evaluating the risk of their behaviour (Table 13.1 is included on the Companion Website in handout format).

Table 13.1 The five stages of substance use

Stage of use	*Motivation for use*
1. Experimental	Curiosity, pleasure seeking, risk-taking, sensation-seeking, poor impulse control
2. Social	Need to be liked, affected by peer group social influence, social attitude, depends on availability
3. Instrumental	Used purposefully to create certain behaviours such as seeking 'highs' or using to 'cope' with stress and negative feelings
4. Habitual	The 'need' to use becomes more regular and frequent
5. Dependent	The substance is constantly 'needed' and misuse is regarded as 'normal' despite negative consequences.

Table 13.2 provides a checklist that allows the therapist and the client to identify problems the client may be experiencing due to their drug use. Items that are endorsed should be used as a basis for further discussion and exploration in sessions. A blank copy is provided in the Companion Website for use in sessions. In time physiological tolerance to substances means the individual must increase their dose to obtain the same effect or stimulation. Dependency is characterized by a state when the drug/alcohol becomes a priority for the individual and no longer causes the desired effect but withdrawal causes undesired effects. Short-term benefits (e.g. the ability to concentrate) are replaced by an increasingly greater need for the drug.

A drug of preference is often augmented by the use of alternative or additional substances, such as an alcoholic 'chaser' drinking strong lager with spirits; poly drug use. In such circumstances, the individual may find themselves operating at different stages in the cycle (outlined in Table 13.3) for different substances. Thus, when a client with ADHD is misusing substances, it is very important to identify the substances they use; the stage of use for each substance; and tease apart the purpose each serves and the consequences of use. Table 13.3 shows an example of how the therapist and client can achieve this to identify potential areas requiring intensive treatment (see Companion Website for a copy suitable to be used in sessions).

An exercise to help the client identify both their goals for improvement and their current vulnerabilities is to ask them to imagine a person with a drug addiction and rate this person's behaviour in the risk domains. They should then imagine a person without an addiction and predict this person's behaviour in the same domains. See Box 13.1 for an example of the exercise completed by Craig (see Companion Website for a blank version for use in sessions).

Craig was asked to look at the ratings for each person and think about what they told him. He decided that the better outcome was for the nonuser and this allowed

Table 13.2 Problems associated with substance misuse

As a result of taking .... do you?	*Circle Y/N*
Engage in verbally aggressive behaviour	(Y) / N
Engage in physically aggressive or violent behaviour	(Y) / N
Often feel irritable	(Y) / N
Often feel temperamental	Y / (N)
Often feel frustrated	Y / (N)
Feel depressed/unhappy	(Y) / N
Feel anxious	Y / (N)
Feel inadequate	(Y) / N
Lack self-control	(Y) / N
Have difficulty communicating with people (i.e. you feel people misunderstand you)	(Y) / N
Fall out with people	Y / (N)
Not look after yourself, e.g. personal hygiene, pride of appearance	Y / (N)
Engage in delinquent and/or criminal behaviour	(Y) / N
Have difficulty studying or working	Y / (N)
Engage in unsafe sex	(Y) / N
Self-harm (ideas or behaviour)	Y / (N)
Have concentration problems	Y / (N)
Have memory problems	(Y) / N
Lack motivation to do anything	(Y) / N
Have loss of appetite	Y / (N)
Have feelings of paranoia	(Y) / N
Have unusual experiences, e.g. visual hallucinations, 'flashbacks'	Y / (N)
Engage in reckless or risky behaviour	(Y) / N
Experience employment problems	Y / (N)
Lack confidence	(Y)/ N
Feel dissatisfied with life	(Y)/ N

Table 13.3 Substance, stage and motivation

Substance	*Stage of use*	*Reason for use*	*Consequence of use*
Alcohol	Habitual	I can't cope in social situations without it	I have hangovers and feel low
Nicotine	Dependent	I can't concentrate without it	I have breathing difficulties
Cannabis	Habitual	It has a calming effect. It allows me to get through the day	I feel edgy and paranoid
Cocaine	Social	I become more entertaining and have more energy	I need more each time I use it
LSD	Experimental	I like the sensation of having a trip. It's exciting.	I have panic attacks
Speed	Instrumental	It calms me down	I feel rough when it wears off

him to reflect on his own drug use and where this was leading him. This process was an influential factor in his decision to stop taking drugs and make changes in his life.

Motivational Interviewing

Encouraging an individual to make important change in their life involves the individual acknowledging that they are dissatisfied with aspects of their life and accepting that alternative possibilities are achievable. In order to do this, the therapist must encourage the individual to think about change as a process. This can be likened to a journey that requires organization and preparation. In these sessions the client will learn about the stages of the journey, in other words the stages of change and the reasons for making the journey. It is hoped that they will recognize that their goal is to achieve a better quality of life.

The readiness of the individual to tackle their addictions will depend on many factors, both environmental (e.g. all their friends being drug users, having to walk past a venue every day where dealers offer them drugs) and psychological (e.g. having insight into their problem, believing that they can function adequately without the substance). Research has shown that people with substance misuse problems can be classified as being at various points on a 'transtheoretical model of change' (Miller and Rollnick, 2002; Prochaska and DiClemente, 1982). In this model, individuals move systematically through a series of five stages in the course of changing their problems: precontemplation, contemplation, preparation, action and maintenance.

Box 13.1 Risk domain exercise

Imagine you are observing two different people, one is a dependent substance user and one is an ordinary person who does not use substances – say a successful person in full-time work with a family. What are they like? How likely are they to have the following problems? Rate them on a scale of 0–4.

0	1	2	3	4
Not at all likely				Highly likely

	Substance user	Non-substance user
Engage in verbally aggressive behaviour	3	1
Engage in physically aggressive or violent behaviour	4	1
Often feel irritable	4	0
Often feel temperamental	4	1
Often feel frustrated	4	2
Feel depressed/unhappy	4	0
Feel anxious	3	1
Feel inadequate	3	1
Lack self-control	4	0
Have difficulty communicating with people	3	0
Fall out with people	2	1
Don't look after themself	3	0
Engage in delinquent and/or criminal behaviour	3	0
Have difficulty studying or working	3	1
Engage in unsafe sex	3	1
Self-harm (ideas or behaviour)	4	2
Have concentration problems	3	1
Have memory problems	4	1
Lack motivation to do anything	4	0
Have loss of appetite	4	1
Have feelings of paranoia	4	1
Have unusual experiences, e.g. visual hallucinations, 'flashbacks'	4	2
Engage in reckless or risky behaviour	4	1
TOTAL PROBLEM SCORE	81	19

Look at the ratings for each person. What does it tell you? Who would you rather be?

Motivational Interviewing is a technique based on the transtheoretical model of change. It is designed to help individuals explore and resolve ambivalence to change and is particularly useful in helping people in the contemplation stage of change, where the task of the therapist is to help 'tip the balance' from ambivalence to favouring change. Motivational Interviewing engages the client in an empathetically supportive but strategically directed conversation about their substance misuse and has received empirical support in the treatment of alcohol and drug abuse (Van Horn and Bux, 2001).

Box 13.2 summarizes these stages, which are also provided in handout format on the Companion Website. The stages are likely to be recognized by the client, particularly with respect to where they get 'stuck' in the process and prevented from moving forward. This is helpful to determine obstacles to progression.

An alternative to the maintenance stage is relapse, when the individual begins another cycle. Most people experience slips or relapses and have to go through the cycle of change again before successfully maintaining change.

It is important to remember that these stages can be 'cyclical' with the client oscillating between stages (and this may occur for some time). For example, the client may revert back a step and waiver between earlier stages by engaging in a stage of 'action' but then relapse and misuse substances again. This may mean that they revert to a stage of preparation or even contemplation before progressing further in the cycle. Being successful in stopping misusing substances takes time, courage and motivation. It is far from easy, and working through the process of stages will involve the support and encouragement from family and friends as well as the therapist.

It is important to introduce the concept of change to the client. This may seem obvious, but to an individual who has physiological and/or psychological dependency, plus poor impulse control, this may seem far from an 'obvious' phenomenon. To encourage 'change', the client and therapist need to identify the clients' future goals, for example, what they desire and what they will plan to achieve. In the Problem-Solving Module (Chapter 7) the importance of breaking down goals into smaller achievable steps was introduced, such as for the goal to get a job – an action plan may be to buy daily newspapers, go to the job centre, register with employment agencies, make enquiries about voluntary work, find out about local training courses organized by the job centre or further education courses and so forth. The substance misusing client must determine not only how to motivate themselves and achieve these steps, but how to do so without using alcohol or drugs. This often means working with the client to improve their self-efficacy and raise their self-esteem. This will involve determining the social support structures around the individual (including those that may be undesirable and negative), what problems may be encountered in achieving the goals and plan how they may be overcome. Box 13.3 provides a structure to help the client identify reasons to engage in a process of change, who is

Box 13.2 Five stages of seeking help

Stage 1: Precontemplative stage
Precontemplative stage is that the core feature of the precontemplative stage is that the problem of substance misuse is not acknowledged and using is considered to be more important than the problems it causes. Individuals in this phase do not consider changing their behaviour as they do not accept that they have a problem. For people with ADHD, it can be difficult to move out of a precontemplative stage to a contemplative stage, as this involves a process of self-reflection and also because their thoughts are often racing ahead so they are unable to stop and consider their situation or needs.

Stage 2: Contemplative stage
At this stage the individual begins to acknowledge that they have a problem and considers making change but finds reasons to justify continued use and/or does not consider themselves able to change. This stage is characterized by ambivalence.

Stage 3: Determination stage (sometimes referred to as the 'preparation' or 'decision-making' phase)
The individual makes a decision to change the problem behaviour. At this stage the individual has the intention to take action to stop substance misuse but may be uncertain about how to follow this through.

Stage 4: Action stage
In the action stage, the individual will stop substance misuse and exhibit a change in their belief system regarding substance misuse. The individual begins to modify the problem behaviour.

Stage 5: Maintenance stage
After successfully negotiating the action phase, individuals move to maintenance or sustained change during which the individual is actively working towards continuing to stop substance use over a period of months and years.

likely to assist, as well as identify potential pitfalls. The Box shows the information completed by Craig (see Companion Website for a format for use in sessions).

It should always be acknowledged that one of the main reasons why individuals continue to use substances is that they perceive it holds some advantage for them, despite the disadvantages. Miller and Rollnick (2002) highlight that the nature of a client's ambivalence can be complex, and can comprise a set of pros and cons for each of the options available. Thus, in order to explore ambivalence to change the client should be asked to discuss the positive and negative aspects of their substance

Box 13.3 The problem of change

Why do you want to stop? I want to stop using because:

Using speed is making me feel edgy and low
I don't get anything done any more
I've lost my job

What do you want? My main goals for making this change are:

I've been evicted from my flat and I need to find a new one
To improve my relationship with Sarah

What can you do about it? This is what I plan to do to achieve my goals:

Action	When?
Look in local newspaper	Thursdays
Register with local estate agents	Saturday
Arrange a special date with Sarah	Saturday
Don't go where the dealers hang out	All week

Who can you get to help you? Other people could help me with change:

Person	Possible ways
Mum	Can store furniture, put me up in short term
Sarah	Doing things together away from places where there are drugs
Steve + Jan	Arrange an evening with Sarah's friends
Dave	Go to the gym

What might stop you succeeding? I anticipate possible obstacles to change:

Possible obstacles	How to respond
Going to a club or party where there are drugs	Leave. Tell Sarah or a friend how I feel
Sarah not trusting me	Reassure her as best I can and stay off drugs. Ask her to help
Bad credit reference	Save up and offer to pay cash in advance

I will know that my plan is working when I see these results

Move into a new flat
No rent arrears
Manage my money
Relationship seems better with Sarah and we see each other on a more regular basis

Table 13.4 Decisional balance sheet

Continuing to use amphetamines	*Making a change and giving up amphetamines*
Benefits	*Benefits*
Stops me from drinking I like it I lose my temper less often I feel relaxed I've got new friends I take it with	I'll save money I won't get in trouble with the police I'll be able to concentrate I'll stop being a bad influence on my younger brother I'll get more motivation
Costs	*Costs*
It's hard to get up for work in the morning I can't concentrate I feel uptight and anxious I think people are looking at me Sarah said she would leave me My mother won't let me stay with her	I might lose my drug taking friends

misuse and generate a list of advantages and disadvantages for continuing to use the substance. Hence, Craig completed a Decisional Balance Sheet in the form of a 4 × 4 matrix (see Table 13.4; a blank version of the table is provided on the Companion Website), which incorporated the costs and benefits of continuing to use substances, and of making a change. It is imperative that the client thinks carefully about the impact of the substance on their health, personal functioning, interpersonal relationships, ability to study or work, and behaviour. Indeed, the therapist must guide the client and ensure they recognize that the costs often outweigh the benefits. In Craig's example, with guidance he generated many more reasons to discontinue taking amphetamines than continuing. While these techniques may appear somewhat repetitive, when introducing the concept of change repetition of the advantages is an important positive reinforcer that should be introduced in sessions.

Miller and Rollnick (2002) argue it is not a simple matter of the number of positive versus negative factors that influence motivation, but the importance of each of the factors. In some cases, the client will insist on emphasizing the positive qualities of using a substance and resist acknowledging the negative qualities. This may result in them identifying just as many reasons to use it as not to use it. In such cases, the client should be invited to weight their reasons in terms of importance. This is illustrated in Box 13.4 when Craig was asked to assign an importance score (0–5) to each of the advantages and disadvantages for continuing to take amphetamines (see Companion Website for blank version for use in sessions). Craig assigned a total importance rating of 15 to the benefits of taking amphetamines and a total importance rating of 25 to the costs. He gave a weighting of 21 to the benefits of giving up amphetamines and only 4 to the cost of giving up. Thus, the outcome clearly

Box 13.4 Weighted advantages/disadvantages worksheet

0	1	2	3	4	5
Not important at all					*Extremely important*

Continuing to take amphetamines		*Making a change and giving up amphetamines*	
Benefits	*Weight*	*Benefits*	*Weight*
Stops me drinking alcohol	5	I'll save money	5
I like it	5	I won't get in trouble with the police	4
I lose my temper less often	3	I'll be able to concentrate	4
I feel relaxed	1	I'll stop being a bad influence on my younger brother	4
I've got new friends I take it with	1	I'll get more motivation	4
TOTAL WEIGHTED SCORE	15	TOTAL WEIGHTED SCORE	21
Costs	*Weight*	*Costs*	*Weight*
It's hard to get up for work in the morning	4	I might lose drug taking friends	4
I can't concentrate	4		
I feel uptight and anxious	5		
I think people are looking at me	4		
Sarah said she would leave me	5		
My mother won't let me stay with her	3		
TOTAL WEIGHTED SCORE	25	TOTAL WEIGHTED SCORE	4

illustrated that the disadvantages far outweighed the advantages both in terms of the number of positives and negatives, and their weighted importance.

COGNITIVE BEHAVIOURAL THERAPY

Psychoeducation: The Five Stages of Substance Use

Substance use can usually be categorized into one of five different stages of use. Individuals may use several substances, each in different stages. Table 13.1 shows the different stages and describes the function or motivation each stage serves to an individual with ADHD (this is also included on the Companion Website in handout format).

A characteristic of ADHD is sensation-seeking and a need for stimulation. The first stage of experimenting with drugs can fulfil these needs as they provide personal gratification in the form of thrills and excitement. For example, Craig described how he first began abusing solvents when truanting from school. This arose partly because, by not attending school, he had more unstructured time on his hands; he became bored and wanted thrills and excitement. He thought he could achieve this by trying new experiences. He made friends with a group of adolescents who spent time at the local park, drinking alcohol and sniffing glue. He also started to steal items from shops. People with ADHD are unlikely to consider the risks attached to taking a mind-altering substance because they do not think about the potential consequences. Apart from damaging his health, Craig ran the risk of being caught and prosecuted but he did not consider this possibility.

The second stage of substance use, the social stage, may be particularly relevant for people with ADHD as they may perceive this to be a way of making friends and increasing their popularity. Drug misuse may be a means of integration with peers, as opposed to being an outsider. The ADHD individual may believe that if they take drugs they will be accepted by their peer group (even if this is a deviant peer group) – a position to which they have long aspired. For example, Craig looked older than his friends and got away with buying alcohol when he was aged 15. For a brief period he found he was very popular with his new friends who requested him to purchase drink on their behalf. He believed he was accepted socially and spent time with these friends in the park drinking to excess. When his new friends became old enough to buy their own alcohol, they were no longer interested in Craig.

Once the individual enters the instrumental stage, the drug provides 'positive reinforcement'. This means the individual feels rewarded by their experience of taking the drug itself and thus increases the likelihood that they will take it again. For example, many young people take ecstasy to stay up and dance all night. They have a great time and do not feel tired, so the next time they go out late, they take ecstasy again. This begins to become a problem when the person believes that they cannot have a good time or enjoy themselves without taking the drug. Ironically, for individuals with ADHD, the positive reinforcement may be that they are better able to concentrate and complete tasks. Their social skills may improve as they engage better in social situations by resisting the urge to flit about in company or frequently change the topic of conversation. For example, after trying speed (amphetamines) Craig felt more confident and believed he was more capable in social interactions. He believed he was wittier and that he engaged in a more meaningful way with his new friends.

However, when a person feels the need to use substances on a daily basis in order to fulfil routine functions, they move to the 'habitual stage'. This can be a costly habit and, for some individuals, this may be the trigger to engage in criminal behaviour in order to fund the addiction. This may commence in a small way, and one which may not always be considered as 'criminal', such as taking money from their mother's purse. However, in time, these behaviours may escalate and include petty crimes of theft or shoplifting. As a young man, Craig used to make excuses and postpone paying his rent to allow him to buy more cannabis and speed as he believed he could not function without it. As the debts stacked up, he borrowed money from his friends, parents and girlfriend, intending to repay them on his next payday, but he never managed to achieve this.

The state of 'dependency' arises when an individual continues to use substances in spite of negative consequences and they feel they cannot manage without it. For example, Craig found that he was not able to get up in the morning to go to work after a night of clubbing and poly drug use. He avoided seeing his girlfriend because she became angry with him for wasting his money and being irritable.

Substance Use Strategies

Bellack and DiClimente (1999) recommend that once a client is engaged in treatment they should be taught the skills necessary to become and remain abstinent. At this stage therapy sessions should include behavioural skills for refusing substances, with emphasis on simple behavioural elements such as making eye contact, not smiling, and saying 'no' clearly. Role-play is helpful in the treatment sessions, as the overt rehearsal of skills has generally been shown to enhance treatment effects (e.g. Kazdin and Mascitelli, 1982). The aim is for the client to learn a few specific skills that may be used automatically, thereby minimizing cognitive load for decision making during stressful interactions.

Once the client has engaged in the action stage, they will be supported to maintain this position and develop the skills to resist temptation. This involves clients developing the confidence to apply successful strategies to overcome physical and psychological cravings. This may be achieved by employing methods such as: distraction and imagery; challenging and controlling dysfunctional beliefs; self-empowerment through the ability to embrace the concept of 'choice'; increasing self-esteem; the application of self-reinforcement techniques; activity scheduling; and motivating social support, rewards and positive feedback.

Controlling Physical Cravings and Urges

A craving is when someone really 'wants' something and an urge is where they 'do' something. For example, cravings for certain foods can occur, because you want to eat them; but you may have urges to eat certain foods because you feel you 'must' eat them. People who have urges feel uncomfortable unless they are able to relieve the sense of wanting something. Physical cravings and urges are linked with negative mood and/or low self-esteem. It is helpful to use distraction techniques to manage cravings, such as talking to someone and listening to music. Urges can be relieved by replacing what is wanted with something else that is less harmful. For example, methadone is commonly provided in place of heroin for people on drug rehabilitation programmes, nicotine patches can be an effective substitute for cigarettes, chewing

Table 13.5 Distraction and replacement techniques

Substance: amphetamines	
Distraction techniques that work for you	*Replacement techniques to manage urges*
go to the gym	drinking caffeinated tea/coffee
play guitar	chew nicotine gum
talk to Sarah and ask for her help	take a caffeine tablet
go for a run	Have a glucose energy drink

Box 13.5 Distraction techniques

Focus on the external environment to distract thoughts from internal cravings – concentrate on the trees, the grass, the people, the shops and so forth.
Engage in some form of mental activity, for example, mental arithmetic, crossword puzzles, reading.
Talk to someone who is unconnected to the substance.
Physical exercise or get out and about, for example, take a brisk walk, visit a friend, go for a drive to escape cravings.
Perform household tasks to keep busy.
Spend some time playing games, such as cards, computer games, board games and so on.

gum and drinking fizzy drinks may also help alleviate urges to misuse drugs and alcohol. The client may have already identified techniques that work; Table 13.5 shows the distraction and replacement techniques Craig identified that had worked for him in the past. He also added to the list some possible techniques that he could try out (see Companion Website for a version for use in sessions).

The distraction techniques outlined in Box 13.5 may prompt ideas for the client to try out. The Companion Website includes this box in handout format and as a flash-card which the client may keep in a wallet and use to remind themselves of a technique they can apply when needed. For example, a cognitive method to help the client cope with cravings is to teach them to say to themselves STOP! Train them to employ visual imagery to do this by imagining a stop sign or a brick wall. They should then focus on their surroundings and describe items in the room in minute detail. Once they have become less tense and more relaxed, encourage the client to conjure up an image in their head. They may wish to think of a *positive image*, for example a place where they have felt safe and happy, such as the seaside, and focus on little details, for example, the sound of the gulls, the lapping of the waves, the sand between their toes. Alternatively, they may wish to use a *negative image*, for example, imagine what it would be like to lose the house, family, friends, health, hurting the people they love and having them feel angry towards them. It may help

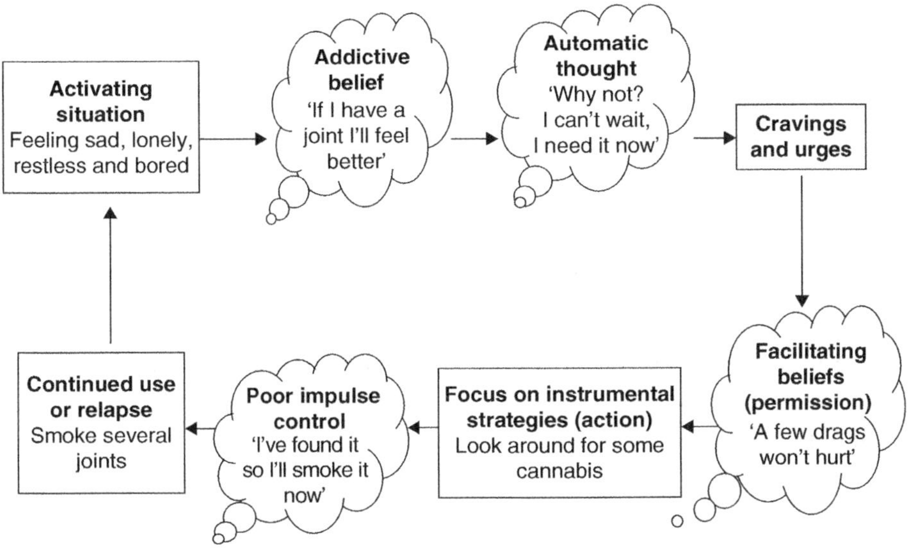

Figure 13.2 The sequence of thoughts and beliefs during cravings and urges

to refer back to the exercise in Box 13.1 when the client imagined a substance user and compared their life with that of a nonuser, and incorporate aspects of the exercise into the imaginal mode.

Dysfunctional Beliefs

Dysfunctional and addictive beliefs are very unhelpful and contribute greatly to the generation of perceived uncontrollable urges for substances. Figure 13.2 demonstrates the negative cyclical relationship between such thoughts, cravings and urges.

This figure can be used in treatment with the client by asking them to complete thoughts and behaviours as appropriate on a blank copy. This will identify thoughts and beliefs that may be cognitively challenged at relevant points in the process. *Dysfunctional beliefs* play an important role in the maintenance of substance misuse. For example, a client Katherine believed that she was only liked when she was being sociable and witty. Katherine formed the dysfunctional belief that drinking alcohol made her more amusing. This reinforced the urge to drink and created an *addictive belief* that alcohol made her more likeable. The relationship between Katherine's dysfunctional beliefs and addictive behaviour is shown in Figure 13.3 (a blank version is provided on the Companion Website).

Table 13.6 gives examples of other addictive beliefs commonly expressed by ADHD clients.

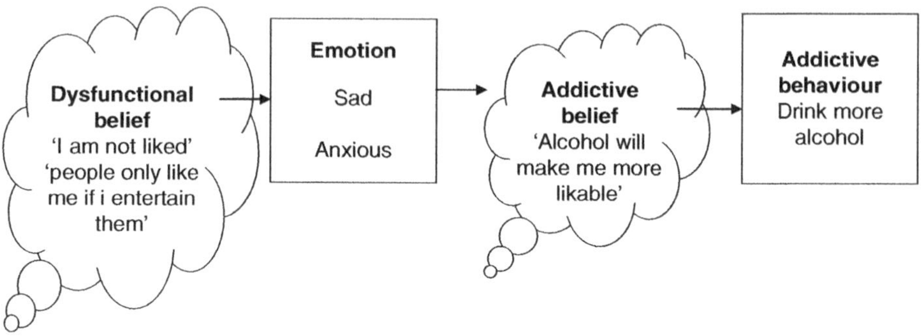

Figure 13.3 Dysfunctional beliefs that can maintain substance misuse

Table 13.6 Addictive beliefs

Taking drugs ...	*Example of addictive belief*
Improves concentration	I can't focus without it
Reduces inner restlessness	I can't feel calm without it
Improves confidence	I can't perform without it
Improves social functioning	I'll be witty and seem dull without it
Improves self-efficacy	I can't achieve without it
Increases pleasure and excitement	Life is boring without it
Increases energy and motivation	It is the only thing that motivates me
Relieves boredom,	The situation won't be so bad if I have it beforehand
Relieves tension, anxiety, and depression	I can't cope without it – it's the only thing that makes me feel better about myself
Maintain psychological and emotional balance	I'll go to pieces without it
Improves social skills	I communicate better and become more extroverted
Relieves craving	If craving is not appeased it will get worse
Justifies dependency	I am addicted so have no option.

Choice and Self-esteem

Individuals who have travelled far in the hierarchy of substance misuse will lose sight of the concept of choice and will. Clients should be asked to think back to a time when they made the choice not to use and had a positive outcome and positive self-esteem. They should then describe how they felt. The therapist should explore what they can do to help themselves get back to this stage again. They should focus on the good qualities such as positive feelings, experiences and behaviours that have occurred during their effort to stop misusing substances. This technique can be particularly empowering for people with ADHD who find themselves at the mercy of

Box 13.6 Flashcards of self-reinforcement

I am in more control without it
I am less aggressive without it
I don't want to hurt my family or friends
I look healthier without it
I don't want it – I want it to stop NOW.

their impulses and incorrectly believe their lack of self-control means they lack choice. This belief is a thinking error.

Self-reinforcement Techniques

Posters can be useful reminders of goals – to reduce and quit using a substance. It may also be helpful to have an advantages/disadvantages table on the wall or a list of distraction techniques that the individual can use as a prompt when an urge or craving arises. Flashcards, kept in a wallet, for example, can be used to remind the individual of the advantages of stopping substance use. The client should carry the card at all times and read it when they feel weak and vulnerable (see Box 13.6). An example that can be used for this purpose is provided on the Companion Website.

It may be helpful to list on the flip side of the flashcard any coping strategies and techniques that have been determined in the course of treatment that will help the client get through the 'risk period' when they feel vulnerable.

Activity Scheduling

Activity scheduling involves making a structured plan to squeeze out risk periods when the client recognizes they may be vulnerable to substance misuse. Pay particular attention to times when the client is most likely to be sensitive to cravings, urges and withdrawal. See the Low-Mood and Depression Module (Chapter 11) for further information about activity scheduling.

Social Support

It is essential that the client does not go it alone. It is really important that they are supported and that they engage the help of friends and family. There are also services that provide support and/or more formal treatment to help reduce excessive emotional reactions, modify self-defeating behaviour and help change beliefs and attitudes concerning the more problematic aspects of substance use. Some are local walk-in services where they can obtain confidential support and advice. Others offer more formal rehabilitation for addiction. However, the client will require ongoing support not only outside treatment but also following treatment, in order to plan and prevent relapse. Internet support groups have also become one source of such support.

Rewards and Positive Feedback

Rewards are a very important part of any treatment program for people with ADHD. Immediate rewards for success include giving themselves a pat on the back, self-praise and/or a more tangible reward for periods where they have succeeded in reducing or rejecting using the substance. The client should inform others about their progress, so that they too can give support and encouragement. This will help to boost their confidence and self-esteem. Treats, rewards, showing off and telling others how well they have done will boost their confidence.

SUMMARY

The process of change requires personal acceptance and once this has been achieved, abstinence and a healthier lifestyle may be maintained by applying specific treatment techniques. Substance misuse is complex and ADHD individuals with sustained long-term use at a level of dependency will require specialist intervention and rehabilitation. This module provides an intervention suitable for individuals who have perhaps long-term but intermittent use. Such individuals will be suitable for treatment using the Motivational Interviewing technique outlined in this module to wean them away from excessive use of drugs and alcohol as a social crutch and/or the risk of damaging their health with unprescribed drugs.

Group Treatment: Substance Misuse Module

It is essential to prepare for group treatment by reading the chapter module. Six group sessions are outlined below, but the number of treatment sessions can be expanded or reduced as required.

Plan

Session 1	Starting activities
Session 2	Psychoeducation – the five stages of change, the transtheoretical model of change, dysfunctional and addictive beliefs, management strategies and rewards.

(Continued)

Session 3–5	Exercises
Session 6	Revision of psychoeducation, techniques and rewards Discussion of homework outcome/experience Obstacles and how to overcome them

Starting Activities

What alcohol/drug(s) do you take? How often do you take them? Discuss relationship between experimentation vs. regular use. Discuss recreational use vs. dependency.
Why do you drink alcohol/take drugs? Discuss reasons for starting to drink alcohol/take drugs (onset). Discuss reasons they continue to drink alcohol/take drugs (maintenance).
What are the consequences of drinking excessive alcohol and/or taking drugs? Discuss past experiences and impact on school or occupation, family relationships, friendships and so forth.
Have you ever tried to cut down or give up? What happened? Group discussion.

Psychoeducation

Describe the five stages of substance use.
  Experimental, social, instrumental, habitual and dependent.
  Describe the link between them.
  Handout Table 13.1 The five stages of substance use.
  Ask participants to identify their stage of use for each substance they use.
Describe the transtheoretical model of change.
  Handout Box 13.2 Five stages of seeking help.
  Discuss 'readiness' for change and cyclical movement between stages.
Describe how dysfunctional and addictive beliefs maintain substance misuse.
  Handout Figures 13.2 and 13.3 on dysfunctional beliefs.
  Handout Table 13.6 Addictive beliefs.
Describe strategies that may help them give up.
  Challenge dysfunctional/negative thoughts (see Anxiety Module in Chapter 9).
  Distraction and replacement techniques to reduce cravings and urges.
  Choice and self-esteem.
  Self-reinforcement techniques (posters, flashcards – Handout Box 13.6).
  Activity scheduling (see Low-Mood and Depression Module in Chapter 11).
  Relaxation strategies (see Anxiety Module in Chapter 9) breathing exercises and progressive muscle relaxation (do in session).
  Social support.
  Rewards.
Identify appropriate rewards for incremental steps leading to completion of goal.

(*Continued*)

Exercises

Discuss outcome of drinking excessive alcohol and/or taking drugs.
- Complete Box 13.1 Risk domain exercise.
- Identify the problems associated with substance abuse (Handout Table 13.2 for completion individually).
- Compare and contrast participant problems identified and relate them to stage of use.
- Ask participants to identify personal goals for improvement.

Discuss advantages and disadvantages of giving up.
- Complete Table 13.4 Decisional balance sheet (individual exercise).
- Complete Box 13.4 Weighted advantages/disadvantages worksheet (individual exercise).

Discuss and identify strategies presented in psychoeducation that may be applied to help give up.
- Complete Figures 13.2 and 13.3 to identify dysfunctional and addictive beliefs that they use (individual exercise). Discuss and compare them with those of others. Discuss challenges (see Module 9).
- Ask selected participant(s) to complete the choice and self-esteem exercise (see text).

Discuss motivation for change.
- Select one participant and work together as a group to complete Box 13.3 The problem of change.

Continue with this participant and as a group discuss and identify strategies presented in psychoeducation that may be applied to give up.
- Set up 'behavioural experiments' by modelling a plan of action for the participant, include contingencies for relapse (as a group produce a draft written template that can be taken home).
- Consider distraction and replacement techniques, cognitive challenges, self-reinforcement techniques, activity scheduling, relaxation strategies, social support.
- Consider rewards to maintain motivation and to reward achievement.
- Discuss obstacles to achievement and methods to overcome them.

Repeat for other participants.

Homework

Handout Boxes 9.4 and 9.5 (relaxation techniques) for homework.

Apply selected intervention(s) as 'behavioural experiments' and amend template as appropriate.

PART IV

THE FUTURE MODULE

14

PREPARING FOR THE FUTURE MODULE

The Preparing for the Future Module is a 'stand alone' module that should always be the final module to a treatment episode in the Young-Bramham Programme. Thus, whatever modules preceded the therapy, treatment always ends with this module. By the time the final stages of treatment have been reached, the therapist is likely to feel that they have shared a journey of self-development with the client. The journey started with the words 'You have ADHD'. To the client, these words were not just a diagnosis, but a framework for self-understanding. Other clients, especially adolescents and young adults, will have been supported through critical periods of uncertainty and/or challenge as they become independent from family or carers and take responsibility for their own welfare and behaviour. Either way, the client is very likely to feel that they have undertaken an emotionally demanding process culminating in self-adjustment, adaptation and, for some, an acceptance of their condition.

As a therapist, the journey's course has involved imparting new psychological techniques in order to develop or enhance the client's skills. The modular design of the Young-Bramham Programme has provided the structure to tailor the psychological intervention to the needs of the client. This began with Parts I and II of the programme, which described the background to the programme and provided treatment modules on the management of core symptoms associated with ADHD; that is difficulties with attention, memory, time management and impulse control. Part III detailed treatment modules providing interventions for the comorbid conditions and associated problems commonly experienced by people with ADHD.

This final module is all about planning and preparing for the future. People with ADHD lack efficiency in their planning skills (Young *et al.*, 2007). Usually adolescents have not been faced with a need to make plans themselves, however, as they grow up and become autonomous they have to make decisions and plans for

Cognitive-Behavioural Therapy for ADHD in Adolescents and Adults: A Psychological Guide to Practice, Second Edition. Susan Young and Jessica Bramham.

their future. It is then that they learn that they do not have good planning skills, which has not been helped in the past by an over reliance on others to organize the world around them. They do not know how much longer they will have ADHD symptoms or the extent to which they will impair their functioning in daily activities. Furthermore these daily activities will not stay the same but change as life changes.

Preparing and planning for the future is extremely important as it entails a shift from problem-resolution towards a more positive position involving the optimization of the client's strengths and their future application. It is important to be mindful, nevertheless, that the end of treatment is always difficult. This may be particularly so for ADHD individuals who have experienced a lifetime of telling their story, yet, feel that no-one has listened or shown interest. The therapist who has conducted the Young-Bramham Programme has not only listened but also provided a programme suitable for their personal needs and development. This level of support or understanding may be new to the client and thus the ending of treatment must be carefully managed.

It is suggested that the final treatment sessions provide a pragmatic review of what has been learned, but also acknowledge and process the emotional journey undertaken by the client. This will involve thinking about the future, raising self-esteem, reviewing achievements and considering how to maximize these in the future to promote healthy mental functioning and instrumental success.

Consistent with the general format of the Young-Bramham Programme modules, the last module begins with a psychoeducational aspect in the form of a discussion regarding the heterogeneous progression of ADHD. There then follows a review of the progress made to date and a discussion about what the client expects in the future. The objective is to increase awareness of how ADHD may impact upon individuals in the years ahead; setting realistic achievable goals; making plans to achieve them in the future; and how best to enlist support in future endeavours. It is important to emphasize the positive aspects of having ADHD such as creativity and resilience, and discuss how the client can apply these characteristics adaptively to achieve success in everyday challenges, as well as in medium- and longer-term plans. In particular it is important to consider how expectations of the self may influence future outcomes and become self-fulfilling prophecies. Many people with ADHD have negative assumptions about themselves and an expectation of failure. Yet, through the reappraisal of their capabilities, people with ADHD can be encouraged to develop a greater sense of self-efficacy and purpose.

Thus, the latter sessions of the Young-Bramham Programme review the potential progression and sequelae of ADHD and summarize salient themes that have arisen in treatment. Cognitive behavioural techniques which have been effective in prior modules should be emphasized and reinforced. Raising self-esteem is an implicit theme in every module throughout the Young-Bramham Programme but, at the end of treatment this becomes more explicit with the introduction of specific techniques to draw attention to past successes and achievements and improve confidence in future performance and self-efficacy. Finally, the therapist should engage the client in a process of transferring the emotional and practical support provided in treatment sessions to outside resources. This may include enlisting the help of friends, family and sometimes the services of other professionals.

Thus, the termination of treatment involves a four-fold process:

1. to review the progression of ADHD and the clients' expectations of the future;
2. to review past achievements and successes during treatment with the objective of raising self-esteem;
3. to identify future goals that are realistic and achievable, and set steps to achieve them; and
4. to put in place methods to access social support outside of the therapeutic environment.

THE PROGRESSION OF ADHD

Different symptoms decline at different rates in ADHD. The course of the disorder usually involves hyperactivity diminishing first, followed by impulsivity. Inattention seems to be the most prominent symptom lasting into adulthood (Bramham *et al.*, in press (Psychological Medicine)). However, even when they no longer have a full complement of symptoms or meet criteria for diagnosis, many clients remain partially symptomatic (Young and Gudjonsson, 2008). This is known as 'ADHD in partial remission' and for some, symptoms may continue into middle age. Thus, some individuals require pharmacological treatment well into adulthood. Others may only require pharmacological treatment if their residual symptoms continue to cause them functional problems in some settings or circumstances.

There are three primary factors that determine the extent that symptoms will cause functional problems follow.

1. *Biological change* affects the symptoms directly, for example, maturation of the brain.
2. *Environmental change*, for example, the ability to change the environment around them so that problems arising from the symptoms are reduced.
3. *Psychological coping strategies*, for example, by the individual recognizing how symptoms affect them and the development of internal techniques to manage their symptoms and problems.

There is not much that the client can do to speed up biological change. Medication serves to relieve symptoms but does not treat the underlying cause of symptoms. An analogy is that spectacles help one to see better but do not change eyesight overall. Similarly medication has been shown to improve concentration and impulse control (to varying degrees) but, once the effects of medication have worn off, the symptoms rebound. Nevertheless, there are methods that one can apply to influence environmental and psychological factors, and many of these have been introduced in the Young-Bramham Programme modules.

Although most people gradually experience an improvement in some symptoms with maturation, some people find that, although their ADHD symptoms no longer cause them problems, they have difficulties due to the 'legacy' of ADHD. For example, some people experience mood-related difficulties due to low self-esteem. They may find that, despite improvement in their ADHD symptoms, they remain caught in a negative cycle of debasement and low self-expectations. They anticipate underachievement. Indeed in spite of ADHD being a heterogeneous syndrome, many clients report consistently that they believe they are not achieving their potential. They feel that they have let themselves down and/or have let others down they care for. Low self-esteem and poor self-efficacy will undoubtedly hamper an individual's ability to succeed in our achievement-orientated society. In other words because people with ADHD have tried and failed at so many projects in the past, they may begin to lose faith in themselves and believe that they will never achieve. In such cases, failure is repeatedly reinforced by further failure. Successes are often minimized, if recognized at all, and people with ADHD no longer believe in themselves. This is a negative cycle, where an individual fails because they expect to fail and thus it becomes a self-fulfilling prophecy.

The outcome for those who do not receive the diagnosis until their late adolescent or adult years is that they have lived and coped (often dysfunctionally) with their symptoms and associated problems for a long time. Some individuals, especially those with a high IQ, develop functional compensatory strategies but find these difficult to apply when they feel overwhelmed by competing demands and/or by stressful life events. Thus, these adults with ADHD are likely to have a different range of problems compared with individuals who were diagnosed and treated in childhood. Even when symptoms remit, internalized failure and learned helplessness may be interpersonally and socially 'ingrained'. The misattribution of the intent and behaviour of others, together with their own maladaptive behaviour, may have become part of a cycle that is difficult to break. Traditionally, the psychological adjustment process of 'graduating' from childhood ADHD is not routinely considered. Yet these individuals often feel that they are 'survivors' of a syndrome that has left them with significant personal, social and occupational consequences. We call this the 'hangover' of ADHD. Once no longer formally classified as suffering with ADHD, family and friends may be unsympathetic and attribute current difficulties to motivational and attitude problems, with little appreciation that these stem from a sense of insecurity and lack of confidence. Graduates of ADHD often need help reappraising their place in life, their skills, capabilities and opportunities. Once they have identified what they want to do, they will need encouragement to put one foot in front of the other and take the first steps towards their goals.

RAISING SELF-ESTEEM

People with ADHD often enter treatment with a chronic sense of failure stemming from a mismatch between actual achievement and potential, and the belief that they have to work harder than others to achieve the same outcome (Ramsay and Rostain, 2005). They may have developed a coping style whereby they react to difficult situations with avoidance or procrastination, often hoping that problems will go away or sort themselves out. Through engaging in therapy, this may have become all the more apparent to them, resulting in them eliciting a more complete recognition of the severity of their problems and feeling regret about lost opportunities. It is therefore crucial when intervening with an individual with ADHD that the therapist remains consistently aware of self-esteem vulnerabilities.

Negative assumptions and expectations about the ability to succeed or simply cope in a given situation are likely to result in the client avoiding situations and exercises, particularly when they perceive these to be anxiety-provoking and unmanageable. One of the most difficult challenges faced by people with ADHD (as well as 'graduates' of ADHD) is to improve self-esteem as the negative experiences of young people with ADHD (whether symptomatic or not) are long-term and deep-rooted. This may sound rather bleak and indeed the future will not always be rosy for people following treatment as they are still likely to encounter various personal and social hurdles. Ironically, self-efficacy does not always appear to be a problem and an underlying belief in their potential (albeit often unmet) most likely forms the basis of the resilient aspect of their personality (see Figure 1.1).

Thus, the experience of ADHD may be characterized as 'the good, the bad and the ugly'. So far the 'bad' and the 'ugly' experiences have been well described, but it is essential to focus on the positive features of ADHD and how these may influence the future prospects of the ADHD client. Indeed, people with ADHD have many strengths to draw on. They are often creative, artistic, witty and entertaining individuals. The most important way forward is to establish an area of expertise in which they can achieve by drawing on their specialized skills. This is often in the form of creative flair such as art, design and/or music, but may also be more practically based, for example, computer skills. Such ADHD strengths can be considered as 'islands of excellence' that form the basis of a fundamental optimism and belief in themselves. Such characteristics are essential catalysts in the process of resilience outlined in the cognitive-behavioural model of ADHD presented in Chapter 1.

Resilience is the factor that helps individuals with ADHD stay the course. Indeed, the motto or rule of people who have ADHD is the adage 'if at first you don't succeed, try, try again'. People who do not try will never have the opportunity to succeed. A negative self-fulfilling prophecy may hold for a short while when life seems bad and nothing seems to work out, but then resilience kicks in. This may occur due to a rigid obstinacy to refuse to head towards despair and/or failure. On the other hand

(and perhaps more likely), this may result from a process of alternative thinking generated from a natural creativity, optimism and interest in new and challenging opportunities. The generation of multiple solutions and/or alternative possibilities to a problem can mean that an individual has access to multiple opportunities of success. If you throw enough mud up on a wall, some of it will stick. Thus, people with ADHD are life's true entrepreneurs but in order to succeed they must find a way of defining their own structures and boundaries.

Low self-esteem is a persistent topic within the Young-Bramham Programme. A separate module has not been included to address this issue because improving self-esteem is so important that this concept is interwoven within each module of the programme. In this final module the therapist will empower the client, lift their confidence for the future and raise self-esteem by (1) working globally with the client by reviewing lifetime achievements and (2) working specifically with the client by re-emphasizing progress and success and reviewing the achievements the client has made during treatment.

Review of Life-Time Achievements

In order to motivate the ADHD client to determine goals and strive to reach their potential in the future, it will be necessary to review past achievements and successes to date. It is important to highlight the individual's strengths and emphasize what they do well. Often, people with ADHD are more familiar with their weaknesses and what they do less well. The 'Top Ten Achievements' exercise in Box 14.1 may be used to draw clients' attention to previous achievements that they are proud of. This is shown for Rebecca, a 32-year-old client, who had a young son Daniel who was also diagnosed with ADHD. This example is included on the Companion Website in a format suitable for use in sessions.

The client should then be encouraged to determine goals for the future. Paperwork often provides external validation of success, so future targets to enrol or become involved with projects that will provide a tangible outcome are very helpful as these provide clear positive reinforcement. In sessions, Rebecca drew up a list of goals she wished to achieve in the future (see Box 14.2). This is also provided on the Companion Website in a format for use in sessions.

Once Rebecca's goals had been identified, Rebecca was asked to suggest how she might achieve these goals, given what she had learned from the Young-Bramham Programme. This involved consideration of how each goal may need to be broken down into smaller achievable steps, as previously outlined in the Organization and Time-Management Module (Chapter 5) in Figure 5.1. Figure 14.1 shows the list of steps Rebecca determined she needed to complete to achieve three of her goals (see Figure 5.1 on the Companion Website for a blank version).

Box 14.1 Top ten achievements

List your top 10 achievements to date …

1. Having Daniel and raising him as a single mother.
2. Training as a nursery supervisor.
3. Being featured in local newspaper for fundraising.
4. Passing the driving test.
5. Buying a car.
6. Winning swimming competitions at school.
7. Art work being exhibited in a school exhibition.
8. Giving up smoking.
9. Gradually renovating the house.
10. Sitting exams at school and leaving with qualifications.

Box 14.2 Future goals

List five goals you wish to achieve in the next year

1. Become a qualified nursery teacher.
2. Go to art classes.
3. Buy a newer car.
4. Refurbish the kitchen.
5. Take up swimming again and obtain a life saving certificate.

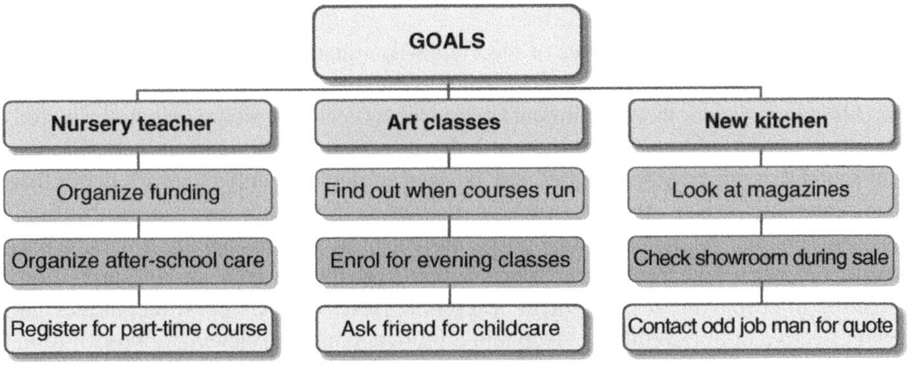

Figure 14.1 Steps towards goals

Completion of this exercise, 'Steps Towards Goals', helped Rebecca prepare for disengagement of treatment as she shifted her focus from supportive therapy in planning and managing her time to self-management and planning for future goals. Additionally, the sessions provided her with a broader perspective; by looking both back and looking ahead. When reviewing previous achievements, the therapist emphasized how well Rebecca had coped in the past despite her many difficulties and encouraged future achievement based on what she had learnt during the course of treatment. Rebecca was also encouraged to include rewards for achievements at 'step' level in order to motivate her progress towards the desired goals. For Rebecca, it was not long before rewards she had given herself in the past (such as a cup of tea and a biscuit, time off-task, or a walk around the block) became less commonly applied in favour of more process-oriented rewards (such as going for a swim, researching local art classes). These latter rewards were more reinforcing as they made a much greater contribution towards achievement of goals.

Review of Successful Strategies

During the course of therapy, the client will have tried out various strategies to improve symptoms in several domains of function. These strategies will have been met with varying degrees of success. The therapist should review the techniques that have been implemented during the treatment and rate their utility. This, of course, may also include strategies that the client has developed themselves that have yielded a positive (or negative) outcome. The exercise provided in Table 14.1 is designed to remind both the therapist and the client of which techniques have been tested and how effective they have been. It will also provide the client with a list of helpful strategies for use when the intervention has been terminated. These strategies should be rated from 0 (not at all useful) to 10 (extremely useful). Table 14.1 shows the review generated by Graham, a client who had combined type ADHD who presented with poor time-management skills, difficulties controlling his temper, moderate cannabis use and sleep difficulties. (Table 14.1 is also presented on the Companion Website).

By working through the modules of the Young-Bramham Programme, it was possible for the therapist and Graham to review which strategies had been used to tackle each of his difficulties. For Graham, treatment began with a focus on his core symptoms including attention and memory difficulties, impulsivity and poor time-management. Graham had found that practical techniques and external strategies seemed to work better than using internally driven strategies such as distraction. For anger management difficulties, he found the 'ADHD Formula' particularly helpful whereas applying volume control of his voice had been rather more difficult for him to achieve but surprisingly effective in 'behavioural experiment' exercises. Several behavioural techniques had been effective in improving his sleep and a motivational interviewing approach to his substance misuse had helped him to reduce his cannabis use. Graham found that drawing up the list allowed him to systematically review what he had achieved during therapy as well as providing him with a list of a range of strategies for future use. Modules

Table 14.1 Review of successful strategies

In order to improve my. ...	*I can....*	*How useful is this strategy? 0–10*
Attention	Make sure the room is quiet	8
	Use earplugs	6
	Switch off the phone	4
	Use a cue card	5
	Take regular breaks	7
Memory	Write a list of things I need to do	7
	Always keep my diary in my pocket	4
	Set an alarm on my mobile phone for appointments	9
Time-management	Breakdown activities into steps	6
	Make a diary activity planner	8
	Work out rewards	5
Problem-solving	Module not administered	
Impulsivity	Use the IMPULSE CONTROL method	7
	Use double-check questions	9
	Count backwards	3
Social relationships	Module not administered	
Anxiety	Module not administered	
Anger	Monitor how I'm feeling	4
	Use the ADHD formula	8
	Listen to criticism	5
	Keep voice volume low	5
Low mood	Module not administered	
Sleep	Stop sleeping in the day	5
	Regular bedtime	8
	Stop watching TV in bed	8
	Make a worry list	4
	Set two alarms	9
	Leave curtains open	7
Substance misuse	Use decisional balance sheets	7
	Use distraction and replacement techniques	5
	Challenge dysfunctional beliefs	6

that were not completed were initially left blank for this exercise although in the course of the review, Graham found that there were aspects of his learning that he could apply to make more general improvements both intrapersonally and interpersonally.

ACCESSING SUPPORT

A long-term problem for people with ADHD is that they have encountered numerous difficulties in developing and maintaining relationships. They find it difficult to pick up on subtle cues that should prompt them to alter their behaviour. Unfortunately, when interpersonal difficulties are pointed out, these are likely to be received negatively by an individual with ADHD who is sensitive to criticism. By engaging in therapy, a client may be encountering for the first time a relationship in which they feel they have been constructively helped. In this way self-esteem may be fostered. Ending this therapeutic relationship is therefore likely to be difficult and lead to an initial deflation in self-esteem accompanied by feelings of being unable to cope. It is therefore important to spend time preparing the individual for the end of treatment by devising a comprehensive 'relapse prevention' plan that will arm the client with numerous coping options when therapy is discontinued. This has been achieved so far by reviewing what has worked during the intervention, what has facilitated success for them in the past and emphasizing the positive features of ADHD. The final step is to discuss ways of enlisting help and support from family, friends and/or other professionals.

Support from Family and Friends

Throughout this programme it has been emphasized how important it is for clients with ADHD to be educated about their disorder and their experience of living with it. This means they will be forewarned about how they may respond to life events. The underlying premise for this is 'forewarned is forearmed'; that is, by being aware of and understanding their own difficulties, the client is better equipped to anticipate situations when they are likely to require extra help or support. A parallel reason for the importance of psychoeducation is for the client to be able to educate their family and friends about how they are likely to behave and react. While ADHD should not be an excuse for inappropriate behaviour, it is useful that family and friends understand that on occasions such behaviour is not due to a lack of caring about the relationship on the part of the individual with ADHD.

By identifying specific ways in which family and friends can provide support, and also providing an explanation of why this is likely to help, the individual with ADHD and their supporters can benefit from mutual gains. An example is the case of Nick. Prior to being diagnosed with ADHD Nick was frequently criticized by his partner for not shouldering his share of the domestic chores. He insisted that this was not through laziness on his part, but through his lack of organization, and he often requested that his partner made him a list of tasks. This request made his partner even more annoyed with the situation as she felt that he should be able to recognize what needed doing around the house without being told. Following being diagnosed with ADHD, Nick became more aware of his inattentive difficulties and consequently his need for structure. With this explanation, his partner was more able to understand the origin of his difficulties and started to make specific work lists for Nick's share of the housework. At weekends, Nick worked through the list and ticked off each chore as he completed it. The house became tidier and Nick had fewer arguments with his partner.

It is not unusual for family and friends who have known the person with ADHD for many years, to accommodate some of their difficulties, albeit in a begrudging way. However, it is not necessarily helpful to always make allowances. Family and friends are well placed to help the individual with ADHD look at a situation in a constructive way. They might remind the client of how they had coped with a similar difficulty in the past and help the client prepare for the future by talking about how it may be overcome and/or avoided.

One issue that clients often raise is that they are unsure of the extent to which others appreciate how much effort they have gone to in trying to do the right thing or trying to please them. Often, in spite of making a huge effort, the client does not achieve exactly what they hoped for. Even worse, their efforts end up causing upset or distress. In such circumstances the client will feel angry (with themselves and others) and low in mood, which in turn can lead to further difficulties in achieving their quest for success. If family and friends are able to understand that individuals with ADHD do not derive pleasure from being late, behaving irresponsibly or acting inappropriately, then the client is likely to feel far better supported and more able to cope with the knock-backs they will inevitably encounter from people who do not share this understanding.

Whenever possible, family or even close friends are important to have on board in a treatment programme as they can help the client apply what they have learnt in the therapy sessions to outside the sessions. They can continue to support the client when the therapy has ended. Additionally they may be helpful in monitoring the effects of treatment and give positive feedback. Such positive feedback will become part of a 'reward system' by providing positive reinforcement. Furthermore they may recognize times when the client has forgotten to take their medication and prompt accordingly.

Professional Help

By the time most young people with ADHD seek treatment, it is unlikely that their ADHD symptoms are the only reason for seeking help. Many people with ADHD have a history of multiple presentations to health services both in childhood and adulthood (Dalsgaard *et al.*, 2002; Young, Toone and Tyson, 2003) so they may have become accustomed to a help-seeking model of coping with their problems. This needs to be transferred to a model that depends less on mental health services and more on self-help and/or accessing community support.

Of course, some individuals may require referral for more specialized treatment, such as detoxification or rehabilitation of addictions, or a more complex pharmacological regimen. Thus, in preparation for termination of therapy, it is recommended that the therapist discusses the range of services available, the grounds for re-referral, and states clearly how and when these services can be accessed.

Waiting lists are an obvious flash point for people with ADHD. Clients need to recognize that, while it is clearly important for them to find out about waiting times and voice their concerns or complaints if they are waiting longer than they would wish, their desire for immediate gratification may cause them to appear unreasonable and/or confrontational. Additionally, responding to their requests may cause further delay in service provision.

Individuals with ADHD are also likely to have high expectations of the outcomes of treatment as they will be hoping for a panacea that requires minimal effort on their behalf but provides immediate gratification. When a treatment falls short of these expectations, the individual may feel that they have (once again) become a 'victim' of services' shortcomings and express their feelings in either general procrastination or by making explicit complaints about services and/or individual service providers. Such behaviours function as a projection or transference of their underlying feelings of anger, frustration and rejection. This propensity should be countertransferred by reassuring clients about the future by preparing them to anticipate and cope with difficulties and challenges. By developing these skills, the client will (hopefully) be prevented from antagonizing the people who may be best placed to help them.

Support Services

An important component of any relapse prevention plan is to determine sources of relevant available support (e.g. learning support, vocational counselling, social services, housing). Clients with ADHD may have difficulty knowing where to start in order to find information about such support provision, so the therapist should prepare a list of available local resources such as the internet, local libraries, local council offices and so forth.

Resources that may benefit clients with ADHD who are studying include learning support and assignment/examination dispensations. These may be particularly relevant for clients with comorbid dyslexia. Similar support structures may be available in the workplace of large organizations. Clients with employment problems may gain benefit from vocational counselling services. In sessions, the therapist can prepare the client for this by drawing up a list of likes and dislikes from previous jobs and determine a skills repertoire. This will help the client to reflect on what they would like to do and where they would excel.

Before attempting to access local support services, clients need to make contact and find out what the service can offer. However, individuals with ADHD may expect immediate responses to their requests and if these are not forthcoming they may become irritated and dismissive of the support service provided. This may fuel underlying negative dysfunctional assumptions that nobody really cares about them.

They are likely to give up trying to get help. In particular, people with ADHD can be particularly infuriated by services that have no knowledge of the disorder. The therapist may need to revise sections of the Interpersonal Relationships Module (Chapter 8) and role-play appropriate responses to requests for information that may irritate them and/or cause long delays.

Support Groups

Today there are numerous ADHD support groups available, ranging from face-to-face contact meetings to internet chat lines and networks. Gaining support from others with the disorder is beneficial for many reasons. The most important, yet most obvious, reason for joining support groups is to access peer support. People with ADHD are more likely to be able to understand the experience of their peers and find it both reassuring and empowering to offer advice to others. It is often a relief for clients to meet people who share similar histories and experiences. It can also be useful to share strategies for coping with ADHD symptoms. People with ADHD have often developed specific expertise to accommodate their difficulties and can provide advice regarding adaptive compensatory strategies to others.

Some people report feeling nervous in the first instance about joining a group that requires face-to-face contact. They worry that they will not have anything to say or be too embarrassed to speak. Also people may be fearful that they may not be able to concentrate. However, when running the Young-Bramham Programme in group workshop format, these apprehensions seem to rapidly dissipate in the face of shared understanding and experiences. One outcome is that the groups often become mutually supportive between sessions and group members are able to swap their contact details if they wish. In some cases, some clients have linked up as 'buddies' to help support each other on a more regular basis.

SUMMARY

This chapter has described the final module of the Young-Bramham Programme. In these sessions, the client will review the past, look towards the future and make constructive plans for this to be successful. For those in symptom remission, the legacy of ADHD may outlive the disorder in the form of low self-esteem and anticipated failure. The Young-Bramham Programme has outlined modules and techniques to address these problems. The natural ebullience and resilience of the ADHD client will considerably further the endeavours of the therapist. People with ADHD are engaging to work with, in spite of a tendency to procrastinate. They have great potential to make positive change and when this occurs it is a rewarding experience for both the client and therapist.

Group Treatment: Preparing for the Future Module

It is essential to prepare for group treatment by reading the chapter module. Six group sessions are outlined below, but the number of treatment sessions can be expanded or reduced as required.

Plan

Session 1	Starting activities
Session 2	Psychoeducation – progression, mediation, preparation for the future, accessing support.
Session 3–5	Exercises
Session 6	Revision of psychoeducation, techniques and rewards Discussion of homework outcome/experience Obstacles and how to overcome them End of treatment activities

Starting Activities

What have you learned from the Young-Bramham Programme? What has changed? Identify global change (self-esteem, confidence, self-efficacy, coping strategies) and specific changes (study skills, emotional control, relationships).

What do you want in the future? How are you going to get this? Encourage participants to set realistic achievable goals. Break goals down into steps and make lists.

What may prevent you from reaching your goals? *What can you do about this?* Discuss difficulties with planning and revise techniques that may help participants stay on task (make written plans, rewards).

What will assist you to reach our goals? *How can you set this up?* Draw on what they have learned in previous sessions (techniques, strategies, plans, rewards and so forth). Explore support structures.

What challenges or difficulties do you think you will face in the coming months/years? Remind participants that forewarned is forearmed. How can they prepare for eventualities? If they prepare, will this help?

Group discussion.

Psychoeducation

Preparing for the future.

Describe the progression of ADHD, heterogeneity and individual differences.

Discuss partial remission of symptoms and link symptoms to functional problems.

Discuss 'graduating' from ADHD and the 'legacy' or 'hangover' of ADHD.

Discuss mediating effects of emotional health, self-esteem, confidence and self-efficacy.

Forewarned is forearmed – we know that some things will happen.

Discuss the importance of thinking about the future.

(Continued)

Change will happen and can be predictable (leaving school, further education, job interviews, leaving home, bereavement, arguments).

Making plans.

Emphasise they need to identify tangible goals. To achieve their goals they must break them down into steps, make written plans and 'to do' lists (revise Organization and Time-Management Module in Chapter 5).

Motivation and rewards.

Accessing support.

Psychoeducation for family and friends – open discussion, constructive criticism, positive feedback, reward systems.

Learning to be independent.

Professional help – realistic expectations.

Support services – provide a handout listing useful local services and activities.

Resources – provide a handout about what help is available and how to access it.

Support groups – provide a handout listing contact details for local and national support groups.

Exercises

Review successful strategies.

Complete Table 14.1 Review of successful strategies (individual exercise).

What can participants learn from this exercise?

Compare and contrast participants' successful strategies.

Discuss whether these were obtained by 'behavioural experiments' and if so how did this help?

Each participant presents in turn to the group:

Present one major or important positive change the participant has experienced by participating in the Young-Bramham Programme. What made this possible (change in attitude, applying strategies, planning etc.)?

Review life time achievements.

Complete Box 14.1 Top ten achievements (individual exercise).

Complete Box14.2 Future goals (individual exercise).

Complete Figure 14.1 Steps towards goals (complete for top 3 goals).

Compare and contrast participants' achievements, goals and steps.

Select the work of one participant:

Will the participant achieve the goals by initiating this plan? Discuss and rework goals/steps if necessary as a group exercise.

Identify rewards to motivate achievement.

Identify support that may be required and factor this in to the plan.

Devise a written plan of action to achieve one of the goals. Include contingencies for obstacles to success (i.e. as a group, produce a draft written template that can be taken home).

Repeat exercise for other participants.

(*Continued*)

End of Treatment Activities:

Identify and discuss appropriate rewards for reaching the end of the programme.

Tape paper to the back of each participant. Ask other participants to write something positive about that person on the paper (e.g. something they like about them, something they learned from them).

Homework

Revise successful strategies. Add new strategies as they arise.

Regularly review future goal plan and steps. Transfer steps into a 'to do' list. Add rewards. Complete steps. Add new steps as required.

Using the skills you have learned set up another goal plan and steps (see goals identified in Box 14.2 completed in session).

Find a 'buddy' partner to help you.

Join a support group. If there is no local support group, start one!

REFERENCES

American Psychiatric Association (APA) (2000) *Diagnostic and Statistical Manual of Mental Disorders*, 4th edn, Washington, DC: APA.

Anderson, J.C., Williams, S., McGee, R., and Silva, P.A. (1987) DSM-III-R disorders in a preadolescent children: Prevalence in a large sample from the general population. *Archives of General Psychiatry*, 44, 69–76.

Asherson, P. (2005) Clinical assessment and treatment of attention deficit hyperactivity disorder in adults. *Expert Review of Neurotherapeutics*, 5, 525–539.

Asherson, P., Adamou, M., Bolea, B., Mueller, U., Dunn-Morua, S., Pitts, M., Thome, J., and Young, S. (2010) Is ADHD a valid diagnosis in adults? Yes. *British Medical Journal*, 340, C549.

Baddeley, A. (1986) *Working Memory*, Oxford: Clarendon/Oxford University Press.

Baddeley, A. and Wilson, B. (1988) Frontal amnesia and dysexecutive syndrome. *Brain and Cognition*, 7, 212–230.

Barkley, R.A. (1998) *Attention Deficit Hyperactivity Disorder. A Handbook for Diagnosis and Treatment*, New York: The Guildford Press.

Barkley, R.A. (2002) Major life activity and health outcomes associated with attention deficit/hyperactivity disorder. *Journal of Clinical Psychiatry*, 63, 10–15.

Barkley, R.A. and Biederman, J. (1997) Towards a broader definition of the age-of-onset criterion for attention-deficit hyperactivity disorder. *Journal of American Academy of Child and Adolescent Psychiatry*, 36(9), 1204–1210.

Barkley, R.A., Guevremont, D.C., Anastropoulos, A.D., DePaul, G.J. and Shelton, T.L. (1993) Driving-related risks and outcomes of attention deficit hyperactivity disorder in adolescents and young adults: a 3–5 year follow-up study. *Pediatrics*, 92, 212–218.

Beck, A.T. (1963) Thinking and depression. I. Idiosyncratic content and cognitive distortions. *Archives of General Psychiatry*, 14, 324–333.

Beck A.T. (1976) *Cognitive Therapy and the Emotional Disorders*, New York, International Universities Press.

Bellack, A.S. and DiClimente, C.C. (1999) Treating substance abuse among patients with schizophrenia. *Psychiatric Services*, 50(1), 75–80.

Biederman, J., Faraone, S.V., Keenan, K., Steingard, R., and Tsuang, M.T. (1991) Familial association between attention deficit disorder and anxiety disorder. *American Journal of Psychiatry*, 148, 251–256.

Biederman, J., Faraone, S.V., Mick, E., Williamson, S., Wilens, T.E., Spencer, T.J., Weber, W., Jetton, J., Kraus, I., Pert, J., and Zallen, B. (1999) Clinical correlates of ADHD in

Cognitive-Behavioural Therapy for ADHD in Adolescents and Adults: A Psychological Guide to Practice, Second Edition. Susan Young and Jessica Bramham.

females: Findings from a large group of girls ascertained from pediatric and psychiatric referral sources. *Journal of the American Academy of Child and Adolescent Psychiatry*, 38, 966–975.

Biederman, J., Faraone, S.V., Spencer, T., Wilens, T., Norman, D., Lapey, K.A., Mick, E., Lehman, B.K., and Doyle, A. (1993) Patterns of psychiatric comorbidity, cognition, and psychosocial functioning in adults with attention deficit hyperactivity disorder. *American Journal of Pyschiatry*, 150, 1792–1798.

Biederman, J., Newcorn, J., and Sprich, S. (1991) Comorbidity of attention deficit hyperactivity disorder with conduct, depressive, anxiety, and other disorders. *American Journal of Psychiatry*, 148, 564–577.

Bramham, J., Young, S., Bickerdike, A., Spain, D., MacCartan, D., and Xenitidis, K. (2009) Evaluation of group cognitive behavioural therapy for adults with *ADHD. Journal of Attention Disorders*, 12(5), 434–441.

Bramham, J., Young, S.J., Morris, R.G., Asherson, P., and Toone, B.K. (2005a) Neuropsychological deficits in adults with ADHD: do they improve with age? British Neuropsychiatry Association Conference.

Bramham, J., Young, S.J., Morris, R.G., Asherson, P., and Toone, B.K. (2005b) Behavioural symptoms and cognitive deficits in adults with ADHD: What changes with age? Division of Clinical Psychology, British Psychological Society Conference.

Bramham, J., Murphy, D., Xenitidis, K., Asherson, P., Hopkin, G., and Young, S. (in press) Adults with ADHD; An investigation of age-related differences in behavioural symptoms, neuropsychological function and comorbidity. *Psychological Medicine*. Epub ahead of print.

Brown, T.E. (1996) *Brown Attention-Deficit Disorder Scales,* San Antonio, TX: Harcourt Brace.

Brown, T.E. and McMullen, W.J. (2001) Attention deficit disorders and sleep/arousal disturbance. *Annals of the New York Academy of Sciences*, 931, 271–286.

Burgess, P.W., Veitch, E., de Lacy Costello, A., and Shallice, T. (2000) The cognitive and neuroanatomical correlates of multitasking. *Neuropsychologia*, 38(6), 848–863.

Cairnes, E. and Cammock, T. (1978) Development of a more reliable version of the Matching Familiar Figures Test. *Developmental Psychology*, 14, 555–556.

Chervin, R.D., Dillon, J.E., Bassetti, C., Ganoczy, D.A., and Pituch, K.J. (1997) Symptoms of sleep disorders, inattention, and hyperactivity in children. *Sleep*, 20(12), 1185–1192.

Clark, D.M. (1986) A cognitive approach to panic. *Behaviour Research and Therapy,* 24, 461–470.

Conners, C.K. (2000) *Conners' Rating-Scales-Revised: Technical Manual*, New York: MHS.

Conners, C., Erhardt, D., and Sparrow, E. (1998) *The Conners Adult ADHD Rating Scale (CAARS)*, Toronto: Multi-Health Systems Inc.

Cortese, S., Konofal, E., Lecendreux, M., Arnulf, I., Mouren, M.C., Darra, F., and Dalla Bernardina, B. (2005) Restless legs syndrome and attention-deficit/hyperactivity disorder: A review of the literature. *Sleep*, 28(8), 1007–1013.

Dalsgaard, S., Mortensen, P.B., Frydenberg, M., and Thomsen, P.H. (2002) Conduct problems, gender and adult psychiatric outcome of children with attention-deficit hyperactivity disorder. *British Journal of Psychiatry*, 181, 416–421.

Deci, E.L., Koestner, R., and Ryan, R.M. (1999) A meta-analytic review of experiments examining the effects of extrinsic rewards on intrinsic motivation. *Psychological Bulletin*, 125(6), 627–668.

Denkla, M.B. (1996) Research on executive function in a neurodevelopmental context: Application of clinical measures. *Developmental Neuropsychology*, 12, 5–15.

Duncan, C.C., Rumsey, J.M., Wilkniss, S.M., Denckla, M.B., Hamburger, S.D., and Odou-Potkin, M. (1994) Developmental dyslexia and attention dysfunction in adults: brain potential indices of information processing. *Psychophysiology*, 31(4), 386–401.

D'Zurilla, T.J. and Nezu, A.M. (1999) *Problem-Solving Therapy: A Social Competence Approach to Clinical Intervention*. New York: Springer Publishing Company.

Ebbinghaus, H. (1885) *Memory: A Contribution to Experimental Psychology*, New York: Teachers College, Columbia University.

Efron, D., Jarman, F., Barker, M. (1997) Side effects of methylphenidate and dexamphetamine in children with attention deficit hyperactivity disorder: a double-blind, crossover trial. *Pediatrics*, 100(4), 662–666.

Elia, J., Ambrosini, P., and Berrettini, W. (2008) ADHD characteristics: I. Concurrent co-morbidity patterns in children and adolescents. *Child and Adolescent Psychiatry and Mental Health*, 2(1), 15.

Emilsson, B., Gudjonsson, G., Sigurdsson, J.F., Einarsson, E., Baldursson, G., Olafsdottir, H. and Young., S. (2011) R&R2 Cognitive behaviour therapy in medication-treated adults with ADHD and persistent symptoms: A randomized controlled trial. *BMC Psychiatry*, 11(116), available at: www.biomedcentral.com/1471-244X/11/ (accessed 21 November 2011).

Faraone, S., Biederman, J., and Mick, E. (2006) The age-dependent decline of attention deficit hyperactivity disorder: A meta-analysis of follow-up studies. *Psychological Medicine*, 36, 159–165.

Faraone, S.V., Wilens, T.E., Petty, C., Antshel, K., Spencer, T., and Biederman, J. (2007) Substance use among ADHD adults: Implications of late onset and subthreshold diagnoses. *American Journal on Addictions*, 16, Suppl 1: 24–32.

Fox, R.A. and Wade, E.J. (1998) Attention deficit hyperactivity disorder among adults with severe and profound mental retardation. *Research in Developmental Disabilities*, 19, 275–280.

Gau, S.S., Kessler, R.C., Tseng, W.L., Wu, Y.Y., Chiu, Y.N., Yeh, C.B., and Hwu, H.G. (2007) Association between sleep problems and symptoms of attention-deficit/hyperactivity disorder in young adults. *Sleep*, 30(2), 195–201.

Gaub, M. and Carlson, C.L. (1997) Gender differences in ADHD: A meta-analysis and clinical review. *Journal of the American Academy of Child and Adolescent Psychiatry*, 36, 1036–1045.

Goldman, L. S., Genel, M., Bezman, R. J., and Slanetz, P. J. (1998) Diagnosis and treatment of attention-deficit/hyperactivity disorder in children and adolescents. *Journal of the American Medical Association*, 279(14), 1100–1107.

Goldstein, S. and Schwebach, A.J. (2004) The comorbidity of Pervasive Developmental Disorder and Attention Deficit Hyperactivity Disorder: Results of a retrospective chart review. *Journal of Autism and Developmental Disorders*, 34(3), 329–339.

Goldstein, S. and Teeter-Ellison, P.A. (eds) (2002) *Clinician's Guide to Adult ADHD: Assessment and Intervention*, New York: Academic Press.

Goodwin, G.M. (2009) Evidence-based guidelines for treating bipolar disorder: Revised second edition recommendations from the British Association of Psychopharmacology. *Journal of Psychopharmacology*, 4, 346–388.

Gudjonsson, G.H., Sigurdsson, J.F., Bragason, O.O., Newton, A.K., and Einarsson, E. (2008). Interrogative suggestibility, compliance and false confessions among prisoners and their relationship with attention deficit hyperactivity disorder (ADHD) symptoms, Psychological Medicine, 38, 1037–1044

Gudjonsson, G.H., Sigurdsson, J.F., Eyjolfsdottir, G.A., Smari, A., and Young, S. (2009) The relationship between satisfaction life, ADHD symptoms and associated problems among university students. *Journal of Attention Disorders*, 12(6), 507–515.

Gudjonsson, G.H., Sigurdsson, J.F., Sigfusdottir, I.D., and Young, S. (forthcoming) An epidemiological study of ADHD Symptoms among young persons and its relationship with cigarette smoking, alcohol consumption, and illicit drug use. *Journal of Child Psychology and Psychiatry*. DOI: 10.1111/j.1469-7610.2011.02489

Hafner, H. and An Der, H. W. (1997) Epidemiology of Schizophrenia. *Canadian Journal of Psychiatry*, 42, 139–151.

Hervey, A.S., Epstein, J.N., and Curry, J.F. (2004) Neuropsychology of adults with attention-deficit/hyperactivity disorder: a meta-analytic review. *Neuropsychology*, 18(3), 485–503.

Hirvikoski, T., Waaler, E., Alfredsson, J., Pihlgren, C., Holmström, A., Johnson, A., Rück, J., Wiwe, C., Bothén, P., and Nordström, A. L. (2011) Reduced ADHD symptoms in adults with ADHD after structured skills training group: Results from a randomized controlled trial. *Behavior Research and Therapy*, 49(Suppl 3), 175–85.

Hull, C.L. (1943) *Principles of Behaviour*, New York: Appleton-Century-Crofts.

Huntley, Z., Maltezos, S., Williams, C., Morinan, A., Brinsford, A., Ball, D., Marshall, E.J., Keaney, F., Porter, S., Young, S., Bolton, P., Glaser, K., Howe-Forbes, R., Kuntsi, J., Simonoff, E., Xenitidis, K., Murphy, D., and Asherson, P. (submitted) Rates of undiagnosed attention deficit hyperactivity disorder in UK substance misuse services.

Huntley, Z. and Young, S. (submitted) Alcohol and substance use history among ADHD adults: The relationship with persistent remitting symptoms, personality, employment and history of service use.

Jackson, B. and Farrugia, D. (1997) Diagnosis and treatment of adults with Attention Deficit Hyperactivity Disorder. *Journal of Counselling and Development*, 75, 312–319.

Jensen, P.S., Arnold, L.E., Swanson, J.M., Vitiello, B., Abikoff, H.B., Greenhill, L.L., Hechtman, L., Hinshaw, S.P., Pelham, W.E., Wells, K.C., Conners, C.K., Elliott, G.R., Epstein, J.N., Hoza, B., March, J.S., Molina, B.S., Newcorn, J.H., Severe, J.B., Wigal, T., Gibbons, R.D., and Hur, K. (2007), 3-year follow-up of the NIMH MTA study. *Journal of American Academy of Child and Adolescent Psychiatry*, 46(8), 989–1002.

Jou, R., Handen, B., and Hardan, A. (2004) Psychostimulant treatment of adults with mental retardation and attention-deficit hyperactivity disorder. *Australasian Psychiatry*, 12(4), 376–379.

Kaplan, B.J., Dewey, D., Crawford, S.G., and Fisher, G.C. (1998) Deficits in long-term memory are not characteristic of ADHD. *Journal of Clinical and Experimental Neuropsychology*, 20(4), 518–528.

Kassel, J.D. (1997) Smoking and attention: A review and reformulation of the stimulus-filter hypothesis. *Clinical Psychology Review*, 17, 451–478.

Kazdin, A.E. and Mascitelli, S. (1982) Covert and overt rehearsal and homework practice in developing assertiveness. *Journal of Consulting Clinical Psychology*, 50(2), 250–258.

Keller, M.B., Lavori, P.W., Wunder, J., Beardslee, W.R., Schwartz, C.E., and Roth, J. (1992) Chronic course of anxiety disorders in children and adolescents. *Journal of American Academy of Child and Adolescent Psychiatry*, 31, 595–599.

Kerns, K.A. and Price, K.J. (2001) An investigation of prospective memory in children with ADHD. *Child Neuropsychology*, 7(3), 162–171.

Kessler, R.C., Adler, L., Berkley, R., Biederman, J., Conners, C.K., Demler, O., and Zaslavsky, A.M. (2006) The prevalence and correlates of adult ADHD in the United States: Results from the National Comorbidity Survey Replication. *American Journal of Psychiatry*, 163(4), 716–723.

Konofal, E., Lecendreux, M., Bouvard, M.P., and Mouren-Simeoni, M.C. (2001) High levels of nocturnal activity in children with attention-deficit hyperactivity disorder: A video analysis. *Psychiatry and Clinical Neuroscience*, 55(2), 97–103.

Kooij, S.J.J., Bejerot, S., Blackwell, A., Caci, H., Casas-Brugues, M., Carpentier, P.J., Edvinsson, D., Fayyad, J., Foeken, K., Fitzgerald, M., Gaillac, V., Ginsberg, Y., Henry, C., Krause, J., Lensing, M.B., Manor, I., Niederhofer, H., Nunes-Filipe, C., Ohlmeier, M.D., Oswald, P., Pallanti, S., Pehlivanidis, A., Ramos-Quiroga, J.A., Rastam, M., Ryffel-Rawak, D., Stes, S., and Asherson, P. (2010) European consensus statement on diagnosis and treatment of adult ADHD: The European Network Adult ADHD. *BMC Psychiatry*, 10, 67.

Lazarus, R.S. and Folkman, S. (1984) *Stress, Appraisal and Coping*, New York: Springer Publishing.

Levin, E.D., Conners, C.K., Sparrow, E., Hinton, S.C., Erhardt, D., Meck, W.H., Rose, J.E., and March, J. (1996) Nicotine effects on adults with attention-deficit/hyperactivity disorder. *Psychopharmacology*, 123(1), 55–63.

MacLean, A., Dowson, J., Toone, B., Young, S., Bazanis, E., Robbins, T.W., and Sahakian, B.J. (2004) Characteristic neurocognitive profile associated with adult attention-deficit/hyperactivity disorder. *Psychological Medicine*, 34, 681–692.

Marsh, P.J. and Williams, L.M. (2004) An investigation of individual typologies of Attention-Deficit Hyperactivity Disorder using cluster analysis of DSM-IV criteria. *Personality and Individual Differences*, 36(5), 1187–1195.

Matsumoto, T., Kamijo, A., Yamaguchi, A., Iseki, E., and Hiravasu, Y. (2005) Childhood histories of attention-deficit hyperactivity disorders in Japanese methamphetamine and inhalant abusers: Preliminary report. *Psychiatry Clinical Neuroscience*, 59(1), 102–105.

Mayes, S.D., Calhoun, S.L., Bixler, E.O., Vgontzas, A.N., Mahr, F., Hillwig-Garcia, J., Elamir, B., Edhere-Ekezie, L., and Parvin, M. (2008) ADHD subtypes and comorbid anxiety, depression, and oppositional-defiant disorder: differences in sleep problems. *Journal of Pediatric Psychology*, 34(3), 328–337.

Mazza, S., Pepin, J.L., Naegele, B., Plante, J., Deschaux, C., and Levy, P. (2005) Most obstructive sleep apnoea patients exhibit vigilance and attention deficits on an extended battery of tests. *The European Respiratory Journal*, 25(1), 75–80.

McCarthy, S., Asherson, P., Coghill, D., Hollis, C., Murray, M., Potts, L., Sayal, K., De Soysa, R., Taylor, E., Williams, T., and Wong, I.C.K. (2009) Attention-deficit hyperactivity disorder: Treatment discontinuation in adolescents and young adults. *The British Journal of Psychiatry,* 194, 273–277.

Miller, W.R. and Rollnick, S. (2002) *Motivational Interviewing: Preparing People for Change*, 2nd edn, New York: Guildford Press.

Millstein, R.B., Wilens, T.E., Biederman J., and Spencer, T.J. (1997) Presenting ADHD symptoms and subtypes in clinically referred adults with ADHD. *Journal of Attention Disorders*, 2(3), 159–166.

Moffitt, T.E. (1993) 'Life-course-persistent' and 'adolescence-limited' antisocial behavior: A developmental taxonomy. *Psychological Review*, 100, 674–701.

Morris, R.G., Downes, J.J., Sahakian, B.J., Evenden, J.L., Heald, A., and Robbins, T.W. (1988) Planning and spatial working memory in Parkinson's disease. *Journal of Neurology, Neurosurgery and Psychiatry*, 51, 757–766.

Murphy, K.R. (1995) Empowering the adult with ADHD, in *A Comprehensive Guide to Attention Deficit Disorder in Adults* (ed. K. Nadeau), New York: Brunner/ Mazel Publishers, pp. 135–145.

Murphy, K.R. (1998) Psychological treatment of adults with ADHD, in *Attention Deficit Hyperactivity Disorder. A Handbook for Diagnosis and Treatment* (ed. R.A. Barkley). New York: The Guildford Press, pp. 692–703.

Murphy, K.R. and Barkley, R.A. (1996) Attention Deficit Hyperactivity Disorder in adults. *Comprehensive Psychiatry*, 37, 393–401.

Nadeau, K.G. (ed.) (1995) *A Comprehensive Guide to Attention Deficit Disorder in Adults*. New York: Brunner/ Mazel Publishers.

Naseem, S., Chaudhary, B., and Collop, N. (2001) Attention deficit hyperactivity disorder in adults and obstructive sleep apnea. *Chest*, 119(1), 294–296.

NICE (National Institute for Health and Clinical Excellence) (2009) *Attention Deficit Hyperactivity Disorder: Diagnosis and Management of ADHD in Children, Young People and Adults*, London: The British Psychological Society and The Royal College of Psychiatrists.

Norman D.A. and Shallice T. (1986) Attention to action: Willed and automatic control of behavior, in *Consciousness and Self-Regulation: Advances in Research and Theory*, vol. 4 (eds R.J. Davidson, G.E. Schwartz and D. Shapiro), New York: Plenum Press, pp. 1–18.

Nutt, D.J., Fone, K., Asherson, P., Bramble, D., Hill, P., Matthews, K., Morris, K.A., Santosh, P., Sonuga-Barke, E., Taylor, E., Weiss, M., and Young, S. (2007) Evidence-based guidelines for management of attention-deficit/hyperactivity disorder in adolescents in transition to adult services and in adults: recommendations from the British Association for Psychopharmacology. *Journal of Psychopharmacology*, 21(1), 10–41.

Owens, J.A. (2005) The ADHD and sleep conundrum: A review. *Journal of Developmental Behavioral Pediatrics*, 26(4), 312–322.

Park, M.J., Paul Mulye, T., Adams, S.H., Brindis, C.D., and Irwin, C.E. (2006) The health status of young adults in the United States. *Journal of Adolescent Health*, 39, 305–317.

Parnes, S.J., Noller, R.B., and Biondi, A.M. (1977) *Guide to Creative Action: Revised Edition of Creative Behavior Guidebook*, New York: Charles Scribner's Sons.

Pauls, D.L. and Leckman, J.F. (1986) The inheritance of Gilles de la Tourette syndrome and associated behaviors: Evidence for autosomal dominant transmission. *New England Journal of Medicine*, 315, 993–997.

Pliszka, S.R (1989) Effect of anxiety on cognition, behaviour, and stimulant response in ADHD. *Journal of American Academy of Child and Adolescent Psychiatry*, 28, 882–887.

Pliszka, S.R. (1998) Comorbidity of attention-deficit/hyperactivity disorder with psychiatric disorder: An overview. *Journal of Clinical Psychiatry*, 59(Suppl 7), 50–58.

Pliszka, S.R. (2003) Non-stimulant treatment of attention-deficit/hyperactivity disorder. *CNS Spectrums*, 8(4), 253–258.

Pliszka, S.R., Hatch, J.P., Borcherding, S.H., and Rogeness, G.A. (1993) Classical conditioning in children with attention deficit hyperactivity disorder (ADHD) and anxiety disorders: A test of Quay's model. *Journal of Abnormal Child Psychology*, 21, 411–423.

Powell, J. (2004a) Effects of medication on cognitive functioning, in *Clinical Neuropsychology: A Practical Guide to Assessment and Management for Clinicians* (eds L.H. Goldsteinand J.E. McNeil), Chichester: Wiley, Chapter 5.

Powell, T. (2004b) *Head Injury*, Bicester: Speechmark Publishing Ltd.

Prior, M. and Sanson, A. (1986) Attention deficit disorder with hyperactivity: A critique. *Journal of Child Psychology and Psychiatry*, 27(3), 307–319.

Prochaska, J.O. and DiClemente, C.C. (1982) Transtheoretical therapy: Toward a more integrative model of change. *Psychotherapy: Theory, Research, and Practice*, 19, 276–288.

Rabiner, D. and Cole, J.D. (2000) Early attention problems and children's reading achievement: A longitudinal investigation. *Journal of the American Academy of Children and Adolescent Psychiatry*, 39, 859–867.

Ramsay, J.R. and Rostain, A.L. (2005) Adapting psychotherapy to meet the needs of adults with attention-deficit/hyperactivity disorder. *Psychotherapy: Theory, Research, Practice, Training*, 42(1), 72–84.

Riccio, C.A., Wolfe, M.E., Romine, C., Davis, B., and Sullivan, J.R. (2004) The Tower of London and neuropsychological assessment of ADHD in adults. *Archives of Clinical Neuropsychology*, 19(5), 661–671.

Rose, E.D., Bramham, J., Young, S.J., Paliokosta, E., and Xenitidis, K. (2009). Neuropsychological characteristics of adults with comorbid ADHD and borderline/mild intellectual disability. *Research in Developmental Disabilities*, 30(3), 496–502

Rosler, M., Retz, W., Retz-Junginger, P., Hengesch, G., Schneider, M., Supprian, T., Schwitzgebel, P., Pinhard, K., Dovi-Akue, N., Wender, P., and Thome, J. (2004) Prevalence of attention deficit/hyperactivity disorder (ADHD) and comorbid disorders in young male prison inmates. *European Archives of Psychiatry and Clinical Neuroscience*, 254, 365–371.

Roth, A. and Fonagy, P. (1996) *What works for whom?* New York: The Guilford Press.

Rubia, K., Oosterlaan, J., Sergeant, J.A., Brandeis, D., and Leeuwen, T. (1998) Inhibitory dysfunction in hyperactive boys. *Behavioural Brain Research*, 94, 25–32.

Rubia, K., Overmeyer, S., Taylor, E., Brammer, M, Williams, S.C.R., Simmons, A., and Bullmore, E.T. (1999) Hypofrontality in Attention Deficit Hyperactivity Disorder during higher-order motor control: A study with functional MRI. *American Journal of Psychiatry*, 156(6), 891–896.

Rubia, K., Overmeyer, S., Taylor, E., Brammer, M, Williams S.C.R., Simmons, A., Andrew, C., and Bullmore, E.T. (2000) Functional frontalisation with age: Mapping neurodevelopmental trajectories with fMRI. *Neuroscience and Biobehavioural Reviews*, 24, 13–19.

Rucklidge, J.J. and Tannock, R. (2001) Psychiatric, psychosocial, and cognitive functioning of female adolescents with ADHD. *Journal of American Academy of Child and Adolescent Psychiatry*, 40(5), 530–540.

Rutter, M. (2005) Environmentally mediated risks for psychopathology: Research strategies and findings. *Journal of Child Psychology and Psychiatry*, 44(1), 3–18.

Sadeh, A., Pergamin, L., and Bar-Haim, Y. (2006) Sleep in children with attention-deficit hyperactivity disorder: A meta-analysis of polysomnographic studies. *Sleep Medicine Reviews*, 10(6) 381–398.

Safren, S.A., Otto, M.W., Sprich, S., Perlman, C.L., Wilens, T.E., and Biederman, J. (2005a) Cognitive behavioral therapy for ADHD in medication-treated adults with continued symptoms. *Behavior Research and Therapy*, 43(7), 831–842.

Safren, S.A., Perlman, C.A., Sprich, S., and Otto M.W. (2005b) *Mastering Your Adult ADHD: A Cognitive-Behavioral Treatment Program*, New York: Oxford University Press.

Safren, S.A., Sprich, S., Mimiaga, M.J., Surman, C., Knouse, L., Groves, M., and Otto, M.W. (2010) Cognitive behavioural therapy vs. relaxation with educational support for medication-treated adults with ADHD and persistent symptoms: A randomized controlled trial. *The Journal of the American Medical Association*, 304(Suppl 8), 875–880.

Satterfield, T., Swanson, J., Schell, A., and Lee, F. (1994) Prediction of anti-social behaviour in attention-deficit hyperactivity disorder boys from aggression/defiance scores. *Journal of American Academy of Child and Adolescent Psychiatry*, 33(2), 185–190.

Seixas, M., Weiss, M., and Muller, U. (2011) Systematic review of national and international guidelines on attentional-deficit hyperactivity disorder. *Journal of Psychopharmacology* (ePub), available at http://jop.sagepub.com/content/early/2011/09/24/0269881111412095.abstract?rss=1 (accessed 22 November 2011).

Shallice, T. and Burgess, P.W. (1996) The domain of supervisory processes and temporal organization of behaviour. *Philosophical Transactions of the Royal Society London*, 351, 1405–1411.

Sizoo, B., van den Brink, W., Koeter, M., van Eenige, M.G., van Wijngaarden-Cremers, P., and van der Gaag, R.J. (2010) Treatment seeking adults with autism or ADHD and co-morbid substance use disorder: Prevalence, risk factors and functional disability. *Drug and Alcohol Dependence*, 107, 44–50.

Sobanski, E. (2006) Psychiatric comorbidity in adults with attention-deficit/hyperactivity disorder (ADHD). *European Archives of Psychiatry and Clinical Neuroscience*, 256(Suppl 1), i26–31.

Solanto, M.V., Marks, D.J., Wasserstein, J., Mitchell, K., Abikoff, H., Alvir, J.M., and Kofman, M.D. (2010) Efficacy of meta-cognitive therapy for adult ADHD. *The American Journal of Psychiatry,* 167(Suppl 8), 958–968.

Sonuga-Barke, E.J.S., Daley, D., and Thompson, M. (2002) Does maternal ADHD reduce the effectiveness of parent training for preschool children's ADHD? *Journal of the American Academy of Child and Adolescent Psychiatry*, 41, 696–702.

Sonuga-Barke, E.J., Taylor, E., Sembi, S., and Smith, J. (1992) Hyperactivity and delay aversion – I: The effect of delay on choice. *Journal of Child Psychology and Psychiatry*, 33(2), 387–398.

Sprich-Buchminster, S., Biederman, J., Milberger, S., Faraone, S.V., and Lehman, B.K. (1993) Are perinatal complications relevant to the manifestation of ADD? Issues of comorbidity and familiarity. *Journal of American Academy of Child and Adolescent Psychiatry*, 32, 1032–1037.

Staller, J.A. and Faraone, S.V. (2007) Targeting the dopamine system in the treatment of attention-deficit/hyperactivity disorder. *Expert Review of Neurotherapeutics*, 7(4), 351–362.

Steinhausen, H-C. (2009) The heterogeneity of causes and courses of attention-deficit hyperactivity disorder. *Acta Psychiatrica Scandinavica*, 120, 392–399.

Stergiakouli, E. and Thapar, A. (2010) Fitting the pieces together: Current research on the genetic basis of attention-deficit/hyperactivity disorder (ADHD). *Journal of Neuropsychiatric Disease and Treatment*, 6, 551–560.

Stevenson, C.S., Whitmont, S., Bornholt, L., Livesey, D., and Stevenson, R.J. (2002) A cognitive remediation programme for adults with Attention Deficit Hyperactivity Disorder. *Australian and New Zealand Journal of Psychiatry*, 36, 610–616.

Sullivan, M.A. and Rudnik-Levin, F. (2001) Attention deficit/hyperactivity disorder and substance abuse. Diagnostic and therapeutic considerations. *Annals of the New York Academy of Science*, 931, 251–270.

Tannock, R. (2000) Attention deficit disorders with anxiety disorders, in *Attention Deficit Disorders and Comorbidities in Children, Adolescents and Adults* (ed. S. Brown), New York: American Psychiatric Press, pp. 125–170.

Taylor, E., Chadwick, O., Heptinstall, E., and Danckaerts, M. (1996) Hyperactivity and conduct problems as risk factors for adolescent development. *Journal of American Academy of Child and Adolescent Psychiatry*, 35(9), 1213–1226.

Teasdale, J.D. and Fogarty, S.J. (1979) Differential effects of induced mood on retrieval of pleasant and unpleasant events from episodic memory. *Journal of Abnormal Psychology*, 88(3), 248–257.

Thapar, A., Harrington, R., and McGuffin, P. (2001) Examining the comorbidity of ADHD-related behaviours and conduct problems using a twin study design. *British Journal of Psychiatry*, 179, 224–229.

Upadhyaya, H.P. (2008) Substance use disorders in children and adolescents with attention-deficit/hyperactivity disorder: Implications for treatment and the role of the primary care physician. *Primary Care Companion to the Journal of Clinincal Psychiatry*, 10, 211–221.

Uzun, N. and Kendirli, Y. (2005) Clinical, social-demographic, neurophysiological and neuropsychiatric evaluation of children with volatile substance addiction. *Child Care Health Development*, 31(4), 425–443.

Van Horn, D.H. and Bux, D.A. (2001) A pilot test of motivational interviewing groups for dually diagnosed inpatients. *Journal of Substance Abuse Treatment*, 20(2), 191–195.

Van Veen, M.M., Kooij, J.J., Boonstra, A.M., Gordijn, M.C., and Van Someren, E.J. (2010) Delayed circadian rhythm in adults with attention-deficit/hyperactivity disorder and chronic sleep-onset insomnia. *Biological Psychiatry*, 67(11), 1091–1096.

Vance, A.L., Luk, E.S., Costin, J., Tonge, B.J., and Pantelis, C. (1999) Attention deficit hyperactivity disorder: anxiety phenomena in children treated with psychostimulant medication for 6 months or more. *Australia New Zealand Journal of Psychiatry*, 33(3), 399–406.

Virta, M., Salakari, A., Antila, M., Chydenius, E., Partinen, M., Kaski, M., Vataja, R., Kalska, H., and Iivanainen, M. (2010) Short cognitive behavioural therapy and cognitive training for adults with ADHD – a randomized controlled pilot study. *Neuropsychiatric Disease and Treatment*, 7(Suppl 6), 443–453.

Wagner, M.L., Walters, A.S., and Fisher, B.C. (2004) Symptoms of attention-deficit/hyperactivity disorder in adults with restless legs syndrome. *Sleep*, 15:27(8), 1499–1504.

Weinstein, C. (1994) Cognitive remediation strategies: An adjunct to psychotherapy of adults with attention deficit hyperactivity disorder. *Journal of Psychotherapy Practice and Research*, 3(1), 44–57.

Weiss, M., Hechtman, L., Milroy, T., and Perlman, T. (1985) Psychiatric status of hyperactives as adults: a controlled perspective. 15 year follow up of 63 hyperactive children. *Journal of the American Academy of Child Psychiatry*, 24, 211–220.

Weiss, M., Hechtman, L., and Weiss, G. (1999) *ADHD in Adulthood: A Guide to Current Theory, Diagnosis and Treatment*, Baltimore: Johns Hopkins University Press.

While, A., Forbes, A., Ullman, R., Lewis, S., Mathes, L., and Griffiths, P. (2004) Good practices that address continuity during transition fromchild to adult care: Synthesis of the evidence. *Child Care Health Development*, 30, 439–452.

Wilens, T.E., Faraone, A.V., Biederman, J., and Gunawardene, S. (2003) Does stimulant therapy of attention-deficit/hyperactivity disorders beget later substance misuse? A meta-analytic review of the literature. *Pediatrics*, 111, 179–185.

Wilens, T.E., McDermott, S.P., Biederman, J., Abrantes, A., Hahesy, A., and Spencer, T.J. (1999) Cognitive therapy in the treatment of adults with ADHD: A systematic chart review of 26 cases. *Journal of Cognitive Psychotherapy: An International Quarterly,* 13, 215–226.

Wilson, B.A., Alderman, N., Burgess, P.W., Emslie, H., and Evans, J.J. (1996) *Behavioural Assessment of the Dysexecutive Syndrome (BADS)*, Bury St. Edmunds: Thames Valley Test Company.

World Health Organisation (WHO) (1992) *ICD–10 Classification of Mental and Behavioural Disorders*, Geneva: WHO.

Wu, L.T., Pilowsky, D.J., and Schlenger, W.E. (2005) High prevalence of substance use disorders among adolescents who use marijuana and inhalants. *Drug and Alcohol Dependence*, 78(1), 23–32.

Young, S.J. (1999) Psychological therapy for adults with Attention Deficit Hyperactivity Disorder. *Counselling Psychology Quarterly*, 12(2), 183–190.
Young, S.J. (2002) A model of psychotherapy for adults with ADHD, in *A Clinician's Guide to Adult ADHD: Assessment and Intervention* (eds S. Goldstein and R. Brooks), New York: Academic Press.
Young, S. (2005) Coping strategies used by adults with ADHD. *Personality and Individual Differences*, 38(4), 809–816.
Young, S., Adamou, M., Bolea, B., Müller, U., Pitts, M., Thome, J., and Asherson, P. (2011) The identification and management of ADHD offenders within the criminal justice system: a consensus statement from the UK Adult ADHD Network and criminal justice agencies, *BMC Psychiatry*, 11(1), 32.
Young. S. and Amarasinghe. J.A. (2010) Practitioner review: Non-pharmacological treatments for ADHD: A lifespan approach. *Journal of Child Psychology and Psychiatry*, 51(2), 116–133.
Young, S., Bramham, J., and Gray, K. (2009) A phenomenological analysis of the experience of receiving a diagnosis and treatment of ADHD in adulthood. A partner's perspective. *Journal of Attention Disorders*, 12(4), 299–307.
Young, S., Bramham, J., Gray, K., and Rose, E. (2008) The experience of receiving a diagnosis and treatment of ADHD in adulthood. A qualitative study of clinically referred patients using Interpretative Phenomenological Analysis. *Journal of Attention Disorders*, 11(4), 493–504.
Young, S., Chadwick, O., Heptinstall, E., Taylor, E., and Sonuga-Barke, E.J. (2005a) The adolescent outcome of hyperactive girls. Self-reported interpersonal relationships and coping mechanisms. *European Journal of Child and Adolescent Psychiatry*, 14(5), 245–253.
Young, S., Channon, S., and Toone, B.K. (2000) Neuropsychological assessment of Attention Deficit Hyperactivity Disorder in adulthood. *Clinical Neuropsychological Assessment*, 1(4), 283–294.
Young, S. and Gudjonsson, G. (2008) Growing out of Attention-Deficit/Hyperactivity Disorder: The relationship between functioning and symptoms, *Journal of Attention Disorders*, 12(2), 162–169.
Young, S., Gudjonsson, G.H., Misch, P., Collins, P., Carter, P., Redfern, J., and Goodwin, E. (2010) Prevalence of ADHD symptoms among youth in a secure facility: The consistency and accuracy of self- and informant-report ratings. *Journal of Forensic Psychiatry and Psychology*, 21(2), 238–246.
Young, S., Heptinstall, E., Sonuga-Barke, E.J.S., Chadwick, O., and Taylor, E. (2005b) The adolescent outcome of hyperactive girls: Self-report of psychosocial status. *Journal of Child Psychology and Psychiatry*, 46(3), 255–262.
Young, S., Hopkin, G., Perkins, D., Farr, C., Doidge, A., and Gudjonsson, G.H. (forthcoming) A controlled trial of a cognitive skills program for personality disordered offenders. *Journal of Attention Disorders*. DOI:10.1177/1087054711430333
Young, S., Morris, R.G., Toone, B.K., and Tyson, C. (2006) Spatial working memory and strategy formation in adults diagnosed with Attention Deficit Hyperactivity Disorder. *Personality and Individual Differences*, 41, 653–661.
Young, S., Morris, R.G., Toone, B.K., and Tyson, C. (2007) Planning ability in adults diagnosed with Attention-Deficit/Hyperactivity Disorder: A deficit in planning ability. *Neuropsychology*, 21(5), 581–589.
Young, S., Murphy, C.M., and Coghill, D. (2011) Avoiding the 'twilight zone': Guidance and recommendations on ADHD and the transition between child and adult services. *BMC Psychiatry*. 11:174 http://www.biomedcentral.com/qc/1471-244X/11/174 doi:10.1186/1471-244X-11-174
Young, S.J. and Ross, R.R. (2007) *R&R2 for ADHD Youths and Adults with ADHD: A Prosocial Competence Training Program*. Ottawa: Cognitive Centre of Canada. Retrieved from www.cognitivecentre.ca
Young, S., Toone, B., and Tyson, C. (2003) Comorbidity and psychosocial profile of adults with Attention Deficit Hyperactivity Disorder. *Personality and Individual Differences*, 35(4), 743–755.

INDEX

Cognitive-Behavioural Therapy for ADHD in Adolescents and Adults: A Psychological Guide to Practice, Second Edition. Susan Young and Jessica Bramham.

Printed and bound by CPI Group (UK) Ltd, Croydon, CR0 4YY
23/09/2025
14740121-0001